THE EERDMANS CRITICAL COMMENTARY

David Noel Freedman, *General Editor*

Astrid B. Beck, *Associate Editor*

THE EERDMANS CRITICAL COMMENTARY offers the best of contemporary Old and New Testament scholarship, seeking to give modern readers clear insight into the biblical text, including its background, its interpretation, and its application.

Contributors to the ECC series are among the foremost authorities in biblical scholarship worldwide. Representing a broad range of confessional backgrounds, authors are charged to remain sensitive to the original meaning of the text and to bring alive its relevance for today. Each volume includes the author's own translation, critical notes, and commentary on literary, historical, cultural, and theological aspects of the text.

Accessible to serious general readers and scholars alike, these commentaries reflect the contributions of recent textual, philological, literary, historical, and archeological inquiry, benefiting as well from newer methodological approaches. ECC volumes are "critical" in terms of their detailed, systematic explanation of the biblical text. Although exposition is based on the original and cognate languages, English translations provide complete access to the discussion and interpretation of these primary sources.

Other Works by Samuel Terrien

The Psalms and Their Meaning for Today (Indianapolis and New York, 1952)

"Introduction and Exegesis: The Book of Job," in *The Interpreter's Bible*, III (New York & Nashville, 1954)

Job: Poet of Existence (Indianapolis and New York, 1957)

Lands of the Bible (New York, 1958)

Job: Traduction et commentaire (Neuchâtel, 1963)

The Bible and the Church (Philadelphia, 1963)

The Power to Bring Forth (Philadelphia, 1968)

The New Testament in Shorter Form (New York and London, 1970)

"Le Livre de Job, Introduction et Notes," in collaboration with Dominique Barthélemy, O.P., *Traduction Œcuménique de la Bible* (Paris, 1972, 1988)

"The Book of Job: Introduction and Notes," in *The New Oxford Annotated Bible* (New York, 1973)

The Elusive Presence: Toward a New Biblical Theology (San Francisco and New York, 1978, 1983)

Till the Heart Sings: A Biblical Theology of Manhood and Womanhood (Philadelphia, 1985)

Proclamation: Holy Week (Philadelphia, 1986)

The Magnificat: Musicians as Biblical Interpreters (New York, 1995)

The Iconography of Job through the Centuries: Artists as Biblical Interpreters (University Park, Penn., 1996)

Associate Editor:

The Interpreter's Bible, I-XII (New York and Nashville, 1952-57)

The Interpreter's Dictionary of the Bible, I-IV (New York and Nashville, 1962)

THE PSALMS

Strophic Structure and
Theological Commentary

SAMUEL TERRIEN

WILLIAM B. EERDMANS PUBLISHING COMPANY
GRAND RAPIDS, MICHIGAN / CAMBRIDGE, U.K.

Wm. B. Eerdmans Publishing Co.
2140 Oak Industrial Drive N.E., Grand Rapids, Michigan 49505 /
P.O. Box 163, Cambridge CB3 9PU U.K.

Printed in the United States of America

08 07 06 05 04 03   7 6 5 4 3 2 1

Note: This title, originally published in a single hardcover volume,
has now been produced in two paperback volumes.

Library of Congress Cataloging-in-Publication Data

Terrien, Samuel L., 1911-2001
The Psalms: strophic structure and theological commentary / Samuel Terrien.
p.   cm.   — (The Eerdmans critical commentary)
Includes bibliographical references and index.
ISBN-10: 0-8028-2744-6 / ISBN-13: 978-0-8028-2744-9 (cloth: alk. paper)
1. Bible. O.T. Psalms — Commentaries.
2. Hebrew poetry, Biblical — History and criticism.
2. Hebrew language — Metrics and rhythmics.
4. Bible. O.T. Psalms — Theology.
I. Title.   II. Series.

BS1430.53 T47   2002
223'.207 — dc21

2002033899

www.eerdmans.com

For Alys and Christopher Queen

Contents

COMMENTARY

Book One

Contents

Contents

Contents

Book Five

Contents

PSALM 73

From Doubt to Glory

1. *Psalm. For Asaph.*

PART ONE
I

   Surely God is good to Israel,
     At least to the pure of heart.
2. *But as for me, my feet almost slipped;*
     They nearly skidded, my steps.

II

3. *For I envied those who boasted,*
     When I saw the health of the scoundrels.
4. *There is no agony for them;*
     Sound and plump is their belly.
5. *They know no pain as other mortals,*
     Neither are they plagued as all humans.
6. *Thus they wear their pride as a necklace;*
     Violence drapes them as a vestment.

III

7. *Their eyes bulge from their fat faces;*
     They exceed the lust of their hearts.
8. *They scoff and speak evil words,*
     And decree oppression with arrogance.

9.   *They set their mouth against heaven,*
        And their tongues walk about the earth!
10.   *This is why they extort pressed grapes from their people*
        And sip their wine until they are drunk.

IV

11.   *And they say, How could God know?*
        Is there any knowledge in the Most High?
12.   *Behold! These are the scoundrels:*
        Serene forever, they amass their wealth.

PART TWO
I

13.   *Surely it was in vain that I kept my heart pure,*
        And washed my hands in innocence,
14.   *For I was hit every day,*
        And beaten up every morning.

II

15.   *If I had said, I shall sing in this manner,*
        Behold! I would have betrayed the generation of thy children!
16.   *As I strove to figure this out,*
        It was only misery in my eyes,
17.   *Until I came to the sacred places of God,*
        And grasped the ultimate fate of the scoundrels.

III

18.   *Surely thou settest them in slippery places,*
        And thou wilt fell them into ruin and desolation.
19.   *How they are destined to nought, in an instant!*
        They will vanish, swept away by their own terrors!
20.   *As a dream when one wakes up, O my Sovereign;*
        As one stirs up from a nightmare, thou despisest their shades.

IV

21.   *Thus my mind had become embittered,*
        And my loins had shriveled up!
22.   *But as for me, I was a beast, I did not know!*
        I was with thee like a hippopotamus.

PART THREE

I

23. *But I am always with thee!*
     Thou hast held me by my right hand,
24. *By thy counsel thou wilt guide me,*
     And afterward thou wilt take me into glory.

II

25. *Whom have I in heaven but thee?*
     If I am with thee, I seek no other delight on earth.
26. *My flesh and my heart may waste away;*
     God is the rock of my heart, and my lot, forever.

III

27. *For behold, those who are far from thee perish;*
     Thou hast annihilated those hustlers away from thee.
28. *But as for me, the nearness of God, this is my good.*
     I have placed my trust in the Lord Yahweh,
     That I may proclaim all thy works!

BIBLIOGRAPHY

S. E. Balentine, *The Hidden God: The Hidden Face of God in the Old Testament* (Oxford, 1983); E. Beaucamp, "Voie nouvelle pour l'exégèse du Psaume 73," in *Festschrift P. G. G. Bagatti* (Jerusalem, 1976), pp. 44-46; H. Birkeland, "The Chief Problems of Ps. 17ff," *ZAW*, LXVII (1955), pp. 99-103; P. E. Bonnard, *Le Psautier selon Jérémie* (Paris, 1960), pp. 140-45; M. Buber, "The Heart Determines," in *Right and Wrong: The Interpretation of Some Psalms*, tr. R. G. Smith (London, 1952), pp. 34ff.; idem, "The Heart Determines Psalm 73," in *Theodicy and the Old Testament*, ed. J. L. Crenshaw (Philadelphia, 1983), pp. 100-108; A. Caquot, "Le Psaume LXXIII," *Semitica*, XXI (1971), pp. 29-55; G. Castellino, "Salmo 73,19," in *Studia orientalia . . . G. Levi della Vida*, I (Rome, 1956), pp. 141-50; J. L. Crenshaw, *A Whirlpool of Torments: Israelite Traditions of God as an Oppressive Presence* (Philadelphia, 1984), pp. 109-18; P. A. H. de Boer, "The Meaning of Psalm LXXIII 9," *VT*, XVIII (1968), pp. 260-64; H. Donner, "Ugaritischen in der Psalmenforschung," LXXIX (1967), p. 336; M. Görg, "'Ich bin mit dir': Gewicht und Anspruch einer Redeform im Alten Testament," *Theologie und Glaube*, LXX (1980), pp. 214-40; H. Graf Reventlow, *Gebet im Alten Testament* (Stuttgart, 1986); J. Guillet, "L'entrée du juste dans la gloire," *BVC*, IX (1955), pp. 58ff.; K. J. Illman, "Pour l'interpretation du Psaume 73," *SEÅ*, XLI-XLII (1976-77), pp. 120-29; F. James, *Thirty Psalmists* (New York, 1938), pp. 204-12; S. Jellicoe, "The Interpretation of Ps. 73, 24," *EvT*, LXVII (1955-56), pp. 209-10; J. Krašovec, *Antithetic Structure in Biblical Hebrew*

Poetry (Leiden, 1984), pp. 38-59; see review in *CBQ*, XLVIII (1986), pp. 528-30; H.-J. Kraus, "Psalm 73," *Bethel*, XI (1973), pp. 3-12; G. Kuhn, "Bemerkungen zu Psalm 73," *ZAW*, LV (1937), pp. 307-8; D. M. Lloyd-Jones, *Faith on Trial: Studies on Ps 73* (London, 1965); J. Luyten, "Psalm 73 and Wisdom," in *La sagesse de l'Ancien Testament*, ed. M. Gilbert (Gembloux & Leuven, 1979), pp. 59-81; M. Mannati, "Sur le quadruple *avec toi* de Psaume LXXIII, 21-26," *VT*, XXI (1971), pp. 59-67; idem, "Les adorateurs de Môt dans le Psaume LXXIII," *VT*, XXII (1972), pp. 420-25; J. C. McCann, *A Theological Introduction to the Book of Psalms* (Nashville, 1993), pp. 140-45; idem, "Psalm 73: A Microcosm of Old Testament Theology," in *Festschrift R. E. Murphy*, ed. K. G. Hoglund et al., JSOTSup LVIII (Sheffield, 1987), pp. 247-57; P. A. Munch, "Das Problem des Reichtums in den Ps 37, 49, 73," *ZAW*, LV (1937), pp. 36-46; H. P. Nasuti, *Tradition and History in the Psalms of Asaph* (Atlanta, 1988), pp. 63-66; E. Otto, "Der Vorwurf an Gott: Zur Entstehung der ägyptischen Auseinandersetzungsliteratur," in *Vorträge der orientalischen Tagung in Marburg . . . 1950* (1951); B. Renaud, "Le Psaume 73: méditation individuelle ou prière collective? [Mélanges E. Jacob]," *RHPR*, LIX (1979), pp. 541-50; H. Ringgren, "Einige Bemerkungen zum lxxiii. Psalm," *VT*, III (1953), pp. 265-72; J. F. Ross, "Psalm 73," in *Israelite Wisdom: Theological and Literary Essays . . .*, Festschrift S. Terrien, ed. J. G. Gammie et al. (New York, 1978), pp. 161-75; N. H. Snaith, "The Asaphite Psalmist," in *Studies in the Psalter* (London, 1934), pp. 25ff.; idem, *Hymns of the Temple* (Ps 42/43; 44; 46; 50; 70) (London, 1951), pp. 102-19; R. J. Tournay, "Le Psaume LXXIII: Relectures et interprétation," *RB*, XCII (1985), pp. 187-99; E. Würthwein, "Erwägungen zu Ps 73," in *Festschrift A. G. Bertholet* (Tübingen, 1950), pp. 532-49.

FORM

On account of its form and its contents, Psalm 73 differs from collective and individual laments, as well as hymns of praise, thanksgiving songs, and other *Gattungen*. Observing its affinities with Psalms 37, 49, and 139, many commentators call it a Wisdom Psalm or a didactic poem. Others, on the contrary, think of it as a song of autobiographical confession, or again, with its reminiscences of royal ideology, as a piece for the New Year Festival. Indeed, like the poem of Job, it may represent a paracultic, parasapiential poem for the celebration of Rosh Hashanah, at the nascent efflorescence of this adoption of an ancient festival: the early Jews, in a foreign land, questioned bitterly the retributive justice of God that had gone awry.

Within a near uniformity of meter (mostly 3+3) and strophic construction (3 or 4 bicola), except for the final declaration (a tricolon, v. 23), Psalm 73 presents three parts, as follows: Part One (vv. 1b-12) comprises four strophes that bemoan the happiness and the health of the scoundrels; Part Two (vv. 13-22) contains four strophes in which an objective meditation becomes subjective and turns into a prayer. The pace slightly accelerates as the two main strophes (vv. 3-6, 7-10) of Part One, made up of four bicola respectively, are shortened into three bicola respectively (vv. 15-17; and vv. 18-20). Parts One and Two begin and end with a strophe of two bicola (vv. 1b-2, 11-12; and 13-14, 21-22). Moreover, both parts begin with the key word, "Surely"!

Part Three (vv. 23-28) comprehends only three strophes of two bicola, two bicola, and a final bicolon slowing down into a tricolon (vv. 23-24, 25-26, and 27-28). The pathetic protest and skeptical bewilderment of Parts One and Two are now absorbed and transmuted into a lyrical exultation of mystical originality. The thematic discovery predicates the form and the evolution of Parts One, Two, and Three. (See the diagram on p. 528.)

COMMENTARY

Superscription: Psalm. For Asaph (v. 1a)

Psalm 73 may have belonged originally to a proto-collection of second-temple or synagogue hymnals that was ascribed to a musical guild (cf. Pss 50; 73–83; cf. 1 Chr 25:1-2).

Part One: Strophe I: Prelude (vv. 1b-2)

The first word, "Surely," emphasizes the need to affirm categorically regained certainty after critical torment on the part of the poet. Was it religious agony after he had doubted the fidelity and the justice of God? Perhaps even an intellectual revolt over the atrocities of the Babylonian exile? Is God really good to Israel? Or to the just of heart? The expression "at least" is implied by the context, which equates the pure of heart with true Israel.

Several translators and commentators believe that the name "Israel" represents the choral use of the psalm from a written psalter, in a later age, when the Hebrew text was read without space between words, *leyisrael,* while the original intent is "to the pure of heart . . . God. . . ." The bicolon, then, would obtain a syntactical balance between its two stichoi, with the word "El" in parallelism with "Elohim," both meaning "God."

According to this view, the Prelude permits one to observe how a psalm, first conceived as an individual meditation, becomes a collective song through congregational singing. In any case, the psalmist does not affirm a traditional dogma of retribution. He merely reiterates that God is good, but he does not define the meaning of this goodness. This restraint may be the reason for which he composes this autobiographical confession of a skepticism now overcome.

Psalm 73

Part One

I

1. — — — — — — — —
— — — — — — —

2. — — — — — — — —
— — — — — —

II

3. — — — — — — — —
— — — — — —

4. — — — — — — — —
— — — — — —

5. — — — — — — — —
— — — — — —

6. — — — — — — — —
— — — — — —

III

7. — — — — — — — —
— — — — — —

8. — — — — — — — —
— — — — — —

9. — — — — — — — —
— — — — — —

10. — — — — — — — —
— — — — — —

IV

11. — — — — — — — —
— — — — — —

12. — — — — — — — —
— — — — — —

Part Two

I

13. — — — — — — — —
— — — — — —

14. — — — — — — — —
— — — — — —

II

15. — — — — — — — —
— — — — — —

16. — — — — — — — —
— — — — — —

17. — — — — — — — —
— — — — — —

III

18. — — — — — — — —
— — — — — —

19. — — — — — — — —
— — — — — —

20. — — — — — — — —
— — — — — —

IV

21. — — — — — — — —
— — — — — —

22. — — — — — — — —
— — — — — —

Part Three

I

23. — — — — — — — —
— — — — — —

24. — — — — — — — —
— — — — — —

II

25. — — — — — — — —
— — — — — —

26. — — — — — — — —
— — — — — —

III

27. — — — — — — — —
— — — — — —

28. — — — — — — — —
— — — — — —
— — — — — —

"They nearly skidded, my steps." The poet feels that he has had a narrow escape, for he might have fallen into a spiritual abyss. The word for "my steps" is akin to the notion of dynamic happiness, a beatitude in movement. His forward élan and his zest for living, which made him perhaps a born leader of men, had almost gone astray. He reeled at the edge of a cliff. His mental equilibrium was close to chaos.

Strophe II: Envying the Boasters (vv. 3-6)

There are within Israel evil men, scoundrels or good-for-nothings, godless individuals who boast of their misdeeds and never mind committing acts of violence against the poor or their neighbors. They are at peace, serene, healthy, and go on unpunished. Why not envy them? They do not seem to share the fate of other "mortals." They think that they do not belong to the descendants of Adam (v. 5). They have lived with evil so intimately that it has become an ornamental necklace for them. Their act of violence fits them neatly, like a tailored garment. Their ignoble habits or "customs" have become their "costumes."

Strophe III: Lustful Excesses (vv. 7-10)

The evildoers are so accustomed to immorality that their inner desires stretch even beyond the imagination of their hearts.[1] The last bicolon of the strophe (v. 10) is obscure: "His people returns hither *(Qerê)*" or "I will bring back his people." Some read, "they are sated with their festive meals, and water in abundance is wrung for them." A possible translation might be, "This is why they extort pressed grapes" (cf. the verb "to smite," especially grapes at vintage wine pressing) "from their people, and drink till complete intoxication" (lit., "till they are full," a common euphemism for "drunken").

Strophe IV: Denial of Divine Knowledge (vv. 11-12)

The scoundrels still believe there is a God, but they do not have faith in him. They assert that the Deity does not know their crimes. Untroubled by their misdeeds, they amass their wealth. An ignorant God is a powerless God. The denial of divine knowledge leads ipso facto to the surrender of the belief that there is justice in the Most High. This could be called practical atheism. It has nothing in common with the prophets' apprehension of divine suffering, divine self-abasement, or divine embrace of human pain.

---

1. P. A. H. de Boer, "The Meaning of Psalm LXXIII, 9," *VT*, XVIII (1968), pp. 260-64.

Part Two: Strophe I: Is It Useless to Serve God? (vv. 13-14)

The second part of the psalm echoes the first, with a difference: it hints at a progressive development. "Surely" in both vv. 1 and 13 implies a reaction against the lassitude of those who have sought purity of heart by their veracity and refused to admit the hidden intrusion of ulterior motives. Such rectitude has earned them no gain.

The poet mirrors almost word for word the oracle of the prophet Malachi: "It is vain to serve God. What profit that we have kept his ordinances? . . . And now we call the arrogant happy. They are prosperous, the scoundrels! They put God to the test and they get away with it" (Mal 3:14-15). Both the prophet and the psalmist are about to discover indirectly the falsehood of mercantile religion.

Strophe II: The Solidarity of Believers (vv. 15-17)

Here is a chorister who hopes to express poetically, in metrics, strophes, and metaphors, his rebellion against what he mistook for divine immorality or impotence. His laborious search for purity of heart covered his envy for the fate of criminals, unpunished and serene. At the very same instant, such a search for virtue concealed a brutal desire to exchange a singleness of motivation for divine favor in material and social reward. Infinity can be bought! Tit for tat! Piety is an investment. Morality is a scheme for grasping happiness. God is good when man is good.

"If I had said, I shall sing in this manner" (v. 15; the verb introduces an aesthetic touch to the repetition). "I would have been a traitor." The verse maker suddenly senses that he was going to prostitute his poetic gifts by using his art in what amounted to blasphemous, vulgar selfishness. "I would have betrayed" my fellow choristers and many more who are similarly hit by poverty, famine, disease, and bereavement, yet maintain courageously their trust in the almighty and loving Deity. The individual doubts expressed in Part One have become in Part Two the cause of fear that a spiritual panic — therefore a collective terror — might weaken, undermine, and even annihilate all trust among "the generation of *thy* children" (v. 15b).

The poet's aversion to such a possibility has abruptly transmuted the meditation into a dialogue! God is no longer a bystander within a poetic monologue. The psalmist has now regained divine intimacy. His responsibility toward his brothers, perhaps his disciples, is now restored. The pseudo-philosophical dissertation or diatribe turns into a most personal subject of introspection: the presence of infinity. The intellectual reflection of Part One is now, in Part Two, a theological and spiritual tournament.

What are "the sacred places of God"? Or perhaps "things" or even "thoughts" of God? Is the Hebrew word not a real plural but a *pluralis majestatis* meaning "sanctuary"? Does the psalmist refer to the rebuilt temple in Zion? Or, if the plural is likely, to nascent synagogues throughout the Persian empire where congregations gather informally, on Sabbath and during festivals? If so, the accent lies on the human and social element rather than on an edifice situated in geography. The people who worship constitute the *qāhāl*, later translated *ekklēsia*, or "church." In the warmth of brotherhood now felt by the singer, a hasty conclusion is to be avoided. One will take a long view of history: Are the scoundrels ultimately condemned or unconditionally spared?

Divine justice is reaffirmed, for — in the end, perhaps a premature end — the evildoers will walk on slippery places. Like trees of majestic appearance belied by the rottenness of their core, they will be felled by the rush of a storm.

A note of subtle psychology is quietly but ferociously added: they will be "swept away by their own terrors" (v. 19). A self-accusing guilt is not a modern discovery. In ancient Near Eastern literature as well as in Greek tragedies, moral conscience slowly and invincibly gnaws at the sense of well-being when this self-satisfaction is based on repressed memories of aggression or cowardice, or even varnishes of serene arrogance. For a while incipient terrors may be covered up, but eventually they surface with a vengeance, and in the end the scoundrels vanish like a nightmare.

Does the poet anticipate, in the last line of the strophe, the stunning illumination of Part Three (v. 24), when he again addresses his God in the second person instead of thinking of him in the third person (v. 20a)? "Thou despisest their image," or "their shades." Are these hints of retribution beyond death? Does Part II flow into Part III as a counterpoint to an expectation of living at last "with God" in glory?

Strophe IV: Philosophical Quest or Plain Stupidity? (vv. 21-22)

"My mind had become embittered" (v. 21), literally, "my heart" not as the seat of an emotional upset but as the symbol of intelligent reason and of the volitive power to pursue a decision to act. "My loins" (lit. "my kidneys" but also "my sexual desires") refers metaphorically to the instinctual power of realizing and acting out an intention. The whole personality of the psalmist has been shattered, and the recognition of this devastating weakness leads him to confess that his sapiential questioning lowered him to the level of a beast. "I was with thee like a hippopotamus," perhaps even a swampy, muddy, grossly arguing behemoth, a metaphysical problem for the Lord Almighty.

The admission of stupidity in discoursing about divine justice verges on the admission of cosmic hubris. I was with thee like an obtuse antagonist (cf.

Job 40:15-24). The "with thee" anticipates the reverse parallel that, in Part III, will bring the psalm to a climax of sublimity.

Part Three:
Strophe I: Afterward Thou Wilt Take Me into Glory (vv. 23-24)

Immediately, and with the swiftness of an epiphany, the poet in Part III exults at the very opening of Strophe I, "But I am always with thee" (v. 23a). The expression "with thee" occurs three times in quick succession: first, at the end of Part Two (v. 22), in a self-derogatory sense; second, "thou wilt guide me" (v. 24a), as a shepherd leads his flock (Ps 23:3) or Yahweh his people (Deut 32:12). Because it is modified by "thy counsel," the verb may suggest the style of sapiential thinking (Job 12:13; 38:2; Prov 12:15; 21:20); and third, in a supraterrestrial mood, "Afterward thou wilt take me into glory" (v. 24b). The adverb 'aḥar (Gen 10:13; 18:15; 24:55; 30:21) has often been understood as indicating the end of the religious crisis endured by the psalmist, and not as the perspective of an afterlife. Perhaps, as Calvin shrewdly observed, the poet is not excluding one or the other prospect. "It comprehends the whole course of our happiness from the commencement, which is seen here upon earth, even to the consummation which we expect to realize in heaven." In other words, the man who is nearest to God upon this earth receives a foretaste of eternal felicity.

While Israel did not speculate on human immortality, and for many years did not expect individual life in heaven, perhaps in reaction to the mortuary culture of Egypt, and took death as an abrupt and final reality, two exceptional characters have escaped this national disbelief, at least in the most astonishing bit of folklore. "And Enoch walked with God, and he was not, for God took him" (Gen 5:24). The same verb is used in the ancient tradition and in the present psalm. No specific indication is given of the mode of this translation or transmutation from terrestrial to eternal life. A similar motif appears in the early prophetic stories of Elijah: "And it came to pass, as [Elijah and Elisha] still went on, and talked, that, behold, there appeared a chariot of fire, and horses of fire, and parted them both asunder: and Elijah went up by a whirlwind into heaven" (2 Kgs 2:11). The second story is circumstantially different, but Psalm 73 possesses the essential ingredients of the same line of thinking. "Heaven" is explicitly mentioned in the next strophe (v. 25a), and "glory" becomes a link between the temporal and the eternal — an accusative of direction and final destination. No allusion is made to sleep, awakening, or resurrection. A Hellenistic influence on the *psychē*, "soul," that will survive a decaying *sarx*, "flesh," is absent. The whole discourse is bound or molded by the recurring "with thee."

Divine love in heaven continues divine nearness on earth. The ultimate destination of the psalmist's life is heaven forever, but not at the expense of happiness on earth in the here and now. It is on earth that eternal life begins.

Strophe II: No One Else in Heaven and on Earth (vv. 25-26)

The presence of the God who alone is sufficient to the poet's deepest needs appears to belong to him. The line, "Whom have I in heaven but thee?" amounts indeed to a daring, almost blasphemous attack on egocentricity, not theocentricity. God is spoken of as a human possession. The *summum mysteriosum* is here reached by man's attempt to express the ineffable. He verges on a claim to own God. The transcendence of the God who owns his servant has been reversed, at least in words. The mystic in rapture tends to absorb the divine.

The line of demarcation is blurred. The I-Thou dialogue in prayer reaches almost the level of identification. The psalmist may not have intended to produce such an impression. Nevertheless, the communion is so intense and so continuous that, although he does not speak of "my God" in the sense of proprietorship, he knows that he possesses none in heaven, no saint, no angel, no member of the heavenly council, besides the Lord.

The nearness of God can hardly be expressed in human terms.[2] It necessitates metaphors of powerful origin and implication. "The rock of my heart" (v. 26) refers not to the hardness of egocentricity, but to the solidity and the endurance of a divine quality lent to man (cf. Ps 18:3). "My lot forever" sounds like the cry of exaltation that a long-suffering wanderer and a nomadic landless man might shout when he suddenly becomes the proprietor of luxurious real estate. His word for an allotted portion of land may indicate that, as a chorister, he remains landless, but he now knows that he abounds in a possession far superior to the riches of land. For he is the inheritor of God's treasure (cf. Pss 16:5; 119:57; 142:6).

Strophe III: Nearness of God: The Supreme Good (vv. 27-28)

The poet has not forgotten his vocation as a sacred chorister. He winds up the sapiential questioning with which he began with exquisite, yet sober, hints of ecstasy, to the eminence of which he has climbed. The would-be philosopher has turned into a pensioner of sanctity. To place one's trust in Yahweh and to call him the rock of my heart and my lot forever (v. 26) is now secondary to "my good" (v. 28), for this declaration expresses anew the meaningful purpose of his future life on earth: the chorister will excel in his professional vocation, to pro-

---

2. S. Blank, "The Nearness of God and Psalm Seventy-three," in *Festschrift C. H. Pyatt* (Lexington, 1953), pp. 1-13.

claim in words and music the deeds of God. The disciple of the sages is an evangelist within the cultus. He gives beauty to sing of the good news.

DATE AND THEOLOGY

As in the disquisitions of Jeremiah (12:1-5) and the protests of Job (21:7-33), the poet of Psalm 73 attacks the seeming injustice, indifference, or impotence of God. He pleads indirectly for deliverance from his own misery when he mocks the prosperity of evildoers. In a thematic style close to the Jeremianic strains, he declares that Yahweh is so distantly removed from the human plight that the cynicism of the fat and prosperous about divine ignorance is quite understandable (Jer 12:1-2). Yet both the prophet and the psalmist know that such human arrogance verges on the abyss of blasphemy. At the same time, the most intimate hope (Ps 73:24) ends with the motif of divine inheritance (Ps 73:26; Jer 10:16). Indeed, the many sapiential elements[3] culminate in rapture. It is therefore probable that, like the poem of Job, Psalm 73 belongs to the Jeremianic circles that have collected and transmitted the prophet's tradition of his agonies and triumphs.

If the poem of Job was chanted and acted during the Babylonian exile as a drama that substituted for a cultic celebration of the New Year Festival, one may legitimately suppose that Psalm 73 was composed in the same cultural and religious environment, after the end of the Judahite monarchy.[4]

In the psalmodic confession of spiritual turmoil, originally individual but eventually collective (see vv. 1 and 28), the philosophical boldness and the theological restraint of such a poet opens a vista on the birth of synagogal worship. The religion of Judah, with its Zion-centricity, is not open to a universal horizon. By going to the "sacred places" of God (v. 17) the poet discovers his responsibility to the *ekklēsia*. He is not alone. Worship is togetherness with "the children of God." Then theology moves solitary questioning to collective adoration.[5] The creed arises when reflection leads to contemplation.

The nearness of God becomes the supreme good. It is both a desire (Isa

---

3. See J. K. Kuntz, "The Canonical Wisdom Psalms of Ancient Israel — Their Rhetorical, Thematic, and Formal Dimensions," in *Rhetorical Criticism* . . . , Festschrift J. Muilenburg (Pittsburgh, 1974), pp. 186-222. It will be noted that while the Jobian poet uses more *hapax legomena* than any other in the Hebrew Bible, the psalmist is also fond of words employed only once or rarely (vv. 2, 4, 5, 6, 8, 14, 18, 27, 28).

4. S. Terrien, "Le poème de Job: Drame para-rituel du Nouvel-An?" VTSup XVII (Leiden, 1969), pp. 226-27.

5. J. G. Gammie, "Behemoth and Leviathan: On the Didactic and Theological Significance of Job 40:15–41:26," in *Israelite Wisdom* . . . , Festschrift . . . S. Terrien (Missoula and New York, 1978), pp. 217-31.

58:2) and a gift (Ps 73:28). Philosophical questioning on the awful banality of evil precedes the mystical refusal to fight the Lord (Job 40:1-8), but poetic formulation and elaboration, thanks to the psalmodic theologian, can follow the memory of a spiritual kidnapping at the very threshold of infinity.[6] Theology is born out of the quest for truth and its doubts. It matures into creedal statements after the sublimity of divine possession.

PSALM 74

Lament over the Loss of Zion

1. Maskil. For Asaph.

PART ONE

I

	O God, why hast thou rejected us? Is it forever?
	Why does thy wrath burn against the sheep of thy pasture?
2.	*Remember thy people, that you purchased long ago!*
	Thou didst redeem them! They are thy firstborn tribe!
	And this Mount Zion, where thou dwellest!

II

3.	*Walk up step by step throughout this utter desolation,*
	The ruins that the enemy wrought to the sanctuary!
4.	*Thy foes roared like beasts in the midst of thy tabernacle!*
	They set up their emblems as signs!
5.	*They hacked at everything as if brandishing*
	A double axe in a jungle thicket.

III

6.	*They hammered down its carved ornaments,*
	And battered them with mattocks and hoes.

---

6. W. Brueggemann, "Shape for Old Testament Theology, II: Embrace of Pain," *CBQ*, XLVII (1985), p. 298.

7.   *They set thy sanctuary on fire,*
       And profaned the shelter of thy name down to the ground.
8.   *They said in their hearts, we'll smash it all!*
       They scorched to ashes all the meeting places of God in the land.

PART TWO
I

9.   *We do not see our signs; there is no longer a prophet!*
       Neither is there among us any that knows, How long?
10.   *How long, O God, shall the enemy scoff?*
       Or shall the foe despise thy name; forever?
11.   *Why dost thou withdraw thy hand,*
       Even hide thy right hand in thy bosom?

II

12.   *Nevertheless, God is my king of old,*
       Working salvation in the midst of the earth.
13.   *It was thou, yes, who didst frighten the Sea by thy power;*
       Thou didst crack the heads of the dragons in the waters.
14.   *It was thou, yes, who didst crush the heads of Leviathan;*
       Thou didst offer them as food to the desert creatures.

III

15.   *It was thou, yes, who didst cleave fountain and torrent,*
       Thou who didst dry up overflowing streams!
16.   *Thine is the day, and thine is the night!*
       It was thou, yes, who didst set up the light and the sun!
17.   *It was thou, yes, who didst fix all the borders of the earth;*
       It was thou, yes, who didst set summer and autumn!

PART THREE
I

18.   *Remember this: The enemy mocks the Lord!*
       An insane people despises thy name!
19.   *Do not deliver the soul of thy turtledove to the beasts!*
       Do not forget forever the life of thine afflicted ones!

II

20.   *Look after thy covenant!*
       For they filled the caves of the land with violence.

21. *Let not the oppressed be turned away, deceived!*
    The humble and the poor, let them praise thy name!

III

22. *Arise, O God! Plead thy case!*
    Remember how fools are scoffing at thee every day!
23. *Do not forget the clamor of thy foes,*
    The increasing din of those who rise against thee!

BIBLIOGRAPHY

P. R. Ackroyd, "Some Notes on the Psalms [Ps 74:4]," *JTS*, XVII (1966), pp. 392-99; idem, "נצח — εἰς τέλος [Ps 74:3]," *EvT*, LXXX (1968-69), p. 264; J.-N. Aletti and J. Trublet, *Approche poétique et théologique des Psaumes: Analyses et méthodes* (Paris, 1983), pp. 21-22; P. Auffret, "Essai sur la structure littéraire du Psaume LXXIV," *VT*, XXXIII (1983), pp. 129-48; C. Begg, "The Covenantal Dove in Psalm lxxiv," *VT*, XXXVII (1987), pp. 19-20; E. Beaucamp and P. de Relles, "S'il s'écroulait le temple, donjon de justice, Ps. 74," *BVC*, LXVI (1965), pp. 26-31; E. Donner, "Argumente zur Datierung des 74. Psalms," in *Wort, Lied und Gottesspruch*, Festschrift J. Ziegler (Würzburg, 1972), p. 45; O. Eissfeldt, "Gott und das Meer in der Bibel," in *Festschrift J. Pedersen* (Hauniae, 1953), pp. 75-84; M. Eliash, "Cuthites and Psalm 74," *Journal of the Palestine Oriental Society*, IV (1925), pp. 51-57; J. A. Emerton, "Notes on Three Passages of the Psalms [Ps 74:5; 11 . . .]," *JTS*, XIV (1963); idem, "Spring and Torrent in Psalm LXXIV," VTSup XV (Leiden, 1966), pp. 122-33; T. H. Gaster, "Note on Ps. 74:14," *EvT*, LXVIII (1956-57), p. 382; A. Guillaume, "Note," *JTS*, XLIX (1948), p. 55; J. P. Hyatt, "A Note on YIWWADA,'" *AJSL*, LVIII (1941), pp. 99-100; A. Lelièvre, "YHWH et la Mer dans les Psaumes," *RHPR*, LVI (1976), pp. 253-75; A. Malamat, "Mari and the Bible: Some Patterns of Tribal Organization and Institutions," *JAOS*, LXXXII (1962), p. 149; J. L. McKenzie, "A Note on Ps. 74:13-15," *TS*, II (1950), pp. 275-82; H. P. Nasuti, *Tradition History and the Psalms of Asaph* (Atlanta, 1988), pp. 66-71; G. A. Rendsburg, *Linguistic Evidence for the Northern Origin of Selected Psalms* (Atlanta, 1990), pp. 69-71; J. J. M. Roberts, "Of Signs, Prophets. and Time Limits: A Note on Ps 74:9," *CBQ*, XXXIX (1977), pp. 474-81; A. Robinson, "A Possible Solution to the Problems of Psalm 74 5," *ZAW*, LXXX (1977), pp. 120-21; H. Spieckermann, *Heilsgegenwart: Eine Theologie der Psalmen* (Göttingen, 1989), pp. 123-31; S. Terrien, "Creation, Cultus, and Faith, in the Psalter," in *Theological Education*, Festschrift C. L. Taylor (Dayton, 1966), pp. 116-28; J. P. M. van der Ploeg, "Psalm 74 and Its Structure," in *Festschrift M. A. Beek* (Assen, 1974), pp. 204-10; C. Westermann, *The Praise of God in the Psalms*, tr. K. R. Crim (Richmond, 1965), pp. 55, 59; F. Willesen, "The Cultic Situation of Ps. LXXIV,4," *VT*, II (1952), pp. 289-306; M. Zeidel, "Leḥayath — A Vulture," *Bulletin of the Jewish Palestine Exploration Society*, VI (1939), p. 144.

FORM

Several words in Psalm 74 are obscure, and the rhythm is quite irregular, as it changes to 2+2, 2+3, 3+3, and even to 3+4. Yet its overall structure presents a masterly architecture, reflecting the semantic progression in a collective lament on the destruction of the Jerusalem temple by Babylon in 587 B.C.E.

PART ONE
I
1b. – – – – – – – –
– – – – – –
2. – – – – – – – –
– – – – – –
– – – – – –

PART TWO
I
9. – – – – – – –
– – – – – –
10. – – – – – – –
– – – – – –
11. – – – – – – –
– – – – – –

II
3. – – – – – – – –
– – – – – –
4. – – – – – – – –
– – – – – –
5. – – – – – – – –
– – – – – –

II
12. – – – – – – – –
– – – – – –
13. – – – – – – – –
– – – – – –
14. – – – – – – – –
– – – – – –

III
6. – – – – – – – –
– – – – – –
7. – – – – – – – –
– – – – – –
8. – – – – – – – –
– – – – – –

III
15. – – – – – – – –
– – – – – –
16. – – – – – – – –
– – – – – –
17. – – – – – – – –
– – – – – –

PART THREE
I
18. – – – – – – – –
– – – – – –
19. – – – – – – – –
– – – – – –

II
20. – – – – – – – –
– – – – – –
21. – – – – – – – –
– – – – – –

III
22. – – – – – – – –
– – – – – –
23. – – – – – – – –
– – – – – –

Like other psalms in the protocollection of Asaph, this poem presents three parts of three strophes each. The only irregularity appears at the exordium: one bicolon followed by one tricolon, both lines announcing the thematic development that follows. Part One offers a plaintive rehearsal, sharing with Yahweh, in the style of a prayer, the horrors of the situation (vv. 1-8). In Part Two, a third person meditation, turning into a second person address to God, questions his seeming indifference, and yet observes God's awesome display of creative power (vv. 9-17). These two parts, with regular strophes of three bicola, precede and prepare for Part Three, also made up of three strophes, each of which contains only two bicola, for it appeals bluntly to the Deity and requires a swift pace of definite urgency.

COMMENTARY

Part One: Strophe I: Exordium (vv. 1b-2)

God's apparent inaction at the time of the Babylonian invasion has stunned the community of Yahweh. Conjectures abound: Why a rejection of "us"? Is it forever? (The Hebrew original has coalesced the two questions into a single sentence.) Deliverance from Egyptian slavery remains in Israel's memory. The psalmist's rebuke conceals a fervent faith: we are "thy people," literally, "thy congregation," namely, those assembled at "appointed times." More than this, still, "thy firstborn tribe," literally, the clan or extended family that inherits from thee, thy eldest son. Finally, "*this* Mount Zion," defined with a demonstrative pronoun, as if the poet were pointing verbally, using his finger, to the site of desolation. This is a programmatic preface to the whole psalm.

Strophe II: A Depiction of the Disaster (vv. 3-5)

The injunction pronounced at once to the Lord, to "walk up steps" (precative intensive), through the ruins of the sanctuary, may simply be a daring metaphor, conceived in the desolate land during the long exile. It is probably the prayer of an actual survivor who remained at the very site of the ruins. He may have been one of the choristers holding ceremonial laments and rites of mourning on regular days (Jer 41:5; cf. Zech 7:2; 8:19). "The midst of thy tabernacle" (v. 4), literally, "the center of thy appointed meeting." The word occasionally came to mean "a place of assembly" (Zeph 3:18), perhaps as an abbreviation of "the tent of meeting" (Exod 33:7). The sense of "they removed our signs" (v. 4) is unclear. Many exegetes and translators believe that the MT is corrupt and correct it in various ways. However, the "signs" may refer to indications of festivals as well as Sabbaths (cf. Exod 31:13, 17), or emblems of the tribes (Num 2:2). The "jungle thicket" shows the ferocity of those who brandish the double axe through an impenetrable forest.

Strophe III: Scorched Policy of Profanation (vv. 6-8)

A fanatic fury of annihilating by fire not only destroyed the Zion temple but also attacked its aesthetic beauty. The wood carvings (v. 6) were for the sanctuary; even the "meeting places" of the open country probably designate the earliest synagogues (v. 8; cf. 2 Kgs 25:9, 12).

Part Two: Strophe I: Questioning Divine Inaction (vv. 9-11)

The "why" of the prologue (v. 1b) is renewed with more intensity. The psalmist appears to maintain the theology of the name rather than the theology of glory. The mention of God's dwelling indicates that a tension is preserved on the paradox of divine transcendence and spiritual presence. While the language of the whole strophe is metaphorical, as shown by such an expression as "the withdrawing of God's hand," the psalmist belongs to the cultic officers of the sanctuary. Nevertheless, a similar tension is implied by the juxtaposition of "residence" and "holiness," a symbolic mystery of collective worship (cf. Exod 15:13; Jer 25:30).

The prophets whose lack is now mourned are cultic diviners, adversaries of the great prophets like Jeremiah. They had nationalistically announced the permanent security of Jerusalem (Jer 3:8; 28:11). The signs, which are no more, differ from the concrete objects mentioned in Part One (v. 4). These designate the optimistic predictions of the cultic diviners.

Strophe II: My King and the Master of the Sea (vv. 12-14)

The tone is abruptly altered without warning, as the poet passes from the plural "us" (v. 1b) to the singular pronominal suffix, "my" (v. 12a). Yahweh is addressed as "my king of old." The suddenness and the uniqueness of this individual outburst of trust and even joy do not justify a correction to read "the kings of the east." "In the midst of the earth" (v. 12b) is a reference to the myth of the navel of the earth, of Canaanite origin. Mount Zion was viewed not only as the center of the dry land but also the vertical linkage from earth to heaven and from earth to the underworld. The strophe proceeds with a subtle transition from a doxology of the most personal character ("my king of old") to the ascription of power to the Creator. We are invited to witness the triumph of Yahweh over Leviathan: this also displays the influence of Canaanite singers on the Hebrew poet. The Leviathan is neither a crocodile (cf. Job 40:25) nor a whale (cf. Ps 104:26), and the multiplicity of its heads confirms its cosmic dimensions (Job 3:8; Isa 27:1). The whole scene is parallel to the other Near Eastern pictures of the watery chaos (cf. Ps 89:9-10). The inhabitants of the wilderness are not forgotten (v. 14b).

Strophe III: The Equilibrium of the Seasons (vv. 15-17)

The Creator also established a balance between fast and moderate streams, days and nights, through the cycle of the sun and the even more extraordinary clarity of the night "luminary," not designated as the moon. The sequence between light and darkness reflects the Hebrew usage of placing the evening at the beginning of the new day (cf. Gen 1:5b).

Summer is followed by autumn (v. 17b), which inaugurates the New Year when its first rains at last terminate the long drought and prepare for the steady showers of winter. The emphatic repetition of the pronoun "thou" (vv. 15a, 16b, 17a, and 17b), in addition to the second person contained in the verbal forms, is rendered in this translation simply by "yes!" This insistence might conceal a lyrical hint of tenderness, from the possessiveness implied by "my king of old" (v. 12) to the admiring familiarity of "thine is the day, and thine is the night!" (v. 16a). One discerns an exceptional undertone of loving intent in the alternation of the creative acts, different from but similar to an ultimate connection in the making of a livable universe and the working out of salvation (v. 12). Creation as a deed of love for humankind may underline the complaint, for the psalm later on blossoms forth in a proclamation of hope (cf. Isa 51:9-15; Ezek 29:1-3).

Part Three: Strophe I: The Covenantal Turtledove (vv. 18-19)

The third part of the psalm concludes with a veritable explosion of demands, commands, peremptory orders hurled at the Lord in a style that is sometimes typical of some mystics in other cultures and times. The poet addresses God as if man could be a military commander: "Remember this . . . , Do not deliver . . . ; Do not forget . . . , Look after . . . ; Let not the oppressed . . . , Arise, God!" And once more, "Remember . . . ! Do not forget!" The multiplicity and the intensity of the petitions may surprise, but it fits the acuteness of the psalmist's agony over the loss of Zion. Appeals to a God whose power is not doubted present a sharp contrast to the sapiential skepticism of other psalms of Asaph.

The observation that the invader who has perpetrated such savage destruction represents a people wicked enough to despise the divine name (v. 18; cf. vv. 10, 22) is reiterated. The comparison between the chosen people, beloved of Yahweh, and "thy turtledove" (v. 19; cf. Hos 7:11) is uncertain, and several commentators correct the MT. Yet this term of endearment designates a bird offered in sacrifice (Lev 1:14; cf. Gen 15:4-10). The allusion to a holocaust that hurts the survivors may not be missed.

Strophe II: The Plight of the Poor (vv. 20-21)

This appeal, more pressing than ever, is based on the Mosaic covenant. The psalmist has not accepted the great prophets' denunciations of the national corruption. He does not believe that the covenant has been annulled (Jer 31:32), although he expresses concern for the poor and the oppressed.

Strophe III: The Final Plea (vv. 22-23)

The third strophe concludes the prayer with the injunction, "Arise!" (v. 22). This outspokenness does not express doubt in Yahweh's power (cf. vv. 12-17!), but it certainly addresses the Deity as if God were unwilling to act. Was he lazy, or asleep? The implied tone is slightly softened by the demand, "Plead thy case!" This borrowing from the language of jurisprudence might intimate that the Lord is a defendant wrongly accused and brought to trial. The last word amounts to a most unexpected transference: criminal injustice committed against us. The people of the covenant are now viewed as if they had rebelled like a foreign tyrant, a blasphemer who rises against the Master of heaven, sea, and earth.

DATE AND THEOLOGY

Many critics have dated Psalm 74 in Maccabean times (2nd cent. b.c.e.). For the temple was then profaned but not devastated by the forces of Antiochus Epiphanes. Although the theology of this complaint differs in several aspects from that of the prophet Jeremiah, its language closely recalls that of the Jeremianic circles: "the head of thy pasture" (Jer 23:1-8), "the tribe of its inheritance" (Jer 10:16; 51:19; cf. 12:1-9; 16:18), meaning in both places "the tribe of the firstborn inheritance." The exceptional thrust of this poem leads to a brilliant integration of cultus, creation, and faith. It follows formal patterns and prosodic canons, but it could not be viewed as the product of impersonal forces operating under cultic institutionalism.

The creation myths, which are of foreign origin, become purified when they are brought in as the manifestation of a personal commitment of trust in the sovereign Lord, Enabler of the world, "my King of old!" The inner life of the singer participates in the stability that the Creator and Re-creator constantly inserts in nature. The theogonic cosmology becomes the macro-mirror of the micro-security of all human beings whose courage in adversity will not vanish.

At the same time a passionate attachment to the geographic center of divine presence, appropriated from the pseudo-magical myth of the omphalos, risks losing the universal sweep that Isaiah and Jeremiah have envisioned and forcefully proclaimed. The wonder of common worship in a common sanctuary should not degenerate into a lust for territorial claims or imperialistic conquest. Common worship, with its social warmth, must remain attuned to the universal scope, without a sectarian sense of superiority over other human beings. The standards of behavior issued from divine salvation cannot and should not deviate into a sociology of exclusion. The unresolved ambiguity of Psalm 74 reveals the tension that threatens both Judaism and Christendom.

PSALM 75

A Prophetic Oracle

1. *To the choirmaster. "Do Not Destroy." Psalm. For Asaph. Song.*

Invocation

2.   *We praise thee, O God, we praise thee!*
   Those who invoke thy name celebrate thy marvels.

Oracle

3.   *[God says:] I, myself, judge with rectitude*
   At my appointed time!
4.   *The earth may totter with all its peoples,*
   Yet it was I who made its pillars firm.   Selah
5.   *I tell the arrogant, No more arrogance!*
   And the evildoers, Raise not your horn!
6.   *Raise not your horn so high and stiff;*
   Speak not rudely with such smugness!

Response

7.   *No! He will not come from east or west,*
       From the southern desert or the northern hills!
8.   *God is the judge:*
       He brings one low and exalts another.

9.   *In the hand of the Lord there is a cup of wine,*
       Full of foam and heavily spiced;
       All the evildoers of the earth will drink it,
       Even lap it up to the dregs.

Commitment

10.   *As for me, I shall forever proclaim*
       And celebrate the God of Jacob.
11.   *And all the horns of the evildoers [he] will smash,*
       But the horns of the righteous shall be exalted.

BIBLIOGRAPHY

E. Beaucamp and J. P. de Relles, "Psaume 75 (74): La coupe de Yahweh," *Feu nouveau,* VIII (1965), pp. 21-27; E. Bonnard, *Le Psautier selon Jérémie* (Paris, 1960), pp. 151-55; F. Crüsemann, *Studien zur Formgeschichte von Hymnus und Danklied in Israel,* WMANT XXXII (Neukirchen, 1969), p. 208; M. Dahood, "The Four Cardinal Points in Psalm 75 and Joel 2, 20," *Bib,* LII (1971), p. 397; J. Jeremias, *Kultprophetie und Gerichtsverkündigung in der späten Königszeit Israels,* WMANT XXXV (Neukirchen, 1970), pp. 117-18; S. Mowinckel, *Psalmenstudien,* III: *Kultprophetie und prophetische Psalmen* (Oslo, 1923), pp. 47ff.; idem, "The Prophetic Word in the Psalms and the Prophetic Psalms," in *The Psalms in Israel's Worship,* II, tr. D. R. Ap-Thomas (Nashville, 1962), pp. 53ff.; H. P. Nasuti, "A Linguistic Analysis of the Psalms of Asaph," in *Tradition History of the Psalms of Asaph* (Atlanta, 1988), pp. 71-75; E. Wiesenberg, "A Note on *m.z.l.* in Psalm LXXV 9," *VT,* IV (1954), p. 434.

FORM

The structure of Psalm 75 is peculiar, for it combines, on the first day, a doxology collectively sung and, on the last day, individually chanted with a prophetic oracle in two quatrains and a response, also in two quatrains. The meter varies for no discernible reason, but the unity of composition, which the form clearly reveals, introduces a liturgical coherence among its various parts. The cultic prophecy concentrates on Yahweh, the judge on the last day. The doxology transmutes a desperate situation into an era of peace and happiness.

COMMENTARY

Superscription (v. 1)

A psalm of the Asaphite precollection, to be sung to a popular tune, "Do Not Destroy." The piece is thematically related to Psalms 74 and 76, but it fulfills a special function in the liturgical mode.

Invocation: The Praise of God's Marvels (v. 2)

Dividing the body of the psalm that follows (vv. 3-6 and 7-8), the invocation announces a celebration of God's marvels and indicates a hymn of thanksgiving throughout the poem's sweep. The genre, however, is altogether different. The Hebrew text of v. 2b seems to mean, "and close is thy name," but the verb that follows is plural, "they celebrate," which is syntactically incoherent. Thanks to the Greek translation of the LXX, one should probably read, "those who invoke thy name."

Oracle (vv. 3-6)

Without any rhetorical warning, a prophetic oracle is now ascribed to the Deity. The words "God says," absent in the MT, have been inserted in the translation for the sake of clarity. A self-declaration of divine rectitude may surprise. This may suggest that the author of this oracle is not an inspired prophet. The next sequence of thought seems to be, "The earth may totter with all its peoples, yet it was I who made its pillars firm," rather than "but I shall strengthen its pillars" (v. 4). God announces a day of judgment, even if he feels divided within himself. Did he not promise to Noah, after the great Flood, that he would not again annihilate most of the living creatures (Gen 8:21-22). Nevertheless, the eighth- and seventh-century prophets predicted the end of a corrupt history before a renewed creation.

Response (vv. 7-9)

Since the sovereign Judge has universal jurisdiction, no one else will come from any of the four corners or main points of the horizon. Is this a hidden way to convey belief in the uniqueness of Zion? (Cf. comment on Ps 74:2, 7.) In the hand of the Lord, a cup of wine, foaming and heavily spiced, will be drunk with greed by the evildoers. Their intoxication will precede their annihilation. The cup of judgment will then become the cup of wrath (cf. Ps 60:4-5; Isa 51:17; Jer 25:15-18; Ezek 23:32-34).

Commitment (vv. 10-11)

The psalm finally returns to the first person singular style. Is this the psalmist or some prominent individual who now sings, "As for me"? If the MT is correctly preserved, the last words are those of the Lord, continuing the previous oracle, "I shall smash all the horns of the evildoers" (v. 11a; cf. v. 5).

Through the image of a bull in fury that is compelled to lower his horns ready to strike, or even the smashing of this symbol of brutal arrogance, the psalmist affirms once more the power and the rectitude of God's judgment. Puzzling, however, is the following clause, "The horns of the righteous shall be exalted" (v. 11b). Is there a hidden meaning in the use of the masculine gender for the evildoers' horns and the feminine gender for the horns of the righteous?

DATE AND THEOLOGY

Like other pieces of the Asaph collection, Psalm 75 displays a striking affinity with the Jeremianic book. The cup of judgment that becomes the cup of wrath resembles that which Yahweh asks Jeremiah to pour for all the nations to which he sends him, so that they will drink, stumble, and be crazed (Jer 25:15-29; cf. 49:12; 51:39). This cup is not only for the nations but also for the evildoers of the holy land (Jer 13:12-14). Both in the psalm and in Jeremiah, the lowering of the horns becomes the symbol of retribution (Jer 48:25-26). "Yes, it is God [alone] who judges with equity" (Jer 11:20).

Was Psalm 75 composed before or after the destruction of the temple in 587 B.C.E.? The allusion to the point of convergence for the four main points implies that the poet is passionately devoted to the omphalos of the earth as the geographical center of worship, but he remains completely silent on the edifice of Mount Zion. The date may very well be that of the late exile, when Second Isaiah proclaimed the hope of renewal (549-545 B.C.E.).

PSALM 76

Paean of Praise after a Victory

1. *To the choirmaster, with stringed instruments. Psalm of Asaph. A song.*

I

2.   God is renowned in Judah;
         His name is great in Israel.
3.   His tent came to be in Salem,
         And he resides in Zion.
4.   There he broke the bow in a flash of fire,
         Buckler and battle scimitar!   Selah

II

5.   Magnificent art thou, more majestic
         Than the eternal hills!
6.   The stalwart of heart were impotent;
         They went to sleep,
         All the valiant warriors!
7.   At thy menace, O God of Jacob,
         Horsemen and charioteers froze up stiff.

III

8.   For thou! Awesome art thou!
         Who is able to resist thee
         When thy wrath explodes?
9.   From the heavens thou sayest the verdict;
         The earth, terrified, is stunned
10.   When God rises in judgment
         To deliver the oppressed of the world.   Selah

IV

11.   Even man's fury brings out thy splendor!
         Those who survive thy wrath celebrate thee!
12.   Make your vows to the Lord your God, and fulfill them,
         All those who surround him!
         Bring your gifts to the awesome one!
13.   For he abases the pride of princes,
         And terrifies the kings of the earth.

BIBLIOGRAPHY

J. Dat, "Shear-jashub (Isaiah vi 3) and the Remnant of Wrath (Psalm lxxvi 9)," *VT,* XXXI (1981), pp. 76-77; O. Eissfeldt, "Psalm 76," *TLT,* pp. 901-3; idem, *Kleine Schriften,* III (Tübingen, 1966), pp. 448-57; J. A. Emerson, "A Neglected Solution of a Problem in Psalm 76, 11," *VT,* XXIV (1974), pp. 136-46; S. L. Kelly, "The Zion-Victory Songs: Psalms 46, 48 and 76" (diss., Vanderbilt, 1968); H. P. Nasuti, "A Linguistic Analysis of the Psalms of Asaph," in *The Psalms of Asaph* (Atlanta, 1988), pp. 75-78, 151-154; E. Slovonic, "Toward an Understanding of the Formation of Historical Titles in the Book of Psalms," *ZAW,* XCI (1979), pp. 359-60; N. H. Snaith, "The Asaphite Psalms," in *Studies in the Hebrew Psalter* (London, 1934), pp. 26ff.; J. S. Strugnell, "A Note on Ps 76.1," *JTS,* VII (1956), pp. 231-43; R. Tournay, "Psalm 76, Nouvel essai d'interprétation," in *Studia Hierosolymitana,* Festschrift P. G. Bagatti, ed. E. Testa et al. (Jerusalem, 1976), pp. 20-26.

FORM

The meter is irregular, but the structure of the four strophes that form the psalm is precise:

Strophe I: three bicola (vv. 2-4)
Strophe II: one bicolon, one tricolon, one bicolon (vv. 5-7)
Strophe III: one tricolon, two bicola (vv. 8-10)
Strophe IV: one bicolon, one tricolon, one bicolon (vv. 11-13).

The first strophe is meditative in appraising the Deity's actions, told in the third person; the middle strophes are prayers addressed to the Lord in the second person, although they are not petitions but praises of divinity (vv. 5-7, 8-10); the last strophe continues initially in the second person (v. 11), but it soon shifts back to the third person meditative style of the first strophe.

COMMENTARY

Superscription (v. 1)

Postexilic editors of provisional psalters may have recorded all the titles that had been given orally to Psalm 76, and it may have been viewed as a hymn of military triumph at various festivals. The LXX adds, "For the Assyrians," which may have indicated an allusion to a historical event: Sennacherib's sudden lifting of the siege of Jerusalem (701 B.C.E.). Syr. adds, "For the Ammonites" and appears to refer to 2 Sam 12:26, and thus relates the hymn to the wars of David.

Strophe I: Salem and Zion (vv. 2-4)

Like other psalms of Asaph, this poem is concerned with the northern kingdom of Israel, although it proclaims the unity of the chosen people under the centrality of Zion. The intention of the hymnist was to celebrate the Jerusalem temple, but he recognized a chronological sequence from Salem to Zion, for the name *Salem,* "health," a cognate of *shalôm,* "peace," was at one time mentioned as the city of Melchizedek (Gen 14:18). The text of Ps 76:3 does not suggest an identity between Salem and Zion. The distinction is shown by the syntax and chronological opposition between "His tent came to be in Salem" and the verbless sequence, indicating the present tense, "and he resides in Zion" (Ps 78:3). This implies a "then" for the tent and a "now" for the habitation in Zion. The LXX, Syr., and Vulg. support views of Eusebius and Jerome.[1] Salem was a Canaanite sanctuary, soon adopted by the Hebrews when they entered the land of Canaan. It was perhaps at Bethshan, more probably at Shechem, a site that then claimed the mythical status of "earth-navel," later attributed to Zion.[2] If these views are correct, they would explain in part the long tension between Judah and northern Israel, a tension that was not really resolved by the reform of Josiah (622 B.C.E.). The religious and cultural conflict between north and south continued for centuries, for Jews continued to discriminate against Samaria and the Samaritans.

While the psalmist subscribes to the theology of the holy name, he is also inspired by a passionate acceptance of the omphalos myth on "the Rock" of Zion.[3] The tent of Yahweh evokes the seminomadic character of early Israel (cf. Ps 27:5).

The psalm glides into the magnificent memory of the time when the Lord intervened in a flash of fire (the lightning of a mythicized thunderstorm). The weapons of destruction aimed at Jerusalem have themselves been destroyed, and peace renewed for the people of the covenant (cf. Psalms 46 and 48).

The poet brought together a daring conjunction of words, "There he broke the bow in a flash of fire" (v. 4), a visual image of the frightening advance of the invading warriors, with the visceral terror of a thunderstorm.

Strophe II: The Majesty of Yahweh (vv. 5-7)

A vivid reminiscence of this fright, still described in the third person, soon elicits the style of prayer in the second person. The emotion abruptly revived brings the poet back to direct address to a God ever present, or at least a God

1. Cf. F.-M. Abel, *Géographie de la Palestine,* II (Paris, 1938), pp. 441-42; H. Vincent, *Jérusalem de l'Ancien Testament,* II (Paris, 1950), pp. 612-13.

2. M. D. Goulder, "Salem," in *The Psalms of Asaph and the Pentateuch: Studies in the Psalter,* III, JSOTSup CCXXXIII (Sheffield, 1996), pp. 86-95.

3. S. Terrien, "The Omphalos Myth and Hebrew Religion," *VT,* XX (1970), pp. 315-16.

who is at this moment as close as ever. "Magnificent art thou." (v. 5), literally, "brilliant" or "luminous." This outplays the flash of lightning evoked in the first strophe to produce a new effect of dread: the intervention of the Lord is even more striking. While viewed most realistically, it does not altogether ignore the element of awe, quite metaphysical, that always terrorizes in a theophany. To say "magnificent" is not sufficient, for this God is more "majestic" than nature's wonders, as shown especially by the snowy top of Mount Hermon.

The arms of the invaders are useless, for they cannot be held or manipulated. The God of the covenant renders ineffectual the most modern weapons; literally, "the men of war could not find their hands!" (v. 6).

Strophe III: The Earth Is Stunned (vv. 8-10)

The poem offers a gradation in its appraisal of Yahweh: from "brilliant" and majestic" (v. 5) to "awesome" (v. 9) so that the neighboring princes and kings are terrified and even the earth is stunned. The unexpected deliverance of Jerusalem has become a token for the oppressed of the world. The nationalistic stress is tempered by an international horizon (v. 10).

Strophe IV: Man's Fury, God's Splendor (vv. 11-12)

The antithesis between humanity and divinity continues to concern the poet, but an unexpected twist alters the awesomeness of the judge into a splendor, and man's fury becomes the very cause of praise!

The MT of v. 11b is obscure: literally, "the remnant of wrath shalt thou restrain." The "remnant of wrath" may well be an intended counter-allusion to the name of Isaiah's son, Shear-yashub (Isa 7:3).

A musician of the temple, writing the psalm in its final form, knows that his poetic inspiration about the grandeur of his God cannot distract his attention from cultic responsibilities. He therefore reminds the faithful of their obligations to fulfill the vows they have made in times of crisis (v. 12). His final word returns to the main theme of his call for the praise of the Lord, but his celebration retains an apprehension caused by the pride of princes and foreign kings. He knows that his Lord will crush them forever.

DATE AND THEOLOGY

It is unlikely that the poetic impulse that prompted the composition of Psalm 76 was other than the memory of Jerusalem's deliverance from the vast and well-equipped army of Sennacherib (2 Kgs 20:36), The story of the siege is so vivid and the Isaianic oracles are so picturesque (Isa 37:36) that an eighth-century date for the composition of Psalm 76 is not impossible (cf. the fear of the Assyrian chariot and the two thousand horses; 2 Kgs 19:23: cf. Psalm 76 and Isa 36:8). Nevertheless, the Hebraic sense of cultic reenacting of distant events, such as the exodus at the Passover (Deut 16:1-8), may well survive the passing of time.

Even if the composition of Psalm 76 was originally due to the recall of Sennacherib's siege of Jerusalem (701 B.C.E.), the author is moved chiefly by the majesty of the sovereign Judge not only of Israel but also of all the oppressed peoples of the world. In addition, he did not neglect his own professional responsibility. As a chorister of the temple, he inserted, almost surreptitiously, an invitation — almost a demand — from the assembly of worshipers for the payment of their vows. Hence the date might oscillate between the time of the late monarchy and that of postexilic Judaism.

A third concern of the author might have been eschatological.[4] The proximate future is bleak, but history moves toward the Last Day. Divine splendor will receive its fulfillment on a new earth from a new heaven. On that day the whole earth may be "stunned," but the famished, landless, and even persecuted "poor" will receive a new life and enjoy at last a peaceful destiny (v. 10).

PSALM 77

I Remember the Deeds of the Lord

1. *To the choirmaster. On the air of Jeduthun. Psalm of Asaph.*

I

2.   *I cried to God in full voice,*
       Even to God in full voice, and he listened to me.
3.   *In my day of distress I sought the Lord;*
       At night without fail I stretched out my hands;
       My deeper self refused to be comforted.
4.   *I think of God and I groan,*
       I meditate and my spirit faints.   Selah

---

4. Cf. D. C. Mitchell, *The Message of the Psalter: An Eschatological Programme in the Book of Psalms,"* JSOTSup CCLII (Sheffield, 1997), pp. 97, 106, 166 [?].

II

5. *Thou keepest my eyelids from sleep;*
  I am in such trouble I don't speak.
6. *But I recall the days of old,*
  And the years of long ago.
7. *The music I played comes back to me in the night;*
  I meditate and my spirit ponders.

III

8. *Will the sovereign Lord cast me off forever,*
  And never again show mercy?
9. *Has his grace disappeared forevermore?*
  Or will his word be muted for all generations?
10. *Has God forgotten to be gracious?*
  In anger has he stifled his tender mercies? Selah

IV

11. *I said, This is the cause of my chagrin:*
  The right hand of the Most High has changed!
12. *I remember the deeds of the Lord!*
  Yes, I recall thy wonders of old;
13. *I meditate also on all thy exploits,*
  And I ponder thy marvelous deeds.

III′

14. *Thy way, O God, is [traced by thy] holiness.*
  Who is a god as great as God?
15. *It is thou, the God who workest wonders!*
  Thou hast shown thy strength among the nations;
16. *Thou hast released thy people with thy arm;*
  The sons of Jacob and of Joseph! Selah

II′

17. *The waters have seen thee, O God! They writhe;*
  The waters have seen thee.
  Indeed, the abysses tremble!
18. *The clouds have poured out their torrential rains.*
  Heavy clouds sounded their thunderclaps,
  And thy arrows flew everywhere.

I'

19.   The rumbling of thy thunder rolled in;
      The flashes of lightning illuminated the world;
      The earth shook and quivered.
20.   In the sea was thy way, in the great waters were thy paths;
      But the traces of thy steps are unknown.
21.   Thou didst lead thy people like a flock,
      By the hands of Moses and of Aaron.

BIBLIOGRAPHY

Y. Feenstra, "Le Dieu qui fait merveille (Ps 77,15," *Revue du Clergé africain*, XXII (1967), pp. 252-57; W. A. Goy, "Has God Changed? Psalm 77," in *Festschrift W. Vischer* (Montpellier, 1960), pp. 56-64; H. G. Jefferson, "Psalm 77," *VT*, XIII (1963), pp. 87ff.; J. Jeremias, *Theophanie*, WMANT X (Neukirchen, 1965), pp. 26ff.; A. Lauha, "Die Geschichtsmotive in den alttestamentlichen Psalmen," *Annales academiae scientiarum Fennicae* (Helsinki, 1945), pp. 68ff.; I. Löw, "Psalm 77,3," in *Festschrift für Karl Marti* (Giessen, 1925), pp. 194-96; H. P. Nasuti, *Tradition History and the Psalms of Asaph* (Atlanta, 1988), pp. 78-81; W. Schottroff, *Gedenken im alten Orient und im Alten Testament*, WMANT XV (Neukirchen, 1964), pp. 131ff.; F. Stolz, *Psalmen im nachkultischen Raum* (Zürich, 1983); B. Weber, *Psalm 77 und seine Umwelt: Eine poetologische Studie* (Weinheim, 1995); A. Weiser, "Psalm 77: Ein Beitrag nach dem Verhältnis von Kult und Heilsgeschichte," *TLZ*, LXXII (1947), pp. 133-40.

FORM

The metrical irregularity of Psalm 77 has led several scholars to consider it a composite poem of at least two or three diverse elements: a prayer, a complaint, and a hymn:

      I. vv. 2-3: 3+4, 4+4+3
      II. vv. 4-16: mostly 3+3
      III. vv. 17-21: mostly 3+3

However, an analysis that discerns four tricola (vv. 3, 17, 18, 20) in the midst of an accumulation of bicola seems to indicate a strict regularity of triads throughout the psalm, forming altogether seven strophes organized around a core strophe (IV). Such a composition is common for individual complaints that shift into hymns of praise. This appears especially among the so-called "psalms of Asaph."

I. The Day of My Distress (vv. 2-4)
II. My Music Playing (vv. 5-7)
III. Has God Rejected His People? (vv. 8-10)
      IV. I Remember the Deeds of the Lord (vv. 11-13)
III'. Thou Hast Redeemed (vv. 14-16)
II'. The Waters Have Seen Thee (vv. 17-18)
I'. Thou Didst Lead Thy People (vv. 19-21)

Not only is the number "seven" a significant feature, but also the core strophe IV (vv. 11-13) offers the clue to the meaning and unity of the entire poem: "I remember the deeds of the Lord" (v. 12).

Before and after the central verse, ascendant and descendant strophes offer a mirrorlike or echolike construction: I and I' form a contrast between psychological distress and the myth of cosmic creation (vv. 2 and 19); II and II' oppose the musical harmonies in the night and the thunderclaps of the theophany at creation (vv. 5-7 and 17-18); III and III' contrast divine muteness and apparent impotence with divine creative power. The core verse binds together the lament in distress that precedes the hymnic elation and the restrained exultation that follows. Psalm 77 may be considered a masterpiece of poetic and theological composition.

COMMENTARY

Superscription (v. 1)

Psalm 77 is a lament that turns into a hymn of praise by sober allusion to the Creator's omnipotence. The tune of Jeduthun could be used with an introspective meditation (cf. Pss 39:1; 62:1).

Strophe I: The Day of My Distress (vv. 2-4)

The poet's vocabulary seems more varied than that of other psalmists of complaint. It may have been enlarged by wisdom teaching. The psalm begins as a confession of despair over the admission that prayer is unanswered. Yet the suppliant shouts in a deep, full voice in order to be heard, and he performs the ritual gesture of prayer: a body language that underlines his integrity and candor.

God is named *Elohim* throughout, with the exception of *Yah* only in the core strophe (v. 12). Like other psalms of Asaph, the origin of Psalm 77 may have been in northern Israel.

Strophe II: My Music Playing (vv. 5-7)

A bold query interrogates God Almighty. It is implied at first by the reproach, "Thou keepest my eyelids from sleep." A devoted worshiper cannot speak about God for long: God is too close to be talked about. The second person is imperative. Even if the Deity is mute, divine presence is still recognized, as in the days of old, and the freedom born from long intimacy does not resist accusing such a God! The psalmist dares to ascribe his insomnia to divine silence.

Instead of "I remember" or "I recall" (MT), LXX and Syr. read (v. 6), "I commune with my heart." The "spirit"[1] is here used to describe the faculty of meditating and even reasoning, although the word "heart" is sufficient to designate the activity of the mind. The MT needs no correction, for the whole psalm deals with the psychology of memory recalled. Musical tunes possess the power to evoke the ideas to which they were connected.

Strophe III: Has God Rejected His People? (vv. 8-10)

To express a doubt on the catechism of the covenant represents such an enormous break with the traditions of Yahwism that the thought grows like the invading surf of the sea in a storm. The implied accusation explaining insomnia and distress now bursts forth explicitly as a near-blasphemy, leading to the charge of divine forgetfulness. Could the "word" of God, which amounts to a solemn promise, be muted and thus broken for all future generations?

Strophe IV: I Remember the Deeds of the Lord! (vv. 11-13)

The nerve center of the psalm connects the ascending strophes with the descending strophes. The core verse in the central strophe also differentiates between the psalmist's distress and the omnipotence of the Creator. The name *Yah* is found about 25 times in the Hebrew Bible, including the cultic exclamation "Hallelu-Yah," "Praise ye the Lord!" It is not certain that the monosyllabic designation is anterior to the name *Yahweh*, revealed to Moses at the time of his prophetic vocation (Exod 3:13-14). It may well have been a ritual cry during a cultic and symbolic reenacting of God's intervention in the choice and salvation of the holy people.

Strophe III': Thou Hast Redeemed (vv. 14-16)

The way of the Lord differs widely from the ways of the nations. The meaning of the MT, however, is uncertain. It may refer to the sanctuary, for the word

---

1. Cf. D. Hill, *Greek Word and Hebrew Meaning* (Cambridge, 1976), pp. 205-17.

"holy" may designate a holy place, the temple, or even the tabernacle.[2] It is used of God's way in the sense of this frightful quality, also mystically embracing and dynamically energetic. It is the way of God that is traced by holiness. As the parallel of "great" (v. 14b), it probably describes the uniqueness of Yahweh in terms of his strength among the nations. The selection of the Hebrew slaves in Egypt, and the wonders of the exodus, manifestly display God's power in redemption. The verb "to redeem" implies the payment of a ransom; since no price has been granted to the Pharaoh, the verb must include the idea of "liberation."[3] The presentation of the sons of Jacob and Joseph is exceptional, and the presence of "Joseph" strengthens the conjecture of a northern origin for the psalm.

Strophe II': The Waters Have Seen Thee (vv. 17-18)

It is unlikely that the language of the theophany with thunder and flooding rains alludes to the crossing of the Sea of Reeds, for it is accompanied by the trembling of these waters, there personified, and the shaking of the abysses. These allusions bring up reminiscences of the ancient Near Eastern myth of creation and the triumph of light and order over darkness and chaos. The primal Ocean lies at the bottom of the earth, which it somehow supports on solid foundations. The poet has softened the details of a cosmic combat, but he has not rejected the notion of an eternal abyss, which therefore antedated the creative word.

Strophe I': Thou Didst Lead Thy People (vv. 19-21)

The final strophe, antithesis of Strophe I, recalls the traditions of the desert and of the conquest of the land of Canaan. Skillfully, the psalmist terminates his disquisition with a dramatic evocation of the creative power of God. The illumination of the world through flashes of lightning offers a stunning contrast with the miracle of light (Gen 1:3). Darkness precedes creation.

The theme of God's way, first introduced in the attribution of holiness to the God who frightens the primal Sea, is now taken up again in its metaphoric suggestion. Having illuminated the cosmos, God has nothing more to accomplish. For his departure he "cuts" or "splits" a way through the sea, but the traces of his path are unknown. The myth of God's way through the primal Ocean becomes the background for the historic picture of God's leading his people through the wilderness of Sinai and the hostile nations. The people are compared to a flock of obstinate sheep, prone to panic, which do not discover

2. Cf. J. G. Gammie, *Holiness in Israel* (Minneapolis, 1989), p. 63, n. 32.
3. Hill, *Greek Word and Hebrew Meaning*, p. 54.

the correct direction, but details are not furnished, as in other psalms. Moses and Aaron are merely mentioned as the intermediaries of the omnipotent and omniscient leader.

DATE AND THEOLOGY

If Psalm 77 has been adapted from an earlier prayer of doubt that emerged in northern Israel, the determination of a date of composition would extend from the tenth century B.C.E. to the eighth. The mention of Jacob and Joseph and of Aaron, after Moses, leads to this tentative conclusion.

Unlike the great prophets of the eighth and seventh centuries, the psalmist omitted to mention the corruption of Israel and the violation of the Sinai Covenant — a conditional contract that was annulled. A sacred singer of the Zion temple, as a royal functionary, like many other psalmists, believed in the unconditional character of the Davidic covenant. The myth of an eternal Zion stood above and beyond the notions of national integrity.

A passionate attachment to the election and mission of the holy people displays the poet's spirituality more than his acceptance of theological dogmatism. The silent and hidden God is not an absent God. He holds himself inactive in the protection of his people, and the psalmist is profoundly distressed by this inactivity, but his memory of the glorious past will enable him to wait and to hope. This memory, as in the poem of Job, is crowned by the contemplation of the universe. The greatness of the Creator may not be denied. The omnipotence of the Creator is not independent of his holiness. He threatens the primal ocean; even the earth quakes at his approach. The way of God across the deep sea is a secret inaccessible to human beings, but the grandeur of God, who maintains the universe in equilibrium, is that of the God who presides over the birth of Israel.

Psalm 77, whose strophic structure in its harmonious architecture does not permit any additional meditation, now ends with an open lack of any affirmation. A leap from the wondrous past to the dismal present does not necessarily promise for Israel a priestly destiny of saving humankind (Exod 19:5). The psalmist relies on the notion of divine omnipotence, but the future agony of Judah may reveal a God of weakness and vulnerability that may promote a more brilliant form of divine splendor.　　　　•

PSALM 78

The Enigma of Sacred History

1. *Meditation of Asaph.*

Exordium

O my people, listen to my instruction!
Incline your ears to the words of my mouth!
2.   *I shall open my mouth for a parable,*
And draw enigmas from the distant past.

PART ONE
I

3.   *We have heard them and known them,*
For our fathers have told us.
4.   *We will not conceal them from their children.*
But narrate them for a generation to come,
The praises of the Lord and his power,
And the wonderful works he has done.

II

5.   *He has established a rule in Jacob,*
And appointed a law in Israel,
Which he commanded our fathers
To teach to their own children;
6.   *So that a new generation might know it;*
These still unborn children should arise,
And they would teach their own children!

III

7.   *These might then set their hope in God,*
And not forget the works of God,
And keep his commandments,
8.   *And might not be, like their fathers,*
A stubborn and rebellious generation,
A generation that set not their heart aright,
And whose spirit was not steadfast with God.

PART TWO

I

9.   *The sons of Ephraim, well-equipped archers,*
      Turned back on the day of battle.

10.   *They did not keep the covenant of God,*
      And refused to walk in his law.

11.   *They had forgotten his works,*
      And the wonders he had shown them.

II

12.   *A miracle he did in the sight of their fathers,*
      In the land of Egypt, the country of Zoan:

13.   *He split the sea in two to let them pass through,*
      Making the sea stand up like a cascade.

14.   *During the day also, he led them with a cloud,*
      And at nighttime with the light of a fire.

III

15.   *He clave the rocks in the wilderness,*
      To give them drink from the great abysses.

16.   *He brought streams out of the rock,*
      And caused water to flow like rivers,

17.   *But they sinned against him the more*
      By provoking the Most High in the desert.

PART THREE

I

18.   *They tested God in their heart*
      By demanding meat, in their appetite;

19.   *Yea, they spoke against God;*
      They said, Can God set a table in the wilderness?

20.   *Behold, he smote the rock,*
      So that water gushed out
      And the streams overflowed.
   Can he give bread also,
      And prepare meat for his people?

II

21.   *When the Lord heard this, he became enraged;*
      So a fire was kindled against Jacob,

And anger came up against Israel,
22. Because they did not believe in God,
       Nor trust in his salvation.
23. And he commanded the clouds from above,
       And opened the gates of heaven,
24. And rained down manna for them to eat;
       He gave them the wheat of heaven.

III

25. Man did eat the food of angels!
       He sent them meat aplenty;
26. He raised in the heaven an east wind,
       And by his power brought in the south wind;
27. He rained meat upon them as if it were dust,
       And fowls as numerous as the sands of the sea,
28. And let these fall in the midst of their camp,
       Round about their bivouac.

PART FOUR
I

29. So they did eat to satiety,
       And he fulfilled their desires;
30. But their appetite was not appeased
       While their meat was still in their mouth;
31. And the wrath of God came upon them,
       And he slew the noble among them,
       He smote down the youth of Israel!
32. In spite of this, they were sinning still,
       For they did not believe in his wondrous works.

II

33. So he made their days vanish like a breath,
       And their years in dismay and terror.
34. When he was about to slay them, they sought him,
       And repented, and followed God.
35. They remembered that God was their rock,
       And the Most High God, their redeemer.
36. They tried to flatter him with their mouth,
       To lie to him with their tongue;
37. Their heart was not steadfast with him.
       They did not have trust in his covenant.

III

38.   *But he, being full of compassion,*
       Forgave their transgression,
       And he did not destroy them;
    Many times he restrained his anger,
       And did not stir up all his wrath.
39.   *For he remembered that they were flesh,*
       A mere breath that goes and does not return.
40.   *Again in the wilderness they provoked him to anger,*
       And in the desert offended him.

PART FIVE
I

41.   *Yea, they turned back and tested God,*
       And grieved the Holy One of Israel.
42.   *They did not remember [the work of] his hand,*
       Nor the day when he saved them from the enemy.
43.   *How he had wrought his signs in Egypt,*
       And his wonders in the land of Zoan;
44.   *And had turned their rivers into blood,*
       So that they could not drink from their canals.

II

45.   *He sent among them swarms of flies that devoured them,*
       And frogs that infested them.
46.   *He also exposed their harvests to vermin,*
       And the fruit of their work to locusts.
47.   *He ruined their vines with hailstones,*
       And their sycamore trees with frost.
48.   *He delivered their cattle to hailstorms,*
       And their flocks to thunderbolts.

III

49.   *He threw upon them the fierceness of his anger,*
       His wrath, his indignation, and his horror.
    He sent evil angels to them;
50.   *He gave free course to his wrath,*
    And spared not their souls from death.
       He gave their lives over to the black plague;
51.   *And he smote all the firstborn of Egypt,*
       The prize of their potency in the tents of Ham.

PART SIX
I

52.   *However, he drove his people like a flock,*
     Guided them in the wilderness like a herd,
53.   *And led them safely without panic;*
     And the sea drowned their enemies.
54.   *And he brought them to the holy land!*
     This is the mountain that his right hand created.
55.   *He chased the nations before them,*
     And he distributed by lots their inheritance.

II

     He installed in their tents the tribes of Israel;
56.   *[Yet] they provoked him and tested their God,*
     The Most High, and did not keep his injunctions;
57.   *They turned back, and betrayed, like their fathers.*
     They reversed themselves, like a faulty bow;
58.   *They incited him to anger with their high places,*
     And with their graven images moved him to jealousy.
59.   *God heard, and he was angry;*
     He abhorred Israel greatly.

III

60.   *He forsook his sanctuary at Shiloh,*
     The tabernacle he had used to dwell among men.
61.   *He let his strength go into captivity;*
     And also his majesty into the hand of the enemy.
62.   *He gave his people over to the sword,*
     For he was angry against his inheritance.
63.   *A fire consumed their young men,*
     And none praised their virgins anymore.

PART SEVEN
I

64.   *Their priests fell under the sword,*
     And their widows did not chant laments.
65.   *Then the Lord woke up, as out of a sleep,*
     Or like a war hero, garrulous from wine;
66.   *And he smote his enemies in the back;*
     He put them into an eternal shame.

II

67.   He refused [to dwell in] the tent of Joseph,
  And did not choose the tribe of Ephraim,
68.   But he chose the tribe of Judah,
  The mount of Zion that he loves.
69.   And he built his sanctuary like the high heavens,
  Like the earth that he established forever.

III

70.   Also, he chose David, his servant,
  And took him from the sheepfolds;
71.   From following the ewes with lambs he took him,
  To tend Jacob his people,
  And Israel his inheritance.
72.   And [David] tended them with an upright heart,
  And guided them with the skillfulness of his hands.

BIBLIOGRAPHY

P. Auffret, "Lui et Eux: Étude structurelle du Psaume 78," in *Voyez de vos yeux . . . ,*" VTSup LXVIII (Leiden, 1993), pp. 175-236; P. Bonnard, *Le Psautier selon Jérémie* (Paris, 1960), pp. 160-65; E. F. Campbell, "Psalm 78: A Contribution to the Theology of Tenth Century Israel," *CBQ,* XL (1979), pp. 51-79; R. P. Carroll, "Psalm LXXVIII: Vestiges of a Tribal Polemic," *VT,* XXI (1971), pp. 133-50; R. J. Clifford, "In Zion and David: A New Beginning: An Interpretation of Psalm 78," in *Traditions in Transformation,* ed. F. M. Cross (Winona Lake, Ind., 1981), 121-41; G. W. Coats, *Rebellion in the Wilderness (on Ps. 78,17)* (Nashville, 1968), pp. 211ff.; M. Dahood, "Sîr 'Emissary' in Psalm 78, 49," *Bib,* LIX (1978), p. 264; O. Eissfeldt, *Das Lied Moses Deuteronomium 32:1-43 und Lehrgedicht Asaphs Psalm 78 . . .* (Berlin, 1958); D. N. Freedman, "God Almighty in Psalm 78, 59," *Bib,* LIV (1973), p. 268; idem, "Divine Names and Titles in Early Hebrew Poetry," in *Magnalia Dei . . . ,* Festschrift G. P. Wright (Garden City, N.Y., 1976); S. D. Goiten, "The City of Adam in the Book of Psalms," *Bulletin of the Jewish Exploration Society,* XIII (1946-47), pp. 86-88; H. Junker, "Die Entstehungszeit des Ps 78 und des Deuteronomiums," *Bib,* XXIV (1953), pp. 487-500; A. Lauha, *Die Geschichtsmotive in der alttestamentlichen Psalmen* (Helsinki, 1945); A. C. C. Lee, "The Context and Function in Psalm 78," *JSOT,* XLVIII (1990), pp. 83-89; H. P. Nasuti, *Tradition History and the Psalms of Asaph* (Atlanta, 1988) pp. 81-93; M. O'Connor, Hebrew Verse Structure (Winona Lake, Ind., 1980), pp. 263-78; D. A. Robertson, *Linguistic Evidence for Dating Hebrew Poetry* (Philadelphia, 1972); J. Schildenberger, "Psalm 78 (77) und die Pentateuchquellen," in *Festschrift für H. Junker* (Trier, 1961), pp. 231-56; B. A. Shafer, "The Root *bhr* and Pre-exilic Concepts of Chosenness in the Hebrew Bible," *ZAW,* LXXX (1977), pp. 20-21; H. Spieckermann, *Heilsgegenwort: Eine Theologie der Psalmen*

(Göttingen, 1989), pp. 133-49; T. Vargas, "Panem angelicum . . . , Ps 77 (78)," *VD*, XIX (1939), pp. 161-66; G. von Rad, "Die levitische Predigt in den Büchern der Chronik," in *Festschrift O. Procksch* (1934), pp. 113-24; J. Wolverton, "Sermons in the Psalms," *CJT*, X (1964), pp. 166-76.

FORM

Psalm 78 is perhaps unique in the hymnology of ancient Israel. Its form is neither that of individual complaints, prayers of supplication, or hymns of praise. Partly influenced by wisdom poetry, it must have been chanted with musical accompaniment since it is now incorporated in the Psalter. A kind of ballad with an exordium of two bicola, it presents itself in seven parts of triads and tetrads. This unusual disposition suggests an intentionality on the part of the poet. The following scheme is based on these sequences:

> *Exordium:* Parable and enigma (vv. 1b-2)
> *Part One:* Three triads (vv. 3-8)
> *Part Two:* Three triads (vv. 9-17)
> *Part Three:* Three triads (vv. 18-28)
> *Part Four:* Three tetrads (vv. 29-40)
> *Part Five:* Three tetrads (vv. 41-51)
> *Part Six:* Three tetrads (vv. 52-63)
> *Part Seven:* Three triads (64-72)

Partly influenced by wisdom poetry, the poet recites, with prolixity and redundancy, a legendary history of Israel, from the exodus to David. The use of four triads (Parts One, Two, Three, and Seven) surrounds the main recitals in three tetrads (Parts Four, Five, and Six). This development seems to indicate the poet's intention to stress the importance of vv. 29-63.

Other form-analysis schemes have been proposed, some of which are extremely skillful,[1] but they seem to be far too complex for the poet's own composition.

---

1. Cf. Auffret, "Etude structurelle du Psaume 78," esp. pp. 208-9.

COMMENTARY

Superscription (v. 1a)

The title *maskîl* is used for other psalms, chiefly pieces attributed to Asaph. The probable meaning of this title is "meditation" or "instruction," if it derived from the verb *ś k l*, "to be wise" or skillful.

Exordium: Parable and Enigma (vv. 1b-2)

The opening invitation to listen is addressed to "my people," just as the epigraph of the book of Proverbs is sometimes spoken to "my son" by an older teacher. The word *tôrâ*, "law," originally meant "instruction," from the verb "to teach." "My people" may indicate that the singer was a prophetic, perhaps even a royal figure, using wisdom vocabulary. A parable might be a longer succession of riddles or enigmas. In this context the speaker would announce a selective review of the wonders of Yahweh from the times of the liberation of Hebrew slaves from Egypt, the passage of the Sea of Reeds, the wandering in the wilderness of Sinai, the conquest of the land of Canaan, and finally the election of David as king of a united people of Israel. Reminiscences of these wonders are expressed in ways similar to the traditions of the Pentateuch but not identical.

These recitals of divine wonder are countered more than twelve times by statements on the people's lack of faith, their ingratitude, and even their rebellion. The poem itself, following the Exordium, was probably divided into seven parts or chants, as an amalgam of two contrasting *legends,* the obduracy of the people and the extraordinary compassion of the Lord. This tapestry, which enmeshes two different sets of memories or theological judgments, may explain what appears prolix and redundant to a modern and Western mind.

Hidden wisdom may be the enigmas lying behind a festival of covenant renewal. It might well be the voice of God commanding, "Hear, my people," in anticipation of the Decalogue (cf. Deut 5:1; cf. Psalms 50; 81; 95).

Part One: Enigmas Revealed (vv. 3-8)

Fathers have transmitted to their sons the extraordinary gift of the law, the observance of which insures the continuity of the covenant from generation to generation, although Sinai and Moses are ignored.

The condemnation of Israel is repeated and stressed, not in a sort of ballad of praise but as a litany of guilt, not only for the fathers but also for their descendants. Notice the use of the first person plural, which includes the present generation (vv. 3 and 4).

Part Two: The Betrayal of Ephraim (vv. 9-17)

The sons of Ephraim may not actually have betrayed, but the wording implies disapproval of their rout since they were well-armed and apparently skillful archers.

Some commentators find that v. 9, like v. 67, interrupts the recital of woe and grace, especially since the condemnation of Ephraim involves the whole of Israel. It has been suggested that v. 9 should be removed as a late addition, or that the text is corrupt. Gunkel emended "sons of Ephraim" into "arrogant sons"; a graphic correction is not impossible. However, such manipulations of the MT miss the whole purpose of the ballad, which is precisely found in vv. 9 and 67! Psalm 78 seeks to link the Sinai Covenant to the Davidic Covenant, and to displace the central cult from Mount Sinai to Mount Zion. By so intending, the poet wishes to affirm the triumph of the tribe of Judah over all the other tribes — the original source of the birth of Judaism.[2]

The observation that "Ephraim turned back on the day of battle" (v. 9) most probably refers to the sons of Ephraim, well armed (cf. 1 Chr 12:2; 2 Chr 17:17), who "fled before the Philistines" (1 Sam 4:17), and even lost the ark of the covenant, so that it was said, "Glory is departed from Israel, for the ark of God is taken" (1 Sam 4:22). Ephraim, known as a younger son of Joseph, became identified with Israel (Jer. 7:15; Hos 4:17). The rout of Ephraim-Israel may also have been remembered as the defeat of the northern kingdom in the so-called Syro-Ephraimite War (734-732).

This litany continues with hymnic references to Yahweh's wonders at the exodus from Egypt (vv. 12-13), the gushing of water from the rock in the wilderness (vv. 15-16), and the constant ingratitude of Israel (v. 17).

Part Three: Doubting and Testing God's Bounty (vv. 18-28)

Ephraim-Israel "spoke against God" (v. 19). Having their thirst now quenched, they demanded bread and meat (v. 20). Divine reaction, always ambivalent before human unbelief (v. 22), was to kindle a fire against "Jacob," whose name was changed to Israel (Gen 32:28). The psalmist appears to follow here a peculiar recollection. But, in a sudden reversal, Yahweh's wrath once more subsided under compassion: clouds opened, manna came down

2. Carroll, "Psalm LXXVIII," pp. 143-47.

from heaven, and Israel was flooded with the wheat of heaven, "the food of angels" (vv. 23-28).

Part Four: God's Compassion for Human Mortality (vv. 29-40)

The dual attitude of the Lord reaches an astounding level, which may be due to the psalmist's reciting a second litany on Israel's corruption. A kind of holy dancing seems to oppose and yet to embrace man's perennial transgression.

Sated, Ephraim-Israel persists in begging for the satisfaction of an obsessive appetite (vv. 29-30). This time divine wrath will kill the youth of Israel, but this evidence of dramatic retribution does not convert them, for "they were sinning still" (v. 32). In the third strophe of Part Four, however, the people repented (v. 35), but they "did not trust in his covenant" (v. 37). Yet the Lord did not destroy, for he remembered that they were only "flesh and mere breath" that were in any case destined to mortality. When they die, they do not return to life. Here is no intimation of immortality. Once again the holy dance sounding like a cosmic pas-de-deux will produce only provocation and offense (v. 40). At this climactic moment of horror, the emphasis mobilizes a strophic enlargement from triads to tetrads.

Part Five: The Plagues of Egypt (vv. 41-51)

The singing over the people's recidivism is renewed: they have forgotten the acts of the benevolent Lord in their favor. The wonders in the land of Zoan (East Nile Delta) were signs of his attempts to demoralize the most powerful empire on earth at that time: the canals turn their water into blood (v. 44), flies and frogs infest human bodies (v. 45), vermin and locusts ruin crops and cattle (v. 46), vines and trees are devastated by hailstorms and frost (v. 47). Instead of the angels' food that the Lord sent later on to the Hebrews in the Sinai desert (cf. v. 24), the Egyptians received "evil angels," demonic messengers who threatened their existence (v. 49). On top of these calamities, the firstborn children, pride of their warrants of a brilliant future, were exterminated. The land of Ham (a name for Egypt; cf. Ps 105:23) was doomed.

Part Six: The Conquest of Canaan (vv. 52-63)

Again, in spite of the fathers' forgetfulness, the help of Yahweh amazingly abides, as the psalmist looks forward in his chronological sequence of recollections. From the plagues of Egypt, he jumps toward the settlement of the tribes in the land of Canaan. Yet the memory of the exodus lingers. The Pharaoh's army, pursuing the fugitives, is now drowned in the sea (v. 53). Like sheep, the Hebrews might have yielded to panic, but they were safely guided by a vigilant shepherd (v. 52). The poet compresses the events of a distant past with those of a relatively recent future, now past; the many obstacles that delayed the final migration from the Sinai desert to the Promised Land are merely summarized in one sentence, "[God] chased the nations before them" (v. 55). Zion is not yet mentioned, but the chorus is told that Yahweh had "acquired" the mountain with his right hand (v. 54). Is this an allusion to Zion?

Nevertheless, the sinfulness of Israel persists, as Canaanite culture seduces the chosen people with "high places" and "graven images," a fateful violation of God's covenant law (v. 56). An abrupt verdict is pronounced against "the tribes of Israel." They once more provoke the wrath of Yahweh. Is this the Israel of the north, the tribes of Zebulun, Manasseh, and Ephraim, all related to Joseph, or the pre-Davidic kingdom of Saul and Samuel, or, again, the post-Solomonic kingdom of the north after the schism of Jeroboam, a kingdom that lasted two centuries (922-722 B.C.E.)? Joshua was credited with having brought to Shiloh the tabernacle and the tent of meeting (Josh 18:1).

Part Seven: David and Zion (vv. 64-72)

By an astounding "enjambment" from Part Six to Part Seven, the psalmist concludes his ballad with a dramatic volte-face of the Lord in the election of David and Zion. The murder of the priests, presumably of Shiloh, prepares for the sudden contrast between Yahweh's rejection of Israel and his waking up from sleep (vv. 64-66). The theme of the condemnation of Ephraim, which began the severe litany (v. 9), is now, at the end of the ballad, bluntly restated: Ephraim is repelled, but Judah is chosen. The tribe of Judah becomes the center of Yahweh's attention, for it promotes Mount Zion, "which [God] loves" (vv. 67-68) and the royalty of David, from Bethlehem in Judah (vv. 70-72). Thus the entire psalm is articulated between the initial charge against Ephraim and its final evocation. Zion will be tended by David. A trinity of divine attention becomes the crown of the ballad. The temple of Solomon in Jerusalem was mythically built by God himself. The comparison of this edifice to "the high heavens" and the enduring solidity of the earth, symbol of eternity (v. 69), amounts to being the most hyperbolic endorsement of early Zionism.

King David, the vigilant shepherd, is now the guide of Israel, the name that embraces all the tribes. They form "the house of Jacob," designation of "the sons of Israel" (Exod 19:2-3).

From Sinai to Zion: the bond of continuity is now established, religiously and politically. David fed his flock "with an upright heart" (v. 72; cf. 1 Kgs 9:4).

He has become the true servant of the Lord. The idealization of the royal head of the Davidic dynasty matches that of the Zion sanctuary.

DATE AND THEOLOGY

The antagonism of Judah for Ephraim led to postexilic Judaism and its hostility to the Samaritans (Zech 11:14). Its origins were ancient. Only the prophet Jeremiah dared to mention, besides Psalm 78, the fall of Shiloh as the retribution of God: "Go therefore to my place in Shiloh; I long ago made my name reside there. See how I have treated it, on account of the perversity of my people Israel . . ." (Jer 7:13-15). Jerusalem will meet the same doom, for the Lord has rejected his people, just as he had rejected the posterity of Ephraim (Jer 7:15).

Since then, Yahweh's indignation was raised by their "high places" and "graven images" (v. 57). Similarly, Jeremiah declared that on the high places the people poured libations for foreign gods and provoked the Lord of the covenant to anger (Jer 7:18). He will reject them (Ps 78:50, 67; cf. Jer 7:29). As Yahweh is compared to a war hero "drunk with wine," so also Jeremiah thought of himself as a war hero "intoxicated with wine" (23:9). There are other literal and thematic affinities that indicate that the psalm belonged to the same milieu as the prophet.

While the date of Psalm 78 remains uncertain, it preceded the destruction of the temple (587 B.C.E.) and even the agony of the Davidic dynasty. The weeks and months that followed the reform of Josiah (622 B.C.E.) witnessed a purification of worship not only in Jerusalem but also in the holy land at large. Even if the reports were exaggerated by legendary enthusiasm (2 Kgs 22:11–23:27), the Canaanitish practices of several generations still colored the religion of the people: "They did not have trust in his covenant" (vv. 36-37; cf. Jer 31:31-34).

It can hardly be through sheer coincidence that this key to the understanding of the whole ballad is to be found only once, and at the very center, halfway from its total length (v. 37 within the 72 verses). Should not such an expectation of peace and harmony depend on the writing of a "new covenant" law on the hearts of men (Jer 31:32)? The God of Psalm 78 is still conceived anthropomorphically as an omnipotent and omniscient lord. It does not hint at a theology of new creation. Divine self-offering, which forms a dialectic with divine power, has to wait for the eschatological messiah. The Davidic dynasty and its mythology still pursue the image of "the vigilant shepherd" at the expense of "the good shepherd" of Johannine Christology.

Psalm 78 is not a theology of the broken covenant. It is "theo-logy" properly speaking, an entrance into the heart of "divinehood." Human pride and human greed, especially those of any holy people, whether synagogue or church, hurt, wound, and even smother the holy God.

This theology knows also about the dark, the evil, the negative, the futile things of this world, and yet . . . it is written out of a grand trust that the good and compassionate God will himself have the last word.[3]

PSALM 79

The Ruin of the Temple

1. *Psalm. From Asaph.*

I

    O God! The goyim have come into thine inheritance;
      They have defiled the temple of thy holiness;
      They have laid Jerusalem in ruins.

2.   *The dead bodies of thy servants they have given*
      To be meat for the fowls of the heavens,
      The flesh of thy saints for the beasts of the earth.

3.   *Their blood have they shed like water,*
      Round about Jerusalem,
      And there was none to bury them.

II

4.   *We have become a gibe to our neighbors,*
      A scorn and a derision to those around us.

5.   *How long, O Lord? Wilt thou be angry with us forever?*
      Shall thy jealousy burn like fire?

6.   *Pour out thy wrath upon the goyim*
      That have not known thee,
    And upon the kingdoms
      That have not called upon thy name.

3. H. Küng, *Theology for the Third Millennium: An Ecumenical View* (New York, 1988), p. 284.

III

7.   *Indeed, they have devoured Jacob*
       And laid waste his dwelling place;
8.   *Remember not against us former iniquities;*
       Let thy compassion come speedily to meet us,
       For we are brought very low.
9.   *Help us, O God of our salvation,*
       For the glory of thy name;
    Deliver us, purge away our sins,
       For thy name's sake!

IV

10.   *Why should the goyim say,*
       Where is their God?
    Let it be known in our sight among the goyim
       That the shed blood of thy servants is avenged!
11.   *Let the groans of the prisoners come before thy face!*
       Through the greatness of thine arm,
       Preserve thou those condemned to die!

V

12.   *Return seven times unto our neighbors' bosom*
       The insults they have leveled at thee, Lord,
13.   *So that we, thy people and the sheep of thy pasture,*
       Will give thanks to thee forever!
    We will show forth thy praise
       From generation to generation.

BIBLIOGRAPHY

P. R. Ackroyd, *Exile and Restoration* (London, 1968), pp. 20-31; P. E. Bonnard, *Le Psautier selon Jérémie* . . . (Paris, 1960), pp. 166-72; W. Brueggemann, *The Message of the Psalms* . . . (Minneapolis, 1984), pp. 71-74; idem, *Theology of the Old Testament* (Minneapolis, 1997), pp. 319-21; E. Janssen, *Juda in der Exilzeit*, FRLANT LXIX (Göttingen, 1956); H. P. Nasuti, *Tradition History and the Psalms of Asaph* (Atlanta, 1988), pp. 97ff.; J. Rhyme, *The Babylonian Experience: The Exile* (London, 1971).

FORM

Psalm 79 is a community lament, which appears to have been composed soon after the destruction of Jerusalem (587 B.C.E.) by the Babylonians. Not unlike the individual complaints, many of which were articulated around a core verse, Psalm 79 contains a core strophe at the center of five strophes:

> I. Defilement and Massacre; three triads (vv. 1b-3)
> II. How Long, O Lord? four dyads (vv. 4-6)
> III. For Thy Name's Sake; three dyads (vv. 7-9)
> II'. Where Is Their God? two dyads and one triad (vv. 10-11)
> I'. God's Avenging and the People's Thanks; three dyads (vv. 12-13)

The meter is quite irregular, but this does not suggest that the poem is composed of many fragments, for the strophic structure seems to be intentionally symmetrical: the question of the people, "How long, O Lord?" is echoed by the interrogative protest of the goyim, "Where is their God?" The lament over the disaster is reversed by the promise of thanks. Moreover, the goyim, "nations," a term about to receive a pejorative sense, here meaning "pagans" or "heathens," is spread throughout the poem (vv. 1, 5, 19, 20). The repetition of this motif seems to suggest a single hand.

COMMENTARY

Superscription (v. 1a)

The attribution of the psalm to Asaph does not suggest a northern origin, for the situation indicates Jerusalem and Judah (see below).

Strophe I: Defilement and Massacre (vv. 1b-3)

It appears that the psalmist has witnessed the siege and fall of Jerusalem with the burning of the temple of Solomon as well as the palaces of the city (2 Kgs 25:1-10), and the murder or exile of its people. The initial cause for horror and revulsion is that the qoyim have invaded God's property (v. 1b); the second is that they have defiled his holy temple; (v. 1c); the third is that they have burned the palaces and mansions of Jerusalem (v. 1c); the fourth is that the dead bodies have been left unburied, as prey to the birds and animals of the earth (v. 2). However terrible the defilement of the temple, their lack of sepulture of the "saints" of Yahweh seems to be their major offense (cf. Deut 28:26; 2 Sam 21:10; Jer 7:32).

Strophe II: How Long, O God? (vv. 4-6)

The lament turns from complaint to supplication. Such an extremity of misfortune defies any explanation, unless the ire of Yahweh has been kindled against his own people, guilty of national disruption. No confession of collective sins is explicitly offered; it is implicitly suggested most clearly by the use of the word "jealousy" — the zeal of a passionate love that the covenant God has lavished on Israel, which is now scoffed at and rejected. Let divine wrath, at first aroused by the covenanted community, be now oriented against the goyim for their unspeakable crimes. The goyim perpetrated these crimes because they did not know Yahweh. Perhaps the meaning should be that they refused to know.

Strophe III: For Thy Name's Sake (vv. 7-9)

The core of the lament and its turning point are now torn open: the name[1] of Yahweh represents far more than his reputation. It molds the very beingness of one whose name means "He causes to be." Now the plea is ardently made that the fathers' transgressions should be forgotten. The psalmist knows that the verb, here translated "purge," means "cover up." The psalmist asks that the cultic act of atonement be performed by the Lord, not by humankind (cf. Jer 18:29). He demands the total gift for dealing with total failure and total inability. This is rather unprecedented daring in the worship of Yahweh.

Strophe II': Where Is Their God? (vv. 10-11)

The prayer of Israel, "How long?" in Strophe II is contrasted in Strophe II' with the scoffing question of the goyim, "Where is their God?" The plight of Judah and of the surviving Judahites is interpreted by the goyim as a crisis in divinity. Is the God of the chosen people now hidden or even powerless? Is the hidden God also the absent God? The defeat of Judah and the defilement of the temple place in doubt the divinity of the Hebrew God. The attack is now shifted from a human to a divine scandal.

Such an act of mockery has become a blasphemy. The new phase of the prayers asks that the blood of God's servants be avenged, and that the prisoners doomed to die now be saved from death.

---

1. J. Pedersen, *Israel*, I-II (London, 1925), pp. 245-59; O. Grether, *Name und Wort Gottes*, BZAW LXIV (Giessen, 1934), p. 53; E. Jacob, "The Name of God," in *Theology of the Old Testament* (London, 1958), pp. 82-85; R. Abba, "For His Name's Sake," in "Name," *IDB*, III (1962), pp. 82-85; S. Terrien, *The Elusive Presence* (San Francisco, 1978), pp. 113-22.

Strophe I′: God's Avenging and the People's Thanks (vv. 12-13)

The Lord himself has been attacked by the question of the goyim. Incredible insults have been leveled at him. A sevenfold retribution is now demanded against the enemy. Far more, God himself has been attacked when his inheritance was invaded and his "saints" tortured and murdered. Avenging belongs to the heavenly Master and needs to be done for his own glory.

In a sudden transformation, the petitioner becomes a hymnist of praise. Committing future generations to the singing of thanks, the poet of Psalm 79 affirms his faith in the power and compassion of Yahweh. He also proclaims the continuity of the chosen people in history.

DATE AND THEOLOGY

The identification of the defilement of the sanctuary with the disaster of 587 has been challenged because the poet of Psalm 79 is totally silent on a siege of Jerusalem, any military invasion of Judah, any mention of the king or the deportation of many inhabitants. Such an argument *e silentio* is not valid in elegiac poetry. A poet is free to select salient features of an event to which he alludes. Moreover, affinities between Psalm 79 and the writings of the Jeremianic circle as well as Psalms 44, 74, 89, and 142 are too numerous to be ignored. Although words are not always identical, the similarities are exceptionally frequent. The goyim have invaded Yahweh's inheritance (Jer 9:10). The dead bodies are left unburied to become prey of the birds of heaven and the beasts of the earth (Jer 8:2; 14:16; 23:33). The goyim are mocking the survivors of massacres, just as Jeremiah or his disciples declare in the name of the Lord, "I shall make of them an opprobrium, a fable, a derision" (Jer 24:9). The old iniquities are the transgressions of the fathers, which should be forgotten (Jer 11:10; 14:20). The contemporaries are deeply sunk in sinfulness. Yet the main request of the entire psalm is that Yahweh should forgive, and even *atone*, for the sake of the glory of his name (Jer 14:20-21). God's ire must now turn away from Judah to the goyim, whose retribution should be sevenfold in the very depth of their being (v. 12). The expression is paralleled in Jeremiah (32:18).

In the power of a faith that brings future hope to a present reality of certitude, the poem ends with the discovery of the Lord's unchanging tenderness (Jer 23:1-8; cf. Pss 95:7; 100:3). The sacred singer who composed Psalm 79 may have survived in the Judean hills, or been deported to the land between the rivers of Babylon (cf. Ps 137:1), but he contributed to maintaining worship alive, away from wasted Zion. He may have been one who, unaware, created the synagogue, a source of religious nationalism and exclusivism of foreigners.[2] Psalm 79 may have favored the universal outlook still evident in Judaism.

PSALM 80

Let Thy Face Shine Forth

1. *To the choirmaster. "On the Lilies." Testimony from Asaph. Psalm.*

I

2.   Shepherd of Israel, give ear,
            Thou who didst guide Joseph like a flock of sheep,
        And art enthroned upon the cherubim,
            Shine forth ahead of Ephraim, Benjamin, and Manasseh!
3.   *Stir up thy bravura,*
            And come to save us!
4.   God, make us turn back,
            And let thy face shine forth, and we shall be saved.

II

5.   *Lord God of hosts, how long wilt thou be angry*
            With thy people's prayer?
6.   *Thou didst feed them the bread of tears,*
            And drenched their thirst with floods of weeping.
7.   *Thou madest us a jest for our neighbors,*
            And our enemies laugh among themselves.
8.   Lord God of hosts, make us turn back!
            Let thy face shine forth, and we shall be saved.

III

9.   *Thou didst bring from Egypt a vine,*
            Expelled the goyim and planted it.

2. S. Terrien, "The Omphalos Myth and Hebrew Religion," *VT*, XX (1970), pp. 319-38.

10.   *Thou didst clear the ground for it,*
        And it took root, and filled the land;

11.   *The hills were covered with its shade;*
        Its branches were like the divine cedars!

12.   *It sent out its boughs to the Sea,*
        And its shoots as far as the River!

IV

13.   *Why, then, hast thou ruptured its enclosures?*
        Any passerby can pluck its grapes;

14.   *The wild boar of the forest tears it apart,*
        And the beasts of the savannah graze upon it!

17. [*]   *Burnt by fire like refuse,*
        At the rebuke of thy countenance it will perish.

15.   Lord God of hosts, come back!
        Look down from the heavens and see!

V

    Visit this vine and its branches,

16.   *Which thou didst plant with thy right hand.*

18.   *Let thy hand remain on the man of thy right,*
        The son of Adam thou madest strong for thyself!

19.   *And we shall not depart from thee.*
        Thou wilt revive us, and we shall call upon thy name!

20.   Lord God of hosts, make us turn back!
        Let thy face shine forth, and we shall be saved.

[*] See below.

BIBLIOGRAPHY

P. Auffret, *Voyez de vos yeux . . .*, VTSup XLVIII (Leiden, 1993), pp. 247-61; W. Beyerlin, "Schichten im 80. Psalm," in *Festschrift G. Friedrich* (Stuttgart, 1973), pp. 9-19; O. Eissfeldt, "Psalm 80," in *Festschrift A. Alt* (1953), pp. 75-78; A. Gelston, "A Sidelight on 'The Son of Man,'" *SJT*, XXII (1969), pp. 189-96; H. Heinemann, "The Date of Psalm 80," *JQR*, XL (1949-50), pp. 297-302; H. P. Nasuti, *Tradition History and the Psalms of Asaph*, SBLMS (Atlanta, 1988), pp. 97-102; P. R. Raabe, *Psalm Structures: A Study of Psalms with Refrains*, JSOTSup CIV (Sheffield, 1990), pp. 200-203; J. Schreiner, "Hirte Israels, stelle uns wieder her! Auslegung von Psalm 80," *BibLeb*, X (1969), pp. 95-111; D. W. Thomas, "The Meaning of *ziz* in Ps 80.14," *Expository Times*, LXXVI (1964-65), pp. 307-8; T. K. Thordarson, "The Metric Dimension: Hermeneutical Remarks on the Language of the Psalter," *VT*, XXIV (1974), pp. 218-19; N. J.

Tromp, "Psalm LXXX: Form of Expression and Form of Contents," in *New Avenues in the Study of the Old Testament,* Festschrift M. J. Mulder (Leiden, 1989); P. Victor, "On Psalm LXXX,13," *Expository Times,* LXXVI (1964-65), p. 294; H. Wagner, "Der Menschensohn des 80. Psalms," *JQR,* XL (1940-50), pp. 297-302.

FORM

Psalm 80 is a national prayer in five strophes of three bicola each, with one exception (v. 12), thus creating in the MT a third strophe of four bicola (vv. 9-12). Moreover, each strophe ends with a refrain (vv. 4, 8, 15, 20), with the exception of the same, third strophe. This peculiarity may be due to the jubilation inspired by the legend of Solomon's empire, which extended — so it was claimed — from the Mediterranean Sea to the Euphrates ("the River"). The reminiscence was so exhilarating that it was sung as a refrain, now the core verse of the entire psalm.

The proposed transposition of v. 17 between vv. 14 and 15[1] clarifies and explains the syntactic incoherence (vv. 14-18) and reconstitutes the three-bicola structures of the fourth and fifth strophes (vv. 13-15 and 15-29). The rhythm of many cola, more than elsewhere, is irregular, which suggests compositional errors or manipulation.

COMMENTARY

Superscription (v. 1)

"On the Lilies" is probably the title of a popular song. The LXX adds, like the MT in a similar poem (Ps 60:1), "About Assyria." The unusual word "testimony" may also mean "attestation" or even "commandment" (cf. the Mosaic Decalogue, Exod 20:1-17). It may indicate the catechetical character of the psalm.

Strophe I: Invocation (vv. 2-4)

The Hebrew text presents the first two verbs as present participles, literally "leading" and "being enthroned," thus qualifying adjuncts of "Shepherd of Israel." The mention of Joseph and his descendants, Ephraim and Manasseh,

---

1. See M. Mannati, *Les Psaumes,* III (Paris, 1967), p. 83, n. 2; P. Auffret rejects this conjecture (*Voyez de vos yeux,* pp. 247-48) but fails to offer a better solution.

clearly indicates the northern origin of this poem, and probably also of the other psalms of Asaph. Enthronement on the cherubim does not necessarily suggest that Elohim's terrestrial presence is confined to a sanctuary of the north like those at Dan, Shechem, or Shiloh, for the symbol of God's proximity to his people may have been the nomadic tabernacle or tent.

In the patronymic traditions of the north, Jacob, blessing Joseph, calls his Elohim "the shepherd" (Gen 48:15), and elsewhere Jacob compares Joseph to a fruitful tree (Gen 49:22). Such a memory may have influenced the poet of Psalm 80 when he compared Israel to "a vine" with branches in the third and fifth strophes (vv. 9, 16).

At once the supplication demands that the shepherd of Israel stir up his "bravura" or "heroic valiance" as if the Lord God of hosts had somehow lost his daring in battles or at least weakened and softened his courage to lead his people from Sinai to Canaan. But, *mirabile dictu,* the request for the renewal or awakening of divine stamina is not directed against the goyim: it is "to make us turn back," and to "convert" us. Here is a psalmist who, like a prophet, is asking for the people's conversion.[2]

No confession of national guilt is here expressed, but the refrain presupposed that the way of Israel needed to be "turned around," away from its state of constant transgression that led to a national misery that provoked the supplication. There is no transition for this startling prayer demanding conversion. To the magnificent hope, "Let thy face shine forth," is added a theological statement implied between despair and steadfastness of faith, with the hint of a bargain with the Almighty. Centuries later open "commercialism" became the bane of Judaism and church acceptance of semi-Pelagianism.

Strophe II: A Complaint against God? (vv. 5-8)

The national calamity from which the people needs to be saved is not described, but it is apparently considered to be a justified retribution, caused by divine anger. After the request for the people's return to God, the refrain calls for a direct and immediate vision of God himself, the shining light that mystics of many religious traditions have associated with a theophany.

In the traditions of Aaron and others who had ascended the mount of the covenant at Sinai, the stress is laid on the actual visibility of the transcendental Deity, "And they saw the God of Israel; and under his feet a pavement of sapphire, something like a dazzling splendor, heaven itself for purity" (Exod 14:10). The repetition, "they saw God," stresses the concreteness of the sight although

---

2. The LXX and other ancient versions, as well as two MSS of the MT, read *lanû,* "at us," instead of *lamô,* "at themselves."

its illumination prevented any human eye from perceiving clearly any divine feature, except the feet (cf. Deut 33:2; Pss 50:2; 94:1).

Strophe II: The Corruption of Israel's Cult (vv. 5-8)

The supplication notably continues and asks, "How long?" It appears that divine wrath arises against the people's prayer. Is it that the psalmist, similar to the great prophets and the editors of the books of Kings, condemned the way Israel worshiped God? Was it on account of the troubling syncretism that early and late corrupted Israel's cult with Canaanite practices?

Strophe III: The Allegory of the Imperial Vine (vv. 9-12)

For the central strophe of the psalm, the sacred history of the liberation from Egypt and the conquest of the Holy Land are then reviewed in grateful terms that soon become hyperbolic: the goyim were expelled from the territory of the promise and — most patriotically remembered — the highly imaginative memory of Solomon's empire: Canaan and Syria from the Phoenician coast to the Mesopotamian border of the Assyrian kingdom and its dominions. The vine was the symbol of God's inheritance! For this glorious reminiscence of a Golden Age, the refrain with its desperate petition for deliverance was inappropriate. Instead of these words, was not the congregation to sing a rousing chorus on a past exhilaration? This is the core verse of the psalm.

Strophe IV: The Hidden God and the Crisis (vv. 13-15)

The psalmist shows here a bit of literary mastery. The contrast strikes the singers in a veritable "coup de théâtre" with the abrupt question, "Why, then, hast thou ruptured the enclosures [of this vineyard]?" Indeed, the hyperbolic geography, which included far more than the Holy Land (v. 12), summons a marvelous past against a dismal present. No vintner would be as careless as a divine protector, liberator, and generalissimo who did not preserve the frontiers of his domain. The metaphor of the vine reflects the pride and love of a vintner for his vineyard (cf. the love song of the prophet, Isa 5:1-5).

Not a word is added to the description of the crisis. This God must have been away, hidden and probably absent. Even his omniscience is doubted.

Strophe V: Prayer for a New Life (vv. 16-20)

Ardently, the poet petitions the vintner to "visit" "this" vineyard — namely, to take care of it and to nurse it back to health. The primary sense of the verb "to visit" is negative, "to encounter in order to punish." Perhaps this meaning still haunts the background of the psalmist's mind, and the ambivalence is partly preserved, but the notion that dominates is positive: "to visit in order to heal and to bring back to life."

The mention of "the son of Adam" remains enigmatic. The expression may designate the tribe of Benjamin (cf. v. 3) or it may prepare for the next person, called "the son of man," a possible designation of a royal figure (Ps 2:7). In the latter case, who would be this future king whom God would nurture for himself? Perhaps the man of God's right is not a king of present history, but, fortified by God "for himself," has to be understood, even at an early date, as the eschatological Messiah for the end of history. Then the people will not again depart from his sustainer, who will revive Israel. The last refrain (v. 20) concludes hopefully by asking for the people's conversion,

DATE AND THEOLOGY

It is not possible to date the composition of this psalm. If it was first intended for a sanctuary of the north, with special attention given to the Joseph tribes, the date may be ancient. However, the reminiscence of a grandiose empire, from the Mediterranean Sea to the Euphrates, can hardly precede sometime after Solomon (10th cent. B.C.E.). Following the seizure of the northern kingdom by the Assyrians, the migration of its priests and prophets to the kingdom of Judah, and eventually the reform of Josiah (622 B.C.E.), the poem may have been adopted by the sacred singers of the Zion temple before the burning of this edifice by the Babylonians (587 B.C.E.). The date of the psalm may also be the sequel of Benjamin's partial association with the kingdom of Judah. The identification of "the son of Adam," whom God must have been affirming for himself, if the conjectural interpretation of a future king is correct, remains uncertain.

The God who hides himself is at the end the God who reveals himself. In later Judaism and Christianity, the eschatological nature of this royal figure prevails. For example, the Aramaic prayer known as the *Qaddish* demands, "Let the name of the Lord be glorified and sanctified, for he will renew the world and vivify the dead."

An early Christian theologian was led to link the motif of "the Good Shepherd" (John 10:7-18) to that of divine absence (John 16:16, 19, 22) through the image of the Vine and its branches (John 15:1-7). However the use of this imagery was sublimated and totally cleansed from the territorial claims of Psalm 80. The eschatological understanding of the "son of [God's] right hand" has succeeded in joining divine election with universalism.

This prayer of the people is quite remarkably composed. The power of God is not really doubted; it is only questioned. Its absence creates an agony of search that precisely requires a supplication for God to appear, not necessarily in a spectacular theophany with fire and thunder, but an enlightenment, and possibly a vision of blinding light. The nationalism of the poet's faith magnifies the success of the conquest of the land. God expels the goyim in order to provide fertile soil in this divine inheritance. This nationalism does not include xenophobia, but it conceives the God of Israel as entirely partial to his election. Yet, why indeed has he neglected to protect the frontiers of his vineyard, thus allowing various sorts of strangers to invade? Divine absence or even divine carelessness stands as a mystery that the power of faith will demand the Holy Shepherd to overcome.

PSALM 81

From Hymn to Oracle

1. *For the choirmaster. On the Gittith. For Asaph.*

I

2.   *Sing with gladness to God, our strength!*
          Make a joyful noise for the God of Jacob!
3.   *Intone the psalmody, strike the timbrel,*
          The melodious harp with the lute!
4.   *Blow the shofar in the new moon,*
          And in the full moon, the day of our feast!

II

5.   *For that is a law in Israel,*
          An ordinance from the God of Jacob;
6.   *He made a statute [for the tribes of] Joseph,*
          In his exodus from the land of Egypt;
          I heard a language I did not understand:
7.   *"I removed the burden from his shoulder;*

III

Thy hands were free from the weight of the baskets;
8.   In thy distress thou didst cry,
    And I delivered thee.
I answered thee in the secret of the thunder;
    I tested thee at the waters of Meribah.   Selah
9.   Listen, my people, and I shall warn thee;
    Israel! If only thou wouldst listen to me!

IV

10.   There shall not be in thy midst any foreign god,
    Nor wilt thou worship a god of strangers.
11.   I am the Lord thy God!
    I brought thee up from the land of Egypt!
    Open wide thy mouth, and I shall fill it!"
12.   But my people did not listen to my voice,
    Israel would have none of me.

V

13.   I therefore let them go after the desires of their heart;
    They followed their own advice.
14.   Oh! If only my people listened to me,
    If Israel walked in my ways!
15.   In a little while I would subdue their enemies,
    And turn my hand against their adversaries.

VI

16.   Those who hate the Lord would seek his favor,
17.   And their life span would last forever.
18.   I would feed them with the finest wheat,
    And satisfy them with honey from the rock.

BIBLIOGRAPHY

W. Beyerlin, *Herkunft und Geschichte der ältesten Sinaitraditionen* (Tübingen, 1961); P. E. Bonnard, *Le Psautier selon Jérémie* (Paris, 1960), pp. 173-78; H. Buckers, "Zum Verwertung der Sinaitraditionen in den Psalmen," *Bib,* XXXII (1951), pp. 401-22; S. Mowinckel, *Psalmenstudien,* III: *Kultprophetie und prophetische Psalmen* (Oslo, 1923), pp. 39-40; idem, *The Psalms in Israel's Worship,* vol. II, tr. D. R. Ap-Thomas (Nashville, 1962), pp. 53-73; N. P. Nasuti, *Tradition History and the Psalms of Asaph,* SBLMS (Atlanta, 1988), pp. 102-8; W. H. Schmidt, "Das Erste Gebot," *TEx,* CLXV (1970), pp. 17ff.; N. H. Snaith, "The Asaphite Psalms," in *Studies in the Psalter* (London, 1934), pp. 27ff.; G. von Rad, *The Problem of the Hexateuch* (London, 1966), pp. 13-20; E. Würthwein, "Der Ursprung der prophetischen Gerichtsrede," *ZTK*, XLIX (1952), pp. 1-16.

FORM

Psalm 81 is a liturgical composition that links the beginning of a hymn (vv. 2-4) with a prophetic oracle (vv. 5-18). It was intended to be sung especially at "our feast," probably the festival of Sukkoth, "Tabernacles" (v. 4b). Structural analysis is uncertain because the transition from praise to admonition may have been written with an accidentally misplaced verse (v. 8), and proposals for transposition are quite diverse, but none is demonstrated with any degree of validity.

The poem appears to be constituted of five strophes of three bicola each (vv. 2-4, 5-7a, 7b-9, 10-12, 13-15), followed by a sixth strophe of only two bicola (vv. 16-18), which may have been added later on.

COMMENTARY

Superscription (v. 1)

The postexilic editors of the Psalter did not insert at the head of this poem the title "Psalm" and merely stated "for Asaph." They may have been conscious of its exceptional *Gattung* among the other psalms of Asaph.

Strophe I: An Invitation to Cultic Gladness (vv. 2-4)

Orchestration is clearly indicated. It is accompanied with a summons to the chorus, and perhaps the whole congregation, to give a full blast of the ritual shout as a symbolic manifestation of "the strength" of God (v. 2). The instrumental fanfare, which also respects the calendar of the new and full moons (Lev 23:34-43; Deut 16:13-15; cf. 2 Chr 8:13), reaches its climactic amplitude with the blowing of the ram's horn *(shofar)* — a full-throated uproar of sound. This is the autumn season, a time for rejoicing over the fruits of the earth.

Strophe II: The Renewal of the Covenant (vv. 5-7a)

Thanksgiving glee brings to mind the memory of the Sinai Covenant, with its fiery "deafeningness" of thunder (Exod 16:16-19). In turn, the announcement of the "law in Israel" surrounds the splendor of natural wonders — all of them within the power of God — with the solemn conditions of the contract thus sealed between the Creator of the world and the Master of history.

"If you keep my covenant, you, from among all nations,
    Will belong to me, for the whole earth is mine;
You will be for me a kingdom of priests
    And a holy nation."
                                                    (Exod 19:5)

The people of Israel are elected, for they receive the vocation of a sacerdotal mediation with the peoples of humankind. Their holiness is due not only to their election but also to their vocation. On the day of "our feast," thankfulness for abundance allies itself to a worldwide mission. The law in Israel, together with its synonyms, ordinance and statute, designates at first not a vast body of prescriptions and prohibitions written on scrolls, but the Decalogue, carved on stone, and possibly other decalogues remembered orally (cf. Exod 20:1ff.; 34:17-27) and likewise written in lapidary form. A decalogue is clearly implied in the fourth strophe (v. 11).

Israel, as the people of the covenant, has been liberated from Egyptian slavery (v. 6cd). It seems to include only the northern tribes (of Joseph). Most of the land of Judah was still in the hands of the Canaanites until it was conquered completely by David in the tenth century.

Strophe III: Israel's Ingratitude (vv. 7b-9)

The Feast of Tabernacles means not only rejoicing over the plentiful harvest but also a severe admonition to hear, and therefore obey, the voice of the divine Liberator. The prophetic interpretation, quite independent of the verdicts of Amos, Hosea, and Isaiah, charges Israel with lack of gratitude and even skeptical questioning of the divinity, as a reference to the provocation recalled in the episode of Meribah (Exod 17:1-7). Devoured by thirst, the people had asked, "Is Yahweh in the midst of us or is he not?" (v. 7).

Strophe IV: The Covenantal Decalogue (vv. 10-12)

When the psalmist cites, "I am the Lord thy God!" the people of the covenant understand the meaning of divine uniqueness. The admonition, however, does not cancel the purpose of the feast, which celebrates physical satiety (v. 11c).

Strophe V: Israel's Self-deviation (vv. 13-15)

The prophetic oracle recognizes the moral freedom of the contract. The people may follow the desires of their heart, but at the price of breaking the conditional covenant. The omnipotence of the covenant God is not to be doubted, for divine providence follows human obedience (v. 15).

Strophe VI: The Double Significance of the Feast (vv. 16-18)

Does the declaration on "those who hate the Lord" refer only to the enemies of Israel? Might there be here a declaration of xenophobia and an implication that ingratitude toward the Lord covers a hatred of that Lord? Is the seeking of the Lord's favor self-centered flattery to obtain long life? If the "time" of the MT probably means "life span," the enemies of God would not be foreigners but individuals within the holy people. In any case, the annual miracle of the autumn (Deut 32:13-14) is once more proclaimed as a final flourish of psalmody.

DATE AND THEOLOGY

Since the naming of the Lord as God of Jacob and the designation of Israel as Joseph suggest that Psalm 81 has a northern origin, it is possible that it was first sung in a sanctuary like Dan, Shechem, or Shiloh. In its present form, the psalm must have been preserved in the temple of Zion in Jerusalem. The Deity is called "Yahweh" (vv. 11, 16). Allusions to the exodus and the desert of Sinai probably reflect mixed traditions. The psalmist is aware of Israel's enemies (v. 15). The final date may have been the time of the monarchy, from Solomon to Josiah. Since the poem ignores the agony of Judah and the destruction of the temple by the Babylonians (587 B.C.E.) a *terminus ad quem* must be anterior to the battle of Megiddo (609 B.C.E.). Examples of close affinities with the book of Jeremiah are notable. The divine imperative, "Open wide thy mouth, and I shall fill it" (v. 11), which may have been fitting for the Feast of Tabernacles, the harvest festival, must have been adopted and spiritualized by the prophet. "Yahweh extending his hand touched my mouth and said to me, Behold! I place my words in thy mouth" (Jer 1:9). The metaphoric image of eating divine words became quite common (Isa 51:16; Jer 15:10), as well as the prophetic admonition, "Listen, my people!" in the sense of "Listen and obey!"

Again, "a strange god" may be a god of strangers and surely a source of religious seduction radically prohibited (Jer 2:25; 3:13; 30:8). "My people did not listen to my voice" was expressed in the plural, "They have not listened or given an ear" (Jer 7:24). In arrogance "They followed their own advice" appears in the prophetic book verbatim with the rare word for "their own advice" (v. 13; Jer 7:24). The sentence, "They go after the desires of their heart" (v. 13) became a fashionable cliché in Jeremianic speech (Jer 3:17; 7:24; 9:13; 11:8; 13:10; 16:12; 18:12; 23:17-18).

In several psalms attributed to the sons of Asaph, similarities of this nature suggest a one-way influence from the prophet to the psalmist. In the case of Psalm 81, such a conclusion is not evident. Perhaps Jeremiah, who must have known the Psalms by heart, may well have been influenced by its poetry, although not necessarily by its theology.

The hymn for "our feast" is sung by the whole community of the elect. They know their distinctive mission in history. They eat, drink, and are merry, but the memory of the covenant at Sinai recalls to them the conditions of their abundance. Their raison d'être, among warring nations, is rehearsed as it implicitly predicts a glorious future, but the oracular mediator respects the mystery of God's power. The secret in the midst of thunder reveals divine strength, which the feast celebrates, but God's presence and intervention have to be proclaimed in a language often so restrained that it may be incomprehensible. God defends and God guides, but he never becomes the tool of human desires. The covenant, severed by human folly, brings about a reversal of historical favor. The miracle of liberation becomes the curse of enslavement. Israel will prove to be a cosmic tragedy: its would-be grandeur becomes the cause of its misfortune.

If the church claimed to be the *ekklēsia* honored by its *klēsis* to be a light of the nations, a moral and political model for the renewal of the world, its hidden corruption through pride and self-deception might reduce it to a drama of indifference or self-destruction. The psalm, however, leaves open a door of hope, for the last strophe (vv. 17-18) expects repentance and conversion. The Lord would then, symbolically, feed humankind with the finest wheat and satisfy even the poor with honey from the rock.

PSALM 82

The Death of the Gods

1. *Psalm of Asaph.*

Prologue

God takes his stand in the divine assembly.
In the midst of the gods he holds judgment:

I

2.   *How long will you judge unjustly*
      In favor of those who are guilty?   Selah

3.   *Render justice to the dispossessed and the orphans;*
      Respect the rights of the weak and the destitute!

4.   *Acquit the miserable and the poor;*
      Deliver them from the hands of scoundrels!

II

5.   *They do not know, they do not understand;*
      They move back and forth in darkness;
      The foundations of the earth are all trembling.

III

6.   *I even declare it, You are gods,*
      The sons of the Most High, all of you;

7.   *Nevertheless, you will die, just like men,*
      And you will fall, like any of the princes.

Epilogue

8.   Arise, O God! Judge the earth!
      Thou art indeed the Master of the nations.

BIBLIOGRAPHY

J. S. Ackermann, "The Rabbinic Interpretation of Psalm 82 and the Gospel of John . . . ," *HTR*, LIV (1966); F. I. Andersen, "A Short Note on Psalm 82, 5," *Bib*, L (1969), pp. 393-94; M. Buber, "Judgment on the Judges," in *The Interpretation of Some Psalms* (London, 1952), pp. 23ff.; G. Cooke, "The Son(s) of (the) God(s)," *ZAW*, LXXVI (1964), pp. 22-47; O. Eissfeldt, "El and Yahweh," *JSS*, I (1956); pp. 25-37; H.-J. Fabry, "'Ihr alle seid Söhne des Allerhöchsten' (Ps 82, 6)," *BibLeb*, XV (1974), pp. 135-47; A. Gonzalez, "Le Psaume LXXXII," *VT*, XIII (1963), pp. 293-309; C. H. Gordon, "History of Religion in Ps. 82," in *Biblical and Near Eastern Studies*, ed. G. A. Tuttle (Grand Rapids, 1978); L. K. Handy, "Sounds, Words and Meanings in Psalm 82," *JSOT*, XLVII (1990), pp. 51-66; A. T. Hanson, "John's Citation of Psalm 82 Reconsidered," *NTS*, XIII (1967), pp. 363-67; H. W. Jüngling, *Der Tod der Götter: Eine Untersuchung zu Psalm 82* (Stuttgart, 1969); note in *RB*, LXXVIII (1971), p. 115; P. D. Miller, *Interpreting the Psalms* (Philadelphia, 1986), pp. 120-24; J. Morgenstern, "The Mythological Background of Psalm 82," *HUCA*, XIV (1939), pp. 29-126; H. P. Nasuti, *Tradition, History, and the Psalms of Asaph*, SBLMS (Atlanta, 1988), pp. 108-15; R. T. O'Callaghan, "A Note on the Canaanite Background of Ps. 82," *CBQ*, XV (1953), pp. 311-14; G. Rinaldi,

"Synagoga Deorum (Salmo 82)," *Biblia orientalia*, VI (1964), pp. 9-11; R. B. Salters, "Psalm 82:1 and the Septuagint," *ZAW*, CIII (1991), pp. 225-39; N. M. Sarna, "Ps. 82: A Judgment on the Judges," in *Songs of the Heart* (New York, 1993), pp. 167-75; R. Tournay, "Les Psaumes complexes," *RB*, LIV (1949), pp. 521-42; M. Tsevat, "God and the Gods in Assembly: An Interpretation of Ps 82," *HUCA*, XL-L (1969-70), pp. 123-37; G. E. Wright, *The Old Testament against Its Environment* (Naperville, 1950), pp. 30-41.

FORM

Both in its form and in its contents, Psalm 82 differs from the rest of the Psalter. It portrays God in the midst of the gods, the supreme Judge in the heavenly council. The singing parts seem to be ascribed not to a chorus "all-the-way-through" but to various individuals: God, an observer, and a final suppliant. Perhaps the text should be considered as a sacred play, a brief equivalent of Egyptian scenic theater or Greek tragedy. One might also think of the Baroque cantata, by J. S. Bach and others, which alternated between choir and solo aria.

The meter amplifies the spread of the musical phrasing, from 3+3 (vv. 1bc-4) to 3+3+3 (v. 5) and 4+3 (v. 6), restrains itself briefly in 3+3 (v. 7), but widens for the prayer in a grand finale (v. 8).

The body of the poem is framed with an exordium and the prayer:

    I. Exordium: The Council of the Gods (v. 1bc)
      II. The Indictment of the Gods (vv. 2-4)
        III. The Stupidity of the Gods (v. 5)
      IV. The Death of the Gods (vv. 6-7)
    V. Epilogue: Prayer for Peace in the Whole Earth (v. 8)

The theme of the psalm is so momentous — the death of the gods — that the words of condemnation need not only to be heard but also to be seen, so to speak, or heard in a visual way. The psalm becomes a mini-spectacle, a one-minute "opera."

COMMENTARY

I. Exordium: The Council of the Gods (v. 1bc)

God rises and takes his stand in the heavenly council amid "the gods." Ancient witnesses and some modern interpreters, Jewish and Christian, believe that the gods are human magistrates and other administrators of high rank, princes, or even priests, but the psalmist clearly distinguishes between gods or sons of God and human judges since he announces later on that these gods are going to die, just like men and princes (v. 7).

The mythological belief in a divine assembly is well attested. The folkloric story of Job tells of the heavenly council attended by "the sons of God," and also the "prosecutor general" with the definite article, not the proper name "Satan." There is little doubt that the early Hebrews, even before entering the land of Canaan, had been exposed to the beliefs and practices of the Canaanites.[1]

II. The Indictment of the Gods (vv. 2-4)

The gods are charged with social oppression. They have inspired human judges and other public officials to favor the wealthy and to condemn the poor. The eighth-century prophets uttered similar accusations, but theirs were different in style and wording. For example, the psalm mentioned the orphans but not the widows, contrary to conventional tradition. There is also an unusual number of synonyms to describe economic destitution. It seems that the psalmist had suffered, personally, from the venal partiality of those judges. Perhaps he remembered the social brotherhood of tribal communities in the seminomadic ancestry of Israel (Exod 22:22; Deut 10:18; Isa 1:17). He may also have been acquainted with popular wisdom (Job 29:12; Prov 31:9).[2]

III. The Stupidity of the Gods (v. 5)

After a solo voice enunciated the recriminations of God, now comes an aside attempting to explain the gods' malevolence. In spite of the old cliché, "to explicate is to disculpate," the hostile attitude of the gods demands some enlightening comment. The reflection on their ignorance and stupidity may be a soliloquy from a wise observer: How could gods, foreign deities worshiped in grandiose temples with magnificent rituals, lower themselves to inspire evil in human judges? They lack the knowledge of, or elementary concern for, the plight of the masses. A certain intelligence requires a sense of solidarity with other human beings. Knowing and behaving feed each other in the flowering of altruism and veracity. Intelligence and reflection deliver one from the way of abjection (Prov 2:11).

Could it be that foreign gods, living in the splendor of great cities and en-

---

1. Cf. C. H. Gordon, *Ugaritic Textbook* (Rome, 1965), II, 51; III, 14, 2: cf. J. B. Pritchard, *Ancient Near Eastern Texts* (3rd ed.; Princeton, 1969), p. 386.

2. S. Terrien, "Wisdom in the Psalter," in *In Search of Wisdom: In Memory of J. G. Gammie*, ed. L. G. Perdue et al. (Louisville, 1993), pp. 56-72.

joying the power of military supremacy, do not know how to live in a coherent society? They march on tenebrous roads (Prov 2:13); worse still, they find perverse pleasure in choosing tortuous paths (Prov 2:15). Their ignorance is itself the cause of their misdeeds, for it prevents them from comprehending the complexity and the simplicity of social ethics. They do not know: How can they understand? They sometimes try to care for the poor, but their lack of decision prompts them to "move back and forth in darkness."

This parenthesis sounds like the solo voice of a member of the sapiential teachers: they liked to think of the effect of knowledge and ignorance; some of them are similar in many ways to the singers of the chorus in the Greek tragedies. They did not intend to excuse the misdeeds of scoundrels, but they took advantage of perversity to praise the salubrious effects of wisdom.

Divinity was held to be shared by beings other than Yahweh, but the psalmist maintained that unethical "divinity" loses its divine character. Criminality and social irresponsibility upset the stability and goodness of creation. The earth will shake and quake in revulsion to human unfairness. Phenomena of nature are not the cause of human iniquity, but human iniquity is judged by wise men and women in a cosmic context. The so-called "pathetic fallacy" conceives humanity as responsible, with the Creator, for the harmony of the universe.

IV. The Death of the Gods (vv. 6-7)

The gods of the nations may be "the sons of the Most High," but their divine filiality will not protect them from annihilation. The psalmist foresees the triumph of righteousness over the perenniality of wars among nations. The gods fight. They will die.

V. Epilogue: Prayer for Peace in the Whole Earth (v. 8)

Why suddenly and finally a prayer? The psalmist composed this unusual "scenic sketch" for worship in the temple, where singing always presumed a musical dialogue with God Almighty.

A swift sequence, without transition, links this supplication with the sapiential remark on the cosmic extension or perhaps repercussion of human criminality. The foundations of the earth may quake (v. 5c). Nevertheless, God is the Master of the earth. The psalm end in a summons to the Master of the earth.

The MT literally reads, "Thou art the inheritor of the nations." If the verb is used strictly, God is addressed as one who is inheriting the nations. The tense probably designates a continuous present. The general meaning is that God, with the death of the gods, is the inheritor of their jurisdiction. The nations hitherto belonged to the gods. With their death, God alone is the Master of the nations as he is the Ruler of the earth. He is bidden to judge the earth. Judgment, in the Hebrew sense of the word, implies not only a verdict of acquittal or of condemnation; it suggests the pursuit of creation, whose ultimate purpose is to assure the harmony and the peace of humanity.

DATE AND THEOLOGY

Classified as "a psalm of Asaph," this scenic sketch was probably ancient. It presents a satire of the syncretism that many of the early settlers favored when they learned agriculture from the Canaanites. The daring strictures of the Sinai Covenant were, at all events, remembered by an elite of Yahwists through the centuries of the late Bronze Age to the time of the Judges, even during the rise of the monarchy. It was not easy to resist the seduction of the divine representations of nature — sun, moon, earth — in a culture worshiping fertility.

Psalm 82, in its crisp condemnation of the gods, probably preceded by centuries the prophetic polemic of Elijah and Elisha in the ninth century and of Amos, Hosea, and Isaiah in the eighth. The scenic sketch, in which the God of Israel declares the death of the gods, anticipates the hymns of praise and their invitation to declare the glory of Yahweh among the nations. Yet the victory of monotheism over polytheism does not occur as an intellectual belief. The gods are still there since Yahweh "is to be feared among all the gods" (Ps 96:4b[H5]). They are invoked by the imperial powers of the ancient Near East. For Israel, however, the gods of the nations are sheer illusion.

The final prayer, probably intoned by the whole chorus, implies that total devotion derives from total dominion. The oneness of God, incomparable, calls for equality among all humans. The death of the gods opens a new vision of respect for nature (no longer the worship thereof) and a search for a community of nations.

PSALM 83

A War Song

1. *A song. Psalm of Asaph.*

I

2. O God! Do not keep silence!
    Hold not thy peace! Be not still, O God!
3. For lo! thine enemies are stirring noisily,
    Those who hate thee are raising their heads.
4. They hatch a plot against thy people;
    They conspire together against thy favorites;
5. They say, "Come! Let us wipe them out from among the nations,
    And let the name of Israel be remembered no more!"

II

6. For they are all of one mind;
    Against thee they have worked an alliance;
7. The tents of Edom and the Ishmaelites,
    Moab, and the Hagrites,
8. Gebal, Ammon, and Amalek,
    The Philistines with the dwellers of Tyre;
9. Even Assyria has joined them;
    They are the strong arm of the sons of Lot!   Selah

III

10. Do to them as to the Midianites,
    To Sisera and Jabin at the brook of Kishon,
11. They perished at En-dor,
    And became manure for the soil.
12. Treat their nobles like Oreb and Ze'eb,
    All their captains like Zebah and Zalmunna!
13. For they said, "We shall take possession for ourselves
    Of the pastures of God!"

IV

14. O my God! Make them like whirling dust,
    Like stubble before the wind!

15. *Like fire that consumes a forest,*
     And like a flame that sets the hills ablaze!
16. *Then pursue them with thy tempest,*
     And terrify them with thy hurricane!
17. *Cover their faces with ignominy,*
     So that they might seek thy name, O Lord!

Envoi

18. Let them be dishonored and dismayed forever!
     Let them be disgraced and let them perish!
19. May they know that thou alone, Yahweh by name,
     Thou art the Most High over all the earth!

BIBLIOGRAPHY

P. E. Bonnard, *Le Psautier selon Jérémie* (Paris, 1960), pp. 179-84; S. Mowinckel, *Psalmenstudien*, V: *Segen und Fluch in Israels Kult- und Psalmdictum* (Oslo, 1924), pp. 83ff.; idem, *The Psalms in Israel's Worship* (New York and Nashville, 1962), p. 202; G. von Rad, *Der heilige Krieg im alten Israel*, Abhandlungen zur Theologie des Alten und Neuen Testaments XX (Zurich, 1951), pp. 12-14; C. Westermann, *The Living Psalms* (Grand Rapids, 1984), p. 41.

FORM

The text of Psalm 83 divides itself into four strophes of four bicola each. The whole poem then ends with an *envoi* that combines a curse of the enemies and praise of the holy name. The last verses (18-19) are clearly distinct from the fourth strophe on account of the thematic climax: a call for the annihilation of the psalmists' enemies and a celebration of the holy name.

Variations of rhythm fit the development. The poem grows from a community complaint to hymnal invitation: 3+3 (vv. 2-11); 2+2+2 (v. 12); 2+3 (vv. 13-18); 4+3 (v. 19).

In its form and content, the psalm is a hymnal invitation rather than a community lament: it begs for deliverance and total victory.

COMMENTARY

Strophe I: The Name of Israel and the Name of Yahweh (vv. 2-5)

The psalm begins and ends as a prayer for help. A military crisis of mortal proportions menaces the people. Worse, the enemies bind together, for they wish to eradicate even the name of Israel from the memory of future generations. The people is God's people. Israel's enemies are the enemies of Yahweh.

Strophe II: The History of the Enmity against Israel (vv. 6-9)

From the time of the conquest under Joshua and his successors, hostility from the neighboring nations has hardly ever ceased, and examples of such acts of war are now selected from all corners of the country:

(1) Edomites, from the southeast, descendants of Esau, twin brother of Jacob (Gen 25:24-25); a secular hatred (cf. Ps 137:7);

(2) Ishmaelites, descendants of Hagar, Abraham's slave, whom Sarah forced away into the desert (Gen 16:1ff.);

(3) Moabites, east of the Dead Sea, at war with Jehoshaphat (1 Kgs 3:4-27; 2 Chr 20:1-29) and Jehoiakim (2 Kgs 24:2);

(4) Gebal, probably in the south of the Negeb, near Petra, rather than Gebal, on the Mediterranean coast (Byblos);

(5) Hagrites, in the northeast, across the Jordan in Gilead (1 Chr 5:10);

(6) Ammonites, east of the Jordan (Judg 3:13; 2 Kgs 24:2);

(7) Amalekites, in the Negeb, south of Judah (Judg 3:13);

(8) Philistines, who occupied the land before the time of Saul, Samuel, and David (Judg 3:31; 1 Sam 4:1);

(9) Phoenicians, inhabitants of Tyre (2 Sam 5:11; Isa 23:1-18);

(10) Assyrians, the most brutal of the adversaries; their name was used for people of Mesopotamia even during Persian times (Jdt 2:1);

(11) and (12) Moabites and Ammonites, listed again as the descendants of Lot (Deut 2:9, 19).

Strophe III: Those Who Seek the Pastures of God (vv. 10-13)

The hymnist has provided a history of warfare from the time of the conquest to the agony of Judah; in addition to Strophe II, (13) and (14) Midianites and Canaanites are brought together in a new strophe, for the proper names of their chieftains add an element of concreteness to the memories of the past. Sisera and Jabin (Judg 4:2) and the little-known Oreb and Ze'eb (Judg 7:25; cf. Isa 3:9) sharpen the remembrance of mighty battles.[1] The psalmist's audience is readily alerted by the implied poem of Deborah, barbarous but brilliant, which indirectly pleaded for tribal unity.

The very crudeness and vulgarism about the defeated leaders' bones left unburied that had become "dung" for the fertile soil[2] transform the horrors of the battlefield into the wonders of agriculture! No doubt the last touch of the strophe accents the religious aspect of the poem. It claims that with the abundance of the harvests all the enemies were envious for "the pastures of the Lord."

Strophe IV: Death to Them All! (vv. 14-17)

The poet affirms once more his total trust in God by returning to the language of personal prayer, even supplication at the intimate level of "O my God!" The imagery accumulates comparisons, at once cruel and elegant, between mortal maledictions and whirling dust, stubble in the wind, fire in the forests decimating the hillsides, even the semi-personification of the Lord's tempests and hurricane. At the end of this epic "entertainment," the attention of the singers is brought back to the theology of the name, the echo of the fear that Israel might have erased in the minds of future humans (cf. v. 5 with v. 17).

Envoi: Shame and Disgrace over against Yahweh's Name (vv. 18-19)

The key to the psalm lies in a new affirmation of trust in the benevolence of Yahweh, who will show favor to his chosen people. He is able to do this because his name, "Yahweh," means that he causes to be any event he selects. His name itself means, "He who causes to be." God creates when he saves. A review of Israel's past deliverances allows the psalmist to ask for the complete disgrace of any new adversary and — an apparent contradiction — the hope that they will learn to worship the only master of the whole earth. Military victories become a tool of *apologia theologica.*

DATE AND THEOLOGY

Common features abound in Psalm 83 and the oracles of Jeremiah. The machinations of the peoples who plan to destroy Israel are in Jeremiah transmuted

---

1. Zebah and Zalmunna, Midianite rulers, whom Gideon slew in revenge for the killing of his brothers (Judg 8:4-21).
2. Literally, "garbage in the street," "manure"; cf. Zeph 1:17.

into machinations of individuals. "Against me they form plots . . . to make me disappear from the earth of the living" (Jer 11:19). "They say, 'Come, let us plot against Jeremiah'" (Jer 16:18). A similar expression is used against Moab, "Come! let us make it disappear from among the nations!" (Jer 48:2; cf. Gen 37:20). They even wish to eradicate his name forever (v. 19b). Three times the prophet announces that his enemies will be left unburied on the soil as "manure" (Jer 8:2; 18:4; 25:33). The poetic metaphors of "stubble" blown away by the wind also appear in the prophet's oracles on the dispersion of Israel (Jer 13:26).

It is unlikely that Jeremiah preceded the psalmist. It may be that both the psalm and the prophetic words were spoken or written during the last years of the kingdom of Judah. Psalm 83 omits listing the Egyptians and the Babylonians. The psalm must have been composed before the fall of Jerusalem and the first exile (598 B.C.E.).

In any culture, a war song exalts the validity of national power. It expects the death of the enemies. Perhaps the modern mind is unable to imagine the religious aspect of war for survival, although it has experienced the horrors of genocide.

On account of the exile in Babylonia, the Judahites (in the political sense) became the Jews (in the religious sense). Two new religions appeared in the ancient Near East: a Judaism meticulously submissive to the letter of the Torah, and the Judaism of the Diaspora with the synagogue and a worldwide horizon. Psalm 83 was preserved by the singers of the second temple, but it looked for the Master of the whole earth.

A virulent question remains unanswered: Should the ideology of divine chosenness, with its presumption of superiority over other peoples, permit itself to claim innocence and "victimization" from surrounding countries, especially the Canaanites, whom they dispossessed in the name of their God? Psalm 83, with its implied motto of *Gott mit Uns!* demands a solution to the problem of "the just war."

For the psalmist and his audience, the theological situation was relatively simple. The nations are sealing a covenant against the God of the Sinai Covenant. They are the enemies of God. The prayer that opens and terminates the "song" is motivated not by a desire for revenge, but by a passion to glorify the divine name.

International ethics will not establish peace on earth as long as religion remains ambiguous on divine choice and protection. In spite of the attitude of Jesus toward foreigners and his openness to all ethnic groups, Christian churches have meddled with secular imperialism. In effect, they have exalted the implied exclusivism of Psalm 83. The worldwide vision of the gospel, after that of the prophetic and sapiential teaching of ancient Israel, may yet engender an actualization of global morality.

PSALM 84

God's Presence Far from Zion

1. To the choirmaster. On the Gittith. From the sons of Korah. Psalm.

I

2.   *How amiable are thy tabernacles,*
       O Yahweh of hosts!
3.   *My soul languishes, even faints*
       For the courts of the Lord;
    My heart and flesh cry out
       For the living God!

4.   *Even the sparrow has found a house,*
       And the swallow a nest for herself,
    Where she may lay her young;
       . . . Thine altars! . . . O Yahweh of hosts,
    My King and my God!
5.   Happy are they that dwell in thy house!
       They will still praise thee.   Selah

II

6.   Happy is the man whose strength is in thee,
       In whose heart are the highways [to Zion]!
7.   *Passing through the valley of weeping,*
       They make it [a place of] fountains!
       Yea, the early rain covers it with blessings.
8.   *They go from strength to strength*
       To appear before God in Zion.

9.   *Yahweh of hosts, hear my prayer!*
       Give ear, O God of Jacob!   Selah
10.   *Behold our shield, O God,*
       And look upon the face of thine anointed!

III

11.   *Because a day in thy courts*
       Is better than a thousand [elsewhere],
    I had rather be doorkeeper in the mansion of my God
       Than to dwell in the tents of the wicked.

12.   *Because Yahweh is a sun and a shield,*
           He will give grace and glory.
        No good thing will Yahweh withhold
           From those who walk uprightly.
13.   O Yahweh of hosts, happy is the man
           Who trusts in thee.

BIBLIOGRAPHY

E. Baumann, "Struktur-Untersuchungen im Psalter, II," *ZAW*, LXI (1950), pp. 132-36; G. W. Buchanan, "The Courts of the Lord," *VT*, XVI (1966), pp. 231-33; M. J. Buss, "The Psalms of Asaph and Korah," *JBL*, LXXXII (1963), pp. 282-92; J. Fleming, *Thirty Psalmists* (New York, 1938), pp. 68-72; L. Grollenberg, "Post-biblical *ḥeruth* in Ps 84,11?" *VT*, IX (1959), pp. 311-12; F. D. Hubmann, "'Weg' zum Zion: Literar- und stilkritische Beobachtungen zu Jer 35 8-10," in *Festschrift Franz Sauer* (Graz, 1977), pp. 29-41; J. Jeremias, "Lade und Zion," in *Festschrift G. von Rad* (Munich, 1971), pp. 183-98; L. Kunz, "Die Gestalt des Ps 84," in *Textbook zur Geschichte Israels*, XLV (1955), pp. 22-34; idem, "Selah, Titel und authentische Gliederung der Psalmen," in *Textbook zur Geschichte Israels*, XLVI (1956), pp. 363-69; M. J. Mulder, "Huibert Duifuis (1531-1581) et l'exégèse du psaume lxxxiv 4," *OtSt*, XV (1969), pp. 227-50; F. G. Neuberg, "Note," *JNES* (1950), p. 215; J. Schreiner, *Sion-Jerusalem Jahwes Königssitz* (München, 1963), pp. 279-83; E. R. Smothers, "The Coverdale Translation of Psalm 84," *HTR*, XXXVIII (1945), pp. 245-69; T. K. Thordarson, "The Mythical Dimension: Hermeneutical Remarks on the Language of the Psalter," *VT*, XXIV (1974), pp. 212-20; R.-H. Tournay, "Le Psaume 84 et le rituel israélite des pélerinages au temple," *RB*, LIV (1947), pp. 521-33; G. von Rad, "Gerechtigkeit und Leben in der Kultsprache der Psalmen," in *Festschrift A. Bertholet* (Tübingen, 1950), pp. 418-37.

FORM

Psalm 84 has been called a hymn about Zion. Such a designation is misleading, for the poem moves from the enjoyment of temple worship to trust in the non-cultic presence of Yahweh, away from Zion. Also, the word "refrain" (vv. 5, 6, and 13) is ill fitting because the macarisms that it contains are not identical. In spite of their locations, they delineate three strophes, each one of which is divided into substrophes and produces a distinctive stage in the rhetorical development of the psalm. It describes

> *first,* the delight of dwelling *in* Zion (staticity)
> *second,* the risks of "pilgriming" *to* Zion (mobility)
> *third,* the sublime thrill of trusting far *from* Zion (interiority)

The peculiar position of the second macarism (v. 6), at the beginning rather than at the end of the second strophe, is due to an elegant and significant chiasmus in the respective lengths of the two substrophes:

4. – – – – – – – – –	8. – – – – – – – – –
– – – – – – – –	– – – – – – – –
– – – – – – – – –	7. – – – – – – – – –
– – – – – – – –	– – – – – – – –
– – – – – – – –	– – – – – – – –
5. – – – – – – – – –	6. – – – – – – – – –
– – – – – – – – –	– – – – – – – –

It will be observed that Strophes I and II form a mirrorlike identity of tricola, whereas the rest of the poem is entirely composed of bicola. The first macarism (staticity) leads to the second (mobility), and the third expresses the climactic meaning of the entire poem (interiority).

COMMENTARY

Superscription (v. 1)

The postexilic attribution to the sons of Korah indicates that it was in some way associated with the psalms of Asaph, most of which are subjective elegies of northern origin, perhaps even from the temple of Dan.[1] Yet this psalm received its present form in Zion, where it was preserved by a sacred singer of the Jerusalem sanctuary, who was then "far from Zion."

Strophe I: The Happiness of the Temple Residents (vv. 2-5)

From the start the psalmist confesses that he passionately longs for the courts of Yahweh. This means that he is not there. His inner self "faints" on account of his absence from Zion. Was he exiled from Jerusalem for religious or political reasons? He may have dissented from the authorities. Even as a sacred singer, he may have been ambivalent on the validity of a sacred place, as the third strophe probably implies (see below). In any case, he associates habitation on the temple mount with the proximity of the living God. He is a theologian of divine residence on earth, the geographical presence of the Lord giving life. The "tabernacles" in the plural seem to designate the various edifices that stand on either side of the sanctuary.

---

1. Cf. J. B. Peters, *The Psalms as Liturgies* (New York, 1922), pp. 273-95.

The second substrophe (v. 4) goes beyond the poetic intensity of the first. It is so charged with imaginative emotion that the evocation of total homelessness abruptly disturbs the syntactic coherence of the exclamation, ". . . . Thine altars!" This interrupts the speech fluency of the elegy. In its turn, it transmutes a third person meditation on God to a second person address to God, "thy house, thine altars, . . . they praise thee" (vv. 4d-5). Prayer erupts through the style of reflection on God. His absence is always a presence.

The word *beatus,* or "blessed," does not suit the Hebrew of the refrain (v. 5), for it misses the dynamic strength of the original, "Oh! the racing energy," "the alertness," of those who praise Yahweh in his temple (from the verb "to go ahead," "to march toward a goal")! It is a wish for success in a marathon of endurance.

Thus even the static character of the members of the temple chorus is hailed with a textual hint of anticipation when, in the second strophe, the mood changes from residency to pilgrimage.

Strophe II: On the Highways to Zion (vv. 6-10)

The immediate reiteration of a macarism at the beginning of the second strophe warns that the singer has narrowed his attention to a single individual instead of to the community of his fellow psalmists, as in the first strophe. The exclamatory wish for happiness now propels the traveler "from strength to strength" on the tortuous highways. To where? The Hebrew text does not specify, for the present and final form of the poem through its entire context (cf. v. 8) justifies the addition of the name "Zion" to the second refrain (v. 6). At the same time, the omission of any destination to the "highways" shows that the original poet, if he were a northerner, might have had in mind another sanctuary than the Jerusalem temple.

The traditions of the conquest and the early monarchy emphasized the fervor of worship at Bethel (Gen 12:8; 28:10; 31:13; 35:15), Shiloh (1 Sam 1:3; 3:3; 4:4), and several other sites, like Shechem, Gilgal, and Dan. There individuals gathered, especially for the celebration of festivals (cf. Exod 23:17; 34:23). Was Mount Sinai also a center of pilgrimages? It is not probable (cf. Num 33:1-49; 1 Kgs 19:8). The reform of Josiah (622 B.C.E.), and especially the reconstruction of the Jerusalem temple (519-515 B.C.E.) in postexilic times, rendered pilgrimages to Zion most important, in spite of the spread of synagogues throughout the Persian Empire.

In a hilly and semidesert environment, travel on lonely paths or primitive roads was always a dangerous undertaking. Lack of drinking water, especially in the early autumn, as well as robbers lurking in narrow valleys, rendered pilgrimages a risky adventure. The psalmist knows that courage given by the Lord nurtures more courage. He wishes the travelers a physio-psychological willfulness, moving "from strength to strength."

The valley of Baca is not topographically identifiable, but a slight emendation permits reading *bĕkî*, "tear" or "weeping." Passing through a canyon of sinister disrepute (cf. Ps 23:4), the pilgrim, imagined by the poet — possibly a projection of himself — "plays" verbally with the horror of thirst and makes the site "a place of fountains." This mutation becomes more credible precisely when the early autumn rain will at last end the long summer drought.[2]

The risks remain, and the prayer will become more ardent. It is addressed to the "God of Jacob," a northern appellation (v. 9). The petitioner now appeals for his own rest, "Look upon the face of thine anointed!" Is he the king? Or does his poem incarnate the monarch, composed for his use? The word "anointed" did not originally mean an eschatological "messiah" but referred to an anointed leader of Israel. Any interpretation must be held as uncertain.

Strophe III: The Sublimity of Inner Trust in God (vv. 11-13)

The poet now reaches a level of spirituality that does not suppress his love of Zion, but he certainly thinks that distance from a tribal or national sanctuary, far from Zion, becomes endurable (but perhaps such a statement is superfluous). At least, such a spiritual certainty and practice is legitimate. The interiority of trust in the Lord is possible because it plants the seed of a universal worship. The myth of the earth-center or omphalos, with its inherent exclusivism,[3] is now overcome.

Even if the third strophe does not at once admit such an a-cultic mutation, it portrays indirectly a member of the sacred chorus, apparently forced to endure the deprivation of his professional and cherished vocation. He was at first unable to imagine the luminescence of the God who has life and gives life. The holy place in Zion was his entrance into the world of God. He therefore had to claim that "a day in thy courts is better than a thousand [elsewhere, anywhere]." The Hebrew original lacks the adverb of place, but the sense of the sentence requires it. The comparison between the vision of the shrine, its touch, its sounds, its smells, and his own geographic location in remoteness is repeated, although the translation is uncertain (v. 11cd). To be a doorkeeper in the mansion of God does not necessarily indicate subaltern status, for the sons of Korah exercised rather distinguished functions (1 Chr 9:19; 26:1-19; 2 Chr 20:19; cf. Num 26:10-11). Courtly styles confer nobility to

---

2. The author witnessed a summer drought in Jerusalem from April 3 to December 7, 1933.

3. See S. Terrien, "The Omphalos Myth in Hebrew Religion," *VT*, XX (1970), p. 338.

housekeeping names. Moreover, the infinitive verb may mean "to stand tense and uncertain at the threshold" or, simply, "to hesitate at the portals." In the Middle Ages, and even today, beggars would stand at the gates of churches, mosques, and synagogues (Donisarius in Padua, ca. 1310). The psalmist prefers this ordinary attitude to the comfortable and lazy enjoyment provided by the scoundrel; the verb *dûr* may mean "to relax and lounge" (cf. Arabic and Akkadian).

The second substrophe extols the reasons for this preference: the presence of such an admirable God should lead to the unusual appellation of God as "a sun." The enormous star that illuminates, warms, and fertilizes must be hailed as "a shield," protector against sterility and death. To compare Yahweh to the sun was a daring act in view of the sun worship that prevailed throughout the ancient Near East (cf. Deut 4:19; 17:3; Ps 104:1-4).

The God of life is the living God who gives life and lavishes "goods" on all those who "walk uprightly" — a description of moral integrity common to many psalms.

Thus the third and final macarism, at the apex of the poem, offers the decisive clue to its meaning: while ritual worship is deeply appreciated, it is clearly superseded by the faith that trusts. Offer sacrifices, said other singers, but "trust the Lord!" (Ps 4:6). "Those who know thy name trust thee" (Ps 9:11); "As for me, I trust thy goodness" (Ps. 13:6). Trust is the *sine qua non* of faith. One is so much aware of the Lord's fidelity that, in spite of negative appearances, his word — that is to say, his commitment to intervene — is accepted without doubt or afterthought.

Again, the meditation that began the final substrophe turns into a dialogue with the God who is all-involving, even far from Zion.

DATE AND THEOLOGY

Psalm 84 has been viewed for a long time as a Song of Zion. The date ascribed to its composition varies from the time of the Judges to the late monarchy and even to the return of the Judahites exiled in Babylonia. If the original form of Psalm 84 was ancient and northern, the ambiguity of cultic space and cultic activity surmounted Yahwistic purity and universality. Even the early poet had forgotten the priestly duty of the sons of Jacob to spread the mode of life that was intended in the covenant. The original psalmist and his co-composers when the centers of worship moved from Shechem, Shiloh, Gilgal, or Dan to Zion in Judah said nothing about sacrificial offerings or any other gesture of ritual solemnity, but he confessed his rapture over the beauty and comfort of the edifice and its precincts. His theology of majestic obedience to social justice did not insist on the ethical aspect of covenant fidelity. A prophetic critique of Israel's national transgression is entirely missing.

It may have been an uncritical love of the temple ceremonies that vitiated the pedagogical meaning of the rites and saw in them a pre-Pelagian tool of salvation. The psalmist stands afar from the oracles of the eighth- and seventh-century prophets. Amos and his successors questioned the validity of the sacrificial system, libations, and other offerings (Amos 5:4-7; cf. Jer 7:21-33).

Early Christian interpretations of the teaching of Jesus — nonlegalistic and nonexclusivistic — proclaimed that "the Word was made flesh and tabernacled among us," but they also associated the person of Jesus with the new temple, a human temple and a divine temple, before the portal of which human beings may stand, tense and uncertain, waiting for the human-divine doors to open. The story of the passion, a mythos truer than historical but naked accuracy, reflects on the significance of the death of Jesus, and it simply says, "The veil of the temple was rent in twain, from top to bottom" (Mark 15:38). The Gospel writers drew straight lines from Psalm 84 to their trust in the God of life.

PSALM 85

Rectitude Shall Kiss

1. *To the choirmaster. From the sons of Korah. Psalm.*

I

2.   *Thou didst show favor to thy land, O God!*
        Thou didst bring back the captivity of Jacob!
3.   *Thou didst forgive the iniquity of thy people;*
        Thou didst cover all their sins.   Selah

4.   *Thou didst entirely withdraw thy wrath,*
        And turn away from the fierceness of thy anger.

5.   *Restore us, O God of our salvation,*
        And put away thy wrath from us!
6.   *Wilt thou be angry with us forever?*
        And keep thy wrath from generation to generation?

II

7.   *Wilt thou not, yea, thou! make us live again,*
        That thy people may rejoice in thee?

8.   *Show us thy mercy, O Lord!*
        And grant us thy salvation!

9.   I certainly will hear what the Lord God will say;
        For he will speak of peace to his people and to his saints!
        And they will not return to their folly.]

10.   *Surely his salvation is near for those who fear him,*
        And glory will inhabit our land.

11.   *Mercy and Truth will meet each other,*
        Rectitude and Peace shall kiss!

12.   *Truth shall spring up from the earth,*
        And Rectitude shall look down from heaven!

Envoi

13.   *The Lord will grant that which is good,*
        And our land will yield its increase;

14.   *Rectitude will march ahead of him,*
        And his footsteps will trace the way.

BIBLIOGRAPHY

P. Auffret, *La Sagesse a bâti sa maison* . . . (Fribourg and Göttingen, 1982), pp. 285-379; idem, *Voyez de vos yeux* . . . , VTSup XLVIII (Leiden, 1993), pp. 263-78; E. Beaucamp, "L'heure d'une réconciliation totale et universelle," *BVC*, XXIV (1958), pp. 68-79; J. Becker, "Israel deutet seine Psalmen," *Stuttgarter Bibel-Studien*, XVIII (1966), pp. 58ff.; M. Dahood, "Enclitic *mem* and emphatic *lamedh* in Psalm 85," *Bib*, XXXVII (1956), pp. 338-40; E. Lipiński, "Le Psaume [. . .] 85: Le salut est proche," *Assemblées du Seigneur*, V (1966), pp. 24-31; S. Mowinckel, *Psalmenstudien*, III: *Kultprophetie und prophetische Psalmen* (Oslo, 1923), pp. 54ff.; idem, *The Psalms in Israel's Worship*, II (New York, 1962), pp. 58ff.; P. Nober, "Notula lexicalis ad Ps. 85, 14b [Lege possibiliter *wᵉyeš-m*]," *VD*, XXXVIII (1970), pp. 34-35; L. Prijse, "[*shubh*], hiphil cum sensu intransitive in Ps. 85,4 und Ezra 14,6 — umwenden (sich selbst) — zurückkehren," *TZ*, V (1949), pp. 152-53; C. Trautmann, "La citation du Psaume 85 (84), 11-12 et ses commentaires dans la Pistis Sophia," *RHPR*, LIX (1970), pp. 556-57.

Psalm 85

FORM

At first glance, this psalm seems to be composed in three strophes:[1]

I. Yahweh's Past Benevolence (vv. 2-4)
II. Plea for Yahweh's Salvation (vv. 5-8)
III. Deliverance Is Near (vv. 9-14)

The architecture of this poem, however, is far more complex than the structure usually found in national complaints. The intervening declaration of the poet, speaking as an individual (v. 9), suggests that the psalm presents a *Gattung* close to prophetic liturgies.

Moreover, the composition is exceptionally regular, with two strophes, each made of two or three bicola:

I. *Deliverance and Restoration (vv. 2-6)*
Substrophe One: Yahweh's Past Benevolence (vv. 2-4)
Substrophe Two: Plea for Restoration (vv. 5-6)
II. *Righteousness and Harmony Shall Kiss (vv. 7-8, 10-12)*
Substrophe One: Plea for New Life (vv. 7-8)
Substrophe Two: Rectitude and Peace (vv. 10-12)

It will be observed that a mirrorlike reverse order brings the two strophes in symmetrical parallelism:

3 bicola+two bicola
2 bicola+three bicola

In addition, the announcement of the granting of an oracle (v. 9) is not only expressed in the first person singular and formulated in a tricolon, standing out of its bicola context, but is also clearly out of place since it aimed at separating the substrophe in 2+3 bicola from the 3+2 bicola in the two main strophes. Thus a thematic transition unites the two strophes.

Finally, the last two bicola (vv. 13-14) conclude magnificently with a dynamic *Envoi* that affirms the certitude of "our land's increase" and the march forward of rectitude on the right way in the Lord's footsteps. (See diagram on p. 606.)

The conjecture of the misplacing of the oracular announcement by some early copyist needs no manuscript support. In any case, the Hebrew text is un-

1. R. Meynet, "L'enfant de l'amour (Ps. 85)," *NRT* (1990), pp. 843-58; Auffret, *Voyez de vos yeux . . .* , pp. 262-75.

Psalm 85

ENVOI

13. – – – – – – – –
– – – – – – –
14. – – – – – – – –
– – – – – – –

I

2. – – – – – – – –
– – – – – – –
3. – – – – – – – –
– – – – – – –
4. – – – – – – – –
– – – – – – –

5. – – – – – – – –
– – – – – – –
6. – – – – – – – –
– – – – – – –

II

10. – – – – – – – –
– – – – – – –
11. – – – – – – – –
– – – – – – –
12. – – – – – – – –
– – – – – – –

7. – – – – – – – –
– – – – – – –
8. – – – – – – – –
– – – – – – –

9. – – – – – – – –
– – – – – – –
– – – – – – –

certain since, instead of the MT, "and they will not return to their folly" (v. 9c), the LXX reads, "even to those who turn their hearts to him." The tone of the poem indeed progresses or even transmutes from Strophe I, which is a request, to Strophe II, which envelops the foreseeable future with the marriage of mercy and truth, or even rectitude and peace.

The ending quite appropriately closes a complete circle. It balances the motif of "thy land" (v. 2) with "our land" (v. 13) and flourishes into a sort of musical fugue for marching in a way traced by the divine footsteps (v. 14).

The meter is regular (3+3), except for the tricolon (v. 9), which seems to be 3+4; 2+2; 2+2. This discrepancy confirms the distinctive nature of the individual confession and may support the hypothesis of its misplacement.

COMMENTARY

Superscription (v. 1)

The attribution of Psalm 85 to "the sons of Korah" probably originated in a preliminary collection of postexilic times (cf. Psalms 42–49; 84; 87–88). The Korahites, with the Kohathites, were singers in the second temple, and some of them were also doorkeepers of the sanctuary (2 Chr 20:19; 26:1, 19; cf. 1 Chr 9:19; Ps 84:10).

Strophe I: Prayer for Deliverance and Restoration (vv. 2-6)

Reflecting on the Lord's benevolence in his permitting the return from the captivity (from Babylon?), but appalled by a continuous state of poverty, famine, and oppression apparently due to administrators of the Persian Empire, the poet begs not only for deliverance but also for the recovery of peace and prosperity.

The verb "to return," in the Hiphil "to bring back," is most common for expressing the end of the "captivity," while the word for "return" is used in the prophetic literature with various meanings[2] (cf. Pss 14:7; 53:6; 126:4; also Deut 30:3; Jer 29:14; Ezek 16:53; Hos 6:11; Amos 9:14; Zeph 2:7; 3:20).

The psalmist, with the great prophets, recognized that Israel's sinfulness at all levels of society had angered the Lord. He knew that the captivity was a legitimate retribution for the national iniquity. Now he appeals for complete restoration. He asks for the granting of a new life (v. 7).

Interjected Confession: A Prophetic Oracle (v. 9)

Suddenly the poet confesses as an individual his openness and yet his apprehension before listening to an oracle of Yahweh. The Lord will speak, perhaps only whisper in secret, a message destined not only to his people in general but also to his saintly devotee. Such a word defines more closely the notion of true peoplehood; it is derived from the word for divine mercy, compassion, and love, which a few individuals can exchange in response to divine intimacy.

The "hearing" of God's words, preparing for Strophe II, demands attention, insistence, willingness, and overcoming of non-expressed diffidence on the part of the hearer. The verb "I shall hear" indicates a certain reluctance on the part of the poet, which needs to be conquered: "I will certainly hear." Mystics, in their visions, sometimes feel that words should not be defiled by crass articulation. How is it possible to share the divine communication with others, in a song? Especially when the theme is truly momentous, as it will be when formulated in the ineffability of the oracle?

2. E. Dietrich, *[Shubh shebhûth]: Die endzeitliche Wiederstellung bie den Propheten*, BZAW XL (Giessen, 1925).

Strophe II: Righteousness and Harmony Shall Kiss (vv. 7-8, 10-12)

The final appeal aims at a new life (first substrophe). It receives a startling response: "*Glory* will inhabit our land" (v. 10). The poet indulges in sublime poetry to deal with the recollection of a sublime experience. He transmits a metaphor of the mystical marriage between two virtues that are now personified, "Mercy" and "Truth," even "Rectitude and Peace." They will meet and kiss each other, with an astonishingly double consequence,

> Truth shall germinate and spring up from the earth,
>> And Rectitude shall look down from heaven!

The vicissitudes of the present time will soon be transformed into a full apotheosis for the Grand Play: when "glory will inhabit our land" (v. 10). The symbols of lasting communion between God in his "wholly otherness" and his genuine people, his devotees and his saints, those who fear him in adoration, will at last be united.

The "glory" seen in the temple is also "filling the whole earth" (Isa 6:3), as sung by the seraphim in their trisagion.

In Second Isaiah, Glory is still a mediatory element of divine proximity:

> The glory of Yahweh shall be revealed,
>> And at the same instant all flesh shall see it,
>> For the mouth of Yahweh has spoken. (Isa. 40:5)

In the psalm, Glory has become an actor, a personage, a theatrical character on the stage. *He* will inhabit our earth — namely, "our land."

Likewise the marvel is being amplified: the prosopopoeia presents an acted-out sketch, as if it were the grand finale of a ballet: Mercy and Truth will meet, Rectitude and Peace will kiss one another (v. 11).

Such keywords as "mercy," "truth," and "trust" appear as mouthpieces for living realities that apply to both the character of God and the hoped-for behavior of renewed man. The imagery is unprecedented. On the strength of his prophetic oracle, the psalmist represents "Rectitude" and "Peace" kissing each other! Is it that now united in God, they were, in man, still unrelated and even contradictory or antagonistic? A physical gesture of endearment becomes the symbol of loving mutuality, even of reconciliation.

Righteousness at the divine level or rectitude as the human need for ethical harmony and peace is close to health and also harmony. No wonder! Truth and Trust will germinate, spring up, and flourish from the earth. The fertility of the soil will bring fruit in abundance, which will sustain man for this new economy of beingness, while the right judgment and providence will watch from heaven (v. 12). At the end of time heaven and earth will be united.

The scene is visual as well as auditory.

Envoi: Our Earth and His Footsteps (vv. 13-14)

The psalmist has now completed his disquisition. The earth created by God has now become "our earth." Or is it "our land"? The motif has appeared through-out the song (vv. 2, 10, 12, and 13). And what is "that which is good"? Is it merely an ingredient of happiness? Moreover, what do the "footsteps" mean if the Lord does march symbolically on the earth? No clue permits a precise and certain answer. All that may be affirmed is theologically most important: immobility is not divine. Transcendence may not be expressed in terms of absolute logic. Movement is the core of divinity.[3]

DATE AND THEOLOGY

The date of composition escapes an exact determination. It is, however, postexilic, at the beginning of the Persian domination of the ancient Near East. A new heaven and a new earth were expected for all the peoples of the earth (Isa 51:4). The poet, let us not forget, was a member of the sacred choir in the second temple, at a time when a new prosperity had not yet occurred. Many descendants of the Judahites who had been forced to emigrate to Babylonia had become rather prosperous there, in the land of the two rivers — Mesopotamia — and did not return to Jerusalem. The early "Jews" were the "Judahites" (*yĕhûdîm*) who had remained in the land or those who took advantage of the Persian policy of tolerance toward the displaced populations and were the first "Zionists," in the cultic sense of the word.

They had expected a triumphant restoration. They still hoped for a glorious future, for they lived a half-life, expecting a new life in its fullness. Their expectations took comfort in the oracular poetry that declared the words of Yahweh:

> My deliverance is near;
>   My salvation will appear soon,
>   And my arms will judge the peoples.   (Isa 51:5)

---

3. Heraclitus, not Zeno of Elea, has stated this notion in Greek philosophy.

A similar hope animated the early Christians. Even today the liturgy of Advent and Christmas applies the psalmodic image to the birth of the holy child.

The conquest of "the land" does not prevent the poet from bringing the future into the imagined present. The breadth of his vision is for the benefit of all peoples,

> The grace of God has appeared for the salvation of all men, . . .
> awaiting the glory. . . .
> (Titus 2:11)

A tension rather than an antithesis gets hold of the poet's imagination while he serves the Jerusalem cult, still waiting for the broadest horizon of universal peace.

The "not yet" aspect of the future vigorously strengthens the life of the present. This is faith. The singer of this prophetic liturgy composes for the harvest feast of autumn — Tabernacles — just after dormant exhaustion in summer heat. The community at worship is receiving now the benefits of a goodness that is made effective by the symbolic marriage of Mercy with Truth and the kiss of Rectitude with Peace. These are not the hypostases of divinity as these will be formulated in the philosophic speculations of another age. Yet the novelty and the forcefulness of the language will engender a knowledge of human language for the description of God.

PSALM 86

Unite My Heart to Fear Thy Name

1. *Psalm of David.*

I

> *Bend thine ear, O Lord, answer me!*
> *For I am poor and in great need.*
2.   *Keep and preserve my life,*
> *For I am a pious man.*
> *O thou my God, save thy servant*
> *That trusts in thee;*

3.   *Grace me, Adonai,*
      For I cry unto thee all day long!
4.   *Make joyful the life of thy servant!*
      I trust in thee, Adonai, for I lift my soul to thee.

II

5.   *Thou, Adonai, thou art good,*
      Ready to forgive and plenteous in mercy
      Unto all those who call upon thee.
6.   *Give ear, O Lord, to my prayer,*
      And attend to the voice of my supplications!

III

7.   *In the day of my distress,*
      I call upon thee, for thou wilt answer me.

IV

8.   *Adonai, there is none like thee among the gods,*
      Neither are there any works like thine.
9.   *The nations that thou hast made*
      Shall come to worship before thee, Adonai!
      And they shall all glorify thy name,
10.   *For thou art great and dost wondrous things!*
      For thou, alone, art God!

11.   *Teach me thy way, O Lord!*
      I will march in thy truth;
      Unite my heart to fear thy name.

IV′

12.   *I will praise thee, Adonai my God, with all my heart,*
      And glorify thy name forevermore.
13.   *For great is thy mercy toward me,*
      And thou wilt deliver my life from the lowest realm of death.

III′

14.   *O God, the proud are risen against me,*
      And a group of violent men have sought my life,
      And they have not set thee before them.

II′

15. But thou, Adonai, art a God full of love and grace,
         Long-suffering, and plenteous in mercy and truth.

I′

16. Turn toward me, and grace me!
         Give thy strength to thy servant,
         And save the son of thy handmaid!
17. Show me a sign of thy goodness!
         May those who hate me see it and be ashamed!
         For thou art Yahweh;
         Thou hast succored me and comforted me.

BIBLIOGRAPHY

P. Auffret, "Essai sur la structure littéraire du Psaume LXXXVI," *VT,* XXIX (1974), pp. 395-402; P. E. Bonnard, *Le Psautier selon Jérémie* (Paris, 1960), pp. 185-89; O. Grether, *Name und Wort Gottes im Alten Testament,* BZAW LXIV (Giessen, 1934); G. Giavini, "La struttura litteraria del Salmo 86 (85)," *Rivista biblica,* XIV (1966), pp. 455-58; P. Joüon, "'Ben amatheka' . . . Filius ancillae tuae," *Bib,* XXIII (1942), pp. 190-91; E. F. Lopez, "La exposicion moral sobre el salmo 86," *Bibliographia nacional,* V (1944), pp. 499-523; A. M. Serra, "Appunti sul Salmo 6 (85)," *Rivista biblica,* XVI (1968), pp. 220-46.

FORM

This individual complaint insists on supplications and the promise to praise God. Most commentators divide the poem into three parts, I. Cry for Help (vv. 1b-10); II. Prayer for Learning the Lord's Way (vv. 11-13); III. Deliverance and Promise to Praise (vv. 14-17). However, an exceptional structure is most probable.[1] Some words and expressions are repeated in mirror fashion, around a core verse that constitutes the central petition (v. 11). These words and expressions move ascendingly toward the core verse (vv. 1-10), and away from this core verse with a verbal symmetry that could hardly be coincidental (vv. 12-17):

    I. "thy servant" (vv. 1b-4)
        II. "plenteous in mercy" (vv. 5-6)
            III. "the day of my distress" (v. 7)

---

1. Cf. Auffret, "Essai sur la structure littéraire," p. 125.

IV. "glorify thy name" (vv. 9-10)
  [core verse] "unite my heart" (v. 11)
IV'. "glorify thy name" (vv. 12-13)
 III'. "group of violent men" (v. 14)
 II'. "plenteous in mercy" (v. 15)
 I'. "thy servant" (vv. 16-17)

It will be observed that III and III' do not have identical words, but both deal with the day of distress (vv. 7 and 14).

According to this analysis, the psalm contains two parts separated by the core verse (v. 11). Each part is made up of four substrophes of irregular length, but identifiable by the repeated words or expressions.

Some of the lines are too long, but it does not seem advisable to consider the text as inadvertently corrupted by early copyists. The psalmist may not be a skillful poet, but he finds himself in a state of mortal terror. His prayer for help may be repetitive. The rhythm is certainly irregular, but the composition suffers from highly emotional disturbance. Textual emendations seem superfluous. Other individual laments in the Psalter contain similar or identical elements, but this does not justify the judgment that this piece is only a collection of quotations.

COMMENTARY

Part One: The Ascending Supplications (vv. 1-10)

This poem, a prayer-song, differs from typical laments. Perhaps the early editors showed its difference from the collections of psalms of the sons of Korah (Psalms 84–88) by classifying it as "A prayer" of David.

Substrophe I: Help! Help! (vv. 1b-4)

There is justification for the pressing repetitions of demand, "Bend thine ear," "answer me," and "preserve my life." The Hebrew means "inner being," my "breathing self." This language shows the gravity, even the desperate extremity of the situation. The poet is in mortal danger. The psalm might be part of a ritual of nocturnal judgment in the temple,[2] but there is no evidence that the frightened man enjoys a temporary asylum. Moreover, the profusion of his appeals (vv. 1, 2, 3, 4) and of the names of God (Yahweh, Elohim, Adonai) may be due to emotional disturbance.

2. J. Begrich, "Das priestliche Heilsorakel," *ZAW*, LII (1934), pp. 8-82; W. Beyerlin, *Die Rettung der Bedrängten in den Feindpsalmen* (Göttingen, 1970), pp. 30-31.

The claim of being a "pious man" implies total devotion, and the renderings "holy" or "godly" are inappropriate.

"Grace me!" This transitive verb means far more than "be gracious unto me." It signifies "convey into me divine grace," "fill me with a divine and radiant virtue" that is to be shared with a faithful and beloved "servant." It implies a transformation, a new-birthing, of the petitioner.

The proper name Adonai needs to remain untranslated. It suggests a sovereign lordship for the singer, who is willing to give up earthly ambition, pleasure, and even freedom in order to please the God of all grace. The sense of the word "servant" in this context does not differ from that of "slave."

Substrophe II: Supplication Repeated (vv. 5-6)

The psalmist knows that God transcends nature and humanity. Yet God does not remain remote from the human terror of dying unjustly. He will hear and answer a second supplication because this suppliant is his willing and devoted servant.

Substrophe III: The Day of Distress (v. 7)

God will intervene now. No description offers circumstantial information on the cause of the psalmist's terror, but the time to save him is short. God will act.

Substrophe IV: Praise and Prayer (vv. 8-10)

God is unique, and he respects the appropriate moment.[3] The prayer becomes the praise of the Maker of all nations. These will come to worship. This prediction is peculiar: the nations will worship "at the face," not just celebrate and adore. Is a special meaning implied in the use of *panim* at this juncture? At any rate, does the expression conceal political imperialism as well as religious universalism?

Core Verse: Teach . . . and Unite (v. 11)

The sacred singer conceives his spiritual devotion in sapiential terms. Hearing the way of Yahweh represents the steadfastness of learning. Mystical communion demands ethical and psychological transformation. The praise of God

---

3. The mixture of supplication and praise is common in the individual complaints. See F. Crüsemann, *Studien zur Formgeschichte von Hymn und Danklied,* WMANT XXXII (Neukirchen, 1969), pp. 274-75.

cannot be "hymned" unless the singer absorbs and digests "the way of Yahweh." Education includes far more than instruction. After I learn the way, I need to know how to walk in it. To keep advancing without deviation involves skill and decisiveness at every instant. Ethical behavior depends not only on knowledge but also on constant observation, deliberation, decision, and consistency.

Since the heart is the seat of the intellect and the source of imagination as well as the faculty of decision, it is to be expected that the intensity of the supplications will find in the core verse a climax of petition. The call is at last for gathering, concentrating, assembling together — in one word — in uniting dispersed consciousness. The purpose is "to fear thy name." To unite the heart implies that the heart is divided. To unite is to prepare for action (cf. Gen 49:6; Isa 14:26; Jer 22:21; 35:17). The truth of God, closely related to the trust in which he nurtures his children, produces a single-mindedness "to fear [God's] name." The purpose of existence is far more than to accept the appellation "Yahweh" ("He who causes to be"): it involves the pledge to harmonize with the divine creativity. Thus the core verse in its threefold escalation from spiritual and ethical reality legitimizes prayer.

Part Two: The Descending Echo of the Prayer Song (vv. 12-17)

The word "descending" does not imply that what will now be expressed belongs to motifs of lesser importance; it points to the strophic "mirror" of the ascending part.

Substrophe IV': Praise Undivided (vv. 12-13)

Ahead of its fulfillment, the divine benevolence is anticipated by the promise to praise. To speak of an undivided heart opens a vista on the psychological perceptions of the ancient psalmist. Centuries before Freudian analysis, he called for coherence between *id, ego,* and *superego* in a magnifying, not a refusing submission.

The incomparable God becomes the sublime maker of human beingness. It is the unity of the heart that permits rejoicing, through the overflow of serenity and the elegance of triumph over the terror of death.

Substrophe III': No Harm from the Evil Gang (v. 14)

The poet does not actually backtrack on what he has already said. He adds some details with each repetition. The enemies who caused the crisis are the proud, namely, the arrogant, an organized group (*'edhah*) of violent men who attempt to have the psalmist killed. Yet — and this is the spark of hope — they have not looked at God before them (v. 14c). These "gangsters" are those who raise their heads to claim their rights, but they will eventually fail, for they are godless. No cultic rite, no prayer, no inner dedication, has given their threat any validity.

Baseless evil is doomed evil. Supplications from the menaced individual are strengthened by the brazenness of the plotters, who ignore the power of divine goodness.

Substrophe II': Compassionate Love Is Long-suffering (v. 15)

Long devotion with intimate tenderness is not only giving but also receiving. A mutuality of allegiance between God and man will never prevent a third supplication. Once again the humble begging is concealed under the human admiration of Adonai. To say "Thou art a God full of love and grace" reiterates without repetition the daring thought of the parallel praise (Substrophe II of the first part): God is ready to forgive.

This is the best gift that God may make: "to forgive" even before sin has been confessed. Or is it that an attack on a person is a sign that he is secretly guilty of high misdemeanor, as Job's dogmatic visitors also claimed (Job 11:6)? There is an implied comparison between a God full of love and a mother. The passion of the maternal womb (cf. Ps 51:3), with its wound and its joy, has become an image of divine love. When received by man, it includes the memory, the anticipation, and the present sensation of pain within the exhilaration.

Substrophe I': A Token of Divine Goodness (vv. 16-17)

In their finitude human beings may yield to sudden manifestations of weakness. The psalmist asks for more strength (v. 16b), but why should he refer to himself as the son of God's handmaid? It implies the closeness of divine love and suffering (cf. the semantic association with the womb, its contractions, its agonies, and its giving of life; see the Hebrew for "full of compassion" and "womb"). And why should the notion of abundant grace be followed, right in the following half-line, with the description of God as "long-suffering"?

The demand for a token of God's goodness is soon canceled, for it appeared "to test the Lord" (Isa 7:12). The sublimity of Hebraic spirituality at times was able to discern that faith alone, and the promise of grace alone, would suffice. Yet who would not welcome a demonstration, a proof, a sign, a token of divine answer? Yes, "a modest doubt" (Marianne Moore) would softly dance rather than whirl around the solidity of certitude.

Is there not also the desire to impress and silence the adversary? Perhaps the psalmist has perceived in his own language a contradiction that would cause his whole poem — model of prayer and praise — to stumble and even crumble. He did not end with a crass demand for a sign that would obliterate pure faith with unfaith. He therefore concludes with the reaffirmation of his trust, the only sign or token he will accept. Already, "thou hast succored me and comforted me." Like Job of Uz, the universal man of sorrow, who confesses in the poem his abysmal suffering (Job 42:6), the poet of Psalm 86, in a different context, but with a verb of the same root, acknowledges divine comfort tinged with the pathos of his defection, committed by the demand of a sign of sensorial or rational verification. The comfort inwardly received is the sign of pure religion.

DATE AND THEOLOGY

Like many other laments, Psalm 86 displays affinities of vocabulary and attitude expressed by the great prophets, especially Jeremiah. It also includes parallel formulas of petition from other psalms. The poem, however, should not be dismissed as "an anthology of spirituality." It shows a uniqueness of passionate eagerness for salvation.

First, the poet expresses himself in the presence of God with unusual intensity.[4] He is steeped within a covenantal tradition that unrolls its cadence with an intellectual delight rarely equaled elsewhere. This man has been brought up with a catechism of Mosaic splendor, when Yahweh, descending within a mystical cloud, declares, "I am God, merciful and compassionate, slow to anger, rich in goodness and fidelity" (Exod 34:6; cf. Pss 103:18; 145:8). The psalm reflects the words of nuptial commitment, when God is compared to a baffled but still eager bridegroom who promises: "I shall betroth thee to me forever: I shall betroth thee to me in righteousness, everlasting love, and mercy" (Hos 2:19). A century later, when the Babylonians are within the gates, the metaphor of husband and wife turns into the imagery of father and son: "Ephraim is for me a cherished child, a child that gives me delights. My mercy, which is rooted in the depth of my being [the Hebrew word suggests a comparison with a visceral feeling, "my bowels of mercy"] is moved in his favor" (Jer 31:20).

Secondly, such a God, overflowing with compassion for his children, is incomparable. Mention of Adonai beside other deities gives Hebrew theology a specific significance, for it does not argue with polytheism or affirm it. To claim that Adonai is incomparable corresponds to a formulation of the most intimate spirituality, while the psalmist cries out, "There is none like thee, Adonai,

---

4. Cf. Bonnard, *Le Psautier*, p. 189.

among the gods." The poet does not enter the realm of religious polemic, but his intention is grounded in the hymn of Jeremiah or his disciples, which sings,

> There is none like thee, O Yahweh. (Jer 10:8)

The similarity becomes even more striking when the psalmist immediately adds, "All the nations will come to adore thy face and glorify thy name, . . . for thou art great" (Ps 86:9-10). It looks as if he offered a liturgical response to the Jeremianic pericope,

> Who would not fear thee,
> King of the nations?
> Great is thy powerful name! . . .
> Thou art great! (Jer 10:7 + 6 and 5c)

The most tender love for his people will be the only love the foreign nations will recognize. They will worship such a God.

Thirdly, the incomparable God should be viewed not only as a husband who betroths anew an unfaithful wife but also as the great God, who is ready to forgive. The verb "to forgive" in biblical Hebrew is used only of the divinity (Exod 34:9; Jer 31:31). Usually, pardon is granted to a sinner who recognizes his offense and ritually, or otherwise, begs for forgiveness. For this psalmist, and for him almost alone, the Lord-God-Adonai is so extraordinarily attached to humankind that the faculty of pardon belongs to the very essence of his being.

How wrong are popular readers, or even some biblical exegetes, who think that the Old Testament, unlike the New Testament, presents only a God of vengeance. In Psalm 86 God is named *Adonai*, "my Sovereign," several times because the psalmist is totally devoted to him (vv. 3, 4, 5, 8, 12, 15), and this completeness of devotion is a response to the divine readiness to forgive:[5] the words of this theology abound in strategic places within the psalm:

> "bend . . . answer" (v. 1)
> "preserve . . . save . . ." (v. 2)
>   "be gracious . . ." (v. 3)
> "ready to forgive" (v. 5)
> "turn . . . be gracious . . . strengthen . . . save" (v. 16).

Moreover, such a God is addressed with a vehemence and a familiarity so intimate that the pronoun "thou" is carefully placed within the symmetry of the two parts united by the core verse (v. 11).

5. Cf. W. Brueggemann, *The Message of the Psalms* (Minneapolis, 1984), pp. 60, 62.

> "*Thou* my God (v. 2)
>> *Thou,* my Lord (v. 5)
>>> *Thou* art good (v. 5)
>>>> *Thou* art God alone (v. 10)
>>> *Thou,* my Sovereign (v. 15)
>> *Thou* art Yahweh (v. 17)

The awesomeness and grandeur of the divinity never overwhelms his "humaneness." This paradox, found in prophetic sermons and oracles as well as in Psalm 86, precedes by centuries Christian attempts to formulate what they discerned in Jesus: the fullness of Godhood in manhood, that of a Jewish man who was ready to break geographical and religious boundaries. In a deep sense, mystic Judaism, at the time of the Babylonian exile, when it was precisely born in agony, with Jeremiah and some individual laments preserved in the Psalter, was able to adore the heavenly Father and the living son, both dead, and both living forevermore.

Disrupting the covenantal notion of a chosen people through genealogy and the myth of a Zionist navel of the earth, the singers of Psalm 86 were invited to contemplate the time when all the nations — not through Israel's imperial conquest — would worship "face to face" the incomparable God.

PSALM 87

All Nations Will Delight with Thee

1. *To the sons of Korah. Psalm. Canticle.*

I

2.   His Foundation Was on the Holy Mountains!

> *The Lord loved the gates of Zion*
> *More than any other dwellings of Jacob.*
3. > *Glorious things were told of thee,*
> *O city of God!*   Selah

II

4.   *I shall mention to those who know me,*
        Egypt and Babylon,
     Especially Philistia and Tyre,
        With even Ethiopia [that says:]
     Such and such was born there.

III

5.   *And to Zion it will be said, Mother!*
        In her every man was born,
     And it is He, the Most High,
        Who solidly affirmed her.

IV

6.   *[But] when he writes the book of peoples,*
        The Lord shall count their number,
     [And write] This one was born there!   Selah

7.   How delighted will be all those
     Who feel at home with thee!

Bibliography

E. Beaucamp, "Le problème du psaume 87," *Liber annuus studii biblici Franciscani,* XIII (1962-63), pp. 53-75; T. Booij, "Some Observations on Psalm lxxxvii," *VT,* XXXVII (1987), pp. 16-25; R. G. Castellino, "Psalm 87/86," *VD,* XII (1932), pp. 232-36; G. E. Closen, "Prophetia quaedam de Regno Dei Psalmus 87/86," *VD,* XIV (1934), pp. 231-40; L. Kreisig, "Ps 87," *Die Zeichen der Zeit,* XI (1957), pp. 461-62; S. Mowinckel, *Psalmenstudien,* III: *Kultprophetie und prophetische Psalmen* (Oslo, 1923), pp. 50-51; idem, *The Psalms in Israel's Worship* (New York, 1962), pp. 88, 90; J. Schreiner, *Sion-Jerusalem: Jahwes Königssitz* (Munich, 1963), pp. 288-92; P. W. Skehan, *Studies in Israelite Poetry and Wisdom* (Washington, D.C., 1971), pp. 59-60; R. Sorg, *Ecumenic Psalm 87: Original Form and Two Rereadings* (Fifield, Wisc., 1968); A. Vaccari, "Note critice ed esegetiche," *Bib,* XXVII (1946), pp. 394-406.

FORM

The text and the form of this short poem are uncertain, for the MSS of the MT and those of the ancient versions, which differ from the Hebrew original and also among themselves, suggest that voluntary corrections rather than mere errors in copying have produced such textual diversity. Modern emendations are equally baffling. The translation proposed here is based on hypothetical choices of readings among the Hebrew, Greek, and other renderings of the psalm. These will be mentioned in the course of the commentary.

According to the most reasonable conjecture on the primitive text, Psalm 87 begins with a prelude (v. 2a) and ends with a postlude (v. 7), which together surround four strophes:

Prelude: God's Foundation (v. 2a)
Strophe I: The Love of Zion (vv. 2bc-3)
Strophe II: The Neighboring Nations (v. 4)
Strophe III: Every Man and Zion (v. 5)
Strophe IV: All Nations Born in Zion (v. 6)
Postlude: God's Home to All (v. 7)

The global horizon, which is eschatological, may have been restrained by early editors of the Psalm.

COMMENTARY

Prelude: God's Foundation (v. 2a)

This short logion begins the song as if the masculine pronoun "his" or "of him" refers to God himself rather than to the city of God or Zion, which commands a feminine pronoun, "of her" (vv. 5a and b). From the following context, it appears that God's foundation is just the temple of Zion. Several other sanctuaries (Dan, Shechem, Shiloh, and Mount Gerizim) attracted pilgrimages before Zion did, since Jebus-Jerusalem was not conquered before David in the tenth century. The use of the name "Jacob" instead of "Israel" may be significant.

The opening line is quite independent of the bicola that immediately follow. Thus the prelude is strikingly parallel to the postlude (v. 7), also independent of the context that immediately precedes (v. 6). Since Jerusalem itself was built on only one hill, the plural "holy mountains" most probably refers to the northern sanctuaries (yet cf. 125:2; 133:3).

Strophe I: The Love of Zion (vv. 2bc-3)

Typical of the hymns of Zion (Ps 132:13-17), the verb "to love" means "to love warmly and even passionately," but it is in the participle, and its tense may be the past, just as the implied past of the prelude. When the psalm was composed, the northern sanctuaries were still related to the myth of the omphalos, or navel of the earth, but Zion made a new claim in this direction.[1] The first strophe displays a devotion to "the city of God" (cf. Pss 48:1, 2, 8; 101:4; Isa 60:14): such veneration, for the psalmist, is the springboard for a deeper and wider commitment revealed only in the postlude.

Strophe II: The Neighboring Nations (v. 4)

Without warning the poet cites verbatim a divine oracle. The meaning of the verb "I shall recall" or "I shall mention" is uncertain. The syntactic link between this verb and the double direct object (?) is obscure. Are "those who know me" God's special confidants who are told about Egypt and the like, or is the revelation addressed to these nations "who know me"?

These neighboring countries were not always friendly to Israel and Judah. Why should God assume that they know him? Moreover, why was Assyria omitted, a cruel invader of the country?

The psalmist comes close to the universalism of some psalmists, sages, and prophets (Pss 56:8; 69:28; 130:16; cf. Exod 32:32; Isa 4:3; Mal 3:16). Yet who could have been born in Zion, even metaphorically, except members of the Jewish Diaspora in postexilic times? Did the psalmist admit that even a foreigner, therefore a non-Jew, could be received into the covenantal peoplehood?

Strophe III: Every Man and Zion (v. 5)

The MT does not yield an obvious meaning, "It will be said to Zion, such and such a man will be born in her" (or "by her"). The LXX appears to read, "Mother Zion, it will be said. . . ." While Eve was known as the mother of all living beings, Zion might figuratively and eschatologically be viewed as the spiritual mother of humans other than members of the chosen people. The psalmist, still a Zion devotee, associates new birth with the adoration of Yahweh in his sanctuary. Yet the mystery of rebirth becomes effective in the midst of a new creation, when the law of life will be written upon and within the heart of man (Jer 31:33).

Strophe IV: All Nations Born in Zion (v. 6)

Like the great prophets in general and Jeremiah in particular, the poet of Psalm 87 is bold enough to explode the restrictiveness of covenantal election. The book of the nations, which the Lord God is keeping up-to-date, similar to the

---

1. S. Terrien, "The Omphalos Myth and Hebrew Religion," *VT*, XX (1970), p. 116, n. 4.

census takers of the Persian Empire (2 Chr 2:17; Ezra 2:62; Neh 7:5; Jer 22:30; Ezek 13:9), will include people born abroad, new sons of Zion nevertheless!

One can understand that such a universalism could not be viewed with favor by the editors of the Psalter, hence the variety of texts now preserved in the Masoretic copies and even in the ancient versions.

Postlude: God's Home to All (v. 7)

The Hebrew text concludes with a non sequitur:

> As well the singers and the dancers shall be there;
>   [They shall say]: "All my springs are in thee."

While the LXX, the Syr., and the Vulg. read different texts or propose their own translations, it seems that the most probable reading of v. 7 should be, on account of LXX,

> How delighted will be all those who feel at home with thee!

The members of the sacred choir, confrères of the psalmist, will lead singers and dancers at some unidentifiable feast in a song of Zion with a subtle announcement for the last day of history. "How delighted . . ." [will be] all those who feel at home in thee!" (LXX; cf. Ps 84:7). The word designates not a house but a state of mind, such as "feeling at home with."

This precise wording is significant. "Dwelling in God," or rather "feeling at home with," tactfully contradicts "dwelling in the temple." The Greek word, which translates an unknown Hebrew original, hints not at a geographical location but at the psychological sentiment of happiness in communion. The word κατοικία means not living in a house but enjoying a settlement for a summer or for vacation, for example, being invited to move to a colony. The object "in thee" indicates an interior state, an inward transformation, a direct intimacy with the divinity.

"To feel at home with God" no longer requires a sacred edifice, even sacred in a unique way, but acclimation to the new temple at the end of days.

DATE AND THEOLOGY

From the prelude to the postlude, the psalmist skillfully conveys his admiration, even his veneration, for the Jerusalem shrine, but the conclusion, in v. 7, already prepared for by the intermediary strophes, and supported by the LXX, introduces a mystical consideration of divine presence, beyond pilgrimage or festival, that stands above the traditional theology of Zion.[2] Direct communion with the divine, without the spatial or temporal mediation of a geographical cult, is available not only to Jews of the Diaspora but also to foreign nations.

Attempting to discover a date for the composition of such a short poem with such a wide horizon is difficult. Several scholars have suggested that this poem emerged from the nascent sect of the Samaritans, or from the Jewish community of Qumran. No convincing evidence for either conjecture is available.

The psalmist proves himself to have been a devotee of the Lord. Nothing will separate him from the divine love. Moreover, all nations will someday inhabit the new Jerusalem. Early Christians, meditating on the teachings and attitudes of Jesus, understood that the notion of an elect peoplehood was outdated, and that the temple, beautiful as it may have been, was the symbol of exclusivism. The universal maternity of Zion may have served as a root for the image of a mother church, equally open to all nations.

The "in thee" becomes an answer to "Immanuel, *"God with us."*

PSALM 88

Lament on Lonely Death

1. Canticle. Psalm from the sons of Korah. To the choirmaster. On the melody of Mahalath le'annoth. Maskil of Heman the Ezrahite.

I

2. *O Lord, God of my salvation!*
   I cried day and night before thee;

3. *Let my prayer come to thy presence,*
   Incline thy ear to my cry!

4. *My deeper self is saturated with pain,*
   And my life draws near to the realm of death;

---

2. R. E. Clements, "The Presence of God in Israel's Worship" and "The Presence of God in the Post-Exilic Community," in *God and Temple* (Philadelphia, 1965), pp. 65-78, 123-34.

5. I am listed with those who descend to the pit;
        I have become a hero without strength.

6. Like the corpses that have been slain
        And stretched out in a grave,
    People whom thou rememberest no more,
        I am they, obliterated from thy hand.

7. Thou threwest me down into the lowest pit;
        Into the dark regions, into the deepest.

8. Thy wrath lies heavily upon me;
        Thou hast submerged me with thy primal waters.   Selah

II

9.   Thou chasedst away from me my acquaintances,
            For thou madest me for them a horror.
        I am a shut-in; I cannot escape;

10.   My eyes grow dim with sorrow.

        Every day I call to thee, O Lord!
            I spread my hands toward thee:

11.   Wouldst thou make wonders for the dead?
            Do the shades arise to praise thee?   Selah

III

12. Will thy love be declared in the grave?
        Or thy faithfulness in the deadly abode?

13. Will thy wonders be known in the darkness?
        Or thy righteousness in the land of oblivion?

14. O Lord, it was I who cried to thee;
        Will, in the morning, my prayer reach thee?

15. O Lord, why dost thou reject my existence?
        Or hide thy face from me?

16. I have been struck, and from youth ready to die.
        Terrors of thee overwhelmed me; I am stunned.

17. Thy bursts of anger swept over me;
        Terrors of thee have destroyed me.

18. They cling around me like primal waters;
        They hit me altogether at once.

19. Lover and friend thou hast chased away;
        And my acquaintances thou threwest into darkness.

BIBLIOGRAPHY

C. Barth, *Die Errettung vom Tod in den individuellen Klage- und Dankliedern des Alten Testaments* (Zollikon, 1947); R. C. Culley, "Psalm 88 among the Complaints," in *In Memoriam P. C. Craigie*, JSOTSup LXVII (Sheffield, 1988), pp. 289-301; N. Füglister, "Psalm lxxxviii der Rätsel Lösung," in *Congress Volume: Leuven 1989* (Leiden, 1991), pp. 264-97; M. D. Goulder, *The Psalms of the Sons of Korah* (Sheffield, 1982), pp. 200-204; E. Haag, *Freude und der Weisung des Herrn: Beiträge zur Theologie der Psalmen*, Festschrift H. Gross (Stuttgart, 1986), pp. 170-75; E. Lipiński, "Trois Hébraismes méconnus," *Rivista dagli Studi Orientali*, XLIV (1969), pp. 83-102; R. Martin-Achard, *De la mort à la résurrection: L'origine et développement d'une croyance dans le cadre de l'Ancien Testament* (Neuchâtel, 1956); A. J. Clinton McCann, Jr., *A Theological Introduction to the Psalms* (Nashville, 1993), pp. 98-100; N. Poulssen, [On Psalm 88], *König und Tempel in Glauben Zeugnis des Alten Testaments* (Stuttgart, 1967); H. D. Preuss, "Psalm 88 als Beispiel alttestamentlichen Redens vom Tod," in *Das Tod-ungelöstes Ratsel oder überwundener Feind?* (1974), pp. 63-79; K. Seybold, *Das Gebet des Kranken im Alten Testament: Untersuchungen zur Bestimmung und Zuordnung der Krankheits- und Heilungspsalmen*, BWANT XIX (Stuttgart, 1973); G. von Rad, "Statements of Faith in the Old Testament about Life and Death," in *God at Work in Israel* (Nashville, 1974), pp. 194-209; L. Wachter, [On Ps 88:6], *Der Tod im Alten Testament* (Stuttgart, 1967).

FORM

This is a lament, apparently composed by a man mortally sick. It does not follow an architectural configuration typical of complaints. It contains repetitions that do not mirror each other symmetrically. For example, the crying out of prayer (vv. 2-3, 11, 14), the estrangement of friends (vv. 4, 19), the forgetting of the dead (vv. 6c, 13), the complaints of physical suffering (vv. 4, 5, 8, 10), and the descent to the underworld (vv. 4, 5, 7, 17, 18). These motifs seem to be placed at random — which is understandable for a patient at death's door.

Nevertheless the poet observed a certain sequence of development, for he was a professionally trained versifier. It is probable that the psalm was composed of two strophes of four quatrains, separated and yet linked by a core strophe of two quatrains:

Strophe I: God's Remoteness and Wrath (vv. 2-8)
Core Strophe II: Death's Loneliness (vv. 9-11)
Strophe III: God's Deprivation (vv. 12-19)

Thus, in spite of its seeming disorder, the psalm may silently have called for a new notion of death.

COMMENTARY

Superscription (v. 1)

The editors of the Psalter have introduced an exceptionally long superscription. Was it that the apparent hopelessness of the psalm produced a debate among the singers of the postexilic temple? Heman was known as a sage, belonging to a guild of dancers at the time of Solomon (1 Kgs 4:31; Heb 5:11). He was probably an Edomite or a Canaanite, perhaps the same as a seer who prophesied while playing musical instruments (1 Chr 25:1, 5). The editors of the Psalter may have used the celebrity of the presumed author. Thus they could justify the inclusion of Psalm 88 in the Psalter and may have implied the secret purpose of the lament under its desperate tone.

Strophe I: God's Remoteness and Wrath (vv. 2-8)

Critics who maintain that Psalm 88 is the most pessimistic of all the complaints might admit the glorious affirmation of the initial cry, "O Lord, God of my salvation!" There is no evidence that he refers to past deliverance. He constantly prays and therefore assumes that hope is not a trait of chimerical fancy. He may not ask for the healing of his body, but he is already catching a glimpse of a new side of divinity: the loneliness of God when the shades of his dead singers, who are exterminated, do not arise to praise him, nor is his love any longer declared in the grave.

The first quatrain indicates only that some obstacle prevents his repeated supplication from reaching the divine ear.

Two themes appear in the second quatrain (vv. 4-5): the saturation of physical pain and the approach of death. The word usually translated "soul" designates here the breathing and palpitating body, and even "the inner self."[1] Descent into the realm of the dead is so proximate and certain that it may be considered a fait accompli (Pss 28:1; 107:18; cf. Job 33:22). The pit is both the open tomb and the lower levels of Sheol. Being compared to a hero without strength is the most humiliating fate of a superman.

The third quatrain (v. 6) goes still further. Already looking like the corpses of soldiers who lie on a battlefield, in final immobility, but not with the dignity of medieval "gisants," the dead envisaged by the psalmist may be without sepulture — a fate even more horrible than that of a hero who has lost his strength. And now a theological subject of terror: God does not remember the dead! The battlefield has been spread with the slain (cf. 2 Sam 1:19). Death

---

1. See H.-W. Wolff, *Anthropology of the Old Testament* (Philadelphia, 1974), pp. 11-12.

amounts to a disruption of man from God; in a physical metaphor, "I am obliterated from thy hand." The impotence of the hero receives here the ultimate malediction.

The fourth quatrain (vv. 7-8). Why should God send his devotee to the realm of the dead? He is angry. Only an irresistible access of wrath may explain such a bewildering act on the part of a God of love and justice (Ps 6:2). Death is a retribution for sin, never acknowledged. Is it that divine anger knows no source and no limit? Is the Deity a victim of caprice? The theme is not pursued, but the crescendo of drama, through the entire first strophe, cannot be overlooked: the poet is questioning the righteousness of Yahweh. This theological twist may introduce the final motif of the psalm.

Core Strophe II: Death's Loneliness (vv. 9-11)

The poet has now reached a level of protest and terror, two decisive quatrains (vv. 9-10 and 11) in which the subtle turning point, in Strophe III, is anticipated and prepared for. First, the sufferer feels abandoned by his friends. Human friendship plays a magisterial role in the morality of the international wisdom of the ancient Near East. Although the poet of Job describes at some length and with elegiac mastery the silence of the hitherto faithful God, he does not find his social isolation (Job 19:7-22) to be the result of divine hostility. The psalmist is bolder: he attacks the divinity when he holds him responsible for the social rejection he now endures from his intimate community (vv. 9 and 10). He then takes a step beyond the conventional language of piety: he uses sarcasm.

Having prayed vainly in words and gestures (Ps 143:6; cf. 1 Sam 1:15), the patient attempts to mock God himself in two ironic questions: "Wouldst thou make wonders for the dead?" and "Do the shades arise to praise thee?" (v. 11cd).

God would not think of performing marvels to entertain the dead in their ennui. How could they react emotionally and intellectually to divine acts of prodigy since they have been deprived of human sensitivity or consciousness: they are immobile and have lost all possibility of knowing.

Would God perform a miracle and bring the dead back to life so that he might enjoy the thrill of an actor delighting an audience? The second question offers additional zest to man's teasing of God: the shades or ghosts do not rise to praise! The poet is reaching a theological ultimate when his wit implies that God enjoys being praised.

It is as if the poet states that the dead become nothing, and he is ready to address coarsely the Master of life and death with "The joke is on thee. Thou art a loser!"

Strophe III: God's Deprivation (vv. 12-19)

In four quatrains, parallels to the four quatrains of Strophe I, the psalmist tightens the implications of his sarcastic attack on God's invisibility and thereby asks implicitly for a radically new expectation of life after death. He silently asks for this revolution by meditating on the meaning of praise for God.

The final edition of the Psalter includes — *mirabile dictu* — many individual and rational complaints. Yet in Hebrew it is called *Tehillim*, "Praises." Hymns of praise abound in the Psalter, especially in its last section (Psalms 134–136; 138; 145–150). The worship of God in Israel was dominated by the singing of hymns that celebrated and were conditioned by thanks as well as an exchange of testimonies between the Creator and nature.

Above all, praise revealed the urge to glorify the Lord for his love and fidelity.[2] Praise responded to the dynamic intervention of God in history. Above all, praise symbolized man's ultimate answer to the covenant, which meant an alliance of the universal master with a tiny nation among the empires of the world.

At once the first quatrain explodes with the poet's awareness of God's tender passion for his chosen people. This love must be faithful (v. 19). The Lord God enjoys praise because this exteriorization, by ritual singing and playing, is not flattery to obtain a favor but suggests an exchange that makes the covenant far more than a legal contract. It is a give-and-take conglomeration of feelings, a sacramental dialogue that unites finitude to infinity.

Human beings, who are snuffed out in the dark, abandon God in somewhat metaphysical deprivation, a divine loneliness akin to sepulchral silence. Does God miss the liturgical declarations of his love and — according to the psychology of the poet — the singing of his praise? Is the nothingness into which a life enters, according to the prevailing view of death in Israel as well as in the ancient Near East, *a void*?[3]

---

2. Cf. H. Gunkel and K. J. Begrich, *Einleitung in die Psalmen* (Göttingen, 1933), pp. 32-34; P. Humbert, "Laetari et exultare dans le vocabulaire religieux de l'Ancien Testament," *RHPR*, XXII (1942), pp. 185-214; N. H. Snaith, *Hymns of the Temple* (London, 1951); C. Westermann, *Das Loben Gottes in den Psalmen* (Berlin, 1953); A. Barucq, *L'expression de la Louange divine et de la Prière en Israël et en Égypte* (2 vols., 1957); G. von Rad, "Der Lobpreis Israels," in *Theologie des Alten Testaments*, I (München, 1957), pp. 353-67; G. Henton Davies, "Praise," *IDB* (1962), pp. 856-57; F. Crüsemann, *Studien zur Formgeschichte von Hymn und Danklied*, WMANT XXXII (Neukirchen, 1969), pp. 274-75.

3. A. Lods, *La croyance à la vie future et le culte des morts dans l'antiquité israélite* (1906); G. Quell, *Die Auffassung des Todes in Israel* (Leipzig, 1925); P. H. Menoud, *Le sort des trépassés* (1945); R. Martin-Achard, *De la mort à la résurrection* (Edinburgh, 1956); E. Jacob, "Death," *IDB* (1962), vol. I, pp. 802-904; L. R. Bailey, "Death as a Theological Problem in the Old Testament," *Pastoral Psychology*, XXII (1971), pp. 20-32; W. Brueggemann, "Death, Theology of," *IDB, Sup. Vol.* (1976), pp. 219-22.

Surely, the Lord of the covenant must resent, even hate solitariness. Such a reflection is the result of an imaginative transposition of human sensitivity.

The psalmist is asking, in effect, for a new notion of death. Job will die, and his death is going to be a lonely death. But he knows that his avenger lives and will rise at last from the dust (Job 19:25-27).[4] Another psalmist, against the prevailing opinion of his culture, likewise affirms an intimacy with the divine that cannot be disrupted by the failure of the body. He was a person of international wisdom as well as a singer who could murmur in a musical melody, "Thou wilt receive me into glory" (Ps 73:24).

The poet does not insist on his implicit desire and expectation, but he now feels that, for the very sake of God's social communality, he cannot be exterminated, for the Lord would miss him.

In the second, third, and fourth quatrains, there is nothing to add. The psalmist continues to formulate his existential isolation. Even when he may muse with muteness that God will not abandon him to nothingness, he still fears that "in the morning" (v. 14b), which might well be "death's day breaking" (Jorge Luis Borges), the solitary moment may not be avoided, but will it also be the plight of the God of the ages?

DATE AND THEOLOGY

Conceived regularly in quatrains, this poem presents a strange form of thematic disorder that conceals, however, a theological movement, from disruption to a divine correlation hardly seizable. A psalm on the finality of death compels its composer, a singing sage of the Jeremianic circle and a confrère of the Jobian poet, to penetrate boldly into the mystery of God. He may have taken a foolish stand against the prevailing opinion of his environment on the meaninglessness of death, but he could not avoid questions on the loneliness of God. Some will think that his words were arrested, untold, upon his singing lips.

The date is uncertain, but the disciples of Jeremiah, at the time of the agony of Judah (end of the 7th century or the beginning of the 6th), may well have fostered such an anguished cry, not devoid of a certain black humor that suggests theological renewal. A long time would have to pass before some Jewish men of faith, from the Maccabees to Jesus and Paul, would speculate on the motif of resurrection.

---

4. See Terrien, *Job: Commentaire* (Neuchâtel, 1963), pp. 150-53.

PSALM 89

The Covenant with David

1. Maskil of Ethan, the Ezrahite

I

2.   *I will sing the mercies of the Lord forever,*
      and with my mouth I will make known thy faithfulness in all
         generations.

3.   *For thou didst say, Mercy has eternal foundations;*
      Thou established thy faithfulness like the heavens,

4.   *I made a covenant with the One I chose,*
      This is what I swore to David, my servant.

5.   *I shall render thy posterity firm forever,*
      And set up thy throne for all generations.   Selah

6.   *The heavens celebrate thy marvels, O Lord,*
      And thy faithfulness in the assembly of thy saints.

7.   *For in the firmament who can be compared to thee?*
      Or likened to the Lord among the sons of God?

8.   *God is greatly to be feared in the community of the saints,*
      Great and awesome above all who surround him.

II

9.   *O Lord God of hosts, who is like thee?*
      Who resembles thee in thy power, O Lord?
      Thy faithfulness is all around thee.

10.   *Thou rulest over the raging of the sea.*
      When its waves rise, it is thou who stillest them;

11.   *It was thou who didst crush Rahab like a corpse;*
      And with mighty arm thou didst scatter thine enemies.

12.   *The heavens are thine, and the earth is thine;*
      It was Thou who founded the world, and the fullness thereof.

13.   *The north and the south, it was thou who didst create them;*
      Tabor and Hermon rejoice in thy name.

14.   *Mighty is thine arm, and strong thy hand;*
      To the heights thou raisest thy right hand.

15.   *Justice and Judgment inhabit thy throne;*
      Mercy and Truth advance in front of thee.

III

16. Blessed be the people that know the festal shout;
    They walk, O Lord, in the light of thy countenance.
17. In thy name they rejoice all day long,
    And in thy righteousness they will be exalted,
18. Because thou art the pride of their power,
    And by thy favor our horn is raised up!
19. Our shield is the Lord,
    And the Holy One of Israel is our King!

20. Long ago thou didst speak in a vision,
    And saidst to thy beloved ones:
    "I have placed the crown on one who is my hero;
    I exalted one chosen from the people;
21. I have found David, my servant,
    And have anointed him with my holy oil."

IV

22. Thus my hand shall ever sustain him,
    My arm also shall strengthen him.
23. No enemy shall catch him by surprise,
    Or evildoer afflict him;
24. I shall crush his foes in his presence,
    And I shall plague those who hate him.
25. My faithfulness and my mercy shall be with him,
    And in my name shall his horn be exalted.

26. I will also extend his hand over the sea,
    And his right hand over the rivers.
27. As for him, when he will invoke me, he will say, "Thou art
    My Father, my God, and the Rock of my salvation!"
28. As for me, I shall make him the firstborn,
    The highest of the kings of the earth.

V

29. My mercies will I keep for him evermore,
    And my covenant will stand firm for him.
30. I will make his posterity last forever.
    And his throne, like the days of the heavens.
31. But if his sons abandon my law,
    And they walk not according to my ordinances,

32. *If they violate my statutes,*
    And keep not my commandments . . .

33. *Then will I visit their transgressions with a rod,*
    And their iniquity with stripes.

34. *But I shall not withdraw from him my mercy,*
    Nor shall I betray my faithfulness.

35. *My covenant I will not break,*
    Nor alter what came out from my lips.

VI

36. *Once I have sworn by my holiness;*
    I will not lie to David;

37. *His posterity shall endure forever,*
    And his throne, as long as the sun shines before me.

38. *Like the moon, it shall be established forever,*
    A faithful witness in the firmament.   Selah

39. *But thou hast now surely cast off and rejected,*
    Thou hast been wroth with thy anointed.

40. *Thou hast made void the covenant with thy servant,*
    Thou hast defiled his crown on the ground;

41. *Thou hast uprooted all his hedges,*
    And brought his shelters to ruin.

42. *All that pass by on the way despoil him;*
    He has become the scorn of his neighbors.

VII

43. *Thou hast exalted the right hand of his foes,*
    Thou hast made all his enemies rejoice;

44. *Thou hast blunted the edge of his sword,*
    And thou hast not sustained him in battle.

45. *Thou hast removed his scepter [from his hand],*
    And cast his throne down on the ground.

46. *The days of his youth hast thou shortened,*
    Thou hast covered him with shame.   Selah

47. *How long, O Lord, wilt thou hide thyself? Forever?*
    Will thy wrath burn like fire?

48. *Remember, Adonai, the limits of existence!*
    For what kind of void hast thou created the sons of Adam?

49. *What strong man can live and not see death?*
    Who can deliver his real self from the grasp of the grave?   Selah

Envoi

50.   *Where are thy mercies of old, Adonai,*
        Which thou didst swear to David, in thy faithfulness?
51.   *Remember, Adonai, the opprobrium of thy servants!*
        How I bear in my bosom all the insults of the nations,
52.   *With which thine enemies taunt, O Lord,*
        With which they taunt the footsteps of thine anointed.

53.   *Blessed be the Lord forever!*
                        Amen and Amen

BIBLIOGRAPHY

G. W. Ahlström, *Psalm 89: Eine Liturgie am dem Ritual des leidenden Königs* (Lund, 1959); A. Baumstark, "Zur Textgeschichte von Ps 89 (88)," *Oriens Christianus*, IX (1934), pp. 1-12; G. Cooke, [On Psalm 89], *ZAW*, LXXVI (1964), pp. 26-29; J. Coppens, "Le messianisme royal," *NRT* (1968), pp. 225-51; M. Dahood, "[ʿd] "Thou in Ps 89, 37; 2 Sam. 7,16; Soph. 3,8," *BETL*, XII (1959), pp. 276-78; L. Dequeker, "Les Qᵉdôšim du Psaume 89 à la lumière des croyances sémitiques," *ETL*, XXXIX (1963), pp. 469-84; J.-B. Dumortier, "Un rituel d'introduction: le psaume LXXXIX, 2-38," *VT*, XXII (1972), pp. 76-196; J. H. Eaton, *Kingship and the Psalms* (London, 1976); O. Eissfeldt, "The Promises of Grace to David in Isaiah 55:1-5, in *Festschrift J. Muilenburg* (New York, 1962), pp. 196-207; S. H. Hooke, *Myth, Ritual and Kingship* (Oxford, 1958); A. R. Johnson, "The Role of the King in the Jerusalem Cultus," in *The Labyrinth* (London, 1935), pp. 71-111; R. Johnson, *Sacral Kingship in Ancient Israel* (Cardiff, 1955); E. Lipiński, "Le poème royal du Psaume LXXXIX, 1-5, 20-38," *Cahiers de la Revue Biblique*, VI (1967); J. L. McKenzie, "The Dynastic Oracle [. . . Ps 89:1-39]," *TS*, VIII (1947), pp. 187-218; J. T. Milik, "Fragments d'une source du Psautier (4QPs89) et fragments des Jubilés du Document de Damas, d'une phylactère dans la grotte 4 de Qumran," *RB*, LXXIII (1966), pp. 94-106; P. G. Mosca, "Once Again the Heavenly Witness of Psalm 89:38," *JBL*, CV (1985), pp. 27-37; S. Mowinckel, *Psalmenstudien III: Kultprophetie und prophetische Psalmen* (Oslo, 1923), pp. 34-37; idem, "The Prophetic Word in the Psalms and the Prophetic Psalms," in *The Psalms in Israel's Worship* (New York and Nashville, 1962), II, pp. 53-69; E. T. Muller, Jr., "The Divine Witness and the Davidic Royal Grant: Ps 89:37-38," *JBL*, CII (1983), pp. 207-18; J. Neusner, "The 89th Psalm: Paradigm of Israel's Faith," *Judaism*, VIII (1959), pp. 226-33; E. Podechard, "Notes on the Psalms," *RB*, XXXIX (1925), pp. 5-10; N. M. Sarna, "Ps 89: A Study of Inner Biblical Exegesis," in *Biblical and Other Studies*, ed. A. Altman, II (Cambridge, Mass., 1963), pp. 29-46; W. H. Schmidt, "Kritik am Königtum," in *Probleme biblischer Theologie*, Festschrift G. von Rad (Munich, 1971), pp. 440-61; M. Simon, "La prophétie de Nathan et le temple," *RHPR*, XXXII (1952), pp. 41-58; R. Tournay, "Note sur le psaume LXXXIX, 51-52," *RB*, LXXXIII (1976), pp. 380-89; A. S. van der Woude, "Zwei alte Cruces im Psalter," *OtSt*, XIII (1963), pp. 135-36; T. Veijola, "Davidverheissung und

Staatsverträge," *ZAW*, CXV (1983), pp. 9-31; H. v. d. Bussche, "Le texte de la prophétie de Nathan sur la Dynastie Davidique," *ETL*, XXIV (1948), pp. 354-94; G. von Rad, "Erwägungen zu den Königspsalmen," *ZAW*, LVIII (1940/41), pp. 216-22; idem, "Das judäische Königsritual," *TLZ*, LXXII (1947), pp. 221-23; J. M. Ward, "The Literary Form and Liturgical Background of Psalm 89," *VT* XI (1961), pp. 321-39; C. Westermann, *The Living Psalms* (Grand Rapids, 1984), p. 41.

FORM

Many commentators maintain that Psalm 89 is a collection of two, three, or more poems of distinct genres, like hymn, oracle, and lament. Strophic structure, however, suggests a magnificent architecture that fused elements of diverse origins in order to produce a liturgy for some festive ceremony.

The entire piece effects a regular succession of seven strophes, followed by an *Envoi*. Each strophe is divided into two substrophes of four and three bicola, with an occasional tricolon (v. 9). Such a structure belongs to some techniques of wisdom literature (cf. the discourses of Job's friends).[1]

Such regularity appears without the slightest emendation of the MT; the two substrophes of the fifth strophe seem to disturb syntactic continuity (from v. 32 to v. 33), but they create a rare example of thematic "enjambment." In all probability, such a pause between two substrophes underlines the horror produced by the mention of the corruption of David's posterity.

The *Envoi*, made up of three verses, like the second substrophe of each strophe, offers the key to the purpose of the psalm (vv. 50-52). The final blessing (v. 53) does not belong to this liturgy, for it marks the end of the Third "Book" of the Psalter (cf. Pss 41:13; 72:19; 108:48).

The diversity of meters (4+4; 4+3; 3+3; etc.) overlaps the various genres and does not indicate a diversity of authorship.

COMMENTARY

Superscription (v. 1)

This psalm is called *maskîl*, a title that probably designates "a meditative chant." The postexilic editors attributed it to Ethan the Ezrahite, who was remembered as a wise man in the court of Solomon; his fame was internationally known (1 Kgs 4:31 = Heb 5:11). Such an attribution reflects the literary knowledge of the editors.

---

1. See S. Terrien, *Job: Commentaire* (Neuchâtel, 1952), pp. 33, 68-71.

Strophe I: Divine Mercies and King David (vv. 2-8)

When a psalm begins with such a sentence as "I shall sing the mercies of the Lord forever," in the first person singular, it is possible to suppose, with the Scandinavian school, that the exegete thinks that this poem should be recited by the king on the day of his enthronement. However, the contextual sequence with its oracle does not favor such an interpretation. The singer of the hymn, which later includes an oracle and ends in a lamentation, probably intoned a national chant on the Davidic dynasty at a time of military disaster. The first six strophes build up the emotional cry of the seventh strophe, and it ends with an ultimate prayer.

The word "mercies" in the plural may mean "gracious acts" or "manifestations of love." Such acts or manifestations were part of holy history that the sacred singers must have known. It was enough to include them without specific details. The word for gratuitous love or steadfast love is common throughout the Hebraic traditions.

The mercies of the Lord had "eternal foundations," and they presided over the eternity of a covenant with David and his descendants. While the word "alliance" is not yet used, the memory of David's election is well attested (1 Sam 9:2; 16:13; 17:12; 2 Sam 7:8) and the notion of a covenant with David and his posterity becomes clearly the central motif of the psalm (cf. Ps 132:11, 12). The hymn celebrates the marvels of nature, which include divine faithfulness in granting an eternal covenant to David and his posterity. Truly Yahweh is unique among the sons of the gods, and this uniqueness is recognized by the heavenly assembly. The Davidic Covenant is now inserted into the immensities of the universe.

Strophe II: Grace and Cosmic Power (vv. 9-15)

Yahweh is the King of the world. His cosmic power limits the raging waves of the sea. The Canaanite and Egyptian myths of the fight with Rahab and Yahweh's control of nature are made clear by the dwelling of justice and judgment on the throne. The royalty of God binds nature and history within his royalty over Judah.

Strophe III: Divine and Davidic Royalty (vv. 16-21)

Through a subtle sliding of themes, the motif of divine royalty now moves toward the kingship of Yahweh, which is indeed the central theme of the whole psalm. The cultic setting for which the psalm was composed and sung permitted the poet to consider the place of the elected people in history (v. 16). The psalmist, who celebrated cosmic marvels (v. 2) now involves the whole congregation assembled for worship. "The joyful sound," or "the festal shout" in which the whole community participates (vv. 16-17), confirms the interrelation of divine and Davidic kingship.[2]

The horn is not the ritual shofar that may accompany the festal shout, but is summoned as the symbol of earthly strength. The psalmist bids a united people, elected by a unique God, to rally around the Davidic son, king of the moment, by remembering how David had been selected and anointed (v. 21). Such a people is not "blessed" in the priestly sense *(barak)* but hurled joyfully toward a goal of moral and spiritual fulfillment (v. 16).

Strophe IV: The Oracle on David's Kingship (vv. 22-28)

There is no identification of the God who now intervenes. He declares that his hand and his arm will ever sustain his anointed (v. 22). Delivered from his enemies, and the bearer of divine mercy now doubled with faithfulness, the king will hold his horn high, implying that the people's successes are due to his victories, so that a time will come when the chosen king will call the King of the universe: "My Father, my God, and the Rock of my salvation" (cf. 2 Sam 7:11; Pss 28:1-2; 103:13). In reciprocity, the human king will be called "my firstborn" and "the highest of all the kings of the earth" (v. 28; cf. Gen 28:13-20; Exod 4:22; Deut 21:13-17; Jer 31:9).

Strophe V: Divine Promise and Royal Transgression (vv. 29-35)

In a dramatic reversal the oracle arrives at its climactic moment, but the divine promise is threatened by the criminal misbehavior of David's descendants. Nevertheless, God will not break his covenant (v. 35). He will chastise the transgressor with a rod, and the worker of iniquity with stripes. The divine sense of justice will provoke catastrophic retribution.

Strophe VI: Oracle Interrupted by Protest (vv. 36-42)

The Lord insists on the firmness of his oath, to sustain both David's posterity and his throne. Like the moon, faithful witness of God's fidelity in its monthly changes across the firmament, the Lord will keep his oath to maintain his covenant, but the last bicolon of the first substrophe, like a sudden thunderclap, instead of acquiescing with humility, attacks the divinity. Those words of recrimination challenge the veracity of God. Punishing human faults, even royal missteps, is one thing, but disrupting the dynasty is another. The psalmist ex-

---

2. See P. Humbert, *Le Terouah* (Neuchâtel, 1946).

plodes into a sort of blasphemous accusation. He does not hesitate to contradict the reiteration of the divine promise with his fateful "But!" (v. 39).

Divine as it may be, the oracle is abruptly cut off by human protest. Some historical event has taken place. A Davidic monarch has been cast off and rejected. The observation of a direst contour has discerned that the wrath of God, which inflamed itself against the anointed son of David, exceeds the proportions of a most severe punishment. Elsewhere in the Psalms, divine ire harasses human deficits and pursues human sin. Here no confession of iniquity is recorded. The king has been forsaken.

The second substrophe is filled with a human pride even more acerbic than the near crimes of lèse-majesté that Job ever dared to hurl at the deity. While Jeremiah or his school admitted that the fathers had broken the covenant (Jer 31:31), the poet of Psalm 89 deliberately charges, "Thou hast made void the covenant with thy servant" (v. 40a).

Still worse, through the double metaphor of street dirt and garbage the psalmist exclaims that the crown had been defiled in a smelly gutter of the pathway (v. 40; Ps 132:18). The theology of protest is now a theology of blasphemy. The psalmist does not become an atheist: he is the antagonist of God.

Strophe VII: Fury Turns into Supplication (vv. 43-49)

The psalmist continues to pile up imputations of divine impropriety against the defeated monarch. The increase of his enemies' power, in addition to the weakening of his military strength, seems an extreme aggravation of the punishment implied by "rod" and "stripes" announced in the preceding strophe (v. 33). For God to remove a scepter from the king's hand must be viewed as a case of lèse-majesté, this time operated by divine anger upon an anointed son of David (v. 44).

The meaning of the MT is uncertain (v. 45; several Hebrew MSS and ancient versions differ). It may be, "Thou hast broken (or, removed) his scepter." The second substrophe suddenly reverses the psalmist's combative outburst to the traditional style of supplication, pressing yet humble. True to the horizon of international wisdom, the singer, who may have been influenced by a school of sages, assumed the position of a son of Adam. He now begs Adonai, the supreme Master of a universal humanity, to reflect on the meaning of death. Is the end of existence completely terminal?

Envoi: The Psalmist Communes with Royalty (vv. 50-52)

The recovery of a certain equilibrium authorizes the poet to restrain his expostulation. In a conscious return to the devotion of the first strophe, he remembers "thy mercies of old." Yet he lives through national shame and in religious ignorance. The opprobrium is now thrown not only on a son of David but also on David's memory. Would Adonai remember "thy mercies of old?" (v. 50; cf. v. 2!). At this most critical juncture, the very end of the psalm, he is named three times (vv. 48, 50, 51). Is not the sovereign master of nature also the marvel maker of history? Without him the events that now afflict Judah are unintelligible.

The opprobrium is now thrown upon the son of David, and also the figure of David himself, as head of the dynasty (v. 50). The very fact, exceptional, that the sons of David remained on the throne more than three-and-a-half centuries was indeed a marvel of divine intervention and benevolence. The military disaster that presently has hit this dynasty has attacked not only a servant of the Lord but also all his servants (notable is the passage of this word from the singular, v. 4, to the plural, v. 50). The entire people suffers from international sarcasm. Mysteriously, the singer of the psalm has become the mouthpiece of all the servants. Is he a veiled prototype of the Deutero-Isaianic "suffering servant"?

DATE AND THEOLOGY

A national calamity has killed the king of Judah, a son of David. No charge of iniquity is made against him. Is this King Josiah, who died after the defeat of Megiddo in 609? A national calamity hit the elected people, from the elected king to an anointed king who has become the suffering servant of the Lord.

No charge of iniquity, transgression, or sin justifies his fate. Sources vary about details of his reign, but he is not accused of misbehavior. The original code of Deuteronomy, presumably found in the temple, which provoked a vast reform in cult and jurisprudence (ca. 622- ?B.C.E.), brought to light the importance of the covenant for both king and people (2 Kgs 23:1-3). A reformed worship attempted to survive through twenty-two years of foreign invasion and domination (609-587 B.C.E.). These years of national agony witnessed, however, the first precursor of the birth of Judaism.

Psalm 89 may have been edited as a liturgy for the annual "celebration" of a royal ritual of death and transfiguration. Its remarkable form of seven strophes with its final *envoi* conferred upon it a singular authority. Beginning with the central significance of the royalty of Yahweh ("our King," v. 19b), the psalmist articulated a meditation on the human king — the terrestrial mirror, and David's descendant is humiliated, defeated, and dying (vv. 47-49; cf. 2 Kgs 13:28-30).

Judaism differs from patriarchal and monarchic Hebraism for many reasons, the most important of which is that the motif of "the King" became eschatological. It is also in this sense that the first interpreters of Jesus spoke of "the son of David," not glorious and omnipotent in a political sense but still royal and glorious in the inner sense of human renewal and social reformation.

If the conjecture of an annual "celebration" of a royal death and transfiguration has any support, Psalm 89 saw "the Anointed One," and its readers came to look for the Anointed One, as "the Messiah" to come as a symbol of the consummation of creation in history.[3]

PSALM 90

The Days of Our Years

1. *Prayer of Moses, man of God.*

Prelude

Lord! Thou hast been a home for us from generation to generation!
2.   *Before the mountains were born,*
Or thou hast brought forth the earth and the world,
     From everlasting to everlasting, thou art God!

I

Thou turnest mortal man into dust,
3.   *And thou sayest, "Return, sons of Adam!"*
4. *For a thousand years in thine eyes*
     Are but as yesterday when it is passed,
     And as a watch in the night.

5. *Thou dost sweep them away to their sleep,*
     They are in the morning as an herb that grows;
6. *In the morning it buds and it grows;*
     Come evening, one cuts it down and it withers.

---

3. D. C. Mitchell, *The Message of the Psalter: An Eschatological Programme in the Book of Psalms*, JSOTSup CCLI (Sheffield, 1997), pp. 253-58.

II

7. For we are consumed by thine anger,
       And in thy wrath we are terrified.
8. Thou hast posted our guilt before thee,
       Our secrets in the light of thy face.

9. For all our days turn away in thy fury;
       We consume our years as a summer lightning.
10. The days of our years are thus seventy,
       Or by extreme vigor eighty years,
       But their pride is only misery and inanity,
       For even if they flee in pleasure, we fly away.

III

11. Who can know the power of thy wrath,
       And in the fear of thee, thy fury?
12. To count our days causes us to know
       That we may regain the inwardness of wisdom.

13. Return I pray thee, O Lord! How long?
       Have pity for thy servants!
14. Satisfy us in the morning with thy loyal love,
       That we may sing aloud and have joy all our days!
15. Give us joy as many days as thou hast afflicted us,
       As many years as we have seen evil.

Postlude

16. Let thy work be seen by thy servants,
       And let thy splendor be over their children.
17. Let the delight of the Lord our God be upon us!
       And establish thou the work of our hands upon us!
       Yea! The work of our hands, establish thou it!

BIBLIOGRAPHY

P. Auffret, "Essai sur la structure littéraire du Psaume 90," *Bib*, LXI (1980), pp. 262-76; W. Brueggemann, *The Message of the Psalms* (Minneapolis, 1984), pp. 110-15; M. Dahood, "Interrogative *kî* in Psalm 90,11; Isaiah 36,15 and Hosea 13,19," *Bib*, LX (1979), pp. 573-74; G. R. Driver, "Old Problems Re-examined," *ZAW*, LXXX (1968), pp. 174-83; S. H. Goitein, "Ma'on — A Reminder of Sin [not 'dwelling' but *'awon*, 'sin']: Ps. 90:9," *JSS*, X (1965), pp. 52-53; W. Harrelson, "A Meditation on the Wrath of God:

Psalm 90," in *Scripture in History and Theology*, Festschrift I. Coert Rylaarsdam, ed. A. L. Merril and T. W. Overholt (Pittsburgh, 1977); J. Hempel, *Gott und Mensch im Alten Testament*, BWANT III (Neukirchen, 1926); K. Koenen, "Jahwe wird kommen, zu herrschen über die Erde," in *Pss. 90–110 als Komposition* (Weinheim, 1995); L. Köhler, *Hebrew Man*, tr. P. Ackroyd (Nashville, 1953); J. L. Kopf, ". . . . 'fürchten et sim. [cf. Arabic *rbb*]," *VT*, IX (1959); J. Clinton McCann, *A Theological Introduction to the Book of Psalms* (Nashville, 1993), pp. 155-62; P. D. Miller, *Interpreting the Psalms* (Philadelphia, 1986), pp. 125-30; J. Reider, "Note on Ps. 90, 10I," *VT*, II (1952), p. 145; D. Robertson, *Literary Criticism of the Bible: Psalm 90* and "Shelley's 'Hymn to Intellectual Beauty,'" *Semeia*, VIII (1977), pp. 35-50; S. Schreiner, "Erwägungen zum Text 90. Psalms," *Bib*, LIX (1978), pp. 80-90; E. F. Sutcliffe, "The Labor and Sorrow of Life," *Scripture*, V (1952), pp. 97-98; M. Tsevat, "Psalm XC 5-6," *VT*, XXXV (1985), pp. 115-16; W. J. Urbrock, "Mortal and Miserable Man: A Form-critical Investigation of Psalm 90," SBLSP (1974), pp. 1-23; B. Vawter, "Post-exilic Prayer and Hope," *CBQ*, XXXVII (1975), pp. 460-70; L. Wächter, "Drei umstrittene Psalmstellen," *ZAW*, LXXVIII (1966), pp. 61-66; C. Westermann, *The Living Psalms*, tr. J. H. Porter (Grand Rapids, 1989), pp. 156-65; idem, "Der 90. Psalm," in *Forschung im Alten Testament* (München, 1964), pp. 344-50; D. Winton Thomas, "A Note on [. . .] Psalm XC,5," *VT*, XVIII (1968), pp. 267-68.

FORM

The structure of this psalm is unusual. It begins with an exordium of two elements (vv. 1b-2), which presides over three strophes. Although it includes praise and laments, Psalm 90 may not be considered a complaint. It is not articulated on a core verse, and it does not mention enemies or a night vigil. It begins and ends with an invocation to God as Adonai (vv. 1 and 17), the sovereign Master of the cosmos.

COMMENTARY

Superscription (v. 1a)

Like Psalm 72, which the editors of the Psalter attributed to Solomon, Psalm 90 is ascribed to a single individual of the glorious and tragic past. The editors may have thought of Moses as the "man of God" par excellence. The Lord of the universe had spoken with a mortal man, who was remembered as the "man of God" (Deut 33:1) and "servant of Yahweh" (Deut 34:5), but who died only within sight of the promised land.

Introit: Our Dwelling Place (vv. 1b-2)

More than the eternity of the Creator is expressed here. The eternity of God lies at the center of Hebrew faith. The jubilant declaration, "Thou art God," comes after the astounding words, "Thou hast been a home for us from generation to generation."

Divine presence is extolled in a spatial symbol that transcends the idea of temple, sanctuary, or refuge. It precedes the psychological apprehension of communion above and beyond the localization and limitation of cult. Although the word "home" or "dwelling place" may have been used with diverse meanings (cf. Isa 13:2; Jer 9:10), from devastated cities to heavenly mansions (Deut 26:15; Zech 2:17) and even to sanctuary and temple (Ps 26:8), it is also the symbol of spirituality for God's people (Pss 71:3; 91:3).

Such a creedal exclamation is in the plural. This is a public prayer of the community. By opening his meditation on the mortality of man, the psalmist affirms that God's eternity is not just in the awe-filled contrast with human transitoriness, for the everlasting character of the Creator goes side by side with "our dwelling place." Moreover, this everlastingness has endured divine pain through the very act of completing creation; the two verbs, "were brought forth" and "thou didst form," apply literally to maternal labor at the moment of a child's birth. This does not mean that the divinity is viewed as a mother-goddess, but it suggests that God suffered strictures of agony when he completed the formation of the earth. After the world came into being by *fiat* (Gen 1:18-19), an earlier tradition describes in anthropomorphic words the vulnerability of the sculptor (Gen 3:16; Job 38:8).

The bicolon on history (Ps 90:1) and the tricolon on cosmic eternity (v. 2) constitute an exordium for the body of the psalm.

Strophe I: The Mortality of Man (vv. 3-6)

Why should the poet immediately stumble on the theme of human death? Is it not because the myths of creation, in Hebrew faith, are more sapiential than cultic? The ontological sinfulness of humankind is understood as a supreme act of hubris. The eating of the forbidden fruit renders man open to death. Love between man and woman not only transforms them into one flesh, but it is also the sublime transfusion of happiness and tragedy (Gen 2:24; 3:19). Fashioned from the dust of the living soil, man will return to the fertile soil (v. 19).

The first strophe of Psalm 90 assumes the myths of creation in Genesis, then compares the everlastingness of the Creator to the fragility of his created agent. "Thou turnest mortal man into dust." Each Hebrew word is advisedly chosen: to turn is also "to repent" and "to be converted." The "*Adham*" is not the strong superman, close to the war hero *(gebher)*, or even the '*ish*, originally the nomadic leader in a caravan, but "'*enôsh*," "mortal man." In addition, the psalmist uses the metaphor of the flower that blooms and withers in a single day.

Mortality is part of nature as well as shockingly the result of the unnatural pride of man, who refuses to accept his finitude and seeks infinity (Gen 3:22). Without a termination for terrestrial existence, the knowledge of infinity leads to the existential urge to possess it. The Hebrew idiom, literally, "good and evil," should be understood not in its ethical significance, but in its unusual meaning "from best to worst," namely, "a totality, the whole." The expression is found only a dozen times and suggests "complete knowledge," including infinity (Gen 3:22).[1]

Strophe II: Sinfulness and Mortality (vv. 7-9)

The disquisition on man's frailty as a result of divine anger is so unexpected and in such contradiction with the naturalness of death, expressed in the preceding strophe, that some exegetes consider it a later addition.

The Genesis myths of creation immediately report the murder of Abel by Cain and continue with examples of humankind's rebelliousness (Gen 6:1-7). These tales provide a strange and convincing background for solidarity in iniquity from generation to generation. Hebrew theology has taken seriously the stormy ambivalence that covered the acts of benevolence with the overtones of barbarian tumult — always the folly of self-centeredness. This nefarious aspect of individual and national envy and hate may also explain why the final editors of the Psalter would have ascribed this realistic appraisal of human nature to Moses himself, the "man of God" and "servant of the Lord," but also someone who unleashed divine wrath (Deut 3:26; 32:51-52).

Strophe IIIa: The Shortness and Distress of Human Life (vv. 11-12)

Wisdom poetry, on the whole, praises the relatively rare phenomenon of aging as evidence of righteous behavior and physical vigor. The sapiential atmosphere of this strophe, however, finds longevity quite independent from happiness since it is "only misery and inanity." Like the Babylonian dialogues, especially those that may have influenced the Jobian poet,[2] Psalm 90 questions the validity of human existence. Why should even a devotee of Yahweh endure, for

---

1. S. Terrien, *Till the Heart Sings: A Biblical Theology of Manhood and Womanhood* (Philadelphia, 1985), p. 26.

2. S. Terrien, *Job: Commentaire* (Neuchâtel, 1963), pp. 11-14.

three- or fourscore years, a destiny as prickly as the cactus or, to the contrary, as insipid as the sap of the purslane (Job 6:6)?

Strophe IIIb: The Prayer of the Sage (vv. 13-15)

The mood changes astonishingly, without transition, to a sapiential prayer. It is addressed in the plural, for the psalmist represents the whole community at worship (v. 12; cf. v. 1). Human reflection on the swift passage of time needs to be initiated and answered by the Lord himself. Humanism may be self-satisfying, but it is a trend of mind that is promulgated by the divine Teacher! Human wisdom is God-activated and God-oriented.

The poet admirably links the initial exclamation of faith with God's dwelling place (v. 1) to his joyful request. In spite of his severe view of terrestrial existence, he never yields to despair. The "inwardness of wisdom" implies a psychology of introspection that eventually makes room for the "satiety" of love. It will be recalled that the heart was the seat of intellectual analysis and decisiveness. The prayer asks that the Lord teach us so much wisdom that we "number" or "count" our days before they slip away, while we remain in unconscious idleness. We are bidden to request from God the faculty of inward vision so that we may "measure" our daily use of the hours that soon pile up into years.

God, the timekeeper, has asked man to "return": wisdom reflection never ignores divine presence. The hiddenness of the Lord must not last: in learning the number and quality of our days, man as a time user discovers that God's eternity may, after all, remain inaccessible to him, yet still be granted to him as the *sine qua non* of God's love.

Postlude: The Work of Our Hands (vv. 16-17)

The secret of "numbering" or "measuring" our days is unveiled when man works; and his work, in whatever field, will receive the strength of the divine Worker. The psalm is not a lament but praise.

DATE AND THEOLOGY

Sapiential affinities do not necessarily point to a postexilic period, when wisdom schools for the education of the young became more or less fashionable in several cities of the Diaspora. Wisdom recitals and rhetorical observations on the meaning of existence were formulated at the royal courts as early as the time of Solomon and Hezekiah. However, the affinities with the Jobian poem might indicate the last years of the kingdom of Judah and even the beginning of the exile, when the catastrophes of 598 and 587 prompted the survivors to reflect on the hiddenness of Yahweh. Like the Jobian poet, who shifted his theological concern from the theme of the people's election to that of the situation of man in the cosmos, the poet of Psalm 90 moved from naming God as Yahweh to the invocation of the divine as Adonai (vv. 1 and 17).

The psalmist passes from acknowledgment of the eternal God to the finitude and sinfulness of man and ends with the marvel of God the Worker. He even compared creation to the painful birthing of a baby from the womb of the mother.

The work of man, far wider in its scope than the specific "work of our hands," confers upon his existence the dignity of living. Psalm 90 is a plea for transitory happiness, in the sharing of divine and human work.

While the afterlife does not unduly concern the poet, he cannot avoid thinking of death as extinction. His repetitive begging for the strengthening of man's work subtly looks for the manifestation of divine glory through the imagination and tenacity of those who, like Adonai, labor. Supplication is never adumbrated by hymnal praise. Existential begging for eternal help may be a rhetorical contradiction, but it gives to individual extinction a contour that differs from the passing moment.

In the words of the sixteenth-century collect, human work strengthened and established by the creating Master of life and death becomes a sacrament of immortality:

> Precede us, O Lord, in all our doings,
>> With thy most gracious favor,
> And further us with thy continual help,
>> That in all our work, begun, continued, and ended in thee,
>> We may glorify thy holy name.

Contradictions remain, in the psalm and its commentary, but the invocation to God, in his beauty, a word that also implies the delight of love, contains a yearning and a hope for eternal glory.

Thus the old collect dares to add:

> And finally, by thy mercy, we may receive everlasting life.

PSALM 91

Courage Aroused by Faith

I

1. He that dwells in the secret place of the Most High
   Shall abide under the shadow of the Almighty.
2. I shall say to the Lord, My refuge and my fortress;
   My God! I will trust in him.
3. For he is the One who will deliver thee
   From the snare of the fowler,
   And from the pestilence of death.

II

4. He shall cover thee with his feathers,
   And under his wings thou wilt be confident.
   His truth shall be thy shield and buckler.
5. Thou shalt not be afraid of terror at night,
   Nor of the arrow that flies by day,
6. Nor of the pestilence that walks in the dark,
   Nor of the plague that strikes at high noon.

III

7. A thousand shall fall at thy side,
   And ten thousand at thy right hand,
   But it shall not come near thee.
8. With thine own eyes, surely thou shalt see
   The retribution of the evildoers.
9. For thou hast the Lord as refuge;
   Thou makest the Most High thy dwelling place.

IV

10. No evil shall ever befall thee,
    Neither pestilence come near thy tent,
11. For he shall give his angels charge over thee
    To protect thee in all thy ways.
12. They shall bear thee up on their hands,
    Lest thou wouldst dash thy foot on a stone.

V

13.   *Thou shalt tread over the lion and the adder,*
        And trample under foot the leopard and the dragon.

14.   *Because he cleaves to me with steadfast love, I shall deliver him,*
        I shall set him on high, for he knows my name.

15.   *He shall invoke me, and I will answer him;*
        I will be with him in his distress.

Envoi

        I will rescue him, even honor him and
16.   *Satisfy him with a long life,*
        And show him my salvation.

BIBLIOGRAPHY

R. Arbesmann, "The *Daemonium meridianum* and Greek and Latin Exegesis," *Traditio*, XIV (1958), pp. 17-31; P. Auffret, "Je suis avec lui: Étude structurelle du Psaume 91," in *Voyez de vos yeux . . .* , VTSup XLVIII (Leiden, 1993), pp. 279-300; E. Beaucamp, "Le repos dans la maison de Dieu, Ps 91," *BVC*, LXXVI (1967), pp. 55-64; A. Caquot, "Le psaume XCI," *Semitica*, VIII (1958), pp. 21-37; M. Dahood, "Hebrew-Ugaritic Lexicography, II," *Bib*, LV (1974), p. 381; J. de Fraine, "Le démon du [sic] midi, Ps 91, 6," *Bib*, XL (1953), pp. 372-83; idem, "Le Psaume 91 (90): Chantez au Seigneur," *Feu nouveau*, IX (1966), pp. 1-15; O. Eissfeldt, "Eine Qumran Textform," in *Bibel und Qumran* (Berlin, 1968), pp. 82-83; idem, "Jahwes Verhältnis zu Eljon und Schaddaj nach Ps 91," *Die Welt des Orients*, II (1950), pp. 343-48; R. Gordis, "The Biblical Root SDY-SD [on Ps 91:6]," *JTS*, XLI (1940), pp. 34-43; P. Hugger, *Jahwe, meine Zuflucht-Gestalt und Theologie des 91. Psalms* (Münster, 1971); Köcher, "[*soḥerah*], cf. acc. *taḥîru*," *Archiv für Orientforschung*, XVIII (1959), p. 311; J. Löw, *Memorial Goldziher*, I (1948), p. 328; A. A. Macintosh, "Psalm XCI 4 and the Root [*sḥr*]," *VT*, XXIII (1973), pp. 56-62; J. Magne, "Répétitions de mots et exégèse dans quelques psaumes et le Pater," *Bib*, XXXIX (1958), pp. 177-97; N. Nikolsky, *Spuren magischer Formeln in den Psalmen*, BZAW XLIX (Giessen, 1927); P. Samain, "Images du psaume 91," *R. Diocèse Tournay*, II (1947), pp. 417-32; K. Seybold, *Das Gebet des Kranken im Alten Testament*, BWANT V (Stuttgart, 1973); J. van der Ploeg, "Le Psaume XCI dans une recension de Qumran, 11QPs Apᵃ," *RB*, LXXII (1965), pp. 210-17.

FORM

Psalm 91 has a simple structure of five regular strophes consisting of three elements each. The second and fourth strophes provide a key to this analysis, through the imagery of feathered wings and the Lord's angels (vv. 4 and 11).

These two strophes (II and IV) determine the central position of Strophe III, which coalesces the motifs of dwelling place and refuge as well as the interiorization of steadfast love with secret space.

> I. Secret Place
>> II. Wings
>>> III. Dwelling Place and Refuge
>> IV. Angels
> V. Name

The *Envoi* (v. 16) transforms the conjunction of refuge and dwelling place with rescue and glorification.

The analysis of the meter confirms the validity of this structure, as Strophe I and Strophe V have identical numbers of accented syllables.

> I 3+3   = V 3+3
>   2+2+2   2+2+2

This structure also allows for a symmetrical disposition of the themes:

> I. Imagery of Secret Places and Fortress (vv. 1-3)
> II. Under the Shadow of the Divine Wings (vv. 4-6)
> III Dwelling Place and Refuge (vv. 7-9)
> IV. Committed Protection (vv. 10-12)
> V. Steadfast Love and the Name (vv. 13-15ab)
>   *Envoi:* Rescue and Glorification (vv. 15c-16)

COMMENTARY

Strophe I: Imagery of Secret Place and Fortress (vv. 1-3)

Dwelling in the secrecy of God does not refer to spending the night in the temple, as in several psalms of vigil and asylum.[1] The "secret" or "secrecy" designates a hiding place and does not associate a temple with a fortress (even cf. Job 22:14; Ps 18:12). The "secret place" may well be the consciousness of psychological security, not a geographical construction of public worship (Pss 32:7; 119:114; cf. Pss 27:8; 31:21; 61:5). Faith delivers from enemies and epidemics of the plague because God responds to human trust in him. "Under the shadow of the Al-

---

1. The LXX and Vulg. have preserved a superscription: "Praise of a canticle of David."

mighty" (v. 1) is an image that anticipates the feathery metaphor of the second strophe (v. 4) and the "angels" of the fourth strophe (v. 4).

Strophe II: Under the Shadow of the Divine Wings (vv. 4-6)

The metaphor of protection, often juxtaposed to the world of defensive warfare ("thy shield and buckler"[2]) with the stunning flight of large birds, leads to the image of feathers and wings. These do not allude to birds of prey in deep and narrow valleys. While these wings do not belong to eagles or hawks,[3] as in much of ancient Near Eastern iconography, they announce the "messengers" or "angels" of God himself.

The statues of two cherubim in the temple (1 Kgs 6:23-27) belong to the realm of cultic worship rather than to the style of personal spirituality. Moreover, the amplitude of the cherubim's wings cannot produce a shadow in the innermost chamber of the temple, which is kept in darkness.

Strophe III: Dwelling Place and Refuge (vv. 7-9)

A cultic interpretation fails to comprehend the warfare aspect of the metaphoric promise, "A thousand shall fall at thy side" (v. 7). The comparisons summon the legendary hyperbole of an open-air battlefield. The promise of safeguard and preservation in the midst of a military engagement announces the revelation of capital punishment for evildoers. Before it winds itself into an oracle, the core strophe repeats the theme of God himself being the refuge. By a bold syntax, it equates the refuge with the divine reality. The poet rises beyond the level of spatiality and temporality into the consciousness of divine presence.

Strophe IV: Committed Protection (vv. 10-12)

In the pit of military violence, the psalmist continues the reassurance of committed protection. This time God's shelter is ascribed to God's "angels" or "messengers." The celestial creatures transmit to humans the divine intentions of benevolence. Angelology developed across the centuries, as when they acted as agents of divine praise (Ps 103:20). In this poem, angels are taking care of the mysterious figure, addressed but unknown. They prevent stumbling in a crisis,

2. The *hapax legomenon* probably derives from a root meaning "to turn around," "to circulate."

3. Yet the mother eagle shelters her young with her spread wings (Deut 32:11; Ruth 2:12; Ps 17:8).

and presumably also the risks of death that in the next strophe leave the hero unscathed (v. 13).

Strophe V: Steadfast Love and the Name (vv. 13-15ab)

In the midst of further examples of the most extraordinary assurance of passing unscathed through perils of certain death, even the fight with a dragon, the mythological monster of destructiveness[4] (whose translation is uncertain), such supernatural ability to triumph over all sorts of perils reveals its origin: the passionate fidelity of God's steadfast love and the human will to abide by the knowledge of the name.

The theology of the name plays a most significant part in the traditions on the Sinai Covenant. To know the name of God is to be immersed in the continuous creativity of Yahweh, "the One who causes to be." The petition of the Lord's Prayer, "Hallowed be thy name," implies total commitment of the self to the will of Yahweh.

Envoi: Rescue and Glorification (vv. 15c-16)

The psalm ends with a rhetorical, thematic, psychological, and theological endorsement of the unknown personality who is addressed in the last three strophes of the psalm. A dual declaration, not an oracle from God but apparently sung by the poet, similar to the first hint (v. 3), engages the divine intention to deliver the unidentified figure. More categorically still, God is cited, this time in oracular fashion, "I will rescue him, even honor him" (v. 15c).

The verb "to rescue" (in its second root) meant originally "to equip for war," and its cognates include fortifications and military belts; the first root, however, means "to withdraw." In the Piel, its sense is more fitting to the context, "to tear out," "to pull out," "to deliver violently from a gripping power," "to rescue" (cf. Ps 116:3). A linguistic family evolves around the two roots, which are sometimes confused and include the noun "loins" as the seat of virility.

Not only will there be deliverance, forcefully, from mortal danger, but the mysterious figure who is addressed in the second person will be granted long life on earth. The verb "to honor" (in the Piel) is generally applied to the divinity (1 Sam 2:30; Ps 22:24; Isa 24:15; 43:30); its use is relatively restricted when it is constructed with a human being (1 Sam 2:30; Ps 15:4; cf. Prov 4:8).

The *Envoi* recapitulates the promises of protection in a most spectacular way, as if the addressee were a king, a royal prince, or a hero of valor. Such a hero, threatened by death, will be saved from harm, but also honored as a demigod.

---

4. The "serpent" sometimes stands for the "dragon," mythological representation of evil.

DATE AND THEOLOGY

Diverse interpretations of this psalm have been proposed in modern times. It is not a hymn, a lament, or even a prayer of trust. It contains signs of meditation and of an oracular genre. It is apparently destined to be sung for a monarch or a daring man of war who has just escaped violent death and is still exposed to future danger.

Several times the psalmist reiterates the certainty that God will intervene in favor of this unknown figure:

a) The Most High will deliver (v. 3)
b) He will overshadow him with wings, like a mother bird (v. 4)
c) Thou shalt be shielded on the battlefield (v. 7)
d) No epidemic will come near thee (v. 10)
e) The angels will bear thee up on their hands (v. 12)
f) Thou wilt pass untouched by animals and monsters (v. 13)

Such a number of hyperbolic previsions becomes doubled in the last three strophes by an oracular citation in which God himself accumulates the signs of his benevolence:

a) He cleaves to me with passionate love (v. 14a)
b) He knows the meaning of my name (v. 14b)
c) He invokes me (v. 15a)
d) I will rescue him (v. 15c)
e) I will even honor him (v. 15c)
f) I will show him the meaning of salvation (v. 16b)

This accumulation of promises may reflect court style, when praise is multiplied on someone who is not divine but attains a ripe old age, like a patriarch.

The date is uncertain, but it could be that of many crowned heads of the monarchy in Judah, even during the dark days of defeat and humiliation. The examples of protection may not have been taken literally. They probably wished to thank the monarch and to strengthen his determination to fight. Courage is aroused by faith.

One can understand why this psalm was applied by the early Christians to Jesus in the gospel of the temptation (v. 11; cf. Matt 4:6; Luke 4:10-11). The power to resist pain is hardly ever sustained, except in communion with infinite compassion.

PSALM 92

Hymn of Praise for God's Acts

1. *Psalm. Canticle for the Sabbath Day.*

I

2.   *How good it is to sing praises to the Lord!*
      And to celebrate thy name, O Most High!
3.   *To announce thy love in the morning,*
      And thy fidelity at night;
4.   *To play on the ten-stringed lute*
      With the modulation of the harp!

II

5.   *Thou givest me joy by thy acts, O Lord!*
      I sing with glee the work of thy hands.
6.   *How great are thy works, O Lord!*
      How profound are thy thoughts!
7.   *The man with a dull mind knows nothing,*
      And the stupid man does not understand this.

III

8.   *If scoundrels are growing like grass, O Lord,*
      And all evildoers are flourishing,
      They will perish forever.
9.   *And thou shalt be exalted forevermore, O Lord!*
10.   *For behold! Here are thy enemies!*
      For behold! Thine enemies will be no more!
      They are dispersed, all the iniquity makers!

IV

11.   *Thou givest me the strength of a buffalo,*
      And I am drenched with fresh oil.
12.   *Mine eye is pleased to confront those who espy me,*
      And mine ear to hear the scoundrels who rebel against me.
13.   *The righteous man blooms like a palm tree;*
      He shall grow like a cedar in Lebanon.

V

14. *Those who are planted in the house of the Lord*
      Shall flourish in the court of our God.
15. *Through his old age he still bears fruit;*
      He is full of sap and greenness.
16. *He will proclaim the rectitude of the Lord!*
      He is my Rock! In him there are no detours.

Bibliography

R. L. Alden, "Chiastic Psalms (II), [. . .]," *JETS*, XXX (1976), pp. 191-200; P. Auffret, "Pour publier qu'il est droit, YHWH: Étude structurelle du Psaume 92," in *Voyez de vos yeux* (Leiden, 1993), pp. 301-18; T. H. Booij, "The Hebrew Text of Psalm XCII, 11," *VT*, XXXVIII (1938), pp. 210-14; H. Donner, "Ugaritismen in der Psalmenforschung," *ZAW*, LXXIX (1967), pp. 344-46; H. J. Jefferson, "Psalm 92," *JBL*, LXXI (1952), p. 151 ; L. Kopf, "*šuray* I attende ar. *ṭarah* ʿalay, gegen Jemanden sich empören [Ps 92:12]," *VT*, IX (1959), p. 284; J. Magonet, "Some Concentric Structures in the Psalms," *Heythrop Journal*, XXIII (1982), pp. 365-76; N. M. Sarna, "The Psalm for the Sabbath Day (Psalm 92)," *JBL*, LXXXI (1962), pp. 155-68; B. Wallner, "An Exposition of 'Qui habitat' and 'Bonum est,' Reviewed by J. P. Smith," *Bib*, XXXVI (1953), p. 33.

FORM

Hymnic elements appear in Strophes I and II, but Strophes III, IV, and V belong to the mixed genre of meditation, with prophetic and sapiential tones. The poem then switches to the personal prayer of trust and thanksgiving. The form subtly follows the structure of a complaint, in which a central or core verse presents the main motif, which seems to be "The Lord is the Master of the just and the unjust."

A mirrorlike construction presents the temple in Strophes I and V (vv. 1 and 14). The two facing strophes, II and IV, introduce the twin themes of God's work of cosmic creation and his act of attention to the unknown hero (vv. 5-7 and 11-12). This thematic twinship then provides the thrust of the core verse, God's triumph against his enemies, with his exaltation (vv. 8-10).

    I. The House of the Lord (vv. 2-4)
      II. God's Work at Creation (vv. 5-7)
        III. God's Triumph (vv. 8-10)
      IV. God's Attention to His Hero (vv. 11-13)
    V. The House of the Lord (vv. 14-16)

The strophes are strictly symmetrical (three bicola each plus one tricolon at the climax of the central verse [v. 10]). The meter is remarkably regular (3+3+3) and becomes more ample for the core verse (3+3+3+3).

COMMENTARY

Strophe I: The House of the Lord (vv. 2-4)

The psalm begins as an exultation of praise, sung with instrumental accompaniment. This hymnic introduction combines vocal and orchestral play![1] The psalmist exceptionally shares with his audience the joy of playing and singing in order to praise the Lord and especially turns to prayer when he tells that his psalmody concerns the name of the Lord.

The artist who has composed this piece enjoys the Lord's work in creation as well as the affinities between theology and aesthetics. To worship God properly requires a sense of beauty. The word *ṭôbh*, "good," also means "beautiful."

Strophe II: God's Work at Creation (vv. 5-7)

The Genesis stories of "the beginning" are made up of six days of work and a seventh day for rest. This seems to explain the postexilic superscription of the psalm, "For the Sabbath Day."

Praise for and joy at the works of God at creation lead to sapiential reflection on the part of those who do sense the greatness thereof. "Dull mind" and "stupidity" are to be understood as hostility to faith in Yahweh.

Strophe III: God's Triumph (vv. 8-10)

The multiplicity of scoundrels has been a grave problem for the keepers of the Sinai Covenant. The "iniquity makers" may include astrologers and magicians, but here the expression covers a much larger area of immorality. The psalmist seems to have softened his astonishment and even his doubt concerning God's righteousness or power by firmly hoping that the evildoers, real enemies of Yahweh, will someday "perish forever." Is this sentence implying that for the righteous death will not be the end? This psalmist is reluctant to affirm that for some devotees of the Lord an afterlife remains an unspoken possibility (cf. Ps 73:24).

---

1. Cf. E. Werner, "Musical Instruments," in *IDB*, vol. II, pp. 474-76.

Strophe IV: God's Attention to His Hero (vv. 11-13)

The Creator's "works" are extended throughout history into "acts" of favor and protection for someone unknown, who might be God's Anointed. Who else is such an individual whom God gives "the strength of a buffalo," or this athlete who maintains his muscles endowed with freshly pressed olive oil? The psalmist himself, using the first person singular and composing a royal canticle destined to be sung by the monarch at a ritual feast, praises and gives thanks. Indeed, the evildoers have rebelled "against me." Indisputably, the enemies of the king are the adversaries of God.

Strophe V: The House of the Lord (vv. 14-16)

The image of an olive tree or perhaps even of a palm tree, planted in the court of the Lord's house, may enlarge support for a royal interpretation. The last strophe has to be sung and played by the psalmist, who then uses the third person singular to emphasize the attractiveness of this unknown personality. He may thank the Lord, who has anointed a king to play a central part in the purification of the cult.

The sapiential style appears in the hope that this hero will live on earth many days, "full of sap and greenness." The palm tree, which is mentioned only here in the entire Psalter was a symbol of elegance and charm (Cant 7:7-8). It may have been selected for a climactic ending to such a hymnic praise and meditation. It perhaps recalls the idyll of the man and woman before the fateful attempt to become, like God, immortal. The palm tree probably adumbrates perfect humanity in the age to come. It will bear fruit, and will also endure as strong as the cedar of Lebanon.[2] God the Rock is as solid and trustworthy as the Lord who knows no failure, no deviation, no detour.

DATE AND THEOLOGY

The ethical aspect of the divine expectation never fails to enhance the expectation of those who keep the Sinai Covenant. They do not, like some sages, raise the bewildering problem of evil, for their sense of divine justice overwhelms their reasonable observation. Thus, if the exegetical suggestion that this canticle is a royal psalm obtains approval, the date of composition may well be the time of Hezekiah or Josiah (8th-7th cent.).

2. G. Widengren, *The King and the Tree of Life* (Uppsala, 1951).

The psalm hails the vitality and the fecundity of the theocratic monarch when his fidelity to Yahweh does not go astray, unlike that of Manasseh, Hezekiah's son, or Amon, Josiah's father. The rectitude of God is to be reflected in the righteousness of his Anointed One. He must be respected and loved like "the Rock," for in him there is no fissure, no deviation, no detour. Psalm 92 sings the weekly rest within the entourage of God the Creator.

By the oil of his anointing the king will be the preacher of divine rectitude, and, as in the celebration of the Sabbath, the singing of this poem will include the advent of the future Messiah. The celebration of the Sabbath may be viewed as the anticipation of rest in the life to come. The Mishnah described this canticle as a song for the future time, the day that shall be all Sabbath and rest in life everlasting (*Tamid* 7.4).

PSALM 93

The Lord Is King!

I

1. *The Lord is King! Clothed in majesty,*
   The Lord is vested with strength!

II

Firmly founded is the world;
It will not stumble.
2. *Thy throne is solidly set from old;*
   Thou art from everlasting.

III

3. *The floods raise, O Lord!*
   The floods raise their voices;
   The floods raise their thundering voices.
4. *More than the roaring of many waters,*
   More than the noble breakers of the sea,
   The Lord is exalted on high!

IV

5.   *Thy testimonies are greatly to be trusted;*
      Holiness is appropriate in thy house,
      O Lord, till the end of time!

BIBLIOGRAPHY

P. R. Ackroyd, "Some Notes on the Psalms," *JTS*, XVII (1966), pp. 392-99; A. Allgeier, "Ein auslegungs- und bedeutungsgeschichtlicher Beitrag," in *Festschrift A. Bertholet* (Tübingen, 1950), pp. 15-28; P. Auffret, "Yahwé règne: Étude structurelle du Psaume 93," *ZAW*, CIII (1991), pp. 101-9; J. H. Eaton, *Psalms of the Way and the Kingdom . . . ,*" JSOTSup CXCIX (Sheffield, 1995); idem, "Some Questions of Philology and Exegesis in the Psalms," *JTS*, XIX (1968), pp. 603-9; O. Eissfeldt, "Jahwe als König," *ZAW*, XLVI (1928), pp. 81-105; A. Gelston, "A Note on [*Yahweh malak*]," *VT*, XVI (1966), pp. 507-12; J. Gray, "The Hebrew Conception of the Kingship of God [. . .]," *VT*, VI (1956), pp. 268-85; H. Gross, "Lasst sich in den Psalmen ein 'Thronbesteigungsfest Gottes' nachweisen?" *TTZ* (1956), pp. 24-40; H. J. Jefferson, "Psalm 93," *JBL*, LXXI (1952), p. 160; O. Kaiser, *Die mythische Bedeutung des Meeres in Ägypten, Ugarit und Israel,* BZAW LXXIII (Giessen, 1959); A. S. Kapelrud, "Nochmals Jahwä malak," *VT*, XIII (1963), pp. 229-31; E. Lipiński, *La royauté de Yahwé dans la poésie et le culte de l'ancien Israël* (Brussels, 1965); D. C. Mitchell, *The Message of the Psalter: An Eschatological Programme in the Book of Psalms,* JSOTSup CLII (Sheffield, 1997); S. Mowinckel, *Psalmenstudien, II: Das Thronbesteigungsfest Jahwäs und der Ursprung der Eschatologie* (Oslo, 1922); idem, "Psalms of the Enthronment Festival of Yahweh," in *The Psalms in Israel's Worship* (New York, 1962), I, pp. 106-92; N. M. Sarna, "The Lord Is King," in *Songs of the Heart* (New York, 1993), pp. 177-88; H. Schmidt, *Die Thronfahrt Jahwes zum Fest der Jahreswende in alten Israel* (Tübingen, 1927); J. P. Shenkel, "An Interpretation of Psalm 93,5," *Bib*, XLVI (1965), pp. 401-16; H. Spieckermann, *Heilsgegenwart: Eine Theologie der Psalmen* (Göttingen, 1989), pp. 180-85.

FORM

This short hymn has been classified with several other psalms (Psalms 47; 92; 99). Several exegetes conjecture that it was sung as the exordium of an enthronement festival that yearly celebrated the kingship of God and of God's Anointed. The time of celebration was thought to be New Year's Day, Rosh Hashanah, in the autumn, when nature is revived after the droughts of the summer season.

The Hebrew text includes no superscription, but the LXX in Alexandria and Antioch during the Hellenistic period states, "For the day preceding the Sabbath, before the world was inhabited." And it adds, "A song of praise by David."

In spite of its brevity, Psalm 93 presents a monument of poetic elation in the course of four succinct strophes that grow in length during the first three strophes before the final strophe (IV) reduces itself into a single exclamation:

I. The Lord Is King, one bicolon (v. 1ab)
II. The Solidity of the Earth and the Throne, two bicola (vv. 1cd-2)
III. The Victory over the Primeval Floods, two tricola (vv. 3-4)
IV. The Sanctity of the Lord's House, one tricolon (v. 5)

The meter is regular (3+3+3).

COMMENTARY

Strophe I: The Lord Is King (v. 1ab)

The exordium sounds like three steps on a temple entrance. Exegetes who accept the Enthronment Festival hypothesis generally translate, "Yahweh *has become* king." Hebrew verbs usually precede rather than follow their subjects. Here, the first stichos of the hymn is a shout of exultation that proclaims, not a renewal every year, but a duration for eternity. It does not seem that the divine royalty needs to be ritually renewed as if it relapsed every summer. Introduced as the war hero on a cosmic scale, Yahweh is girded with strength, as a fighter constantly awaiting combat with the anticosmic forces. The psalmist makes a programmatic declaration growing from the beginning to the end of time (Job 40:2).

Strophe II: The Solidity of the Earth and the Throne (vv. 1cd-2)

At once the majesty and power of God receive an illustrative demonstration from the myth of creation, even before the dawn of light. There was darkness on the surface of the abyss, but the spirit of Elohim, in its breadth, flew over the surface of the waters, which were always ready to engulf any semblance of order.

Strophe III: The Victory over the Primeval Floods (vv. 3-4)

The divine kingship is immediately ascertained by his triumph over the watery abyss. The rising of the floods is mentioned three times in a single tricolon. Emphasis on God's reign, probably inherited from Canaanite mythology, is asserted spatially and audibly (v. 3ab), reaching a fortissimo of thundering strokes.

As a consequence of this preliminary but gigantic act of creation, a firm theater of natural growth and human life becomes assured. The God hero is exalted on high. Human praise is only the echo of the acclamations from the celestial beings. The Lord is superb in the heights. Praise answers to praise. This strophe musically and theologically advances its piercing prow at the very center of the whole poem. The form signals the thought.

Strophe IV: The Sanctity of the Lord's House (v. 5)

As a rational and accurate architect, the Creator proceeds now to the final crowning of his work: a certain quality of awe and moral sublimity enters the house of the Lord on earth.

Holiness is not described, but it clearly determines the fundamental character of God as King! Awe is based on veracity, and the sanctity of the shrine is due not to its geographical location but to the rectitude of God and his worshipers. The testimonies of such a God may be trusted. Divine straightforwardness — as in the lack of a detour at the end of Psalm 92 — issues in the radical demands of ethical behavior. The testimonies to be accepted lead to the genuineness of considering the Torah as a living and changing code, for the nation as well as the individuals who follow its own election.

DATE AND THEOLOGY

Psalm 93 sums up the entire faith of Israel in five succinct cola. Yahweh reigns. The initiator of stability and durability for both the temple and its foundation, the earth, looks at public worship and its musicality of praise as the flowering of his faithfulness, viewed in its double dimension: space and time.

The marriage between theology and ceremony in Zion depends on the trustworthiness of Yahweh's testimonies and the divorce of rite from moral behavior and ethical rectitude. The Torah remains dynamic teaching for the whole of individual and national existence. On account of Canaanite influence on the development of consciousness, the date for "The Lord Is King!" may have evolved from the early days in the Promised Land. It received its final formulation at the birth of Judaism during and after the Babylonian exile. The kings may have vanished, but "The Lord is King!"

An eschatological promise now shines over the beauty of God (cf. Ps 92:2). For a number of different reasons, Mowinckel, Gunkel, and many students of the Psalms at the end of the nineteenth century saw the hymns of Israel as looking toward the future, "till the end of time." Theological archeology, the basis of the Jewish and Christian traditions and hope, tends to lose its dynamics if it does not evolve toward the fulfillment of the Lord's Prayer, "Thy reign arrive!"

PSALM 94

God the Avenger

I

1.   O Lord, God of vengeance,
        O God of vengeance, shine forth!
2.   Arise, Judge of the earth!
        Render to the proud their deserts!
3.   O Lord, how long will the evildoers,
        How long will the evildoers triumph?

II

4.   They belch forth and gossip haughtily,
        They boast, all the makers of iniquity.
5.   O Lord, they crush thy people;
        They oppress thine inheritance.
6.   — They slay widow and immigrant,
        And they slaughter the orphans.

III

7.   They say, The Lord is not looking;
        The God of Jacob does not pay attention!
8.   Pay attention yourselves, stupid men!
        Fools, when will you become wise?
9.   He planted the ear, will he not hear?
        He fashioned the eye, will he not see?

IV

10. He chastised nations, shall he not punish?
        And give to Adam knowledge;
11. The Lord knew the thoughts of Adam,
        For indeed they were vanity.
12. Happy the strong man thou punishest, O Lord!
        And whom thou instructest with thy teaching!

V

13. Give him a respite from the evil day,
        Until a pit is dug for the evildoers.

14. But the Lord will not abandon his people,
     Nor will he reject his inheritance;
15. For judgment will again conform to justice,
     And all the upright of heart will agree.

VI

16. Who will stand for me against the scoundrels?
     Who will defend my cause against the iniquity makers?
17. If the Lord had not come to my help,
     My being would now dwell in the world of silence.
18. If I said, My foot is skidding,
     Thy love, O Lord, would sustain me.

VII

19. In the many fits of my anxiety,
     Thy consolations comforted my soul.
20. Would a criminal throne be thine accomplice,
     Creating havoc against thy laws?
21. These men attack the life of the righteous,
     And they even condemn innocent blood.

VIII

22. But the Lord has become for me a fortress;
     My God is the Rock where I find shelter.
23. He will bring upon them their own guilt,
     And exterminate them through their own evil;
     He will exterminate them,
     The Lord, our God!

BIBLIOGRAPHY

A. Allgeier, "Psalm 93 (94): Ein auslegungs- und bedeutungsgeschichtlicher Beitrag," in *Festschrift A. Bertholet* (Tübingen, 1950), pp. 15-28; P. Auffret, "Essai sur la structure littéraire du Psaume 94," *Biblische Notizen*, XXIV (1984), pp. 44-72; E. de Meyer, "La sagesse psalmodique et le Psaume 94," *Bijdragen*, XLII (1981), pp. 22-45; A. Klawek, "Articuli de Psalmis . . . ," *Bib*, IV (1951), pp. 147-62; K. Koch, "Gibt es ein Vergeltungs-dogma im Alten Testament," *ZTK*, LII (1955), pp. 1-3; S. E. Loewenstamm, "The Expanded Colon in Ugaritic and Biblical Verse," *JSS*, XIV 1969), pp. 176-96; A. Maillot, "La justice contre la justice (Ps 94)," *BVC*, LXXIX (1968), pp. 54-57; F. L. Moriartym, [Note on Ps 94:1], *CBQ*, XIV (1952), p. 62; R. Rios, "A Call to Worship," *Scripture*, I (1946), pp. 74-77; N. M. Sarna, "Psalm 94: How Long Shall Evil Prevail?" in *Songs of the*

Heart (New York, 1993), pp. 189-204; E. Stolz, *Psalmen in nachkultische Raum* (Zürich, 1983).

FORM

The literary genre of this psalm cannot be determined easily, for it contains hymnic praise, national lament, individual supplication, and sapiential questioning. In spite of such diversity, which makes any indication of a cultic ceremonial uncertain, the poem is well constructed, for it is made of eight strophes, each presenting three bicola. Vaguely following the model of many complaints, both individual and communal, it makes two strophes (IV and V) equally central. The function of the core verse is to be a turning point between ascending strophes — accusation of the wicked — and descending strophes — divine protection (vv. 1-9 and 16-23). The meter is most varied (from 3+3+2 to 3+3+3, 2+2+2, and even 4+3). Such metrical modulation may point to a cataloguelike method of construction, which only renders more remarkable the architecture of the entire psalm. It is also, like Psalm 33, a nonalphabetic acrostic.

    I. God the Avenger (vv. 1-3)
        II. The Evildoers (vv. 4-6)
            III. God Accused of Inattention (vv. 7-9)
              IV. The Fault of Adam (vv. 10-12)
              V. The Return of Justice (vv. 13-15)
            VI. God, the Protector (vv. 16-18)
        VII. God's Consolations (vv. 19-21)
    VIII. The Lord, Our God! (vv. 22-23)

The final bicolon shortens its second stichos (v. 23d), for its exultation of praise forms a perfect parallel to the initial exclamation, "God the Avenger" (v. 1a). Here again, formal structure enables the exegete to discover sequences and rhetorical movement.

COMMENTARY

Strophe I: God the Avenger (vv. 1-3)

The psalmist bursts forth with exclamations: first, a categorical confession of faith, "The Lord, God of vengeance," and second, an urgent demand to this

God, "Arise, Judge of the earth!" Yahweh is not only the God of Israel but also the God of the universe, thus bidden to judge all the nations of the earth.

The devotees of the covenant have been mercilessly buffeted by interior as well as exterior enemies, and the psalmist asks that the Lord intervene. Does the poem imply that vengeance is not the province of the worshipers of Yahweh? Does it mean that avenging, as well as vengeance and retribution, are the prerogative of God alone? In any case, the initial petition, self-centeredly demanding, presumes a degree of horror, of terror, and of suffering as well as of national humiliation.

Strophe II: The Evildoers (vv. 4-6)

It seems that the enemies are a mixture of foreign soldiers and domestic opportunists who collaborate with the invaders, out of sheer self-interest. Their arrogance shows their illusions. They oppress the Lord's inheritance; thus they attack the Lord as well as "thy people."

Strophe III: God Accused of Inattention (vv. 7-9)

There may well have been a trace of disputation among the common people, imitating the professional sages. Who are "they" who say, "The Lord is not looking" or "does not pay attention"? Perhaps some rebels from the sapiential circles. If not rebels, perhaps some smart individuals who had sensed the scandal of injustice on earth. To charge God with carelessness or lack of knowledge, blindness, or deafness may not have been intended as blasphemous humor, but it may have been another approach to explain the silence and inaction of Yahweh before human corruption and brutality. A prophet could suggest that the Lord's omnipotence and omniscience could be doubted in the face of the devastating events of history, but such an injunction merely reflects the sinfulness of Israel. The psalmist's questioning of divine knowledge is immediately denounced as human folly, spoken by stupid men deprived of wisdom (v. 8b).

Strophe IV: The Fault of Adam (vv. 10-12)

Sapiential heterodoxy may have inspired the poet to recall the myth of the expulsion from the Garden of Eden. Most scholars render the Hebrew word Adam by "man" or "humankind." A professional hymnist, who was educated in the knowledge and use of the old traditions, most likely used the word as a proper name, "Adam." While rabbinical Judaism and some Christian interpretations developed the dogma of original sin, the myth of the Garden clearly presented the tree of "good and evil" not in the sense of moral conscience but as knowledge of the best and the worst. This absolute knowledge could appropriate immortality (Gen 3:6, 22).

The psalmist was precisely aware that Adam and Eve had entered into the possession of a knowledge of the tree of life, and thus of immortality. Metaphysical arrogance leads Adam to desire life forever. The enemies may not crave for immortality, but their aggressiveness against the people of God conceals extravagant hubris, the swelling of self-centeredness, which is the ultimate revolt against the supreme "teacher" (*moreh,* a cognate of *torah*).

Strophe V: The Return of Justice (vv. 13-15)

Twin brother of the strophe on Adamic folly, Strophe V turns to the corruption of judges who do not decide fairly the verdict of trials. This appears to be similar to what the great prophets, such as Amos, Isaiah, and Micah, deplored in the name of "the just Judge." Again, on account of their dishonesty princes and judiciary officers will be expelled and soon lie in the pit that is now dug for them. Justice will return.

Strophe VI: God, the Protector (vv. 16-18)

The psalm now becomes a personal canticle of supplication, interlined with the memory of the Lord's seemingly miraculous intervention in delivering the hero from mortal peril. The utter loneliness of the psalmist and his sense of abandonment emerge from the shout of despair that is also a challenge, "Who will stand for me against the scoundrels?" (v. 16). Perhaps even among his colleagues and fellow singers, nobody had the courage to defend his cause. "The iniquity makers" may have been magicians and witches who manipulated (they claimed) forces of nature to reach their ends. Yahweh saved the poet from death.

The "inner being" evokes far more than "soul," the psychological center of the human person, which would continue to live on in the grave. It refers here to the fullness of terrestrial existence. While the evildoers in a daring jest accused God of inattention or blindness and deafness, the poet shifts again to the second person singular in an ardent style of prayer. Such a direct address to the Lord (v. 18) reaches the sublime level of a hymn of thanksgiving.

Strophe VII: God's Consolations (vv. 19-21)

The psalmist pursues a discreet confession of gratitude for the Lord who came to his help, without which he would have yielded to his "many fits of anxiety." The Hebrew conveys a much stronger emotion than current translations of "cares" and "concerns." The words "in the abundance," in the midst of my being, point to entangled, thorny brambles *(hapax legomenon)*. Most probably the poet alludes to the haunting nightmares that spoiled his sleep and upset his psychological equilibrium. His distress is not described in detail, but it certainly produced disturbing torments.

"Thy consolations" are not identified. Were they visions or the hearing of soothing words? Did he receive the gift of suprasensorial light? The word "consolations" is found only here in the Psalter (cf. Isa 66:11). Mystics of later times have sometimes sketched "the dark night of the soul" and its subsequent illumination.

A "criminal throne" as God's accomplice offers an obscure meaning; the word "throne" refers here not to a royal government but to the seat of justice. The psalmist expresses his utter bewilderment at the idea that the Lord of righteousness would find accomplices among corrupt judges.

Strophe VIII: The Lord, Our God! (vv. 22-23)

In a display of joyful certitude, Yahweh is compared to a fortress. The Rock is not to be understood as the omphalos or center of the earth, standing in the most sacred room of the Zion sanctuary, but it must be taken as the stony shield that the hills offer warriors and, metaphorically, the defender who brings to justice his moral balance and integrity.

The chiasmus found in the entire psalm and mirrored by the final bicolon (v. 23) from the initial cry of joyful elation (v. 1) so deeply intensified the religious sensitivity of the poet that he did not complete the second stichos of his exclamation, "The Lord, our God!" Close to ecstasy, he can only show that, remembering his own salvation in the past, he thinks again of the community that he represents and says, "*our*" God!

DATE AND THEOLOGY

Rabbinical tradition relates that this psalm was sung on the fourth day after the Sabbath. It adds that the singers were completing the rendition of the psalm and were interrupted by the Babylonian army that seized the city of Jerusalem (in 587?). The singers of the "première" intoning of Psalm 94 could not finish the final stichos, and later copyists respected the dramatic lacuna. If there is any basis for this detail, the psalm belongs to the last days of Judah's agony. Such a date would fit the mixture of foreign and domestic enemies (cf. vv. 4-5).

The shift of concern from communal prayer (vv. 2-3, 14) to individual reminiscence of God's succor (v. 19) with the final return to communality of needs (v. 23) indicates not an editor bringing together originally independent fragments, but the poet's theological acuteness. To convince the sapiential doubters, or at least questioners, of divine omniscience and omnipotence, that the Lord will eventually save his people, the psalmist exclaims, "Look at what God has done for me!" (v. 17).

Objectivity in the theological exteriorization of faith and its temporary fixation into an intellectual belief accessible to others requires the mystic, the oracular prophet, or the would-be leader to indulge in subjectivity. He must testify on the personal authenticity of his *fiducia* (trust), which he is about to translate into *fides* (belief). Biblical theology is the attempt, at a given moment of cultural history, to transmute biblical speech into subjectivity before it is led back, in time and space, to openhanded objectivity.

The psalmodic chiasmus in this poem, from v. 1 to v. 23, stimulates the fragile but indispensable translation of a visual or auditory perception of God's Word *(Verbum Dei)* into the human discipline of thinking. Evasion from "the world of silence" (v. 17) compels experiential formulation intending to edify or at least to alert and stimulate the society of God.

This psalm forces a momentary pause in what A. Chouraqui called "the impatience of the vision of glory."

PSALM 95

Praise God, Never Test Him

Prelude

1.   *O come, let us sing to the Lord!*
    Let us make a joyful noise
    To the Rock of our salvation!

I

2.   *Let us come into his presence with thanksgiving*
      And make a joyful noise unto him with psalms!
3.   *For the Lord is a great God,*
      And a great King above all gods.

II

4.   *In his hand are the abysses of the earth;*
        The crest of the mounts is his also.

5.   *The sea is his, and he made it,*
        And the continents that his hands have formed.

III

6.   *O come, let us worship and bow down,*
        Let us kneel before the Lord, our Maker,

7.   *For he is our God, and we are the people of his pasture,*
        And the sheep of his hand.

IV

     Today, if you hear his voice,

8.   *Harden not your heart as at Meribah,*
         And as on the day of Massah in the wilderness,

9.   *When your fathers tested me,*
        Probed me, and saw my works.

V

10.   *Forty years long was I grieved with this generation,*
       And said, They are people that do err in their heart,
       And they have not known my ways.

11.   *Unto whom I swore in my wrath*
       That they should not enter into my rest.

BIBLIOGRAPHY

W. E. Barnes, "Two Psalm Notes — Ps 22,17; 95,6," *JTS*, XXXVII (1936), pp. 385-87; G. Braulik, "Gottes Ruhe — Das Land oder der Tempel? Zu Psalm 95,11," in *Freude und die Weisung der Herrn*, Festschrift H. Gross (Stuttgart, 1986), pp. 33-34; G. H. Davies, "Psalm 95," *ZAW* LXXXV (1973), pp. 183-95; J. Finkel, "Some Problems Relating to Ps 95," *AJSL*, L (1933), pp. 32-40; M. Girard, "Analyse structurelle du Psaume 95," *Sciences ecclesiastiques*, XXXIII (1981), pp. 182-99; idem, "The Literary Structure of Ps 95," *Theology Digest*, XXX (1982), pp. 55-58; F. James, *Thirty Psalmists* (New York, 1938), pp. 38-43; J. Jeremias, *Kultprophetie und Gerichtsverkündigung in der späten Königszeit Israel*, WMANT XXXV (Neukirchen, 1970), pp. 125-27; S. Lehming, "Massa und Meriba," *ZAW*, LXXIII (1961), pp. 71-77; J. C. McCann, Jr., *A Theological Introduction to the Book of Psalms* (Nashville, 1983), pp. 45-48; J. Racette, "La spiritualité du Ps 95 (94)," *Sciences ecclesiastiques*, X (1958), pp. 385-92; C. B. Riding, "Psalm 95 as a Large

Chiasm," *ZAW,* LXXXVIII (1976), p. 418; S. Schilling, "Die Anbetung Gottes — Wurzel und Konsequenz Auslegung von Ps 95 (94)," *BibLeb,* II (1961), pp. 105-20; R. Tournay, "Notes sur les Psaumes," *RB,* LXXIX (1972), pp. 50-58; G. von Rad, "Es ist noch eine Ruhe vorhanden dem Volke Gottes," *Zwischen den Zeiten,* XI (1933), pp. 104-11.

FORM

This hymn begins as an invitation to worship and repeats the call, "O come . . ." (vv. 1-2), rather imperatively. The modern failure to recognize the preludial character of the first invitation (v. 1) often spoils the strophic analysis, which presents exactly five regular strophes. Strophes I-II contain two bicola each, while Strophes IV and V each include a tricolon and a bicolon. Although the psalm is a hymn of praise instead of a lament, Strophe III (vv. 6-7) may well have been the central prow of the entire poem. The imperative, "O come . . . ," restates the beginning of the prelude (v. 1), for this strophe joyfully affirms the metaphor of the sheep and shepherd, which then reinforces the severe warning of the divine oracle cited in Strophes IV and V.

The meter confirms the movement of the poem, from 3+3 in vv. 1-9 to 4+4 in the prophetic oracle in vv. 8-11.

COMMENTARY

Prelude: Call to Worship (v. 1)

This invitation does not seem to be made for a single event. It is probably a common Introit repeated at the opening of every service with musical instruments and singing.

The "joyful noise" is a ritual shout[1] that mobilizes the attention and the cooperation of the whole assembly. The "Rock of our salvation" is an expression that uses an image derived from the stony asperities that enabled guerrillas to escape attention as well as from arrows from soldiers in the valley (Pss 18:1; 94:22). It should not be confused with the omphalos, or navel of the earth, which stood at the center of the third, most holy room in the temple of Zion. Its Canaanite origin carried with it a whole array of polytheistic rites that rendered it suspect to pure Yahwists.[2] However, God's presence was sensed with strongest intensity by the devotees of Yahweh.

---

1. P. Humbert, *La terou'a: Analyse d'un rite biblique* (Neuchâtel, 1946).
2. S. Terrien, "The Myth of the Omphalos," *VT,* XX (1970), pp. 315-38.

Such abruptness of speech, perhaps even its harshness, was typical of many imperative psalms;[3] such commands to praise may sound out of place to modern minds, but they may indicate that the singing of a hymn of praise may have raised a certain protest, or at least some reluctance among faithful religionists who, in spite of their fidelity, faced the problem of evil with bewilderment. The power of a God who is good may have to be challenged in the dark events of social injustice without punishment, or military disaster without an ethical explanation.

Strophe I: The Presence of King Yahweh (vv. 2-3)

The liturgical order to worship is reiterated, as if there were a sapiential debate among musicians and congregation. This time, however, praise is linked to thanksgiving (cf. the double meaning of the Hebrew *tôdāh*). The Lord's benevolence in the history of election and deliverance from slavery is forever remembered. The ancient Near Eastern milieu of polytheism is recognized, but the kingship of Yahweh is acknowledged as a sign of his incomparability. The divinities of the Egyptians, Canaanites, and Mesopotamians do exist in human architecture and piety, but compared to Yahweh they are nothing. Yahweh is the great King.

Strophe II: The Maker and Master of Nature (vv. 4-5)

Even high peaks and bottomless abysses, as well as the sea, are God's servants. The Hebrews, like other inhabitants of hilly regions, looked at the sea as an unexplored and monstrous part of the world, like the inaccessible mountains and the deepest canyons of the earth. Unlike the Canaanites of the seashore, who were the Phoenicians, they feared the sea, but they knew that Yahweh owned the sea, for he made it.

Hymns of praise commonly summon the theme of creation in admiration for Yahweh.

Strophe III: The Good Shepherd (vv. 6-7)

The comparison of God's people to a flock of sheep is a common metaphor. God is thanked as the keeper of his people. The promised land is the Lord's pasture. The psalmists and other poets never tire of the shepherd image. There is, however, a tension within the leader, who is not only the feeder or even the

---

3. C. Westermann, *The Praise of God in the Psalms,* tr. K. R. Crim (Richmond, Va.), pp. 60-84, 131-32.

nurse (cf. Ps 23:5) but also the heavenly moralist and disciplinarian. God is God: this means both his compassionate fidelity and his severity. It is also one of the reasons why his rod is reassuring. Suddenly the tone will dramatically change.

Strophe IV: Praise, Do Not Test Infinity (vv. 8-9)

Remember the history of salvation! The hymnist has become a prophetic preacher of divine sadness and even horror. The exodus stands at the birth of the nation, but the sojourn in the wilderness in the sands and rocks of Sinai, forty years long, should not be forgotten. Gratitude for protection is now linked to a confession of guilt for rebellion: "Your fathers tested me."

Israel is unique in the history of nations only when it admits the ambivalence of its early and later years, indeed the duplicity between obedience to the ideal of election and self-deception in its centuries of corruption in domestic and international policies.

Yet should not natural catastrophes and cataclysms be traced to the sovereign of nature? At Massah and Meribah (Exod 17:1-7; Num. 20:13; cf. Ps 81:7), the lack of water threatened the life of the people, and they asked, "Is Yahweh among us or not?"

It has been said for a long time, and rightly, that the problem of evil is the creation of monotheism. A positivist humanist looks at natural or biological mysteries but does not try to find any transcendental cause. A polytheist will speak mythologically of a fight between gods or goddesses and let his inquiries end there. A pantheist will enter into the vast horizon of the worlds and avoid digging into the question of cosmic injustice by embracing the forces of good and evil and communing with life in its terrestrial fullness. But the theist, a Hebrew monotheist, who affirms both the omnipotence and the goodness of God, faces an insoluble scandal of theology.

Raising existential doubt about the presence of God, the fathers "tested" God and probed him. Finitude claimed to judge infinity. Did they inaugurate the long *via dolorosa* that led to contemporary agnosticism?

By ascribing mortal thirst to the weakness, ignorance, or decision of their God, the ancient Hebrews debated the divinity as an equal. When finitude questions the motivation of Yahweh, it erects itself as the judge of divinity. The psalmist stresses the urgency of the prophetic warning with "today" (v. 8). He refers not just to the distant past. The psalm declares a contemporary oracle.

Strophe V: The Two-Generation Delay (vv. 10-11)

The long sojourn in the wilderness and the military obstacles to the conquest of the Promised Land are now explained and justified as national retribution for national blasphemy, from generation to generation. The second-generation delay seems to be another injustice or incompetence of God toward his people, but the transhistoricity of Israel as an ethnic unit is thereby affirmed.

While the hostility of various nomads and settled kingdoms, from Edom to Canaan, could have been viewed as the normal, defensive reaction to the Hebrew invaders, the sacred traditions of Israel preferred to remember those forty years of waiting and fighting as the result of divine judgment, "In my wrath" — against not the autochthons but the disturbers of the international state of affairs — "they should not enter into my rest" (v. 11).

Some exegetes have asked why the last word of this psalm should designate the Land of Promise as God's "rest" (v. 11; cf. Deut 3:9). The whole strophe is cited in its Greek (LXX) translation by the writer of Hebrews (3:7-11). "Rest" might be a fitting word for the "green pastures" after the waterless exertions in the Sinai wilderness, but was it a "rest" for the Hebrew tribes who had to conquer the territory inch by inch for several centuries of savage combat in the time of the Judges and the early monarchs, Saul and David?

The Deuteronomists and the psalmists appear to ignore the almost ceaseless battles of "the Conquest." Even during the dual monarchy, the land of Israel finally fell into the hands of the Assyrians and Babylonians.

Or was the word "rest" used for the quiet ceremonies of worship in the sanctuaries inherited from Canaan and eventually from the temple of Zion before it was destroyed by the Babylonians (587 B.C.E.)? The Deuteronomists may have found that God's rest included personal and communal delights, which were also translated into hymns of praise.

DATE AND THEOLOGY

If this interpretation is correct, the date of Psalm 95 may go back to the renewal of Yahwism that seems to have taken place with the reform of Josiah (622 B.C.E.). It may also refer to the postexilic restoration, when services of worship demanded grandiose ceremonies as a climax to pilgrimages and processions.

The admonition to hear the Lord's voice "today" shows that the great prophets of the eighth and seventh centuries spoke with an appropriate effectiveness that was reflected upon through the trial of the exile.

To recall the fathers' blasphemous questioning of Yahweh's presence was perhaps inspired by sapiential debate. The Jobian poet was aware of the deadly threat that events presented against the admission of divine justice and even attention and concern. He may have discovered an area of fluidity in any simplistic theodicy when he represented the Creator as somewhat ambivalent about Behemoth and Leviathan.[4] The psalmist did not choose to enter this dangerous path because, perhaps, his professional vocation was not to question the justice of God but to sing God's praise. Yet he seized the aptness of the prophets' attacks on a worship divorced from national reform and purification (Isa 1:10-17; Amos 5:21-27).

PSALM 96

Song for the New Day

I

1. *O sing to the Lord a song for the new day!*
    Sing to the Lord, all the earth!
2. *Sing to the Lord, bless his name!*
    Show forth his salvation from day to day!
3. *Declare his glory among the nations,*
    And his wonders among all peoples.

II

4. *For the Lord is great, and greatly to be praised;*
    He is to be feared above all the gods;
5. *Since all the gods of the peoples are idols!*
    But the Lord made the heavens.
6. *Honor and majesty are before him;*
    Strength and beauty are in his sanctuary.

III

7. *Ascribe to the Lord, [ye] kindred of nations;*
    Ascribe to the Lord glory and strength.

4. J. G. Gammie, "Behemoth and Leviathan: On the Didactic and Theological Significance of Job 40:15–41:26," in *Israelite Wisdom*, Festschrift S. Terrien (New York, 1978), pp. 217-31.

8.   *Ascribe to the Lord the glory due his name;*
        Bring an offering and come into his courts.
9.   *O worship the Lord in the beauty of holiness;*
        Tremble before him, all the earth!

IV

10.   *Say among the nations that the Lord reigns as king!*
        The world was set also that it cannot be moved.
        [The Lord] shall judge the peoples with justice.
11.   *Let the heavens rejoice and the earth be glad!*
        Let the sea roar and the fullness thereof!
12.   *Let the countryside be joyful and all that is therein!*
        Then shall all the trees of the forest rejoice in the presence of the Lord!

Envoi

13.   *For he cometh, for he cometh, to judge the earth!*
        He shall judge the world with righteousness,
        And the peoples with his truthful faith.

BIBLIOGRAPHY

A. Caquot, "In splendoribus sanctorum (Ps 29; 92,2; I Chron 16,20)," *Syria*, XXXIII (1956), pp. 36-41; G. R. Driver, [Note on Ps 96:8; *ha'erath*, presence], *ETL*, XXV (1950), p. 348; A. Feuillet, "Les psaumes eschatologiques du régne de Yahweh," *NRT*, LXXXIII (1951), pp. 244-60, 352-63; H.-J. Kraus, *Die Königsherrschaft Gottes im Alten Testament*, (Tübingen, 1951); S. Mowinckel, *Psalmenstudien*, II: *Das Thronbesteigungsfest und der Ursprung der Eschatologie* (Oslo, 1922); H. Ringgren, "Behold, Your King Comes," *VT*, XXIV (1970), pp. 207-11; H. Schmidt, *Die Thronfahrt Jahwes zum Fest der Jahreswende im alten Israel* (Tübingen, 1927); R. Tournay, "Le Psaume XCV et ses antécédents," in *Les Psaumes complexes, RB*, XLV (1947), pp. 521-42.

FORM

This hymn contains four strophes of three bicola each (vv. 1-3, 4-6, 7-9, 10-12), followed by an *Envoi* (v. 13). The horizon of praise broadens itself from "all the earth" to "the sea" and "the forest." The blessing of the Lord's name (v. 2) becomes linked to the declaration of the Lord's glory (v. 8). The *Envoi* rehearses the whole (v. 13).

     The meter is irregular even with the regular division of the poem into two parts:

	Part One					Part Two	
v. 1			(3+3)				
v. 2		(4+3)					
v. 3	(3+2)						
v. 4	(4+3)			v. 9			(3+3)
v. 5	(4+3)			v. 10	(4+3)		
v. 6		(2+3)		v. 11	(4+3)		
v. 7		(4+3)		v. 12			(3+3)
v. 8			(3+3)				

Such metrical symmetry does not correspond exactly to the thematic structure and the stichoi regularity, but it may have had its significance for the echo-type singing of the words.

COMMENTARY

Strophe I: The Name and the Glory (vv. 1-3)

The psalmist seems to have been aware of two different theologies of presence: a theology of the name and a theology of the glory.[1] The first favors the mystery of God, conveyed by hearing the word, and proclaiming implicitly God's power to create: "I cause to be whomever and whatever I cause to be" (Exod 3:14). The second seems to have appealed to the sense of sight, especially the symbols of the inner room of the temple. Both ways are brought together (2 Sam 6:14; 7:25-26). The name is to be blessed and the glory proclaimed to the nations.[2] The relatively rare verb *baśar*, here used in the Pi'el, means, "to announce good news" (cf. LXX, "to evangelize"). The mission of Israel is double: to translate the name into life and to preach it abroad.

Strophe II: Foreign Gods Do Not Exist (vv. 4-6)

The perception of divine transcendence expresses God's power in creation with the image of kingship. However, the politico-mystical image of "king," borrowed from the ancient Near East, implies a whole hierarchy of priests, princes, and submissive public servants. This is apparent in the Egyptian literature, which assigned royalty to the Pharaoh and especially to the god Amon, "king of

1. S. Terrien, *The Elusive Presence* (San Francisco, 1978), pp. 448-70.
2. R. Martin-Achard, *Israel and the Nations*, Cahiers théologiques XLII (Neuchâtel, 1939).

the gods." To speak of Yahweh as king is an entirely different proposition. In the Psalter, the gods are nothing. They do not exist.

In contrast to "idols" and their nothingness, the court of Yahweh — heavenly beings and angel — is not the object of human worship, but the greatness of the king is adorned with four "concrete" abstractions, graded in ascending order: from honor and majesty to strength and beauty. These four aspects are to be found in the innermost room of the temple of Zion. Beauty is the highest quality, but like "glory" it goes far beyond the temple and its ceremonial, for it points, as in Second Isaiah, to the final hope of creation and therefore history.

Strophe III: The Beauty of Holiness (vv. 7-9)

Foreign nations are enrolled as missionaries and preachers of the gospel, in a universal eschatology. The pilgrims in procession surround the sanctuary in Yahweh's courts. The LXX and Syr. read not *hadhrath*, "splendor of" or "beauty of," but *haṣrath*, "in the abode of," or even "the green pasture of." The word "holiness," to which "splendor" is grammatically constructed, favors the correctness of the MT. Again, the cultic environment evolved into the supra-quality of an aesthetic emotion mixed with religious ecstasy.

Strophe IV: The Lord Is King (vv. 10-12)

Once more the unique royalty of the Lord is to be proclaimed aloud with singing voices and instrumental accompaniment. The monarchy of Yahweh is to be viewed as a gospel for today and tomorrow. The strength of the Creator is also found today in the juridical righteousness of the last day.

Joy becomes universal. It spreads from the heavens to the earth, and from there even to the sea, with all its strange creatures. More stunning still, as in Second Isaiah, is the gladness of the countryside, which, during the long months of the summer season, looks exhausted from the drought. The last celebration is reserved for the trees — no doubt the cedars of Lebanon — with their shade, solidity, and endurance. The forest becomes an active participant in divine joy and creation. It plays in the supraterrestrial orchestra. Perhaps the anonymous prophet of Isaiah 40–55 and the psalmist reflected on the good that the forests do botanically and geologically for dry regions — an observation revived by the green activists in the twentieth century.

The "new song" (v. 1) is truly "the song for the new day."

Envoi: For He Cometh, For He Cometh! (v. 13)

The hymn has not reached its summit of crescendo before the *Envoi* and its double shout of gladness, "For he cometh, for he cometh" (v. 13a). It is not enough to sing "he comes" (Isa 40:10); God will bring a glorious consummation to the history of pride and imperial conquests. An apotheosis will then harmonize nature, the earth, and "peoples." The curse of womanhood and manhood, pride and self-centeredness, domestic and foreign, will come to an end. The judge will use his "truthful faith."

The original Hebrew text carries only a single word, whose root, *amen,* entered the liturgical vocabulary of Christendom through Greek and Latin. It means far more than "so be it!" It proclaims the certainty of the faith that God has in humankind, and humankind in God, as well as the veracity or "truthfulness" of its trust. It brings out the ultimate "truth."

The last word of the psalm suggests that Yahweh's compassion, not just for an elect people but for the whole of humankind, will reciprocate the trust that men and women place in God.

DATE AND THEOLOGY

Affinities with Deutero-Isaiah in Psalm 96 are so gripping (Isa 44:23; 55:12) that the date might be the late exile with its hope of a restoration, if not actually the postexilic times with the new ceremonial of joy in the second temple.

Divine justice continues to form the major motif, extended to the whole world and transformed by the continuity of a proximate future that is in a dateless end of time. Yahweh will not abandon his people forever. As maker of all — the heavens, the earth, the sea, and the forests — and judge supreme — he will rally the sociopolitical ambition of all the peoples into a universal harmony. The vision of peace and health *(shalom)* no longer results from Israel's self-centered ambition; it blooms from the junction of God's name and glory.

This catechism, which involves the whole cosmos, opens up to both Judaism and Christianity. Such a mythical view of time may or may not be acceptable to contemporary speculations on an eternal universe, but it may symbolically become, for humankind, a musical *vade mecum.*

PSALM 97

From Heaven to Earth

Prelude

1.   *The Lord reigns: may the earth rejoice!*
     Let the many isles be glad!

I

2.   Clouds and darkness are round about him,
        With justice and judgment at the base of his throne!
3.   Fire advances before him,
        And burns up his enemies round about;
4.   His lightnings enlighten the world;
        The earth sees and trembles.

II

5.   The hills melt like wax at the presence of the Lord,
        At the presence of the sovereign of the whole earth.
6.   The heavens proclaim his righteousness;
        And all the peoples see his glory.
7.   Confounded be all they that serve graven images,
        And themselves boast of idols.
        Worship him, all you gods!

III

8.   Zion heard and was glad, and the daughters of Judah rejoiced,
        Because of thy judgments, O Lord;
9.   For thou, Lord, art the Most High above the whole earth;
        Thou art exalted far above all the gods.
10. You that love the Lord, hate evil!
        He preserves the full life of his devotees,
        And delivers them out of the hands of evildoers.

Postlude

11. Light is sown for the righteous,
        And gladness for the upright in heart.
12. You righteous ones, rejoice in the Lord!
        And give thanks at the remembrance of his holiness!

BIBLIOGRAPHY

J. Gray, "The Hebrew Conception of the Kingship of God — Its Origin and Development," *VT*, VI (1956), pp. 268-85; F. James, "The Author of Psalm 97," in *Thirty Psalmists* (New York, 1938), pp. 81-84; J. Jeremias, *Theophanie: Die Geschichte einer alttestamentlichen Gattung*, WMANT X (Neukirchen, 1965), pp. 28-40; E. Lipiński, *La royauté de Yahwé dans la poésie et le culte de l'Ancien Testament* (Brussels, 1968); S. Morag, "Light Is Sown (Ps 97,11)," *Tarbiz*, XXXV (1963-64), pp. 140-48; H. H. Schmid, "Jahwe und die Kulttraditionen von Jerusalem," *ZAW*, LXVII (1955), pp. 168-97; idem, *Gerechtigkeit als Weltordnung*, BHT XL (Tübingen, 1968); A. Weiser, "Zur Frage nach den Beziehungen der Psalmen zum Kult: Die Darstellung der Theophanie in den Psalmen und die Festkult," in *Festschrift A. Bertholet* (Tübingen, 1950), pp. 513-31.

FORM

The form of this hymn presents three strophes of three stichoi each (vv. 2-4, 5-7, 9-10), preceded by a prelude (v. 1) and followed by a postlude (vv. 11-12).

The meter, fairly regular, enlarges the rhythm as the poem moves toward its final climax:

Prelude (4+3); Strophe I (3+4; 3+3); Strophe II (4+2; 3+3); Strophe III (3+3; 4+4; 4+4); Postlude (3+2; 3+3).

The thematic movement seems to determine the metric growth, from a didactic sketch of a theophany, to Zion, love, and hate. Finally, to light and holiness.

COMMENTARY

Prelude: The Kingship of the Lord (v. 1)

As in many other hymns of a similar type, the liturgical ejaculation, "The Lord is King," does not necessarily mean, "The Lord has become king." The MT means, "The Lord reigns."[1] The pedestal of his heavenly throne (v. 5) shows that his royalty concerns highly ethical judgments.[2]

---

1. Cf. A. Gelston, "A Note on [*yhwh mlk*]," *VT*, XVI (1966), pp. 507-12.
2. H. Brunner, "Gerechtigkeit als Fundament des Throns," *VT*, VIII (1968), pp. 79-80.

Strophe I: Darkness and Light (vv. 2-4)

The evocation of a theophany articulates a religious antithesis between "thick darkness," the symbol of God's dwelling, and light, which enlightens the world. From several Hebrew synonyms for obscurity — the shadow of the night and death — the psalmist selects the "heavy clouds" and their invisibility for the divine presence. It is on the whole a theological term (Exod 20:18; Deut 4:11; 5:22; 2 Sam 22:10; 1 Kgs 8:12; cf. Job 22:13) that belongs to the vocabulary of judgment (Jer 13:16). The same word even implies the future Day of the Lord at the fulfillment of creation and the end of history (Zeph 1:11; Ezek 34:12). This is clearly an opening for eschatological interpretation.

Strophe II: The Presence of the Glory (vv. 5-7)

The traditional features of the theophany lead to the vision of the Lord in glory (v. 5). The worship directed to foreign gods creates only chaotic confusion among the nations. A subtle sarcasm underlines an invitation to the gods themselves to worship the Lord. Their existence is not denied, as in other hymns, but they clearly must submit to the Most High. The Hebrew word for "graven images" occurs only here in the entire Psalter.

Strophe III: Love God, Hate Evildoers (vv. 8-10)

Zion — namely, the Jerusalem priests and Levites as well as "the daughters of Judah" (female dancers?) — by its joyful exhilaration directs attention to a cultic ceremonial but also responds to the divine presence anywhere and at any time.

The hymnic praise changes into a prayer (v. 9) that confirms the impression that the blooming of religious ecstasy may occur beyond the time of feasts and the cultic space of a sanctuary.

Postlude: Light Arises, Holiness Is Remembered (vv. 11-12)

From the "darkness" of God's cosmic theophany (v. 2) the psalm reaches the broad "sowing" of a resplendent light for the righteous. Some wish to correct the idea of "sowing" light (Hebrew root I) and prefer the second root, which means, "to rise," "to shine," but the idea of "sowing light," while bizarre, is possible, for sowing implies a gesture of open and wide generosity.[3]

3. J. G. Gammie, *Holiness in Israel* (Minneapolis, 1989), pp. 105-7.

A chiasmus thus closes the poem with thematic coherence, with an emphasis on the joyfulness of those who behave rightly.

Begging the devotees to give thanks at the memory of God's holiness (v. 12b), the psalmist continues to insist on the meaning of presence. Memory of cultic holiness seems to indicate that it is perceived outside the sanctuary and beyond sacred days.

DATE AND THEOLOGY

Like the other hymns in which the Lord is worshiped as the master of the world, Psalm 97 shows the influence of Second Isaiah. The early postexilic period is probable (see Psalms 95; 96). In addition, the final invitation to give thanks "at the remembrance of [God's] holiness" confirms the spirituality of the life of communion beyond sacramental proximity to Zion.

PSALM 98

The Remembrance of Holiness

1. Psalm

Prelude

Sing unto the Lord a song for the new day,
For he has done marvelous things!
His right hand and holy arm gave him victory.

I

2.   *The Lord has made known his salvation;*
In the sight of the nations he revealed his rectitude.
3.   *He remembered his mercy and his faith*
    Toward the house of Israel;
All the ends of the earth have seen
    The salvation of our God.

II

4.　*Make a joyful noise unto the Lord, all the earth!*
　　　Cry the ritual shout and rejoice and praise!
5.　*Celebrate the Lord with a harp,*
　　　With a harp and the voice of a psalm!
6.　*With trumpets and the sound of the shofar!*
　　　Make a joyful noise in the presence or the Lord King!

III

7.　*Let the sea roar, and the fullness thereof!*
　　　The world and those who dwell therein!
8.　*Let the streams clap their hands,*
　　　And all the hills be gleeful together
9.　*In the presence of the Lord, when he comes*
　　　To judge the earth!

Postlude

With equity will he judge the world,
And the peoples with rectitude.

BIBLIOGRAPHY

E. Beaucamp, "L'univers acclame le justicier d'Israel (Ps 98)," *BVC*, LXX (1966), pp. 36-40; E. F. Davis, "Psalm 98: Rejoicing in Judgment," *Int*, XLVI (1992), pp. 171-75; H. Kosmala, "Form and Structure in Ancient Hebrew Poetry," *VT*, XVI (1966), pp. 178-84; H.-J. Kraus, *Die Königsherrschaft Gottes im Alten Israel*, BHT XIII (Tübingen, 1951); S. Mowinckel, "Die Thronfahrt Jahwes . . . ," in *Psalmenstudien*, vol. II (Oslo, 1922); idem, "Psalms at the Enthronement Festival of Yahweh," in *The Psalms in Israel's Worship*, I (New York, 1962), pp. 106-9; H. Ringgren, "Behold, Your King Comes," *VT*, XXIV (1974), pp. 207-21; H. Schmidt, *Die Thronfahrt Jahwes* (Tübingen, 1927).

FORM

Like many other hymns, Psalm 98 begins with a prelude (v. 1) and ends with a postlude (v. 9cd), embracing three strophes of three stichoi each. The meter appears to confirm the structural analysis.

　　v. 1 (4+2; 3+2+2)
　　vv. 2-3 (3+2+2; 3+2; 2+2)

v. 4 (3+3)
v. 5 (3+3)
v. 6 (3+3)
v. 7 (3+3)
v. 8 (2+3)
v. 9 (3+2; 3+2; 3+2)

Irregularity is found, with longer rhythm, at the beginning and at the end, but the rhythm of the body seems regular. The rhythmic distinction may well have been determined by the music of the instruments listed in the second strophe.

COMMENTARY

Prelude: A Song for the New Day (v. 1)

The community at worship is invited to sing praises in honor of the new day. The Hebrew original says, literally, "a new song," but the context of the psalm is inspired by mythological and ardent expectation. The Lord is praised for his cosmic power in the primeval combat that led to his victory.[1] He is thus the decisive master of the created world. Salvation will complete this victory not only in nature but also with humans.

Strophe I: The Many Isles (vv. 2-3)

The other hymns that immediately preceded it show a close affinity with the prophetic oration of Second Isaiah (40:5; 42:10; 51:3; 52:9-10; 55:12). Yahweh has revealed his victory not only to Israel but also to all nations of the world, including the "many islands" that are found at its extremity.

Strophe II: The Musical Accompaniment (vv. 4-6)

The psalmist shows his concern for the aesthetic aspect of praise by listing the musical instruments that support the voice and the ritual shouts. The climax is reached with the blowing of the shofar, which produces a powerful sound and is reserved for special feasts.

---

1. Davis, "Psalm 98," p. 173.

Strophe III: The Sea and the Primal Floods (vv. 7-9ab)

Cosmic victory at creation is won against chaos. The sea is invited to "roar," and the primal floods are bid to applaud (lit., to "clap their hands"; v. 8). Instead of being annihilated, they become actors in the dramatic display of divine power. The Creator's strength includes that of being the Judge of the earth.

Postlude: The Rectitude of the Supreme Judge (v. 9cd)

Tying the theme of judgment with the universalism implied by the invitation of the Prelude, the equity of the Lord is reaffirmed in the final declaration.

DATE AND THEOLOGY

Like Psalms 95, 96, 97, and other hymns, this poem emerged from the early postexilic period, when the second temple had been erected. In spite of its modest structure, the new sanctuary in Jerusalem became the theater of elaborate ceremonies.

The theology of this hymn, like that of the immediately preceding psalm in the final Psalter, is implicitly inspired by the cultic motif of sanctity around and within the sanctuary. It emphasizes the musical solemnity of the ceremonies, singing praises in honor of Yahweh's holiness (Ps 97:12). But the poem also looks forward to the actualization of this holiness in the secular environment of daily behavior.

By its insistence on universal salvation, this theology stressed an openness to foreign peoples beyond Israel. This open door was closed in the Hellenistic and Roman periods, from Antiochus Epiphanes to Vespasian and Titus, except in Galilee and in some communities of the Diaspora. The memory of holiness preserved a Judaic universalism that the Christian church, in spite of the apostle Paul and the Johannine circles, shamelessly restricted for centuries (John 4:22).

With the violent attacks by the great prophets, which Jesus repeated in parabolic style, the expectation of world judgment stirred the imagination and daring of a Jewish minority that understood the juncture of creation and judgment (Rom 8:19-22). The Psalm for the New Day is also "a new song," for the demands it makes address the individual as well as the community (cf. Isa 42:10; 52:10). Centuries before the apostle Paul, who admonished the readers of his epistles to be "always joyful," Psalm 98 makes rejoicing a key to "righteous judgment." It involves both the congregation of the faithful and its individual members.

PSALM 99

The Holy King

I

1. The Lord is King! Let the peoples tremble!
      He sits above the cherubim;
      Let the earth tremble!
2. The Lord is great in Zion;
      He is exalted above all peoples;
3. Let them praise thy great and awesome name!
      For he is holy.

II

4. The King is holy; he loves justice.
      It is thou, thyself, who hast established equity.
    Justice and righteousness
      That thou, thyself, executest in Jacob.
5. Exalt the Lord, our God, and worship at his footstool.
      For he is holy.

III

6. Moses and Aaron among his priests,
      And Samuel among those who call on the Lord's name,
    They cried unto the Lord, and he answered them.
7.   He spoke to them from the pillar of cloud;
      They kept his testimonies and the statutes he gave them.
8. O Lord, our God, it is thou, thyself, who answeredst them.
      Thou hast been for them a forgiving God,
      Although thou didst discipline them for their faults.

Envoi

9. Exalt the Lord, our God, and worship at his holy hill!
      For the Lord, our God, is holy.

BIBLIOGRAPHY

P. E. Bonnard, *Le Psautier selon Jérémie* (Paris, 1960), pp. 190-93; J. H. Eaton, "Proposals in Psalms 99 and 119," *VT*, XVIII (1969), pp. 555-58; A. Feuillet, "Les Psaumes eschatologiques du règne de Yahweh," *NRT*, LXXIII (1951), pp. 244-60; H.-J. Kraus, *Die*

Königsherrschaft Gottes im Alten Testament, BHT XIII (Tübingen, 1951); E. Lipiński, *La royauté de Yahwé dans la poésie et le culte de l'Ancien Testament* (Brussels, 1988); P. Mommer, "Samuel in Ps 99," *Biblische Notizen*, XXX (1985), pp. 27-30; S. Mowinckel, "Das Thronbesteigungsfest Jahwäs . . . ," in *Psalmenstudien*, II (1922); idem, "Psalms at the Enthronement Festival of Yahweh," in *The Psalms in Israel's Worship*, I (New York, 1962), pp. 106-9; P. Raabe, *Psalm Structures: A Study of Psalms with Refrains*, JSOTSup CIV (Sheffield, 1990), pp. 165, 177; A. Rose, "'Le règne du Dieu saint': Lecture juive du Ps 99," *BVC*, XIX (1957), pp. 91-97; H. Schmid, "Jahwe und die Kulttraditionen von Jerusalem," *ZAW*, LXVII (1955), pp. 168-97; H. Schmidt, *Die Thronfahrt Jahwes* (Tübingen, 1927); R. Scoralick, *Trishagion und Gottesherrschaft: Psalm 99 als Neuinterpretation von Tora und Propheten* (Stuttgart, 1989); C. F. Whitley, "Ps 99,8," *ZAW*, LXXXV (1973), pp. 227-30; R. N. Whybray, "'Their Wrongdoings,' in Ps 99,8," *ZAW*, LXXXI (1969), pp. 237-39.

FORM

This hymn is made up of three strophes and an *Envoi*. The strophes contain three stichoi each, and the *Envoi* summarizes the whole in a threefold stichos. Strophes I and II end with a refrain, "For he is holy," and Strophe III withholds this refrain, but the *Envoi* (v. 3b) offers a slightly enlarged form of the refrain, "For the Lord, our God, is holy."

In spite of a remarkably regular strophic structure, the meter is rather unexpected:

I: vv. 1-3	II: vv. 4-5	III: vv. 6-8
(4+4+4)	(4+3)	(3+3)
(3+3)	(4+3+2)	(4+4)
		(4+4; 4+3)
(2+2+2)	(3+2+2)	Envoi:
		(3+3+3)

Such rhythmic diversity suggests that the psalmist assembled citations and composed a regular poem with them.

COMMENTARY

Strophe I: The Lord Is King! (vv. 1-3)

As in the other hymns of praise that shout, "Yahweh is King!" (Pss 93:1; 97:1; cf. 47:8-9), divine royalty first means the lordship of the heavens, and second the judgment of the nations of the earth.[1] Yahweh is also the God of Jerusalem, Master of Zion. The Lord is at once present and absent in his temple. He sits enthroned above the cherubim. These heavenly beings are endowed with wings. The Lord flies on them through the heavens (2 Sam 22:11; Ps 18:11). Their statues, which represent them with wings spread and made of wood and gold, recall the guardians of the Tree of Life (Gen 3:24), which support the throne of God in the temple (Ps 80:1; Isa 37:16). In other traditions, the cultic cherubim spread their wings over the ark (Exod 25:18-20; 1 Kgs 6:23-28; 8:6-7).

In Ps 99:1, no Hebrew preposition indicates their function, "The Lord sits, cherubim." It seems clear that the kingship of the heavens is joined symbolically with the cultic "dwelling" of Yahweh. If the poet declares that Yahweh is enthroned on the cherubim (1 Sam 4:4; 2 Sam 6:2; 2 Kgs 19:15; Ps 80:1), he addresses himself to the community at worship (cf. v. 5). The claim for the Lord's universal mastery (v. 2) becomes an ambivalent theme. Are "the peoples" to be conquered by an imperialistic Israel? This does not seem to be the case, for the invitation is made "to praise [God's] great and awesome name," not his glory, which usually relates visibly to the gold of the cultic accessories.

Strophe II: Holiness and Rectitude in Judgment (vv. 4-5)

The holiness of God is not perceived only in the temple, although it is to be praised there (v. 5). It flows from the divine exercise of judgment with rectitude and righteousness. It has been executed "in Jacob" (v. 4), a name that designates the whole of Israel.[2]

Strophe III: Moses, Aaron, and Samuel (vv. 6-8)

Three heroes of *Heilsgeschichte* are selected among those who called on the Lord and received answers (Exod 32:11-13; 1 Sam 7:8-9; cf. Jer 15:1). Aaron became the first in a hereditary line of priests, and he also supported the hand of Moses in intercession (Exod 17:11-12).

Envoi: Worship at God's Holy Hill (v. 9)

A final appeal to the congregation stresses again the holiness of the Lord and the unique aspect of Zion, which may be related to the myth of the omphalos.[3]

---

1. S. Terrien, *The Elusive Presence* (San Francisco, 1978), pp. 167-71.

2. J. G. Gammie, *Holiness in Israel* (Minneapolis, 1989), pp. 71-101.

3. S. Terrien, "The Myth of the Omphalos and Hebrew Religion," *VT,* XX (1970), pp. 315-38.

DATE AND THEOLOGY

The poet of Psalm 99 differs from the authors of Psalms 96, 97, and 98, for he stresses his professionalism. As a member of the functionaries who sing and play in the cultic ceremonial, he remains rather vague about the relation between the nations and Israel, even in an eschatological perspective. The most likely date for this psalm is the Persian period, when the second temple had been erected and solemn ceremonies had been held there. Some elements of the psalm, however, may have come from preexilic times.

The mention of "Aaron among his priests" in addition to Moses and Samuel, as in the Jeremianic circles (Jer 15:1), may indicate that the sacerdotal class has assumed an unprecedented importance during and after the exile. Nevertheless, the priests are not explicitly viewed as intercessors. In any case, the conjunction of rectitude in judgment with the exaltation of the Lord of the heavens justifies the classification of this poem with the "Yahweh is King" psalms. The Jerusalem Lord is also Master of the world. His holiness should be evaluated through the influence of the great prophets.

The trisagion sung by the seraphim in the vocation of the prophet Isaiah (6:3), and not by the cherubim, may point to a theological emphasis of significance, for it sings of a holiness not restricted to the temple but open to the whole earth. Moreover, Israel — like Judaism and the Christian church — needs forgiveness (Ps 99:8b).

PSALM 100

A Joyful Noise to the Lord

1. *Psalm for praise.*

I

> *Make a joyful noise to the Lord,*
> > *All ye lands!*
2. > *Serve the Lord with gladness!*
> > *Come before his presence with singing!*
3. > *Know ye that the Lord, he is God!*

> It is he that has made us, and not we ourselves;
> We are his people and the sheep of his pasture.

II

4.   Enter into his gates with thanksgiving,
          And into his courts with praise!
       Be thankful to him and bless his name.
5.   For the Lord is good;
       His mercy is everlasting,
          And his truth endures to all generations.

BIBLIOGRAPHY

W. H. Bellinger, Jr., *Psalms: Reading and Studying the Book of Psalms* (Peabody, Mass., 1990), pp. 26-32, 97-98; W. Brueggemann, *The Psalms of Faith* (Minneapolis, 1995), pp. 51-52; C. L. Feinberg, "Old Hundredth," *Bibliotheca sacra*, C (1946), pp. 53-66; K. Koch, "'Denn seine Güte währet ewiglich,'" *EvT*, XXI (1961), pp. 531-44; J. O. Lewis, "An Asseverative [*lô'*] in Psalm 100," *JBL*, LXXXVI (1967), p. 216; J. L. Mays, "Worship, World, and Power: An Interpretation of Ps. 100," *Int*, XXIII (1969), pp. 315-30; J. Clinton McCann, Jr., *The Book of Praises: A Theological Introduction to the Book of Psalms* (Nashville, 1993), pp. 64-70; G. Quell, *Das kultische Problem der Psalmen*, BWANT XI (Neukirchen, 1926); C. Westermann, *The Praise of God in the Psalms* (Richmond, Va., 1965), pp. 148-50; W. Zimmerli, *Erkenntnis Gottes nach dem Buch Ezechiel*, Abhandlungen zur des Alten und Neuen Testaments (Zurich, 1954).

FORM

This short poem contains two strophes of almost identical form:

    I: (vv. 1bc-3): two bicola and one tricolon
    II: (vv. 4-5): three bicola

The meter, however, is irregular, which may indicate that even such a brief psalm may have been composed of diverse quotations: v. 1 (3+3+3); v. 3 (3+3+3+3); v. 4 (3+2+3); v. 5 (4+3).

Superscription (v. 1a)

Psalm 100 begins with an invitation to praise with stringed instrumentalists (*psalmos* may be derived from the verb "to pluck strings").

Strophe I: Call before Him! (vv. 1b-3)

The invitation to praise extends to the entire earth; all the lands are directly addressed as if they were in a universal forum. The ritual shout is to be cried out (Pss 33:3; 89:16). The singing of praise and thanksgiving is to be intoned in the presence of the Lord, after the portals of the temple are opened. Presumably, the congregation is still marching up toward the sacred hill.

The whole catechism of Judaism is already here summed up in four articles: (1) "The Lord is God"; (2) "he has made us"; (3) "we are his people"; (4) "the Lord is good." Most Hebrew MSS read, "He has made us, and not we ourselves." The Qerê and most ancient versions read, "And we are his." Modern translators prefer this text, but they do not recognize that such a reading repeats the idea that "we are his people." The Kethib of the MT should be preserved, for in this sentence the psalmist implicitly denies that human beings procreate their offspring. The stress on our personal, individual creation implies that we are indeed his people, not just by election but also by intention, when we come into life. The image of shepherd and pasture was apparently common (cf. Ps 23:1-2).

Strophe II: Everlasting Mercy (vv. 4-5)

When the procession has reached the gates of the inner courts, other hymns of praise are intoned, and the holy name is blessed. The praise of God's glory is not mentioned, perhaps because the gold objects of the innermost room are not yet visible. The blessing is sung by the congregation: its appropriate emphasis may well reflect a profound respect for the tradition of the revelation of the name to Moses, "I cause to be whatever I cause to be." The name always includes the theme of creation. The freedom of the Creator is thereby exalted.

DATE AND THEOLOGY

It is difficult to suggest a date of composition for the final product. The lack of a precise superscription implies that Psalm 100 did not belong to any preliminary psalters. As a liturgical Introit, it belongs to the ceremonial of the second temple. The "blessing" is not pronounced by priests. The theology of the great prophets that seems to have been absorbed by the poet belongs to the group of psalmists who affirm the universal openness of Deutero-Isaiah. The "Old Hundredth" has been set to music in many lands and may thereby testify to an authentic ecumenicity.

PSALM 101

Ideal Conduct for a King

1. *Psalm. Of David.*

I

> I will sing of loyalty and judgment;
>> It is for thee, O Lord, that I sing a psalm;
2.
> I will behave wisely, in a perfect way;
>> When wilt thou come to me?
> I will walk in my house
>> With full integrity.

II

3.
> I will not keep before my eyes
>> Anything that is base.
> I hate the doing of those who fall away;
>> It will not cling to me.
4.
> A tortuous heart shall stay far from me;
>> I refuse to know any evil.

III

5.
> If one slanders secretly against his friend,
>> I shall reduce him to silence;
> Haughty looks and arrogant hearts
>> I will not endure.
6.
> My eyes will look for trustworthy men
>> In the land, for my ministers.

IV

7.
> One who practices deceit
>> Will not sit in my house;
> Whoever utters lies
>> Will not tarry before my eyes.
8.
> Morning after morning I shall get rid
>> Of all scoundrels in the land.

Envoi

[I plan] to remove any worker of iniquity
From the city of the Lord.

BIBLIOGRAPHY

P. Auffret, *La Sagesse a bâti sa maison* (Fribourg and Göttingen, 1982), pp. 301-12; E. Beaucamp, "L'espoir d'une ère de justice et de paix," *BVC*, LXXIII (1967), pp. 32-42; J. Begrich, "Sōpēr und Mazkia," *ZAW*, LXVIII (1940/41), pp. 1-29; O. Kaiser, "Erwägungen zu Psalm 101," *ZAW*, LXXIV (1962), pp. 185-205; N. A. Kenik, "Code of Conduct for a King: Psalm 101," *JBL*, XCV (1976), pp. 391-403; N. W. Lund, *Chiasmus in the New Testament* (Chapel Hill, N.C., 1942), pp. 101-4; J. Ouellette, "Variantes qumrâniennes du livre des Psaumes," *Revue de Qumrân*, XXV (December 1974), pp. 105-23.

FORM

This unique psalm was presumably destined to be sung by a royal prince about to become king of Judah. It was composed in the form of a hymn, with four strophes of three bicola each and a short but pungent *Envoi* at the end (I: 1b-2; II: vv. 3-4; III: vv. 5-6; IV: 7-8b; *Envoi:* v. 8cd. The *Envoi* is not a part of the fourth strophe, which would then have four bicola instead of three, and in addition would deal crisply with two themes still unused.

COMMENTARY

Superscription (v. 1a)

This royal program was perhaps included in the final Psalter because it began as a hymn (cf. v. 2).

Strophe I: The Steadfast Love and Equity of Yahweh (vv. 1b-2)

The poet intends to sing and at the same time to play a stringed instrument. The word "love" covers a wide range of meanings: steadfast love, fidelity, loyalty, goodness, and mercy (cf. Pss 72:1; 88:1). The term "judgment" implies the qualities of a judge who will respect equity in his verdicts. The two words together describe virtues that belong to the Lord (Hos 12:7; Mic 6:8; cf. Matt 23:23). In singing the first line of this "hymn," the prince hopes to imitate its meaning (cf. Deut 17:14-20). He might also have hoped to honor the dynasty of David (cf. Isa 55:3).

From the hymnic style the poet shifts at once to the sapiential vocabulary. The acquisition of wisdom in a perfect way becomes his goal, not only for himself but also for the members of his company.

Strophe II: Honesty in the Royal Court (vv. 3-4)

The prince knows that a monarch does not govern alone: he needs a "household" whose members reflect his own integrity (cf. Ps 119:11). "A tortuous heart" has chosen the wrong direction (Prov 11:20; 17:20; cf. Deut 32:5; Ps 18:26).

Strophe III: The Selection of Trustworthy Assistants (vv. 5-6)

The future king will not tolerate secret calumnies among his ministers. Arrogant characters shall not dominate his counsels (Prov 21:4; 28:25).

Strophe IV: Veracity in Society-at-large (vv. 7-8b)

Straight relations will be the mark not only of a good government but also of the whole community. The next king promises to seek (and destroy?) all the evildoers of the land. The proto-Babylonian legislator Hammurabi, in the name of the god Marduk, proposes the eradication of evildoers. Judaic kings, likewise, must destroy antisocial elements.

Envoi: Jerusalem, the City of God (v. 8cd)

The MT considers the last bicolon as the fourth part of the last strophe. The purpose of the final intent ("to remove") implies a judiciary promulgation of the death penalty. The exact meaning of the verb "to destroy" is not certain. Yet the sense may well be "capital punishment" if "the workers of iniquity" are actually magicians or sorcerers (S. Mowinckel). A great many of them were condemned for various reasons, the chief of which was probably their claim to possess powers that belonged to God alone The Deuteronomic code lists diviners, soothsayers, charmers, mediums, wizards, and astrologers (Deut 18:9-14).

In any case, these men are not simply workers of iniquity. They make utter misery. Such a condemnation demands a special bicolon on "the city of the Lord."

DATE AND THEOLOGY

This psalm is often classified as a royal hymn, but its destination is quite distinct. It may have been preexilic, coming from the time of the Judahite monarchy. Why was it preserved and included in the final Psalter? The answer is not clear. Since it was attributed to King David, or at least said to have been composed for him, one may easily suppose that it was part of the Davidic legend. At any rate, Psalm 101 combines sapiential ethics with theocentric spirituality. The short but unexpected prayer, "When wilt thou come to me?" may well have been the key to its preservation, not only in the official Judaism of the Persian period but also among the members of the Qumran community (cf. 11Qps^a, cols. 15-16, 135 catena).

Without a monarch the Jerusalem community needed, for its leader, a code of behavior beyond petty corruption (cf. Ezra and Nehemiah). Under its surface of high standards and strange optimism in their fulfillment, the plaintive petition for God's intimate manifestation covers a profound anxiety over the absence of the Lord. A great void lies behind the begging for presence! A new age will create a new society.

Christians as well as Jews interpreted this longing as a passionate hope for the divine kingdom. The Lord's Prayer includes a demand that is not often noticed in depth: "Let thy reign arrive!" At the turn of the twentieth century, Alfred Loisy declared, "Jesus announced the kingdom of God, but it was the church which came." This psalm may urge Christians to pray for an existential messianism.

PSALM 102

Lament and Hymn

1. *Prayer of an afflicted man. When he is overwhelmed and pours out his complaint before the Lord.*

PART ONE
I

2.   *Hear my prayer, O Lord,*
         And let my cry come unto thee!

3. *Hide not thy face from me*
     In a day when I am in trouble.
   Incline thine ear unto me;
     When I call, answer speedily!

II

4. *For my days vanish like smoke,*
     And my bones burn as in a furnace.
5. *My heart is smitten and withered like grass,*
     So that I forget to eat my bread.
6. *As shown by my constant groaning,*
     My bones cleave to my flesh.

III

7. *I have become like the pelican in the wilderness,*
     Like a screech owl among ruins.
8. *I stay awake, and I am feeling*
     Like a lonely sparrow on a roof.
9. *Every day my enemies revile me;*
     Those that are mad at me curse my name.

IV

10. *I eat dust like bread,*
      And mingle my drink with my tears;
11. *On account of thine indignation and thine anger,*
      Thou hast lifted me up and thrown me down.
12. *My days are like the shadow in the twilight;*
      And as for me, I wither away like grass.

PART TWO
I

13. *But thou, O Lord, art enthroned forever,*
      And thy remembrance is to all generations;
14. *Thou wilt surely arise and take pity on Zion,*
      For this is the time to favor her;
      Yea, the set time has come.
15. *For thy servants admire and like her stones,*
      And they pity even the dust thereof.

II

16. And the nations fear the name of the Lord;
    Even all the kings of the earth fear thy glory.
17. For the Lord will build up Zion;
    He will appear in his glory.
18. He will regard the prayer of the destitute,
    And not despise their supplication.

III

19. Let this be written down for a generation to come,
    And a people yet unborn will praise the Lord,
20. For he will look down from his holy place,
    From heaven will the Lord look at the earth
21. To hear the groaning of the prisoners,
    To set free those who are doomed to die.

IV

22. To declare in Zion the name of the Lord,
    And his praise in Jerusalem,
23. When peoples will be gathered together,
    And kingdoms, to serve the Lord,
24. [But] he has broken my strength in midcourse!

PART THREE
I

25. I said, O my God! Take me not away in the midst of my days!
    Thy years shall endure to all generations.
26. Thou didst lay of old the foundations of the earth,
    And the heavens are the work of thy hands;
27. They also shall perish,
    But thou certainly shalt endure.

II

All of them shall wax old like a garment;
    As a vesture thou shalt change them, and they shall change.
28. But thou! The same shalt thou be!
    Thy years will have no end.
29. The children of thy servants shall still be living,
    And their posterity will be secure in thy presence!

BIBLIOGRAPHY

R. Davidson, *The Vitality of Worship* (Grand Rapids, 1998), pp. 108-16; R. Martin-Achard, *Approche des Psaumes* (Neuchâtel, 1969); K. Seybold, *Das Gebet des Kranken im Alten Testament*, BWANT V, 19 (Stuttgart, 1973); N. H. Smith, *The Seven Psalms* (London, 1964), pp. 65-85; O. H. Steck, "Zu Eigenart und Herkunft von Ps 102," *ZAW*, CII (1980), pp. 357-71; A. Urban, "Verrinnendes Leben und ausgeschüttete Klage: Meditation über Psalm 102," *BibLeb*, X (1969), pp. 137-45; C. Westermann, *The Living Psalms* (Grand Rapids, 1989); idem, *The Praise of God in the Psalms* (Richmond, Va., 1965), pp. 66-67; G. Widengren, *The Accadian and Hebrew Psalms of Lamentation as Religious Documents* (Stockholm, 1936).

FORM

The meter is irregular, from 3+3 to 2+2+2 to 3+4; but the structure is not "unusually misshapen," as some critics maintain. To be sure, the genre is complex, for it moves from the complaint of a man sick unto death to a rather extravagant hymn of praise, and it returns to a prayer of a man sick unto death, to conclude in a final outburst of praise. Both the complaint and the hymn are composed chiefly of strophes of three bicola each, with the exception of one tricolon (v. 14) and a single colon (v. 24). There might be thematic reasons for both.

COMMENTARY

Superscription (v. 1)

The title added to this psalm by the editors of the Psalter is unusually long. It may indicate that they considered the praise a liturgical prayer rather than the spontaneous imploring shouted by a man in pain.

Part One: Supplication of a Man Sick unto Death (vv. 2-12)

The first strophe (vv. 2-3) follows the traditional pattern of a prayer by someone afflicted with a terminal disease. Begging for a speedy answer implies that the suppliant is familiarly associated with Yahweh, whom he later calls "my God" (v. 25).

The second strophe (vv. 4-6) describes the symptoms of the disease in hackneyed terms, but the third strophe (vv. 7-9) indulges in highly poetic imagery, and its last bicolon stresses the normal reaction of revulsion sensed by the ancient mind to the spectacle of terminal malady. The fourth strophe (vv. 10-12) spells out the common belief that sickness and early death are willed by

Yahweh. The dying man believes that his ailment is due to divine wrath. He must have imagined that he was guilty of a serious transgression (v. 11).

Part Two: Praise of God Eternal (vv. 13-24)

Some critics believe that the abruptness of the thematic change indicates that the present psalm is an artificial combination of two independent poems, a lament and a hymn. The sick man, however, may also be a shrewd religionist who flatters that angry God in order to appease him. His praise has become a prayer of intervention. He challenges the Master of life and death by opposing the expected shortness of his terrestrial existence to divine immortality: "enthroned forever!" Generations of humans come and go, but the Creator endures.

The eternity of God is played against man's transitoriness. Various themes are then brought, intertwined. The Lord will have mercy on Zion. His name is already feared by many foreign nations. In the second strophe (vv. 16-18) the implicit question is asked: Should not the rebuilding of the Zion temple, the ruins of which are so eloquent, even mean that Yahweh will appear in glory, and also that the destitute will soon be healed?

The praise of God shall continue in the distant future: this is written *now* for its being read *then*. In the third and fourth strophes (vv. 19-24), the Lord's name will be praised, not only by those who will worship in a restored Zion but also by "peoples" and "kingdoms" of the whole world.

The vision of the future, with its extraordinary list of eschatological motifs, is then abruptly interrupted, "[But] he has broken my strength in midcourse!" The bicolon is likewise broken in half (v. 24).[1] Is the divinity moved by caprice? Or is there an ethical or ritual justification that the psalmist carefully omits to tell? The mystery remains. This is no longer a second person singular address to the eternal God. A third person declaration suffices, as if, indeed, such a God does not hear prayers.

Part Three: Lament and Hymn Articulated (vv. 25-29)

The prayer style is not renewed, for the dying man is not seized by despair. He continues to implore, but he merely murmurs, without voice, a final supplication, to himself! The first strophe (vv. 25-27ab) — so the imperfect verb implies — only indicates the word "saying," for the prayer is not spoken aloud but "mouthed" inaudibly.

The psalmist had probably sensed the enormity of what he was about to enunciate. He still admires the Creator, but he dares to entertain a unique

1. Text uncertain. Cf. Qerê, 4QPs[b].

thought: the earth, the symbol of indestructible solidity, and the heavens, God's own dwelling, "also shall perish"! It seems that a Ugaritic text offers an unexpected parallel. Addressing the goddess Anath, a Canaanite poet declares, "The heavens will wear away and even sag like the fastening of a garment."[2] The created world has a beginning and an end. Yet the Lord shall endure forever. The cosmos is ephemeral; God alone is eternal.

The seemingly incoherent second strophe (vv. 27cd-29) actually maintains divine eternity, even without a spatial habitat for heaven and earth. Yet, "the children of thy servants shall still be living" (v. 29a). As if to reach a final, crowning thought, the psalmodic singer perceives that, in spite of universal destruction — the world's end — some human beings will enjoy a form of immortality because they will be "secure" in the presence of Yahweh (v. 29b). It is the metaphor of his "face" that brings the psalm to an end.

DATE AND THEOLOGY

According to this interpretation of Psalm 102, the date of its composition must be at a time following the exile, just before the building of the second temple. The theology of this suffering man does not greatly differ from that of an unknown poet who attributed to King Hezekiah, prey to a serious malady, in similar words, "Now that my days are at rest, I must be going to the abode of the dead, I am deprived of the rest of my years" (Isa 38:10-11). In the Psalter, there are a few allusions to life beyond the grave. Even more astonishing is the hope that some individuals — "the children of thy servants . . . and their posterity" — will be alive when the earth will have perished. The fulfillment of this expectancy depends upon the "security of thy presence." The cosmos is no longer conceived in spatial and material terms.

The second person style of address to the Lord has returned in the second strophe (vv. 27cd-29), as the lament has again become a hymn. The supplication, which began as a subjective complaint on the absence or deafness of the Lord, terminates with the ecstasy of seeing his "face," the best metaphor of his presence. The subjectivity of the lament has been transmuted into the pluralistic altruism of the *ecclesia* to come.[3]

The amazing perspective of the end of the world does not undermine the

---

2. W. F. Albright, "Are the Ephod and the Teraphim Mentioned in Ugaritic Literature?" *BASOR*, LXXXIII (October 1941), p. 40.

3. This *ecclesia* is the eschatological projection of "the church," traditional Christendom. See S. Terrien, "The Metaphor of the Rock in Biblical Theology," in *God in the Fray*, Festschrift W. Brueggemann, ed. T. Linafelt and T. K. Beal (Minneapolis, 1998), pp. 157-71.

courage of the sick man. Like Job, he does not ask for healing, for he remains silent on his eventual destiny. The earth and even the heavens will not be obliterated, for they will be changed like a vestment.

The poet does not go as far as the apostle Paul, wishing to become anathema and even separated from Christ for the sake of his brothers (Rom 8:3). He considers it sufficient to know that God himself shall not change (Heb 1:19-12).

Even the holiness of Zion may be surpassed by a new type of divine activity. Presence is security.

PSALM 103

Bless the Lord, O My Soul!

1. Of David.

Prelude

Bless the Lord, O my soul,
    And all that is within me[1] bless his holy name!
2.   Bless the Lord, O my soul,
    And forget not all his benefits!

I

3.   *He who forgives all thine iniquities,*
    Who heals all thy diseases,
4.   *Who redeems thy life from death,*
    Who crowns thee with lovingkindness and tender mercies,
5.   *Who satisfies thy desires with good things,*
    So that thy youth is renewed like the eagle's!

II

6.   *Lord executes acts of righteousness*
    And judgments for all that are oppressed.

---

1. The plural "my entrails," "all that is within me," is a *hapax legomenon*. The word usually refers to overpowering emotions.

7. *He made known his ways to Moses,*
   His deeds to the children of Israel.
8. *The Lord is merciful and gracious,*
   Slow to anger and plenteous in mercy.

III

9. *He will not always chide,*
   Neither will he keep his anger forever.
10. *He has not dealt with us according to our sins,*
    Nor requited us according to our iniquities;
11. *For as the heaven is high above the earth,*
    So great is his mercy toward those who fear him.

IV

12. *As far as the east is from the west,*
    So far has he removed our transgressions from us.
13. *Like as a father has compassion upon his children,*
    So the Lord has compassion for those who fear him;
14. *For he really knows our frame;*
    He remembers that we are dust.

V

15. *As for man, his days are like grass;*
    As a flower of the field, so he flourishes.
16. *For the wind passes over it, and it is gone;*
    And the place thereof shall know it no more.
17. *For the mercy of the Lord is from everlasting to everlasting*
    On those that fear him,
    And his righteousness unto children's children.

VI

18. *To such as keep his covenant,*
    And to those that remember his commandments to do them,
19. *The Lord has prepared his throne in the heavens;*
    And his kingdom rules over the universe.
20. *Bless the Lord, ye his angels,*
    That excel in strength, that do his commandments,
    Hearkening to the voice of his word.

Postlude

21.   Bless the Lord, all ye his hosts,
                  Ye ministers of his, that do his pleasure!
22.   Bless the Lord, all his works in all places of his dominion!
                  Bless the Lord, O my soul!

BIBLIOGRAPHY

P. R. Ackroyd, "Some Notes on the Psalms," *JTS*, XVII (1966), pp. 392-99; E. Beaucamp, "Guérison et Pardon (Ps 103)," *BVC*, XXIX (1959), pp. 13-25; W. H. Bellinger, Jr., *Psalms* . . . (Peabody, Mass., 1990), pp. 38-39; W. Brueggemann, *The Message of the Psalms* (Minneapolis, 1984), pp. 160-61; idem, *The Psalms and the Life of Faith* (Minneapolis, 1995), pp. 52-54, 200-204; O. Grether, *Name und Wort Gottes im Alten Testament*, BZAW LXIV (Giessen, 1934); J. Herrmann, "Der 103 Psalm: Dienst unter dem Wort," in *Festscrift H. Schreiner* (1953), pp. 82-93; F. Horst, "Segen und Segenshandlungen in der Bibel," *EvT*, I/2 (1947), pp. 23-37; F. James, *Thirty Psalmists* (New York, 1938), pp. 44-48; A. A. MacIntosh, "A Third Root of ['*dh*] in Biblical Hebrew?" *VT*, XXIV (1974), pp. 454-73; N. H. Parker, "Psalm 103: God Is Love: He Will Have Mercy and Abundantly Pardon," *Catholic Journal of Theology*, I (1965), pp. 191-96; K. Seybold, *Das Gebet des Kranken im Alten Testament* . . . , BWANT V, 19 (Stuttgart, 1973); J. J. Stamm, *Erlösen und Vergeben im Alten Testament* (Bern, 1940); C. Westermann, *The Living Psalms* (Grand Rapids, 1989), pp. 236-44; idem, *The Praise of God in the Psalms* (Richmond, Va., 1965), pp. 135-36.

FORM

The form of this psalm is remarkably constructed with six strophes, each of which comprehends three bicola, with the exception of tricola toward the climax (vv. 17 and 20), where a thematic stress entails the lengthening of the rhythm. The body of the poem is surrounded by a Prelude (vv. 1b-2) and a Postlude (vv. 21-22) in which the psalmist dialogues with himself. The sixth strophe ends with the invitation to bless the Lord, as a transitional link toward the Postlude in which the heavenly hosts, the Lord's ministers, and even "all his works" are bidden to praise, as well as the poet's own self.

The meter is generally 3+3. It becomes quite irregular as the psalm progresses toward its end.

COMMENTARY

Superscription (v. 1a)

An editor of the Psalter ascribed this psalm to David, perhaps on account of its personal tone.

Prelude: Dialogue of the Poet with his Soul (vv. 1b-2)

To bless the Lord's holy name is to bless the Lord in action. A theology of glory is absent, perhaps because it did not fit a lyrical hymn with a highly subjective tone. A tradition on the vocation of Moses tells that the name Yahweh remains the unspeakable designation of God's creating power (Exod 3:14). The meaning "I am that I am" comes in part from the Greek translation in post-Alexandrian times. The Hebrew "Yahweh" is probably the causative third person singular of the verb, meaning "I cause to be whatever I cause to be." Yet see Exod 3:14.

Strophe I: The Benefactions of God (vv. 3-5)

The whole catechism of ancient Israel's covenant faith is here summarized. God forgives and he heals (the common belief attributed sickness to the guilt of a transgression); he keeps alive; he crowns with lovingkindness and tender mercies; he fulfills human longings and desires.[2] This last marvel has an uncertain meaning. Literally, "he redeems life from death" is an ambiguous statement; it may allude to the healing of a mortal sickness, or it may allude to life everlasting, after death. The verb "redeem" favors the latter translation (see Job 19:25). This poetic comparison is notable since the eagle was considered to be an impure bird (Lev 4:13; Deut 14:12).

Strophe II: The Sinai Covenant (vv. 6-8)

The benefactions of Yahweh were personal in Strophe I, but they became general in Strophe II. Respect for the covenant mediated by Moses (v. 7) stipulates obedience to the commandments that Yahweh revealed through him. They are not spelled out, but they most likely are the moral decalogue in pithy form (Exod 20:1-24). Fulfilling these commandments rather than those of the ritual decalogue (Exod 34:17-27) is most significant, for the psalmist either referred to an early time, anterior to the Priestly code, or this allusion to the moral decalogue conferred on the poet a nonritual attitude familiar to the great

---

2. The LXX reads the MT, "my mouth?" as "my longing."

prophets. Moreover, the stress on mercy and grace, with slowness to anger
(v. 8), points to an inner religion.

Strophe III: Further Stress on God's Love (vv. 8-11)

The theme of divine compassion is continued and even emphasized quite explicitly. The psalmist clearly objects to a theology of a strict justice based on retribution, in punishment or reward. However, this splendid "God'spel" applies
to "those who fear him" (v. 11). The concept of awe in love meant the scrupu-
lous acceptance of God's compassion. It is a passion to please the beloved.

Strophe IV: The Metaphor of Fatherhood (vv. 12-14)

While the imagery of father-son originated in the supreme bond of God-and-
king, not in the Near Eastern myth of physiological filiation, it may have come
into Israel with the sense of ancestry and lineage alive in family life, still ambivalent about good and evil (2 Sam 7:14; cf. Ps 2:7).

Strophe V: Man's Frailty and God's Pity (vv. 15-17)

The word "dust" in the preceding context formed a transition to the divine
compassion (v. 11; cf. Gen 2:7; Job 10:9).

Man's frailty and transitoriness are like those of flowers, devastated by a
breath of hot wind (Job 14:2; Ps 90:10; Isa 40:6-7). The mortality of humankind
moves the Sovereign of heaven and earth to soften his ideology of high morality
and to have pity on his creatures, especially those who love him with the fearful
desire of not disappointing their loving God.

Strophe VI: From Covenant Observance
to Universal Praise (vv. 18-20)

The ambivalence implied in Strophe V is made clearer now that the heavenly
throne and worldwide dominion are linked to those who keep the covenant and
therefore remember to do its commandments. As in other hymns, the theme of
creation flows into the theme for obedience. This understanding of human salvation closely related to cosmic harmony allows the singer to show the bond
between morality and aesthetics. It is a preparation for the Postlude and its renewed invitation to bless the Lord, but, this time, this exhortation is to the angels at the same moment that it goes to the human servants of Yahweh, who
"excel in [a] strength" that enables them to "do his commandments" and to pay
attention to "the voice of his word."

Postlude: The Sublime Bidding (vv. 21-22)

Now we have the holy marriage between the heavenly hosts, side by side with the angels who minister, doing his pleasure, on the one hand, and "all his works," on the other hand (v. 22).

These are not specifically described, but all the works are personified. They are in some way the living servants of the Creator: moon and stars, clouds and rain, thunderstorms and hail, the sea with its infinite horizon, the high mountains inaccessible to humans, the rivers and the lakes. The whole of nature is summoned to bow and "to bend its knees" before the holy Maker.

In a silent way the poet wants the gods of the foreign nations to join in this universal symphony. "To bless," in the intensive mode, amounts to cosmic worship.

Only a short sentence suffices to tie up the poem, "Bless the Lord, O my soul!" The sick man, now brought back to life and perhaps expecting everlasting communion after his death, will at last convince his "inner self," which may have been, once upon a time, unwilling and reluctant to join not only humankind but also the whole of creation in united lauds.

DATE AND THEOLOGY

From ancient versions to modern translations, readers of the Hebrew text had to harmonize participles in second person clauses with the initial invitation. This magnificent psalm, with the implied debate of the poet with himself, may well have been inspired not just by emotional selfhood but by flagrant emotional self-centeredness. This bit of egotism is understandable if sickness has prompted such a psychological, inward altercation.

The deeper being needs to be told that God heals because he forgives. A prayer of gratitude follows an unexpressed lament. It is God who liberates this man's life from the threat of death. Yet he has to convince not only his breathing self *(nephesh)* but also the deep being within him of his silent terrors. "My entrails" is a metaphor in the song for the instinctive anxiety that tortured him. Evolution from near despair to a rejoicing health shows its culminating point of exhilaration when the ardor of his youth, with an ebullient *joie de vivre,* has returned. He has been crowned with divine love and mercy, as if he had triumphed at the existential stadium.

Respect for the covenant mediated by Moses broadens the horizon of the sick man who has been healed. His personal life has now become the symbol of Israel's *Heilsgeschichte.* Elihu, in the poem of Job, defines the successive aspects of "being forgiven." God warns the sinner with a painful ailment (Job 33:19-22).

God will not accept a man blinded by arrogance or pride. Forgiveness means that thanksgiving, which is so often postponed and forgotten, takes hold of the new man who does not suffer anymore and has received again his youthful energy. It bursts out of his flesh.

The psalmist is now eager to share with others that the Creator, who is the ruler of universal harmony, takes time to enter into a dialogical exchange with a man who is only dust, just as in the book of Job Yahweh enters with the Discourses, which conclude the disquisition of the man of sorrow. Creation opens up the perspective of salvation. The psalmist enters the company of the angels, the heavenly ministers, and all those who belong, on earth and in heaven, to the government of the universe.

The final bidding, "Bless the Lord, O my soul," belongs to the concert in the music of the spheres.

PSALM 104

The Lord of the Seven Wonders

Prelude

1.
> *Bless the Lord, O my soul!*
> *O Lord, my God, thou art exceedingly great,*
> *Clothed in majesty and magnificence!*

I

2.
> *He is wrapping himself with light as a garment.*
> *He spreads out the heavens as a tent,*

3.
> *He lays the beams of his chambers in the waters,*
> *He orders the clouds as his chariot,*
> *He takes a walk on the wings of the wind,*

4.
> *He makes the winds his messengers,*
> *He sends fire aflame as his ministers.*

II

5.
> *He has set the earth on solid foundations,*
> *That it should not be moved, ever and ever.*

6.   *Thou didst cover it with the abyss as a vestment;*
         The waters stood above the mountains.
7.   *At thy rebuke they fled;*
         At the roaring of thy thunder they hastened away.
8.   *They went up the mountains, down in the valleys,*
         To the place thou didst found for them.
9.   *A boundary thou didst set that they should not trespass,*
         So that they would not return to cover the earth.

III

10.   *He sends forth springs into the riverbeds;*
         Between the mountains they run along.
11.   *Thou givest drink to all the beasts of the fields,*
         And even the wild asses quench their thirst.
12.   *Above them, the birds of the sky have their homes;*
         Among the branches they send forth their song.
13.   *He rains on the mountains from his upper chambers!*
         From the fruit of thy works the earth is satisfied.

IV

14.   *He makes grass grow for the cattle,*
         And herbs for the service of man;
       He brings forth food from the soil,
15.   *And wine to rejoice the heart of mortals,*
       And oil to make their face shine,
         And bread to strengthen the heart of men.
16.   *The trees of the Lord are satisfied,*
         The cedars of Lebanon that he planted,
17.   *Where the birds build their nests;*
         As for the stork, her house is under the cypresses.
18.   *High peaks are for the wild goats,*
         And rocky bluffs, a shelter for badgers.

V

19.   *He made the moon to announce feast days;*
         The sun knows when he must go down;
20.   *Thou bringest darkness, and it is night;*
         All the beasts of the forest creep out;
21.   *The young lions roar after their prey;*
         They seek their food from God!

22.   *The sun rises; they retreat*
          And lie down in their dens.
23.   *Man goes to his work,*
          And to his task till evening.

VI

24.   *How manifold are thy works, O Lord!*
          In wisdom thou madest them all.
          The earth is filled with thy creatures.
25.   *Yonder is the sea, great and wide,*
          Wherein swim numerous fish,
          Little ones and big ones;
26.   *There go the ships to and fro,*
          And that Leviathan which thou didst make for play!

VII

27.   *All of them look after thee*
          To receive their food in due season.
28.   *Thou givest them, gather up they do;*
          Thou openest thy hand, they are satisfied with goods;
29.   *Thou hidest thy face, they are in distress;*
          Thou takest away their breath, they expire,
          And they return to their dust.
30.   *Thou sendest thy Spirit, they are created,*
          And thou renewest the face of the ground.

VIII

31.   *Let the glory of the Lord last forever!*
          Let the Lord rejoice in his works!
32.   *He looks at the earth, it trembles;*
          He touches the mountains, they smoke!
33.   *I will sing unto the Lord all my life!*
          I will celebrate my God with my whole being!
34.   *Let my sung meditation be agreeable to him!*
          As for me, I rejoice in the Lord!
       May sinners be consumed from the earth,
35.   *And scoundrels be no more!*

Postlude

Bless the Lord, O my soul!
Alleluia!

BIBLIOGRAPHY

P. Auffret, *Hymnes d'Egypte et d'Israël: Etudes de structures littéraire* (Fribourg and Göttingen, 1981), pp. 137-295; idem, "Note sur la structure du Ps. 104," *RSR*, LXI (1982), pp. 73-82; J. Barr, "Was Everything That God Created Really Good?" in *Festschrift W. Brueggemann* (Minneapolis, 1998), pp. 61-62; K. H. Bernhardt, "Amenophis IV und Ps 104," *Mitteilungen des Instituts für Orientforschung*, XV (1969), pp. 193-205; W. Brueggemann, *Theology of the Old Testament* (Minneapolis, 1997), pp. 155-56; E. Celada, "El salmo 104, et himno de Ameno is IV y ostros documentos egipcios," *Sefarad*, XXXI (1971), pp. 3-26; P. C. Craigie, "The Comparison of Hebrew Poetry: Psalm 104 in the Light of Egyptian and Ugaritic Poetry," *Semitica*, IV (1974), pp. 10-21; A. Deissler, "Mensch und Schöpfung: Eine Auslegung des Ps. 103 (104)," *Bib*, LXI (1960), pp. 15-22; P. E. Dion, "YHWH as Storm God and Sun God: The Legacy of Egypt and Canaan as Reflected in Psalm 104," *ZAW*, CIII (1991), pp. 143-71; G. R. Driver, "The Resurrection of Marine and Terrestrial Creatures: On Ps. 104:24-30," *JSS*, VII (1962), pp. 12-22; O. Eissfeldt, "Alexander von Humboldts 'kosmos' und der 104. Psalm," in *Kleine Schriften*, III (Tübingen, 1966), pp. 471-80; idem, "Gott und das Meer in der Bibel," in *Festschrift J. Pedersen* (Hauniae, 1953), pp. 76-84; S. Grill, "Textkritische Notizen zu Ps 104, 26," *BZ*, III (1959), p. 102; A. Guillaume, "The Hebrew Root [*l.h.ṭ.*]," *JTS*, XLI (1940), pp. 251-52; idem, "Note on the Verb *i.s.h.*," *JTS*, XLIV (1943), p. 23; H.-J. Hermisson, "Observations on the Creation Theology of Wisdom," in *Festschrift Samuel Terrien* (Missoula, Mont., 1978), pp. 43-57; V. Howard, "Psalm 104," *Int* (1992), pp. 176-80; P. Humbert, "La relation de Genèse 1 et du Psaume 104 avec la liturgie du Nouvel an Israélite," *RHPR*, XV (1935), pp. 1-27; P. Joüon, "Les 'reptiles' [*sheres*] et [*remes*] (Ps. 104:25)," *Bib*, XXI (1940), pp. 152-58; O. Kaiser, "Die mythische Bedeutung des Meeres in Ägypten, Ugarit und der 104. Psalm," *Forschungen und Fortschritte*, XXXIII (1959), pp. 112-17; H. Kruse, "Archetypus Psalmi 104? Hymnus solis Echratonis," *VD*, XXIX (1951), pp. 41-43; G. Leonardi, "Note zu alguni versetti del Salmo 104 (6, 8a, 9a, 10-17, 14-15, 18)," *Bib*, XLIX (1968), pp. 238-42; R. Loewe, "The Divine Garment and *Shil'ur Qomah*" [in postbiblical rabbinical mysticism]," *HTR*, LVIII (1965), pp. 153-60; G. Nagel, "À propos des rapports du psaume 104 avec les textes égyptiens," in *Festschrift A. Bertholet* (Tübingen, 1950), pp. 395-403; M. L. Ramlot, "Hymne à la gloire du Créateur, Ps 104," *BVC*, XXXI (1960), pp. 39-49; J. Reider, [Textual Notes on Ps 104:13], *VT*, IV (1954), p. 284; J. H. Scammon, "Another Look at Ps 104," *Journal of Hebrew Studies*, I (1969), pp. 1-12; M. S. Smith, "The Near Eastern Background of Solar Language for Yahweh," *JBL*, CIX (1990), pp. 29-39; H. T. D. Sparks, "A Textual Note on Psalm 104:10," *HTR*, XLVIII (1947), pp. 57-59; H. Spieckermann, *Heilsgegenwart: Eine Theologie der Psalmen* (Göttingen, 1989), pp. 21-49; E. F. Sutcliffe, "A Note on Psalm CIV,8," *VT*, II (1952), pp. 177-79; S. Terrien, "Creation, Cultus, and Faith in the Psalter," in *Horizons of Theological Education* (Dayton, Ohio, 1966), pp. 116ff.; A. van der Voort, "Genèse I à II,4a et Psaume CIV," *RB*, LVIII (1951), pp. 321-47; G. von Rad, "The Theological Problem of the Old Testament Doctrine of Creation," in *The Problem of the Hexateuch and Other Essays* (Edinburgh and London, 1966), pp. 131-35; idem, *Das theologische Problem des alttestamentlichen Schöpfungsglaubens* BZAW, 61 (Giessen, 1936), pp. 135-47.

FORM

Psalm 104 is a hymn of praise to the Creator of the living universe. It contains seven strophes (vv. 1-30) in harmony with the seven days of creation in the Genesis myth (Gen 1:1–2:4a). Strophe I assumes a double function (vv. 2-4), for it shows, first, the magnificent Yahweh, covered with light, and, second, the Maker of nature, in seven wonders:

I. sky; II. earth; III. water; IV. vegetation; V. moon and sun; VI. the great sea; VII. the life-giver.

An eighth strophe (vv. 31-35) differs from those on the natural wonders, for it expresses three wishes: (1) the joy of the Lord; (2) the promise to praise him; and (3) the disappearance of sinners.

The meter varies substantially from the beginning to the end: from 3+3 to 3+4 and 3+3+3. Strophes vary in length but offer an almost regular pattern of three or four stichoi (I, III, VI) to five and six stichoi (II, IV), returning to four (VII) or even five (VIII).

Attempts have been made to discern a linkage of strophic couplets (I and VIII; II and VII; III and VI), thus emphasizing the central importance of Strophe V, which is precisely on the moon and sun. It may also be significant to observe that the use of the divine name, Yahweh, is reserved for the Prelude (v. 1), the Postlude (v. 35c), and, in the body of the psalm, for Strophe IV (v. 16), Strophe VI (v. 24), and Strophe VIII (vv. 31, 33, and 34). The heart of the poem addresses the Deity without name, not in the style of prayer (2nd person singular) but in the style of meditation (3rd person). Thus the two styles are distributed as follows:

Second person	*Participial and third person*
vv. 1, 6, 7, 8, 8, 9, 11, 13, 20, 24, 26, 27, 28, 29, 30	2, 3, 4, 5, 10, 13, 14, 16, 19, 31, 33, 34, 35

Such a distribution may not be accidental. True to the style of meditation (v. 34a), the poet may have suggested in this fashion the absolute independence of the Lord's creative activity with the cosmic elements: light, sky, earth, water, clouds, winds, and fire. The second person style of prayer seems to have been appropriate for the emotional reminiscences of polytheistic myths (vv. 6-9, 26b) and those parts of the world that include human enterprise, such as the art of navigation, always dangerous and aleatory (v. 26a).

The eight strophes correspond to the eight acts of creation in the Yahwist myth (Gen 1:1–2:4).

The structure (see diagram on p. 712) respects almost entirely the number of bicola or tricola from Strophe I to Strophe VIII, when it is discovered on strophic couplings as follows:

I and VIII (vv. 2-4 + 31-34)
II and VII (vv. 5-9 + 27-30)
III and VI (vv. 10-13 + 24-26)
IV and V   (vv. 14-18 + 19-23)

The themes of the coupled strophes also correspond to each other:

I. Light	VIII. Glory
II. Earth	VII. Terrestrial Creatures
III. Spring and Rain	VI. The Great Sea
IV. Vegetation	V. Night and Day

If this superb structure is correct, Psalm 104 received in its form and its motifs an exceptional quality in its development and unity.

COMMENTARY

Prelude: Appeal to the Soul (v. 1)

Shorter than the Prelude to Psalm 103, the opening apostrophe of Psalm 104 introduces at once a personal note on the part of the poet. This poem is to be sung as a hymn of praise to Yahweh, whose joyful presence is at once exultantly proclaimed.[1] This presence is acknowledged by the immediate consecution of two divine names, "Lord" and "my God." These two names symbolize the tension between divine transcendence and divine immanence, or between divine distance and divine proximity (cf. v. 33).

This deity is the fashioner and maintainer of the universal cosmos, but he is also addressed in prayer as the most intimate and yet holy companion. The divine actor, maker, initiator, and originator of the whole world reality is the owner of a majesty and the bearer of a "magnificence" that sets him aside, beyond, and above a divinized force of nature with the status of casual or steady acquaintance, a familiar companion, or a "fellow pal." Yahweh, whose name means "He causes to be," is also "my God."[2]

1. The accent on the poet's inner life is at once amplified and minimized by the address, "O my soul," because the Hebrew word is not the Greek *psychē* but the breathing of life in its greatest intensity and privacy. Thus God is named both the Creator of all, "He who causes to be" (Yahweh), and "my God."

2. O. Eissfeldt, "'Mein Gott' im Alten Testament," *ZAW*, LXI (1945/46), pp. 3-16.

I

2. – – – – – – – –
– – – – – –
3. – – – – – – – –
– – – – – –
4. – – – – – – – –
– – – – – –
– – – – – –

II

5. – – – – – – – –
– – – – – –
6. – – – – – – – –
– – – – – –
7. – – – – – – – –
– – – – – –
8. – – – – – – – –
– – – – – –
9. – – – – – – – –
– – – – – –

III

10. – – – – – – – –
– – – – – –
11. – – – – – – – –
– – – – – –
12. – – – – – – – –
– – – – – –
13. – – – – – – – –
– – – – – –

IV

14. – – – – – – – –
– – – – – –
15. – – – – – – – –
– – – – – –
16. – – – – – – – –
– – – – – –
17. – – – – – – – –
– – – – – –
18. – – – – – – – –
– – – – – –

VIII

31. – – – – – – –
– – – – – –
32. – – – – – – –
– – – – – –
33. – – – – – – –
– – – – – –
34. – – – – – – –
– – – – – –
– – – – – –
– – – – – –
– – – – – –

VII

27. – – – – – – –
– – – – – –
28. – – – – – – –
– – – – – –
29. – – – – – – –
– – – – – –
30. – – – – – – –
– – – – – –

VI

24. – – – – – – –
– – – – – –
25. – – – – – – –
– – – – – –
– – – – – –
26. – – – – – – –
– – – – – –

V

19. – – – – – – –
– – – – – –
20. – – – – – – –
– – – – – –
21. – – – – – – –
– – – – – –
22. – – – – – – –
– – – – – –
23. – – – – – – –
– – – – – –

He is "exceedingly great." He stands without equal or peer. His immensity renders him "one and only." But he comes to me.

Strophe I: Architect of Heaven? He Is Wrapped in Light (vv. 2-4)

Within a Canaanite, Phoenician, Egyptian, and Mesopotamian culture that divinized the forces of nature (pantheism), the Hebrew mind could look with tenacity and wonder at the sky and the light as the creation of Yahweh. Because it is the vastest space and monument in which God dwells, it must be called "heaven." The division between the Prelude and Strophe I is due to the syntactic change from the use of a second person verb to a series of participial sentences that imply an objective statement of divine activity. Yahweh is the continuous Creator. The present tense is required by the participles in the MT of vv. 2-4. The subjective tone of the Prelude is now replaced by the objective character of a description that sketches the various parts of the world, from sky to earth, water, and sea.

The creation of the sky as "the heavens" is often praised in other hymns (Pss 8:4; 33:5; 102:26; 136:6). This sky does not surround God to shelter him, but it looks like the dome of a tent that has been solidly stretched.

In addition, the spreader of this tent is invisible, for he has clothed himself in light. Unlike the Yahwist myth of Genesis, where light is the first response to the Word, "Let there be light!" and the response to the Word, "And there was light" (Gen 1:3), in the psalm the participial verbs hint at a procedure of creation but not for "light." This does not imply that light was uncreated, but the process of its appearance is entirely absent. Simply, light becomes the vestment of God, and its purpose is to produce a blinding effect, rendering God invisible.[3]

The sky is not only the "habitat" made by God for himself, but it also supports the beams for the chambers that contain the heavenly waters. Rain and clouds are related. Clouds provide a ready chariot for the divine maintainer of the cosmos, side by side with his messengers flying in the winds, as well as the zigzagging flames of lightning. Electric storms, or "thunder," are not yet mentioned. There is no "thunder God" — the Baal of the Canaanites — centuries ahead of the Greco-Roman "Zeus" or "Jupiter" of Olympian mythology. Astonishingly, through his imperative faith in the One Yahweh, the psalmist succeeds in ignoring the seduction of treating as gods the forces of natural phenomena.

---

3. Invisibility through blinding luminescence was already observed by ancient Egyptians who covered faience plaques with an aquamarine glaze, whose dazzling light imitated the rays the sun.

Strophe II: The Earth and the Abyss (vv. 5-9)

The wonder of the sky, with its blue ether, its light, its clouds carried by its winds, is followed by a wonder equally astonishing. The stability of the earth is due to its solid foundation although these foundations emerge from the primal waters of the abyss, which presumably rest on nothing. International wisdom probably lies under the paradox of this declaration. In a sense, such cosmological beliefs antedate by centuries the discoveries of Copernicus and Galileo.

> It is [God] who spreads Septentrion on emptiness,
> And suspends the earth on nothing. (Job 26:7)

The mystery deepens and yet softens at the thought that the Lord, who was the master of creation in the distant past, now covers the foundations of the earth with the waters of the abyss. He is indeed the continuous Creator.

The psalmist also alludes to the Near Eastern myth of a cosmic fight of the God of light with the goddess of darkness. He triumphantly states that the primal waters fled at Yahweh's rebuke. He unwittingly, symbolically, subscribes to speculations on an uncreated *tohu-bohu* (Gen 1:3).

Strophe III: Springs and Rains (vv. 10-13)

The next wonder is that of water from springs and water from clouds. The thirst of all living creatures on earth needs to be quenched. Birds also drink; then they sing to the delight of human ears. A soil stultified by long summer droughts is "satisfied" by outbursts of rain, and the hills become green again. This is stressed as a miracle of God; hence the psalmist suddenly turns to the style of prayer in the second person: "From the fruit of thy work, the earth is satisfied." This autumnal revival of nature may have contributed to the origin of the Feast of the New Year.

Strophe IV: Green Pastures and High Peaks (vv. 14-18)

Without transition, the poem glides into the wonder of vegetation. Pastures for goats, sheep, and cattle, food for animals and for humans. Grapes and olives become wine and oil. Here the poet goes beyond the need to satisfy hunger. He praises God for the wine that rejoices the heart of mortals and the oil that adds luster to the skin of women and men.

To the beauty of ordinary trees and their shade stands the supreme grandeur of the cedars of Lebanon, whose majesty and immovability require the fantasy that it was the Creator of the world who planted them. Lebanon made the poet think of Anti-lebanon and its snowy summit, Mount Hermon, outside of human reach, the home of wild goats and badgers.

Harmony or sound, sight, and touch extended the usefulness of plants and vegetables from the realm of necessity to that of play. Economics are crowned by aesthetics and hedonic appreciation.

Strophe V: The Moon and the Sun (vv. 19-23)

As the structure of the entire poem reverses its course from Strophes I–IV to Strophes V–VIII, an equilibrium of themes becomes apparent. The moon and the sun, wonder of wonders, remind the worshipers to celebrate seasonal feasts and to respect the nocturnal and diurnal alternation of sleep and work, while recognizing an opposite schedule for wild animals.

The moon has always fascinated and awed human imagination. Its roughly twenty-nine-day revolution and its cyclical growth to circularity followed by a decrease into obscurity became a way to remember seasonal feasts. Ancient Eastern religions made the moon a goddess, but in the psalm it serves only to mark the passing of calendar time.

With its blinding light and fertile heat, the sun had become the heliocentric mystery of worship, even in the temple of Jerusalem,[4] but the psalmist relegated it to second place and reduced it to obedience in service. Yet a prosopopoeia will make him leave the scene with regular punctuality. Both the moon and the sun are demoted to ancillary status.

The succession of light after darkness deserves notice: "days" begin at sunset; they signal rest for humans.

The question of Egyptian influence upon the psalm was faced after the discovery of the Tell el-Amarna tablets, among which was found the fourteenth-century hymn of the Pharaoh Amen-hotep IV (Akhenaten). Addressed to the sun god, the prayer presents many affinities with Psalm 104.

(a)   When thou settest in the western horizon,
          The land is in darkness, in the manner of death[. . .],
       Every lion is come forth from his den,
       All creeping things, they sting.[5]

The psalmist merely claims promptness and accuracy, as has been seen, but the motif of darkness and that of the nocturnal prowl of wild beasts appear in both documents.

4. S. Terrien, "The Omphalos Myth in Hebrew Religion," *VT*, XX (1970), pp. 324-25.
5. Translation by John A. Wilson, in James B. Pritchard, ed., *The Ancient Near Eastern Texts* (Princeton, 1969), pp. 369-70.

(b)   At daybreak, when thou arisest on the horizon[. . .],
        All the world, they do their work.

The psalmist prefers to reassure workers in the fields, and at the same time praise Yahweh for feeding dangerous animals.

(c)   All beasts are content with their pasturage.
        Trees and plants are flourishing;
        The birds [. . .] fly from their nests. . . .

The psalmist had already admired the satisfaction of earthly creatures, but added his delight with bird songs.

(d)   The ships are sailing north and south,
        For every way is open at their appearance;
        The fishes in the river dart from thy face;
        Thy rays are in the midst of the great green sea.

Navigation on the Nile and on the Mediterranean, likewise, has become the psalmist's admiring concern, but he reserved it for a later strophe, where he would add a significant theme: Leviathan, the ocean monster, symbol of mortal menace for sailors and, elsewhere, a world evil (Job 41:2; cf. Ps 74:14; Isa 27:1).[6] The Hebrew poet wanted to show his care "for those in peril on the sea" who face "the foaming deep," but he has also rendered Leviathan harmless as a pet for the Lord to play with!

The influence of the Akhenaten prayer is undeniable, but was the poet directly acquainted with it? Most probably not. Not only did he insist on the pragmatic employment of the day star, but he also ignored the splendid Egyptian line, "Thou didst create the world according to thy desire."

Moreover, unlike another sacred singer and a sophisticated sage (Job 10:8-11; Ps 139:13-16), he omitted all references to the wonders of embryology that captured the attention of the Egyptian theologian, nor did he praise the ruler of history, with the Egyptian insistence on the geographical distribution of various countries and the diversity of their speech and color. In all probability, he learned about Leviathan, and perhaps the whole Egyptian hymn, from the Phoenicians-Canaanites. The Phoenicians were experienced and daring navigators.

---

6. In the fourteenth-century tablets of Ugarit, Baal defeats *L.t.n*; cf. the late growth of the myth in 2 Esdr 6:52; 2 Bar 29:3-8.

Strophe VI: The Great Green Sea (vv. 24-26)

The sapiential flavor of the entire psalm is now confirmed by an explicit junction between creation and wisdom (v. 24b). The wonder of marine immensity is acknowledged implicitly with a warning of danger. Navigating skill and technology were severely and sometimes tragically tested by Mediterranean storms, and the motif of Leviathan — as it has been seen — was reduced to helplessness with God's playful laugh. The waves of the great green sea are now calmed by the mockery of tempests. The benevolence of spring water in Strophe III is now counterbalanced with the wonder of the sea in Strophe VI.

Strophe VII: The Giver of Life and Joy (vv. 27-30)

The wonder of life on earth reveals that the Lord of life brought humans into existence by sending them his breath, which is also his Spirit in the early sense of the word: "that which palpitates and ennobles emotions." He also maintains his blessings for the upholding of human life. The Creator is the feeder of the famished, thus the giver of health and happiness. He opens his hands, and all creatures gather for the feast of abundance.[7] The end of life in death is not comparable to an impersonal fading, like that of flowers, or the wearing out of animals, but a specific act of the Creator, who gives, and also withholds, his breath. The intimate and ultimate designer confers on the impersonality of death the splendid meaning of divine decision. Master of life and non-life, Yahweh may well, in a later age, grant afterlife for a heavenly communion with divinity in glory (cf. Job 19:26; Ps 73:24).

Again, the subtle equilibrium with parallel positions evokes the wonder of continuous creation. The link of Strophe II, in its establishment of a stable earth upon the abyss, with Strophe III can hardly be accidental. The underworld is the realm of death, but from the uttermost depth of extinction arise the pillars of support with monumental durability.

Strophe VIII: Light and Glory (vv. 31-35a)

The temple singer terminates his poem with a promise to praise as long as the Lord permits him to live. Human rejoicing is endemic, for it communes with the Creator's enjoyment in his works, which in turn fosters human praise with hymns of joy. Such a promise echoes Strophe I in which the Lord is praised for being invisible, clad in glory, but overwhelmingly present.

7. On creation and joy, see S. Terrien, *The Psalms and Their Meaning for Today* (New York and Indianapolis, 1952), pp. 63-64.

A theology of glory is often opposed to a theology of the name. Sight competes with hearing. The vision of a God clothed in blinding luminescence evokes the unapproachable sublimity that belongs to the glory of the working Creator. Life, joy, and glory are joined in a symphony of voices, which the temple choir transmutes, thanks to this amazing hymn, into an act of adoration, instead of a complaint against adversity. Hinting that not every part of the cosmos is the best within the best of things, the psalmist is aware of the dreadful danger at sea that he learned from the Phoenicians, intrepid navigators who sail toward a *terra incognita,* but he chooses a higher course. The psalm, in its cosmogonic structure, looks at creation as essentially "good, very good." The forces of nature are all designed to "satisfy."

A passing reference to earthquakes and volcanic eruptions notes that sapiential knowledge is aware of the problem of evil, but the uncertain drama of history — which is never mentioned — will finally end well (v. 35). In the present time, human evil, worse than natural disasters, will be sublimated in the ecstasy of communal adoration.

Postlude (v. 35bc)

In a responsive parallel to the Prelude, the poet asks his inner self to be wholeheartedly involved in the *Te Deum.* The objective style of contemplation is framed by a subjective intention and reaction. The theologian has become an artist.

DATE AND THEOLOGY

The acquaintance of the psalmist with both the prayer of an Egyptian thinker, who wishes to unify the world of praise, and a Hebrew wise man, who introduces into worship the seven wonders of cosmogony, can hardly be doubted. Like the poet of Job, this poet is an international seeker of God in world culture.

The command to bring forth light belongs to the first day of the Genesis recital (Gen 1:3-5); the spread of the heavenly tent takes place on the second day (1:6-8); the mass of primal waters and its containment fit the third day (1:9-13), as does the growth of vegetation; the fourth day witnesses the birth of stars and planets (1:14-19); the fifth day watches the swimming of sea fishes and monsters as well as the flying of birds (1:20-25). Quadrupeds and human beings appear on the sixth day (1:28-30; cf. 2:15). Minor differences aside, the order of the creative acts in the psalm is clearly that of the Genesis Yahwist myth. The date of both documents seems to be approximately the same, for they were both related to the origin of the New Year Feast: joy at the autumnal revival of greenness in valleys and hills that had been scorched by the summer heat.

Sapiential and cultic aspects of the psalm and the Genesis myth were probably inspired in blissful reaction to the military oppression of Judah under the Egyptian and Babylonian invasions (609-587 B.C.E.). Like the sage of the royal circle and the priest of the temple of Zion, to which the psalmist also belonged, everyone knew, *de visu et de carne,* that creation was not entirely devoid of demonic flaws. Yet the poet wanted to show that, eschatologically, the world would reflect the order, the justice, and the beauty of God.

In the end, it is not *natura rerum* that is admired, but the theater of humanity as a tool of divine love and compassion. The election of Israel as a superior people does not concern the poet. Israel is not even named. The theology inherent in the psalm leads to a universal and totally inclusive anthropology. Only a worldwide humanity makes doxology possible. Woman and man deserve the respect of anyone who reflects on heaven, earth, and the abyss, and will respond to the joy of their maker, the Lord of the seven wonders.

PSALM 105

Hymn to the Lord of the Covenant

I

1.   *Give thanks unto the Lord, call upon his name,*
         Make known his deeds among the peoples!
2.   *Sing unto him! Celebrate him!*
         Tell of all his wonderful works!
3.   *Glory ye in his holy name!*
         Let the heart of those who seek the Lord rejoice!

4.   *Seek the Lord and his strength!*
         Look for his face evermore!
5.   *Remember the marvelous works that he has done,*
         His wonders and the judgments of his mouth!
6.   *O ye seed of Abraham his servant,*
         Ye sons of Jacob, his chosen ones!

II

7. He is the Lord our God,
   His judgments are in all the earth.
8. He has remembered his covenant forever;
   The word that he commanded to a thousand generations,
9. This same covenant he made with Abraham,
   And his oath to Isaac.

10. He confirmed it to Jacob as his statute,
    To Israel as an everlasting covenant,
11. Saying, To thee will I give the land of Canaan,
    As the portion of your inheritance,
12. When they were but a few in number,
    Yea, very few, and in it mere strangers.

III

13. When they went from nation to nation,
    From one kingdom to another people,
14. He suffered no man to oppress them;
    Yea, he rebuked kings for their sakes,
15. Saying, Touch not my anointed ones
    And do my prophets no harm!

16. Then he summoned a famine on the land,
    And broke every staff of bread;
17. He sent a man ahead of them,
    Joseph, who was sold as a slave,
18. Whose feet they hurt in fetters;
    His neck was put in iron.

IV

19. Until the time when his word came to pass,
    The word of the Lord tested him;
20. The king sent and released him;
    Even the ruler of the peoples, and he set him free!
21. He made him lord of his house,
    And ruler of all his possessions,

22. To instruct his princes at his pleasure,
    And to teach his elders wisdom.
23. And Israel came into Egypt,

And Jacob sojourned in the land of Ham,
24. And God made his people very fruitful,
And stronger than their enemies.

V

25. He turned their hearts to hate his people,
To deal cunningly with his servants;
26. He sent Moses his servant,
And Aaron whom he had chosen.
27. He fulfilled through them the signs he had announced,
And wonders in the land of Ham.

28. He sent darkness, and it became dark,
And they rebelled not against his words.
29. He turned their waters into blood,
And caused their fish to die;
30. Their land swarmed with frogs
And invaded the palace of their kings.

VI

31. He spoke, and there came a cloud of flies,
And gnats throughout their country;
32. He gave them hail for rain,
And flaming fire in their land;
33. He smote their vines and fig trees,
And crushed the bushes of their territory.

34. He spoke, and there came the locusts,
And brown beetles without numbers.
35. They devoured all the green leaves of their land,
And they devoured the fruit of their ground.
36. He smote all the firstborn in their land,
The flower of all their vigor.

VII

37. Then he led them forth with silver and gold,
And there was none among their tribes who stumbled.
38. Egypt was glad when they departed,
For dread of them had fallen upon [it].
39. He spread a cloud for a covering,
And a fire to give light in the night.

40. The people asked, and he brought them quails,
       And he satisfied them with bread from heaven.
41. He split open the rock, and waters gushed out,
       And flowed on the dry soil like a river,
42. For he remembered his holy promise
       To Abraham his servant.

Envoi

43. He brought forth his people with joy,
       And his chosen with gladness.
44. And he gave them the lands of the nations;
       And they inherited the labor of the peoples,
45. That they might observe his statutes
       And keep his laws. Hallelujah!

BIBLIOGRAPHY

F. Baumgärtel, "Zur Liturgie in der 'Sektenrolle' vom Toten Meer," *ZAW*, LXV (1953), pp. 263-65; J. Brinktrine, "Zur Übersetzung von Ps 105 (104) . . . ," *ZAW*, LXIV (1952), pp. 251-58; R. Clifford, "Style and Purpose in Psalm 105," *Bib*, LX (1960), pp. 420-27; G. W. Coats, "Despoiling the Egyptians," *VT*, XVIII (1968), pp. 450-57; N. Fügilster, "Psalm 105 und die Väterverheissung in M. Gorg," in *Festschrift J. Scharbert* (Stuttgart, 1989), pp. 41-60; S. L. Holm-Nielsen, "The Exodus Tradition in Psalm 105," *ASTI*, XI (1978), pp. 22-30; H.-J. Kraus, *Theology of the Psalms* (Minneapolis, 1979); A. Lauha, *Die Geschichtsmotive in den alttestamentlichen Psalmen* (Helsinki, 1945); A. C. C. Lee, "Genesis I and the Plagues Tradition in Psalm CV," *VT*, XL (1980), pp. 257-64; E. Loewenstamm, "The Number of Plagues in Ps 105," *Bib*, LII (1971), pp. 38ff.; B. B. Margulis, "The Plague Tradition in Ps 105," *Bib*, L (1969), pp. 491-96; M. Noth, *A History of Pentateuchal Tradition* (Englewood Cliffs, N.J., 1981); G. von Rad, *The Problem of the Hexateuch and Other Essays* (New York, 1966), pp. 1-78; T. C. Vriezen, *Studies on the Psalms* (1963), pp. 5ff.; D. Winton Thomas, "Hebrew ['ani], Captivity," *JTS*, XVI (1965), pp. 444-45; W. Zimmerli, "Zwillingspsalmen," in *Studien zur alttestamentlichen Theologie und Prophetie,* Gesammelte Aufsätze II (Munich, 1974), pp. 261-71.

FORM

Like most other hymns, Psalm 105 contains seven strophes, composed of two substrophes, each of which has three bicola. The poet succeeded in producing this regular form, slightly different from that of other hymns, although some enjambments were apparently unavoidable between vv. 18 and 19, as well as between vv. 21 and 22.

The rhythm is generally 3+3, although it tends to enlarge into 4+3 toward the last part of the psalm.

The strophes succeed one another, sometimes unexpectedly, with thematic coherence, based on the sacred history of Israel, from Abraham to the conquest of Canaan.

I. Invitation to Praise (vv. 1-6)
II. Covenant with the Patriarchs (vv. 7-12)
III. Patriarchal Sojourn in Canaan (vv. 13-18)
IV. Joseph, the Exodus, and the Desert (vv. 19-24)
V. Moses and the First Plague (vv. 25-30)
VI. Successive Plagues (vv. 31-36)
VII. The Exodus and Sojourn in the Wilderness (vv. 37-42)
Envoi: The Promised Land (vv. 43-45)

In each strophe, the psalmist intends to proclaim the greatness and universality of the Lord.

COMMENTARY

Strophe I: Invitation to Praise (vv. 1-6)

Psalm 105 addresses the fellow singers and musicians of the choir, as well as the whole company of worshipers. It urges them to sing a thanksgiving canticle and to play sacred instruments in honor of the Lord of all countries, especially those from Canaan to Egypt.

First of all, the psalmist begs them to call on the Lord, Yahweh, and to make his works known as wondrous deeds "among the peoples" (plural). Like other hymns (cf. Psalms 78, 106, 107, 135, 136), this poem justifies singing the praise of such a Lord for his exploits in sacred history, from Abraham to the conquest of Canaan.

The universal sweep of Yahweh's jurisdiction becomes the leitmotif of the praise. His urging all the peoples "to glory" in God's holy name is exceptional. The formula combines the theology of the name and the theology of glory. This latter usually springs from the temple cult, with its symbolic objects, but it now applies to human beings. Devotees of Yahweh share in the wonders of the name — he causes to be whatever he causes to be — and the congregation, in this most unusual twist of thought, become glory sharers, glory spreaders, and glory singers. Worship transmutes human beings rather than symbolic objects of the cult. Personalism replaces the sacredness of temple.

Strophe II: Covenant with the Patriarchs (vv. 7-12)

Israel's history begins with Abraham and continues with Isaac and Jacob. The traditions of the Pentateuch, still in oral form, were apparently the general source of the psalmist's recollection and selection (cf. Gen 12:1–13:18; 20:1-18; 28:1:29-35). The covenant with Abraham, renewed with Jacob-Israel, is everlasting (vv. 8-10) and unconditional — quite different from the Sinai Covenant (Exod 19:5, 6). The great prophets, likewise, did not espouse the illusion of a covenant "forever" (Jer 31:31-32).

Strophe III: Patriarchs Sojourn in Canaan (vv. 13-18)

Significantly, the psalmist recalls that the covenant with Abraham includes the promise of the land of Canaan. It is to be noted that he omits telling of Abraham's purchase of the cave of Machpelah. It was this business document with the original proprietors of Hebron that later on became the basis of a legal claim for the ownership of the land (Gen 23:1-20).

Psalm 105 also ignores Abraham's marriage to Keturah, with whom he procreated in his old age numerous descendants other than the ancestry of Israel (Gen 25:1-6). Again his posterity through Ishmael is left in oblivion (vv. 9-10).

Patriarchs sojourned in Canaan, but a famine sent them to Egypt (vv. 7-18). Again, Pentateuchal traditions are generally followed.

Strophe IV: Joseph, the Exodus, and the Desert (vv. 19-24)

The fertility of the Nile Delta attracted many nomads from the ironically called "Fertile Crescent," which suffered severe droughts (Gen 37:28). The selected sketches of Joseph are also close to the Pentateuchal traditions.

Strophes V-VI: The Plagues of Egypt (vv. 25-36)

The ninth plague of Egypt in the Pentateuchal traditions (Exod 3:10) is the first mentioned by the psalmist (v. 28), probably because it is the most ominous of all the signs before the final manifestation of God's ultimate power over the most powerful nation on earth at the time. Total darkness over the Egyptian sky could not have failed to impress its court. The tenth plague, however, which killed all the newborn infants of the population, attacked the manhood of the males. The bereaved mothers are not even mentioned.

It is remarkable that Psalm 105 is not interested in the sinfulness of Israel or even its protest against want. The singer appears to think of only one idea: praise for God's omnipotence over the universe.

Seeking divine presence is the next motif of the poet's review of the distant past, together with constant praise for the promise of the land (vv. 7, 11, 12, 16, 23, 27, 30, 31, 32, 33, 35, 36, and 44). The gifts of God in the desert of Sinai contradict the coveted abundance of Egyptian agriculture.

The final theme is that of the amazing protection the Lord offered to Israel, from the patriarchs to the conquest. "Do not touch my anointed ones, and to my prophets do no harm!" Abraham is the first man to be called "the anointed one," while Moses and Aaron are "the chosen ones" (v. 26).

VII: The Exodus and the Sojourn in the Wilderness (vv. 37-42)

No moral judgment is offered on the Hebrew plundering of Egyptian gold and silver (v. 37), or on Israel's rejoicing over the use of labor furnished by the foreign nations (v. 44).

Envoi: The Promised Land (vv. 43-45)

Joyful thanks for the land of Canaan now form the summing up of the thrust of the psalm. The Lord's purpose does not appear without compromise: the work of the peoples (v. 44) is to be accepted gleefully, like the despoiling of the Egyptian jewels, as a way by which Israel may at last keep the ordinances of the covenant and observe God's laws. Religious morality is made possible by extortion from others.

DATE AND THEOLOGY

The pious nationalism of Psalm 105 hardly deserves discussion. To psalmody Yahweh's supreme power over all the earth in favor of the people of Israel in the name of an everlasting covenant with Abraham and his descendants is a noble intention at the cost of misinterpreting the ethical strictness of the Mosaic covenant. Not the slightest allusion is to be found to the Assyrian and Babylonian invasions of the land, nor to the exile of the sixth century B.C.E. with its killing, burning, and the razing of the temple.

Psalm 105 may well represent the mentality of Jeremiah's enemies. In a time of royal and priestly agonies, the psalmist would still proclaim the beneficent power of the Lord, and did not face, in the most indirect way, the inability of avoiding a form of anxious theodicy. He could not understand divine retribution for national corruption.

The task of other psalmists or the Jeremianic circle is to face resolutely the seeming impotence of the Lord of the universe.

PSALM 106

The Fathers' Sins and God's Grace

Prelude

1.

Hallelujah!

Praise the Lord, for he is good,
   For his mercy endures forever!
2. Who can describe the mighty acts of the Lord?
   Who can recount all his triumphs?
3. Happy are those who respect his judgment,
   He who does right at all times!

I

4. *Remember me, O Lord, with the favor thou showest to thy people!*
   Visit me with thy saving help;
5. *That I may see the happiness of thy chosen ones!*
   Rejoice with the gladness of thy nation,
   And find glory in thine inheritance!

6. *We have sinned like our fathers,*
   We have committed iniquity and done evil.
7. *In Egypt, our fathers did not notice thy miracles,*
   Nor did they remember the abundance of thy acts of grace,
   But they rebelled at the sea, the Sea of Reeds.

8. *Nevertheless he saved them for the sake of his name,*
   That he might display his mighty power.
9. *He also rebuked the Sea of Reeds, and it dried up,*
   And he led them through abysses as through a wilderness,
10. *And he saved them from the hand of one who hated them,*
   And redeemed them from the power of the enemy.

II

11. *The waters covered their foes;*
   There was none of them left;
12. *Then they believed his words*
   And sang his praises.
13. *But they soon forgot his deeds;*
   They did not wait for his designs.

14. They lusted exceedingly in the wilderness,
     And they tested God in the desert.
15. And he gave them what they had asked for,
     But he sent them enough to disgust them.
16. They envied Moses in the encampment,
     And Aaron, the holy one of the Lord.

17. The earth opened and swallowed Dathan,
     And buried the company of Abiram;
18. And a fire was kindled in their company;
     The flames burned up the evildoers.

III

19. They made a calf in Horeb,
     And worshiped a molten image;
20. They exchanged the glory of God
     For the image of an ox that eats grass!
21. They forgot God, their Savior,
     One who had done great deeds in Egypt,
22. Wondrous works in the land of Ham,
     Terrible miracles at the Sea of Reeds.

23. And he said he would destroy them,
     Had not Moses, his chosen,
   Stood before him in the breach
     To turn away his wrath from destroying them.
24. Yea, they despised the pleasant land;
     They believed not in his word.

25. They murmured in their tents,
     And did not obey the voice of the Lord.
26. Therefore he lifted up his hand against them,
     To make them fall in the wilderness;
27. To disperse their descendants among the nations,
     And scatter them into foreign lands.

IV

28. They joined themselves to Baal-Peor,
     And ate sacrificial offerings to the dead.
29. Thus they provoked the Lord to anger with their inventions,
     And plague broke in among them:
30. Then Phineas stood up, and he interceded,

And the plague was stayed.

31.   *This was reckoned to him as an act of righteousness,*
      From generation to generation, evermore.

32.   *They also angered the Lord at the waters of Meribah,*
      So that Moses suffered on their account,
33.   *Because they provoked his spirit,*
      And he spoke unadvisedly with his lips.

34.   *Also they did not destroy the peoples*
      As the Lord had told them (to do).
35.   *They intermarried with the nations,*
      And even adopted their customs.
36.   *They worshiped those nations' false gods,*
      For they had been ensnared by them.

V

37.   *Yes, they even sacrificed their sons*
      And their daughters to demons;
38.   *They spilled innocent blood, the blood of their sons and daughters,*
      Which they sacrificed to the idols of Canaan,
      And the land was polluted with bloodshed.

39.   *Thus they became unclean with their own acts,*
      And went a-whoring with their inventions.
40.   *The wrath of the Lord was kindled against his people,*
      And he abhorred his own inheritance.
41.   *So he gave them into the hand of the nations,*
      And those who hated them ruled over them.

42.   *Their enemies also oppressed them,*
      So that [Israel] was brought into subjection.
43.   *Many times he delivered [our fathers],*
      But they indeed opposed [his] counsel
      And were brought low for their iniquity.
44.   *Nevertheless, he saw their distress,*
      And he heard their cry.
45.   *For their sake he remembered his covenant,*
      And relented for the multitude of his mercies.
46.   *He ensured that they would receive pity*
      From all those who held them captive.

Postlude

47.   Save us, O Lord our God!
        And gather us from among the nations
        So that we may give thanks unto thy holy name
        And make our glory from the praise of thee!
48.   Blessed be the Lord, God of Israel,
        From everlasting to everlasting;
        And let all the peoples say, Amen!

Hallelu-Yah!

BIBLIOGRAPHY

F. Baumgärtel, "Zur Liturgie in der 'Sektenrolle' vom Toten Meer," *ZAW*, LXV (1953), pp. 263-65; A. Bentzen, "Die Schwindsucht in Ps 106,15," *ZAW*, LVII (1939), p. 152; W. Beyerlin, "Der *nervus rerum* in Psalm 106," *ZAW*, LXXXVI (1974), pp. 50-64; P. Bonnard, *Le Psautier selon Jérémie* (Paris, 1960), pp. 194-98; G. W. Coats, *Rebellion in the Wilderness: Tradition of the Old Testament* (Nashville, 1968); A. George, "Le sacrifice d'Abraham," in *Études de critique et d'histoire religieuse* (Lyon, 1946), pp. 99-100; J. Hoftijzer, *Die Verheissungen an die drei Erzväter* (Leiden, 1956), pp. 72ff.; F. James, *Thirty Psalmists* (New York, 1938), pp. 228-35; A. Lauha, *Die Geschichtsmotive in den alttestamentlichen Psalmen* (Helsinki, 1945); M. Noth, *A History of Pentateuchal Traditions* (Englewood Cliffs, N.J., 1981); G. von Rad, *The Problem of the Hexateuch and Other Essays* (Edinburgh, 1966), pp. 1-79; W. Zimmerli, "Zwillingspsalmen," in *Studien zur alttestamentlichen Theologie und Prophetie,* Gesammelte Aufsätze II (Munich, 1974), pp. 261-71.

FORM

As in the hymnic form, it has already been observed (cf. Psalms 78, 105; cf. Psalm 136) that the psalmist invites his fellow singers and the whole congregation to praise the Lord. He first presents a Prelude and a Postlude (vv. 1-3 and 47-48) for this purpose, and the Prelude includes a macarism to exalt the congregation, while the Postlude ends in a blessing of the Lord.

In contrast with Psalm 105, the body of this poem is made up of five strophes, slightly irregular, that stress the sins of the fathers and of later times, from the sojourn in Egypt to the corruption and the punishment of Judah at the exile.

The first strophe begins with a personal prayer, "Remember me, O Lord!" which is in a first and a second person of address, most exceptional for a hymn. The main body of the psalm alludes without elaboration to five episodes of corporate rebellion:

While the meter is on the whole regular (3+3), the substrophes do not strictly follow the common structure of three bicola; in any case, the acts of transgression are alluded to, not described.

COMMENTARY

Prelude: Praise of God and Man's Happiness (vv. 1-3)

The expression "for he is good" commonly occurs in the hymnic style (Pss 103; 107:1; 118:2-4; 136:1; cf. 1 Chr 18:34, 41; 2 Chr 5:13; 7:3-6; 20:21) and appears to be familiar to Ezra and Jeremiah (Ezra 3:11; Jer 33:11).

Those who live according to the right standards, dictated by God, are capable of singing, "for he is good," and to add, "Happy are those!" This expostulation of good wishes for the future is not a blessing. Probably of wisdom origin, it is a salutation of dynamic movement. The word 'ashrê probably derives from a verb meaning "to march ahead," The singers will be able to recount God's acts of bravura. The comparison is of divine might with acts of heroism and triumph on the battlefield.

Strophe I: Miracles in Egypt and at the Sea of Reeds (vv. 4-10)

A most personal supplication is exceptional in a hymn. Several MSS read the plural "us," but this seems to be a correction of the scribes, knowing that a personal supplication, in any case, returns to the scale of the nation. The finding of "glory in thine inheritance" marvelously shows how the singers can participate in the rejoicing over God's salvation.

The review of sacred history from the exodus to the exile starts with an unexpected condemnation of the fathers, "We have sinned like our fathers; we have committed iniquity and done evil." The prophet Jeremiah seems to have inspired the psalmist, for he or his circle said, "We know, O Yahweh, that we have done evil; it is the guilt of our fathers; we have sinned against thee" (Jer 14:20).

The strophe ends with an acclamation of the divine miracles at the Sea of Reeds: "He rebuked the Sea of Reeds" (Exod 14:11-12; 15:5-6). The legendary process has been at work over the centuries. The coasts of the Suez Isthmus, which the Hebrews crossed at a number of places, reveal the probability of a simple drying up of the sea level at the equinoctial low tide, instead of "depths" or "abysses," a small difference of a few inches under the coastal level of sand.

Strophe II: Envy toward Moses and Aaron in the Wilderness (vv. 11-18)

The *raconteurs* of the Exodus traditions must have been pleased with the stories of the plagues and the total defeat of the pursuers: "There was none of them left" (v. 11). The fathers forgot God's tender mercies, a peculiarly Deuteronomic theme (Deut 4:9, 23, 31; 9:7; 31:6, 12; 25:19; 28:29). Dathan and Abiram became envious of Moses and Aaron, "the holy ones of the Lord." The later prophets could be called "holy men of God" (2 Kgs 4:9). Apparently the first act of rebellion in the Sinai desert was the people's envy.

Strophe III: The Golden Calf (vv. 19-27)

An indication of the northern and probably Deuteronomic influence on Psalm 106 comes from the use of the name "Horeb" instead of "Sinai" (Exod 3:1; 18:5; Deut 1:4; 4:10; 5:20; cf. 1 Kgs 19:4-8). The worship of the golden calf appears to have been more scandalous than the people's envy of these leaders: "They exchanged the glory of God for the image of an ox that eats grass!" "Their glory" (lit. in MT) could hardly be their own possession (Hos 4:7; cf. Jer 2:11; also Rom. 1:23). They also doubted the attractiveness of Canaan: "They despised the pleasant land" (v. 24; cf. Jer 3:19; 12:20).

Strophe IV: Baal-Peor and Meribah (vv. 28-36)

An even worse transgression seems to have been syncretism with Baal-Peor worship (Num 25:5; Hos 9:10). Intermarriage with the daughters of Moab (Num 23:28) was held to have been its cause. The memories were also referring to the failure of Moses, on account of which he was prevented from entering into Canaan (Deut 32:51). The waters of Meribah (v. 32; cf. Exod 17:1-7; Num 20:10, 12-13), sketchily and succinctly alluded to, were somehow related to the fact that he "spoke unadvisedly with his lips" (v. 33).

Strophe V: The Sacrifice of Sons and Daughters (vv. 37-46)

The truly obscene memories of the sins of the fathers, committed since the conquest of the land, consisted in the sacrifices of their own children, sons and daughters (v. 37; cf. Lev 18:21; Deut 12:31; 2 Kgs 16:3; passim). To "spill innocent blood" (v. 38) is literally used by Jeremiah twice (cf. Prov 6:17) about the sacrifices of children (Jer 2:34; 19:4-5). These most shocking practices were due to an imitation of foreign customs. Instead of destroying the neighboring nations, Israel absorbed their religious techniques, probably in order to force the will of hostile gods by appealing to their emotions. Jeremiah was deeply offended by these sacrifices (Jer 7:31; 19:5). The foreign gods were called "demons" (Deut 32:17), and this revolting form of syncretism had to be called "a-whoring" (v. 39; cf. Hos 1:12).

In spite of the horror induced by this final example from the not distant past, the strophe ends in a spectacle of divine mercy (v. 45). Although the chastisement was severe — it probably caused, in the minds of the prophets, the destruction of the temple and the execution and deportation of the princes and common people — the psalmist lived at a time when the captives, in Mesopotamia and elsewhere, were apparently treated with limited pity (v. 46).

Postlude: Final Prayer, Thanksgiving, and Benediction (vv. 47-48)

The psalmist is living at a time of national disaster and humiliation. Thus, the Postlude concludes, first, with a cry of supplication, "Save us!"; second, with a request for the reunion of the scattered Judahites among foreign nations, explaining that such a salvation would permit and even urge the beneficiaries to thank God's "holy name" (almost a kind of hypostasis); third, such a divine intervention would enable the reassembled people to make their glory arise not from themselves but from divine praise (a splendid sidelight of hymnal intention and meaning, which binds praise to the sharing of God's grace [v. 47]; fourth, pronouncing the benediction of God himself, to be sung by the choir and the congregation, and therefore transformed into a sacrificial offering — implying also the priesthood of all believers; fifth, the responsibility for a united humanity in the wish that "all the peoples" would say, "Amen!" (v. 48).

Some exegetes suggest that the saying of a blessing of God belongs to the final edition of the Psalter, when it was divided into five books. This view supports the interpretation of the final verses when they receive a double significance: at once the Postlude of Psalm 106 and the conclusion of "the fourth book" of the Psalter.

DATE AND THEOLOGY

The time of composition for this psalm seems to be the latter part of the exile, when a new administration of the empire was taking over and a new generation of "Judahites" were beginning to become "the Jews" (*yehudim* in the religious sense rather than in the political meaning of the word). The psalmist suffers from the awareness of the dispersion of Israel, the elected nation, among many peoples of the world, but his last word is precisely, "Let all the peoples say, Amen!"

The psalm may have been conceived as a hymn of praise and thanksgiving, in which both the power and the steadfast love of God prevail over the negative relapses of Israel in the course of the centuries. The poem is therefore not simply a collective confession of unpardonable sins but a paean of wonder before the patience and the long-suffering of the covenant Deity.

Unlike Psalm 105, this psalm rejects nationalism as a caricature of patriotism that hides collective guilt. The psalmist has been nourished by the realism and honesty of the great prophets, from Amos and Hosea to Isaiah and Micah, and above all from Jeremiah. Unlike the psalmist of Psalm 105, God is indeed the sovereign master of history, who knows that Israel is not better than the Egyptians and the Babylonians. Israel continues to act arrogantly, but the Lord will be a model of humility, forgiving offenses movingly, with the faculty of waiting for international triumph over egocentricity.

As long as there stands a Phineas who intercedes on behalf of a blind and obstinate community that shows forgetfulness of divine grace (v. 30), the holy mystery of pardon will place the forgiveness of God over the forgetfulness of man.

The two poems, Psalms 105 and 106, contradict and yet complete each other in the dialectic of sin and grace. Christendom must learn that love of country is not the final aim of humanity. The ecumenical church, whatever be its weaknesses and self-centered history of "converting the pagans" — a history usually corrupted by political colonialism — faces the eternal vocation of behaving with integrity and respect for freedom and diversity, so that, of their own initiative, all the peoples may say, "Amen!"

PSALM 107

Praise from the Redeemed of the Lord

Prelude

1.   Praise the Lord, for he is good,
     And his mercy endures forever!
2.   Thus they may say, the redeemed of the Lord,
     For he delivered them from the hand of the enemy;
3.   And he gathered them from among the lands,
     From the east to the west, from the north and from the south sea.

PART ONE
I
(a)

4.   *Some wandered into desert wastes,*
     And found no way to a habitable city;
5.   *Hungry and thirsty,*
     Their life was fainting within them.

(b)

6.   In their distress, they cried to the Lord,
     And he brought them out from their affliction;
7.   *He led them by a direct route*
     To a city fit to dwell in.

(c)

8.   May they celebrate the Lord for his fidelity,
     And his miracles to the sons of Adam!
9.   *For he quenched their thirst,*
     And filled their hunger with good things.

II
(a)

10.   *Others were seated in darkness, in the shadow of death,*
     Bound in dire sickness and irons,
11.   *For they had rebelled against the words of God,*
     And had despised the counsel of the Most High.
12.   *He had tamed their heart with overwhelming pain,*
     And they had stumbled, but nobody helped.

(b)

13.   In their distress they cried to the Lord,
        And he brought them out from their affliction;

14.   *He made them leave darkness and the shadow of death,*
        And broke off their shackles.

(c)

15.   May they celebrate the Lord for his fidelity,
        And his miracles to the sons of Adam!

16.   *For he shattered portals of bronze*
        And cut asunder bars of iron.

III

(a)

17.   *Still others, rendered insane by their misconduct,*
        Of their own fault made themselves miserable;

18.   *They became disgusted with any nourishment,*
        And drew near enough to touch the gates of death.

(b)

19.   In their distress they cried to the Lord,
        And he brought them out of their affliction.

20.   *He sent his word, and he healed them,*
        And saved their life from the Pit.

(c)

21.   May they celebrate the Lord for his fidelity,
        And for his miracles with the sons of Adam!

22.   *Let them offer sacrifices of praise,*
        And proclaim his works in shouts of joy!

IV

(a)

23.   *Again, others have gone down to the sea in ships,*
        And followed their profession on the high waters;

24.   *These, in truth, have seen the works of the Lord,*
        And his miracles on the ocean depths.

(b)

25. *At his word came a stormy wind*
    That raised enormous waves.
26. *They ascended to the skies*
    And descended into abysses;
    Their courage melted in terror;
27. *They reeled and staggered like drunken men,*
    And all their skill was engulfed.

(c)

28. In their distress they cried to the Lord,
    And he brought them out from their affliction.
29. *He reduced the tempest to stillness,*
    And the waves became silent.
30. *They rejoiced at this return to calm,*
    And God led them to a desired harbor.

(d)

31. May they celebrate the Lord for his fidelity,
    For his miracles with the sons of Adam!
32. *Let them exalt him at people's assemblies,*
    And praise him at sessions of the elders!

PART TWO
I
(a)

33. *He turns rivers into desiccated soil,*
    Springs of water into thirsty ground,
34. *A fertile land into a salty marsh,*
    On account of the evil of its dwellers.
35. *But he turns a desert into pools of water,*
    And parched earth into gushing springs.

(b)

36. *He let the hungry reside there,*
    And they build a city to dwell in;
37. *They sow seeds on new fields,*
    Plant vineyards, and reap their grapes.

(c)

38. *He blesses them and they greatly multiply,*
    And their herds do not diminish.

39. *Yet they are reduced and they decline*
    Through depression, adversity, and grief.

II

40. *He poured contempt on their princes,*
    And they wander on trackless savannas.

41. *But he protects the poor from want,*
    And increases families like flocks;

42. *The upright saw, and they were glad;*
    And all unjust talk shut its mouth.

Postlude

43.   Who wishes to become wise?
        Let him remember these things
        And heed the graciousness of the Lord!

BIBLIOGRAPHY

C. Barth, *Die Errettung vom Tode* (Zollikon, 1947); W. Beyerlin, *Werden und Wesen des 107. Psalms*, BZAW CLIII (Berlin and New York, 1979); M. D. Goulder, *The Psalms of the Return (Pss. 107-150)* (Sheffield, 1998); G. C. Gunn, [On Psalm 107], *God in the Psalms* (Edinburgh, 1956), p. 53; H. Holzmeister, "Clamaverunt ad Dominum cum tribularentur et necessitalibus eorum liberavit eos: Ps 106 (107), 1, 6, 13, 19, 28," *VD*, XXIV (1944), pp. 3-6; M. Lohr, *Psalmenstudien* (Berlin, 1922), pp. 39ff.; J. Mejia, "Some Observations on Psalm 107," *BTB*, V (1975), pp. 56-66; J. W. Michaux, "Le chemin des sources du salut, Ps. 107 (106)," *BVC*, LXXXIII (1968), pp. 46-55; M. O'Connor, *Hebrew Verse Structure* (Winona Lake, Ind., 1980); L. Rabinowitz, "The Existence of a Hitherto Unknown Interpretation of Ps 107 among the Dead Sea Scrolls," *BA*, XIV (1951), pp. 50ff.; S. Sauneron, *Les fêtes religieuses d'Esna* (1962); F. Schneider, "Rettung aus Seenot: Ps 107,23-32 und Mk 4,35-41," in *Festschrift H. Gross* (Stuttgart, 1986), pp. 375-93; N. H. Snaith, [Psalm 107], *Five Psalms* (London, 1938); D. Winton Thomas, "Hebrew ['ani], 'Captivity,'" *JTS*, XVI (1965), pp. 444-45.

FORM

With a Prelude (vv. 1-3) and a Postlude (v. 43), this psalm might have been composed by a single poet. Yet it contains two different parts, Part One with refrains

(vv. 4-32) and Part Two without refrains (vv. 33-42). At the same time, the entire psalm deals with almost the same theme — the supremacy of Yahweh over nature — and both parts have a similar rhythm (3+3). The architecture and length of each part, however, are different. Part One contains four strophes of three substrophes each, and its refrains are placed at special spots, unlike other psalms with refrains (cf. Psalms 42–43; 46; 49; 56; 57; 59).

In Psalm 107 the refrains appear in I, vv. 6 and 8; II, vv. 13 and 15; III, vv. 19 and 21; IV, vv. 28 and 31. Moreover, Strophe IV contains an extra substrophe (vv. 25-27), apparently because the poet, unlike the Phoenicians, was in awe of seafarers.

In Part Two, the text contains two strophes; one is made up of two substrophes (vv. 33-35 and 36-39). The other strophe is much shorter than the first (vv. 40-42). Perhaps the Prelude and Postlude were sung by different artists and not by those who sang the body of the psalm. The Postlude, in addition, presents a sapiential affinity, which may indicate an editorial development.

It is not possible to demonstrate that Psalm 107 was a liturgy to be sung in a festive ceremony on an autumn holy day.

COMMENTARY

Prelude: Praise by the Redeemed of the Lord (vv. 1-3)

As in other hymns, the initial exclamation hails the goodness of Yahweh and addresses those who, having passed through mortal perils, are now God-saved. In addition, the Lord is to be praised for having reunited Jews from among the foreign nations of the four cardinal points of the world. The "south sea" is the Gulf of Aqaba, which widens into the Red Sea. The psalmist pleads for a geographical center at the rebuilt temple of Zion, but his horizon is worldwide.

Strophe I: Some Are Lost in the Desert (vv. 4-9)

The redeemed of the Lord include wanderers who lost their way in a trackless wilderness. God, who then led them by a direct route, will be celebrated for his faithfulness and for the miracles he has accomplished in their favor. The expression "the sons of Adam" is the literal equivalent of the Hebrew, which is often paraphrased into "the children of men." Allusion to the creation myth stresses the unity and diversity of the human race.

Strophe II: Others Are Sick and Sinful (vv. 10-16)

As often believed in ancient times, malady was viewed as a symptom of guilt. Those stricken with a terminal sickness were chained in dark cells. Crying to Yahweh, they were healed and delivered. Had they rebelled against the word of the Lord, their disease was entirely explainable, but their prayer received an answer. Good health and freedom were restored.

Strophe III: Still Others Became Mentally Ill (vv. 17-22)

A prolonged refusal of food, or *anorexia nervosa,* was already recognized as a mental ailment. A form of psychological pathology was not ignored by the ancient mind. Types of folly were attributed to immoral conduct. There is no reason for ruling out of the original text such a statement. Mental illness was here brought by Yahweh to mental sanity.

Strophe IV: Seafarers Risk Their Lives (vv. 25-32)

The story of the prophet Jonah illustrates the Hebraic apprehension of sailing through the high seas. Even when they did not cause perdition, Mediterranean tempests rendered the well-being of sailors most miserable. An extra sub-strophe (vv. 25-27) is required to describe their terror. This time the refrain invites a new expression of gratitude to the Lord. In truth, this group, back in safety, has seen real miracles (v. 24). Their thanksgiving will have to be repeated at people's festive assemblies and at elders' sessions.

Part Two, Strophes I and II: The Lord's Goodness (vv. 33-42)

A further description of the Lord's intervention in favor of the oppressed is told in the same style, without allusion to specific groups of men in peril. Dry land becomes the home of springs of water; agriculture feeds the hungry; human beings and animals multiply. When adversity strikes and princes are corrupt, the Lord of nature and history solves all the problems of existence (v. 41). There will be no reason for comments of protest against adversity.

Postlude: Sapiential Advice (v. 43)

The final expression of musical opportunity differs radically from that of the Prelude. It appeals to the remembrance of the Lord's gracious acts but it also encourages worshipers to "meditate on these things," presumably on the teaching implied in the models of the entire psalm. More unexpectedly, the psalmist makes this final appeal to "anyone who desires wisdom" — a surprising insertion from a sapiential psalmist!

DATE AND THEOLOGY

Perhaps the psalm with its refrains constituted a liturgy for pilgrims assembled from the four corners of the world (v. 3), and the invitation to thank and praise the Lord was made by the *ecclesia* of all the people present at this ceremony. The mention of such an assembly, together with "the sessions of the elders," indicates a postexilic date. Diaspora Judaism could travel freely throughout the Persian Empire.

The theology of the psalm arises from a reaffirmation of an ardent faith and successful supplications. The power of Yahweh manifests itself without obstacle in a world where all is well that ends well. There is no need to hint at the bewildering spectacle of unjustifiable evil. The problem of theodicy is totally absent. Singing thanksgiving is a sacrificial offering to the Lord of nature and history. The proximate and ultimate future is filled with "the graciousness of the Lord."

PSALM 108

I Shall Awaken the Dawn

1. *Song. Psalm of David.*

I

2.   *My heart is ready, O God!*
        I shall sing a hymn;
        I shall play my instruments: it is my glory!
3.   *Awake, my lute and my cither!*
        I shall awaken the dawn.
4.   *I shall praise thee, O Lord, among the peoples,*
        I shall celebrate thee among the nations.

5. For thy goodness is great above the heavens,
    And thy fidelity above the firmament.
6. Stand up above the heavens, O God,
    And let thy glory be over the whole earth!
7. Let thy beloved people be delivered!
    Save with thy right hand! Answer me!

II

8. God has spoken in his holiness:
    I triumph! I shall divide Shechem
    And survey the valley of Succoth;
9. Gilead is mine; Manasseh is mine;
    Ephraim is a helmet for my head,
    And Judah, my scepter.
10. Moab is the basin for my ablutions;
    Upon Edom I shall cast my sandal,
    And over Philistia I shall shout with joy!

11. Who will bring me to the fortified city?
    Who will lead me as far as Edom?
12. Will it be thou, O God, who hadst rejected us,
    Thou, the God who didst not go out with our armies?

13. Come, give us help against our foe,
    For vain is salvation from man;
14. With God we shall do deeds of valor;
    It is he who will trample over our foes.

BIBLIOGRAPHY

See bibliographies for Psalms 57 and 60. In addition: J. Becker, "Israel deutet seine Psalmen," *Stuttgarter Bibelstudien*, XVIII (1966), pp. 65ff.; S. Mowinckel, *Psalmenstudien*, III: *Kultprophetie and kultprophetische Psalmen* (Oslo, 1923), pp. 64ff.; idem, *The Psalms in Israel's Worship* (Nashville, 1962), I, pp. 81-105; C. R. North, "*'eloah 'ahalleqah shekhem*," *VT*, XVII (1976), pp. 242-45.

FORM

Psalm 108 is a copy, with slight alterations, of Ps 57:8-11 and Ps 60:4-12. Through this reedition, the form of Psalm 108 is different from that of the two fragments in Psalms 57 and 60. The new psalm is an individual prayer, with a divine oracle followed by a supplication for a military victory.

DATE AND THEOLOGY

The new prayer celebrates the Lord after, and also during, a military catastrophe. Perhaps the long struggle for the conquest of the land inspired the hymn of thanksgiving. The rather grotesque nationalism within a context of praise may partly be explained by the memory of a long insecurity.

Prayers of thanksgiving remember the darkness that prompted a new supplication for national deliverance. The date must remain uncertain. Even the postexilic situation was not uniformly favorable.

The theology of the piece remains traditionally Yahwistic.

PSALM 109

Supplication of a Persecuted Man

1. To the choirmaster. Psalm. Of David.

I

    O God of my praise, do not keep silent!
2.   *For a mouth of evil and a mouth of deceit*
    Are open against me,
       And speak with a lying tongue.
3.   *They have compassed me about with words of hatred,*
       And they have attacked me without cause.

4.   *In return for my love they accuse me,*
       But I have gone, myself, into prayer.
5.   *They have heaped on me evil for good,*
       And hatred for love.

II

6. Summon against him an evil man,
       And let him be his accuser when he stands trial!
7. May he be condemned when he shall be judged,
       Let his plea be counted as a sin!
8. May his days be few!
       Let another take his place!

9. May his children be fatherless,
       And his wife a widow!
10. Let his children wander about and beg!
       May they be mendicant, out of their ruins!

III

11. Let his creditor seize all that he has,
       And strangers plunder the fruit of his labor!
12. May there be none that has pity for him,
       Nor any to favor his orphan sons!
13. Let his posterity be cut short,
       And in the next generation let their names be blotted out!

14. May the Lord remember the guilt of his fathers,
       And let not the sin of his mother be blotted out!
15. Let them be constantly before the Lord,
       that their memory may vanish from the earth!

IV

16. Because this man did not remember to show mercy,
       And persecuted the poor and needy
       And even slew the broken in heart;
17. He loved to curse, so let curses be on him,
       For he delights not in blessing;
       Let it be far away from him,
18. Because he clothed himself with cursing as a garment,
       Let it come into his bowels like water,
       And like oil into his bones!

19. Let it be to him like a mantle,
       Or a girdle constantly too tight on him;
20. May this be the reward of my accusers,
       And of those who threaten my life.

V

21. *But thou, Lord, my Sovereign, thou wilt*
    Deal on my behalf for the sake of thy name!
    Because thy mercy means goodness, deliver me!
22. *For I am poor and needy,*
    And my heart is wounded within me;
23. *I am like the shadow when light declines;*
    I am tossed up and down, like a locust.

24. *My knees are weak from fasting,*
    And my body has become visibly gaunt.
25. *As for me, I am now an object of scorn;*
    When they look at me, people shake their head!

VI

26. *Succor me, Lord, my God!*
    O save me according to thy mercy!
27. *That they may know this is thy hand,*
    Thou, O Lord, thou hast done it.
28. *Though they should surely curse, yet thou wilt surely bless.*
    When they arise, let them be put to shame!
    But may thy servant rejoice!

29. *Let my foes be clothed in shame!*
    May they wrap themselves in dishonor as a mantle!
30. *I will greatly praise the Lord with my voice,*
    Yea, I will praise him in the multitude,
31. *[For he shall stand at the right hand of the poor,*
    to save him from those who would condemn him to death.]

BIBLIOGRAPHY

F. Baumgärtel, "Der 109. Psalm in der Verkündigung," *Monatsschrift für Pastoraltheologie*, XLII (1953), pp. 244-53; P. E. Bonnard, *Le Psautier selon Jérémie* (Paris, 1960), pp. 199-206; W. Brueggemann, "Psalm 109: "Three Times Steadfast Love," *Word and World*, V (1982), pp. 28-46; idem, "The Costly Loss of Lament," *JSOT*, XXXV (1986), pp. 57-71; W. Brueggemann and P. D. Miller, "Psalm 109: Steadfast Love and Social Solidarity," in *The Psalms and the Life of Faith* (Minneapolis, 1993), pp. 268-82; H. L. Creager, "Note on Ps. 109," *JNES*, VI (1947), pp. 121-22; G. R. Driver, "Note [on Psalm 109]," *ETL*, XXVI (1950), p. 147; P. Hesse, [Note on Psalm 109], in *Festschrift F. Baumgärtel* (Erlangen, 1959), pp. 274-96; P. Hugger, "'Das sei meiner Ankläger Lohn . . .'? Zur Deutung von Psalm 109,20," *BibLeb*, XIV (1973), pp. 105-12; M. Z.

Kaddary, "Note on Ps. 109:22 *ḥll*," *VT*, XIII (1963), pp. 486-89; E. J. Kissane, "The Interpretation of Psalm 109 (108) [*ḥorbag* = Palace]," *Irish Theological Quarterly*, XVIII (1951), pp. 1-8; T. Plassman, "A Note," *American Ecclesiastical Review*, CXVI (1947), pp. 452-55; N. H. Ridderbos, "Psalmen und Kult," in *The Bible and the Politics of Exegesis*, pp. 234-79; H. Schmidt, *Das Gebet der Angeklagten im Alten Testament*, BZAW XLIX (Giessen, 1928), pp. 40-55; idem, *Das Gebet . . .* (summary of 1928 work in *Zur neueren Psalterforschung*, ed. P. H. A. Newmann) (Darmstadt, 1976), pp. 156-67; A. Schultz, *Kritisches zum Psalter* (Münster in Westfalen, 1932), pp. 51ff.; G. T. Sheppard, "Enemies and the Politics of Prayer in the Book of Psalms," in *The Bible and the Politics of Exegesis*, Festschrift N. K. Gottwald, ed. D. Jobling, P. L. Day, and G. T. Sheppard (Cleveland, 1991), pp. 61-82; P. W. Skehan, E. Ulrich, and P. W. Flint, "A Scroll Containing 'Biblical' and 'Apocryphal' Psalms," *CBQ*, LX (1998), pp. 267-77; M. J. Ward, "Psalm 109: David's Poem of Vengeance," *Andrews University Seminary Studies*, XVIII (1980), pp. 163-68; D. P. Wright, "Ritual Analogy in Psalm 109," *JBL*, CXIII (1994), pp. 385-404.

FORM

The chief peculiarity of this psalm lies in a contradiction between its strophic structure, usually used for hymns, and its thematic content, which is that of a complaint.

The symmetry is spectacular: there are five strophes, each of two substrophes of three and two bicola respectively; a sixth strophe appears to have a final substrophe of three bicola instead of two (vv. 29-31), but the final bicolon (v. 31) did not belong to the original poem, for it is a third person reflection presumably written by an early copyist.

The meter is extremely irregular (from 3+2; 3+3; to 4+3; and 4+4), perhaps due to the emotional disturbance of the persecuted poet, who has been falsely accused of serious crimes.

COMMENTARY

Strophe I: Prayer to a Silent God (vv. 1b-5)

The supplication does not immediately petition for help; it invokes the Lord as "God of my praise." Certain commentators translate, "The Lord is my glory" (cf. Deut 10:21; Jer 17:14). In any case, the eloquence of the invocation clearly indicates a long intimacy between the poet and his God. The singer not only asks for help, but his indignation against false accusation begs for immediate succor.

Strophes II and III: A Trial with Corrupted Judges (vv. 6-15)

From the attacks of adversaries, in the plural, suddenly the singular appears: Does this suggest that a mouthpiece for all the foes, an individual accuser, will speak at the session of the tribunal? Several exegetes have suggested that the psalmist did not curse his main foe with such cruelty, but that he was quoting the attacks that were directed against him: the plot of murder, that of his descendants, and the elimination of his name (cf. LXX, Vulg.) from the memory of future generations.

Strophe IV: Curses and Countercurses (vv. 16-20)

According to this interpretation, the psalmist continues to describe the indictment that will be spoken against him. However, the identity of those who curse is not clear. There is no indication that those barbarous threats are quotations from others rather than statements of the poet. Moreover, one should not forget that other psalmists have spoken most harshly of their enemies (cf. Psalms 35 and 38).

More especially, against the malignity of his adversaries Jeremiah replied with violent and even brutal reaction, "They said, Come, let us plot against Jeremiah! . . . May we kill him with our tongue . . ." (Jer 18:18). And the prophet continues, in a prayer with an unusual asperity of request, "Listen to me, Yahweh! Hear the voice of my foes! Should evil be returned for good? . . . Remember I have taken a stand before thee to speak in their favor. . . . Therefore deliver his children to famine. . . . Let their wives be deprived of children, and let them become widows!" (Jer 18:21; cf. Ps 109:9). Is the psalmist's vituperation, though distasteful to moderns, out of place?

In any case, are the arguments intended to support the hypothesis of a long quotation, by the psalmist, of an indictment against him, convincing? (a) If the enemies are now represented in court by a single prosecutor, does it imply an entirely different context? (b) Do vv. 2-5 and 20 imply that vv. 6-19, in which the psalmist laments the evil tactics of his enemies, constitute the equivalent of an open and closed quotation around vv. 6-19? Was not Jeremiah supposed to have said, in prayer, "Listen, Yahweh, and hear the voice of my adversaries, should evil be rendered for good?" (Jer 18:20; cf. Ps 109:6)? (c) A masculine designation of an evil foe (v. 16) does not necessarily suggest that Strophes III and IV (vv. 11-20) are cited by the psalmist as his own indictment. (d) Verse 21, beginning with "But thou," is indeed similar to many other uses of the same apostrophe in a lament, and does not necessarily mark the termination of the quotation (vv. 6-20). (e) A prayer asking God to summon an evil man as an accuser is not incongruous if the psalmist is attacking his adversaries to defend himself.

Jeremiah is represented as being the target of plots (Jer 11:18–12:6; 18:18; cf. 15:15-21), and such a plot was fomented by priests, wise men, and prophets, quite a different crowd, it may be surmised, from the psalmist's foes.

Strophe V: Prayer for Deliverance (vv. 21-25)

The supplication is renewed to Yahweh as "my Sovereign." This prayer is more pressing than the original request (v. 2). The whole psalm rests on the belief that Yahweh is the master of "mercy." This word has a wide range of significations[1] from faithfulness and steadfast love to compassion, fidelity, and pity. Mercy is the divine reality in which the psalmist is living. He now begs for this mercy with an unprecedented intensity. To plead his cause not only in court but especially before God with the most pressing ardor, he now places in balance God's mercy, which is goodness, and his own poverty, his need, his pierced heart (vv. 21-23).

It will be noted that this miserable man, at the extremity of his terror, will not perpetrate vengeance by acting violently toward his accuser. Rather, he asks his loving God to use his justice in order to avenge his servant. The new prayer is unexpected, but it emerges from the deepest confidence that this man projects on his God.

Strophe VI: The Ultimate Cry for Salvation (vv. 26-31)

The supplication reaches its climax with the call for *"Au secours!"* And it precedes the begging *in extremis,* "Save me!" The demand now turns to a surprising subject: the reputation of God. The enemies will look at the psalmist's deliverance as a revelation of God's most unsuspected characteristic: his mercy (v. 27). Invoking salvation and receiving it as a gift from heaven, the psalmist discerns that this will become the preaching of a "gospel": the Good News or "God's spell": God loves man. Yet divine blessing may only seal the curse of man (v. 28). Shame would be a mantle of strangulation, while the psalmist, now saved, will sing a hymn of praise and thanks. Chanted gratitude transforms the lament into the promise of a hymn.

Even the concluding reflection (v. 31), which refers to the psalmist in the third person singular, rehearses Israel's constant concern for the poor, the needy, the pierced heart.

---

1. N. Glueck, *Ḥesed in the Bible* (Cincinnati, 1967); K. Sakenfeld, *The Meaning of Ḥesed in the Hebrew Bible* (Missoula, Mont., 1978).

DATE AND THEOLOGY

The similarity of themes and even the identity of vocabulary display remarkable affinities between this psalm and the Jeremianic circle, perhaps with the prophet Jeremiah himself. However, complaints against enemies were common. Affinities do not necessarily demonstrate that Psalm 109 was directly influenced by the sayings of Jeremiah or those of his disciples. At the same time, the date of its composition could hardly be earlier than the last years of the kingdom of Judah, and might even be around early Judaism in Persian times.

While the persecuted individual did not seek to avenge himself upon the menacing mortals who confronted him, he implored Yahweh, the Lord of justice, to attack his adversaries in the most virulent manner. Human imprecations may be rendered null and void by the God of righteousness, Such an appeal to Yahweh is "clothed" with such ire that, at this instant in the unfolding of the poem, justice may overcome love. Let the scoundrels render evil for good (v. 5). A true devotee of a God of mercy may still ask for the annihilation, not only of his accuser but also of this man's family, with a venom comparable to that of his enemies.

It is here that the theology of the cross might and should intervene. The supplication of authentic Christianity — not, alas, of historical Christendom, neither ecclesiastical nor sectarian — must remain, "Father, forgive them, for they know not what they do" (Luke 23:34). In spite of the violence of his words, produced by his fear and even his terror, the psalmist prays with a supreme confidence. The man's faith at length overcomes his language. The probability and proximity of his death may stretch spirituality to an unfortunate extreme, but it remains unshakable when it declares oracularly, as in the Song of Moses (Deut 32:35), "Vengeance is mine and retribution, . . . for the Lord will vindicate his people . . . and will have mercy on his servants."

The words attributed to Jesus went even further: "Love your enemies, and pray for those who persecute you" (Rom 8:33; 12:19; Heb 10:30).

By placing himself in the ranks of the poor, the needy, and those whose heart has been pierced, the poet of Psalm 109 entered the Hebraic ideal of society that "subverts hatred" by appealing to divine mercy.[2]

---

2. J. Milgrom, "Let Your Love for Me Vanquish Your Hatred: Nonviolence in Modern Judaism," in *Subserving Hatred: The Challenge of Non-Violence in Religious Traditions* (Boston, 1998), pp. 115-39; D. Smith-Christopher, "Political Atheism and Radical Faith: The Challenge of Christian Non-violence in the Third Millennium," in *Subserving Hatred*, pp. 141-65.

PSALM 110

Eternal Priest from Melchizedek

1. *Psalm. Of David.*

I

> Oracle of the Lord to my Lord:
>> Sit down at my right
> Until I make thine enemies
>> A stool for thy feet.

2.   The Lord shall send forth from Zion
>> The scepter of thy power;
>> Rule in the midst of thine enemies.

3.   Thy people will offer themselves freely
>> In the day when thou takest power;
>> In holy splendor from the womb of the dawn,
>> The dew of thy youth will be thine!

II

4.   The Lord has sworn and he will not recant:
>> Thou art a priest forever
>> In the order of Melchizedek!

5.   The Lord will stand at thy right hand;
>> He will shatter kings on the day of his wrath.

6.   He will carry out his verdict among the nations;
>> Those will be full of corpses;
>> And he will shatter their chiefs in the wide earth!

7.   He will drink from the brook along the way,
>> Then he will lift up his head.

BIBLIOGRAPHY

P. Auffret, "Note sur la structure littéraire du Psaume CX," *Semitica*, XXXII (1982), pp. 83-88; J. Becker, "Zur Deutung von Ps 110,7," in *Festschrift H. Gross* (Stuttgart, 1988), pp. 17-32; J. W. Bowker, "Psalm CX," *VT*, XVII (1967), pp. 31-41; W. P. Brown, "A Royal Performance: Critical Notes on Psalm 110:3a-b," *JBL*, CXVII (1998), pp. 93-96; E. Burrows, *The Gospel of the Infancy and Other Essays* (1941); A. Caquot, "Remarques sur le Psaume CX," *Semitica*, VI (1956), pp. 33-62; J. Coppens, "La portée messianique du

Psaume 110," *Analecta Lovianiensia biblica et orientalia,* III (1956), pp. 5-23; idem, "Trois Parallèles ougaritiens du Psautier: Ps. 110, 6b et Ps. 82,7," *ETL,* XXIII (1947), pp. 173-90; J. de Fraine, "L'aspect religieux de la royauté israélite," *Analecta biblica* (1954); J. de Savignac, "Essai d'interprétation du Psaume CX à l'aide de la littérature égyptienne," *OtSt,* IX (1951), pp. 105-35; G. R. Driver, "Psalm CX — Its Form, Meaning, and Purpose," in *Studies in the Bible,* XVII (Jerusalem, 1964), pp. 17-31; L. Dürr, *Psalm 110 im Lichte der neueren altorientalische Forschung* (Münster, 1929/30); J. A. Fitzmyer, "Melchizedek in the MT, LXX, and the NT," *Bib,* LXXXI (2000), pp. 63-69; J. G. Gammie, "A New Setting for Ps 110," *Anglican Theological Review,* LI (1969), pp. 4-17; G. Gerleman, "Psalm CX," *VT,* XXXI (1981), pp. 1-49; M. Gourges, *A la Droite de Dieu: Résurrection de Jesus et actualisation du Psaume 110:1 dans le Nouveau Testament* (Paris, 1979); M. M. Gourgues, "Lecture christologique du Psaume CX et la fête de la Pentecôte," *RB,* LXXXIII (1976), pp. 5-24; J. Gray, "Canaanite Kingship in Theory and Practice," *VT,* II (1952), pp. 193-220; E. R. Hardy, "The Date of Psalm 110," *JBL,* LXIV (1945), pp. 385-90; D. M. Hay, *Glory at the Right Hand: Psalm 110 in Early Christianity,* SBLMS XVIII (Nashville, 1973); H. Herkenne, "Psalm 110/109 — Dixit Dominus domino meo," *Bib,* XI (1930), pp. 450-57; S. Herrmann, "Die Königsnovelle in Ägypten und in Israel," *Wissenschaft Zeitschrift... Leipzig,* III (1953-54), pp. 51-62; K. Homburg, "Psalm 110, im Rahmen des jüdäischen Krönungszeremoniells," *ZAW,* LXXXIV (1972), pp. 243-46; H. L. Jansen, "Den 110. Psalmen," *Svensk teologisk kvartalschrift,* XVI (Lund, 1940), pp. 263-76; H. G. Jefferson, "Is Psalm 110 Canaanite?" *JBL,* LXXIII (1954), pp. 152-56; J. Jelito, "Tu es sacerdos in aeternum," *Ruch Biblijny,* III (1950), pp. 351-64; A. R. Johnson, "Hebrew Conception of Kingship," in *Myth, Ritual and Kingship,* ed. S. H. Hooke (Oxford, 1958), pp. 204-35; idem, *Sacral Kingship in Ancient Israel* (Cardiff, 1955); R. Kilian, "Der 'Tau' in Psalm 110,3 — Ein Missverständnis?" *ZAW,* CII (1990), pp. 417-19; E. Kissane, "The Interpretation of Psalm 110," *Irish Theological Quarterly,* XXI (1954), pp. 103-14; L. Köhler, "Vier Marginalien," *ZAW,* LXIV (1952), p. 196; L. Kunz, "Psalm 110 in massoretischer Darbietung," *Theologie und Glaube,* LXXII (1982), pp. 331-35; M. G. Maurice and S. Pisano, "Ps 110 (109)," *Bib,* LXI (1980), pp. 343-46; H. E. Medico, "Melchisédech," *ZAW,* LXIX (1957), pp. 160-70; R. Möller, "Der Textzusammenhang in Ps 110)," *ZAW,* XCII (1980), pp. 343-58; P. Nober, "De torrente in via bibet — nota ugariticani VT *(drk — regnum),*" *VD,* XXVI (1948), pp. 351-53; E. Podechard, "Psalm 110," in *Études de critique et d'histoire religieuse* (Louvain, 1949), pp. 7-24; A. Rebié, "Psalm 110: Zur Bedeutung von 'Sedet ad dexteram Patris' im AT," *International kirchliche Zeitschrist Communio,* XIII (1884), pp. 14-17; H. Ringgren, "König und Messias," *ZAW,* LXIV (1952), pp. 125-47; M. T. Rondeau, "Le commentaire des Psaumes de Diodore de Tarse et l'exégèse antique du Psaume 109/110," *RHR,* CLXXVI (1969), pp. 1-33; H. H. Rowley, "Melchisedek and David," *VT,* XVII (1976), p. 485; idem, "Melchizedek and Zadok (Gen 14 and Ps 110)," in *Festschrift A. Bertholet* (Tübingen, 1950), pp. 461-72; C. Schedel, "Aus dem Bach am Wege," *ZAW,* LXXIII (1961), pp. 280-97; J. Schildenberger, "Psalm 109 (110): Christus König und Priester," *Bened. Mischr.* (1938), pp. 361-74; W. H. Schmidt, "Kritik am Königtum," in *Festschrift G. von Rad* (München, 1971), pp. 440-61; S. Schreiner, "Psalm CX und die Investitur des Hohenpriesters," *VT,* XXVII (1977), pp. 216-22; A. Schuldenberger, "Der Königs-psalm 110," *Erbe und Auftrag*, LVI (1989), pp. 53-59; A. Schulz, *Kritisches zum Psalter* (Münster in Westfalen, 1932), pp. 53ff.; G. Sisto, "Exegesis Psalmi 110/109," *VD*, X (1930), pp. 169-75, 201-10; H. J. Stoebe, "Erwägungen zu Psalm 110 auf dem Hintergrund von 1 S 21," in *Festschrift F. Baumgärtel* (Erlangen, 1959), pp. 175-91; R. J. Tournay, "Notes sur les Psaumes," *RB*, LII (1945), pp. 214-23; idem, "Le Psaume CX," *RB*, LXVII (1960), pp. 5-41; W. van der Meer, "Psalm 110: A Psalm of Rehabilitation?" in W. van der Meer and J. C. de Moor, *Analysis of Biblical and Canaanite Poetry* (Sheffield, 1988), pp. 207-34; T. C. Vriezen, "Psalm 110," *Vox theologica*, XV (1944), pp. 81-85; S. Wagner, "Das Reich des Messias: Zur Theologie der alttestamentlichen Königspsalmen," *TLZ*, CIX (1984), pp. 865-71; G. Widengren, "Psalm 110 och det sacrala Kungadömet i Israel," *Urkunden des ägyptischen Altertums*, VII (1941).

FORM

This poem is composed of two strophes, each of which is divided into two substrophes of two or three bicola. The last substrophe (v. 7) contains only one bicolon, perhaps because it concludes the psalm with an unexpected and cryptic statement on the hero for whom it is composed. While the structure is relatively simple, the meter is unusually complex (3+2; 4+3; 2+2+3+3; 3+2; 3+3; 4+2+2; 3+3). In addition, syntactic obscurities at times render the meaning unclear.

Some exegetes have proposed two parallel structures, extremely precise, that overlap each other: for example, one concentric over one sequential,[1] or one inner and the other outer.[2] It is doubtful that a psalmist would have consciously created such overlapping symmetry. One should not forget that the psalms were composed to be sung, partly in solo voice and partly in choral ensemble. Structures had to be simple and readily grasped by the singers. The form had to be memorized as a guide before it appeared in a written text.

COMMENTARY

Strophe I: The Lord's Oracle (vv. 1-3)

The expression "oracle of the Lord," spoken at the beginning of a sentence, is found only here in the Hebrew Bible. It appears in Deutero-Isaiah at the end of a whole poem (Isa 56:8; cf. Num 24:3, 4, 15, 16). In this psalm it introduces, in solemn tone, a declaration, possibly of an ecstatic or parapsychic nature, a liter-

---

1. Auffret, "Note sur la structure," pp. 982-83.
2. Kunz, "Psalm 110," p. 334.

ary gem of only five words. The psalmist sings as a prophet, and repeats a message from God to a human sovereign. The whole sequence following presupposes that the sovereign is new, and the word "Zion" indicates that he will be king of Judah.

The invitation for a monarch to sit at the right hand of the Lord is momentous and even stupendous for the Hebrew mind, but it was doubtlessly borrowed from the foreign nations of the ancient Near East. The imagery does not necessarily indicate that Yahweh is cultically represented by the ark, in the innermost hall of the temple (cf. 1 Sam 4:4; 1 Kgs 8:6). The metaphor, however, suggests an exceptional degree of intimacy between God and the new monarch. When he is victorious over his enemies, these will be used as a footstool for the triumphant victor. He then will receive the royal scepter. Similar language was common among the Sumerians, the Assyrians, the Babylonians, the Canaanites, and the Egyptians.

The oracle is at first sung as a quotation of the Lord, but it soon shifts as a reflection from the prophet-singer-psalmist.

The translation "freely" is uncertain. The word is used here as a noun in the plural of majesty. It may allude to something noble (cf. Job 30:16; Isa 13:2). Nobility is not usually the privilege of an elite of chiefs and princes. The new king, as a descendant of David, was born in splendor, not just "adopted as the son of God" (cf. Ps 2:7). He will now appear in wondrous circumstances, poetically described as "the womb of dawn" (cf. Isa 14:12), with a youthfulness compared to a flower or a tree covered with "dew" (v. 3cd). Syntactical links are absent, and this translation represents a likely conjecture, although the mention of dawn connotes sunrise and the marvel of the birth of day (cf. Luke 1:78).

Strophe II: From Kingship to an Eternal Priesthood (vv. 4-7)

An extraordinary change occurs in the second strophe: the human sovereign is not only to triumph as a military commander but he will also be "a priest forever," according to the unique order of Melchizedek. The Hebrew notion of priesthood was ancient but apparently foreign in its origin.

Egyptian priests are mentioned in the patriarchal stories (Gen 46:20; 47:22, 26), and young Moses apparently married a daughter of Jethro, who was the priest of Midian (Exod 2:16; cf. 3:1; 18:1). In Hebrew traditions, priests came near to Yahweh but had to consecrate themselves (Exod 19:22; cf. v. 24), and nothing is told about their sacerdotal tenure. It seems that the Levites fulfilled priestly functions after the awful apostasy of the golden calf (Exod 32:29). Traditions on the covenant speak of Israel as "a people of priests" (Exod 19:6): the plural noun is clearly used to indicate that the chosen nation, as a whole, is called to be a collective agency of intermediacy with the nations of the earth. Even after the entrance into the Promised Land, the "blessing of Moses" represents priests as teachers of the law, as well as ministers of the Urim and Thummim (Deut 33:8). In due course the priests chiefly offered sacrifices on behalf of the "laity" and occupied a middle echelon, in the clerical hierarchy of "high priest and Levite."

The oracle of Psalm 110 sets the king apart from ordinary priesthood. The Lord has taken a solemn oath, irreversible, that the new monarch would be "priest forever in the order of Melchizedek." Nothing else is told of this priestly order in the entire Hebrew Bible. "Forever" may not mean literally "eternally," but "for a long time" or even "life duration."[3] Melchizedek is known as "king of Salem," a city identified with Jerusalem (Josh 18:21). The name Melchizedek is most probably Canaanite (cf. Adoni-zedek and Abi-melek). As "priest of the Most High," he blessed Abraham, whom the Most High had delivered from all enemies; and Abraham apparently "gave Melchizedek a tenth of everything" (Gen 14:20). The priestly order that the psalmist had in mind remains mysterious: its "eternal" quality suggests a tradition of high spirituality that has not been preserved elsewhere by the ancient Hebrews. The early Christians seized the opportunity to apply the name to the status of the Messiah (Matt 22:44; passim).

An eschatological interpretation of this entire motif may already have been implied by the poet: Why should a king, a beneficiary of Yahweh's victories, be named as the eternal priest of the special order of Melchizedek? And why should the final bicolon (v. 7) stress, at the climax of the psalm, a physical act of "drinking from the brook along the way," the explicit cause of his lifting up the head? Is the psalm composed for an autumn festival when rain had failed after the drought of summer? We do not know.

Some exegetes have thought that the ceremonial enthronement of a new monarch in the temple of Zion would be terminated by a ritual drink of water at the spring of the Gihon, which precisely flows near the hill of the sanctuary. Such an interpretation is possible, but identifying clues are missing. Do we have here a mystical or sacramental rite?

The sentence in the future tense, "he will lift up his head," comes at the very end of the psalm in the Hebrew text, and is articulated with the verb "he will drink" in the singular. The precise and emphatic "therefore" implies a relation of cause and effect. The gesture of raising one's head, which elsewhere accompanies an acknowledgment of success and even military triumph, is here the direct result of drinking from the brook along the way.

The Gihon is not only a local spring at the base of a sacred hill (1 Kgs 1:33;

3. E. Jenni, "Das Wort *'olam* im Alten Testament," *ZAW*, LXIV (1952), p. 237.

cf. 2 Chr 32:30), a place associated with the anointing of King Solomon (1 Kgs 1:34), but also one of the rivers of Eden (Gen 2:13). Could it be that the final position of this bicolon, forming an entire substrophe that crowns the whole psalm, calls for an extended meaning of its cryptic significance?

DATE AND THEOLOGY

Even if the poem, which was set to music like any other psalm (see superscription, v. 1), is interpreted as a hymn for the ceremony of a royal enthronement, its mysterious elements require a wider and more inclusive explanation. The mention of Zion makes the date post-Davidic and separates it from the tradition of a Mosaic and Aaronic priesthood. The double status of king and priest could no longer apply to that of the Hasmoneans, especially John Hyrcanus and Alexander Jannaeus (1 Macc 14:41; cf. *Testament of the Twelve Patriarchs, Testament of Levi* 6–7).[4] The LXX shows that the Hebrew text of the psalm was already firmly established.[5] The Davidic dynasty was declared victorious against the nations of the world, and the poetic allusions to the hero of the psalm ("holy splendor," "the womb of the dawn," "the dew of youth") suggest legendary hyperbole in the vision of Yahweh at the end of history. Since the psalmist is a prophet, he adopts an oracular style, not unlike that of the sayings of Second Isaiah, "Thus speaks Yahweh to his anointed one, whom he holds by the hand, and he will throw down the nations before him" (Isa 45:1-2).[6] To be sure, unlike Second Isaiah, he does not refer to Cyrus.

Here Yahweh triumphs over the nations. While his hero, at once monarch and priest after the order of Melchizedek, is not called "my Anointed One," he became the most potent ferment of hope for both Judaism and Christianity.

---

4. P. W. Flint, *The Dead Sea Scrolls and the Book of Psalms* (Leiden, 1997), p. 128.

5. Psalm 110 may have been composed with such care that each of its two strophes contains 74 syllables, according to D. N. Freedman, cited in M. Dahood, *Psalms 101–150* (Garden City, N.Y., 1970), p. 113.

6. Hay, *Glory at the Right Hand*, pp. 19-33, 34-51.

PSALM 111

Praise for the Lord of Wonders

I

1. *Hallelujah!*

	Aleph	*I will praise the Lord with all my heart,*
	Beth	*In the congregation of the upright and the assembly.*
2.	Gimel	*Great are the works of the Lord!*
	Daleth	*They are sought by all those who delight in them.*
3.	Hê	*Splendor and majesty, these are his deeds!*
	Waw	*And his righteousness will endure forever.*
4.	Zayin	*He made a memorial for his wonders;*
	Heth	*Merciful and compassionate is the Lord.*
5.	Ṭeth	*He gave food to those who fear him;*
	Yodh	*He remembers his covenant forever.*

II

6.	Kaph	*He showed the power of his works to his people;*
	Lamedh	*He gave them the inheritance of foreign nations.*
7.	Mêm	*The works of his hands are faithful and just.*
	Nûn	*All his commandments are trustworthy;*
8.	Ṣamekh	*They are a source of strength forever and ever,*
	Ayin	*To be performed with truthfulness and rectitude.*
9.	Peh	*He sent a ransom for his people;*
	Sadhê	*He established his covenant forever.*
	Qôph	*Holy and full of reverence is his name.*
10.	Resh	*The fear of the Lord is the beginning of wisdom!*
	Shîh	*Those who practice it understand what is good.*
	Taw	*His praise will endure forever.*

BIBLIOGRAPHY

P. Auffret, "Essai sur la structure littéraire des Psaumes CXI et CXII," *VT*, XXX (1980), pp. 257-64; J. Becker, *Gottesfurcht im Alten Testament* (Rome, 1965); O. Grether, *Name und Wort Gottes im Alten Testament*, BZAW LXIV (Giessen, 1934); D. Pardee, "Acrostics and Parallelism: The Parallelistic Structure of Psalm 111," in *Memorial S. Gevirtz* (Rollins Estates Hills, Calif., 1993), pp. 117-38; J. J. Stamm, *Erlösen und Vergeben im Alten Testament* (Bern, 1940); G. von Rad, *Wisdom in Israel* (London, 1972), pp. 66ff.;

H.-W. Wolff, "Psalm 111," in *Herr, tue meine Lippen auf,* Bd. 5.2, ed. G. Eichholz (Wuppertal, 1961), pp. 251-57; W. Zimmerli, *Zwillingspsalmen: Studien zur alttestamentlichen Theologie und Prophetie,* Gesammelte Aufsätze, II (Munich, 1974), pp. 261-71.

FORM

The text of this psalm is an acrostic poem covering the 22 letters of the Hebrew alphabet, in 11 bicola. This was probably a sign of elegance as well as a mnemonic device for community singing during pilgrimages. This structure was borrowed from the Canaanites, for it appears in the Ugaritic texts.[1] Such a rigidity of form entailed a certain artificiality of style, in the multiplicity of the themes mentioned but not developed.

One may probably discern in Psalm 111 a structure of two strophes, each of which comprehends two substrophes of two and three bicola. The first strophe introduces the pleasure evoked by the marvelous works of the Lord (vv. 1-2), the greatest of which is the covenant (vv. 4-5). The second strophe finds the wonderful power of this covenant (vv. 6-10).

The meter shows the relative importance of the themes succinctly listed. In the first strophe the meter is moderately subdued (3+3; 3+2; 3+3; 3+3). In the second strophe emphasis is laid on the benefits of the covenant, the inheritance of land from the nations, the certitude issued by the commandments, and the beginning of wisdom (4+4; 4+2; 3+3; 3+2; 3+4; 3+3).

The last substrophe (vv. 9-10) has three bicola (vv. 9-10) on account of the number of letters in the Hebrew alphabet.

COMMENTARY

Strophe I: The Remembrance of God's Wonders (vv. 1-5)

This hymn of praise and memorial, by an individual singer who may have led a pilgrimage, begins with a promise to celebrate with his whole heart. Does he hint at the resolution of some personal crisis? Or is this an echo of a liturgical litany, "Thou shalt love the Lord thy God with all thy heart" (Deut 6:5)? Either supposition is possible for the closed congregation before which he plans at first to sing his hymn in an intimate, perhaps even secret, circle (an unusual

1. On the Ugaritic alphabet, see W. F. Albright, "Alphabetic Origins of the Idrimi Statue," *BASOR,* CXVIII (1950), pp. 1-20; idem, "The Origin of the Alphabet and the Ugaritic ABC Again," *BASOR,* CXIX (1950), pp. 23-25; S. A. Speiser, "A Note on Alphabetic Origins," *BASOR,* CXXI (1951), pp. 17-21.

designation of a community of worshipers), because it is repeated before a large assembly (*synagogē* in the LXX).

The wonders of God's works are observed and perhaps discerned only by those who "delight" in them (v. 2). Divine splendor and majesty reflect the wonders of both nature and history. The covenant, mentioned at the end of the first substrophe (v. 5), is subtly announced at its beginning (v. 4).

The giving of food (Hebrew, "prey") probably refers to the manna in the desert of Sinai (cf. Exod 12:14). That Yahweh "remembers his covenant forever" (v. 5) is a declaration that does not include its conditionality, and therefore its violation by Israel (Exod 19:5; cf. Jer 31:32). The ambiguity of the sentence, with its insistence on "memorial" (v. 4) and "forever" (v. 5), suggests that the psalmist may silently agree to passing from the Mosaic to the Davidic and even Abrahamic covenants, which are unconditional and therefore mythical in the sense of "suprahistorical."

Strophe II: The Lord's Power (vv. 6-10)

It seems that the poet may have qualified an implication of suprahistorical and supraethical nationalism. Although he considered the conquest of Canaan as a gift from the Lord even if that conquest entailed bloody conflict with the nations that Israel invaded and dispossessed (v. 6), nevertheless he also immediately hails the Law of the Lord as a wonder of his work. There can be neither compromise nor any legalistic interpretation of the commandments of Yahweh: they must be fulfilled "with truthfulness and rectitude" (v. 8). Election anticipates and requires morality. The gift of the land is a wonder that may not be divorced from ethical living.

The succinctness of his catechism notwithstanding, the psalmist has accepted obedience to standards of righteousness and solidarity. The poor, the needy, the widows, and the orphans are not mentioned, but when Yahweh "redeemed" the Hebrews from Egyptian slavery, he expected gratitude at the level of tribal seminomadism. The deeds of wonder call for justice in society (v. 7).

A theology of the name (v. 10), which includes reverence for holiness in daily living, is not the same as a theology of glory, which originally implied cultic ritual and "the holy of holies." Reverence for the name leads to holiness in time and space, for it brings obedience in daily living. Thus the résumé of a theology of the name ends with the sapiential motto on wisdom and the fear of Yahweh. In this context, fear is not to be confused with terror of divine judgment. It points to the marvels of love. The word "love" is absent, but, like the pre-Islamic Arabs, the ancient Hebrews knew that a lover "fears" to displease.

The psalm ends as if the "delight" of the first strophe becomes the fear of the Lord, the fear to displease him. The sapiential conclusion (v. 10ab) comments on the well-known proverb with a reflection on the results of practical wisdom; those who practice it (lit., "those who make it happen") obtain a psychological faculty often absent from those who are not sages: they are unable to understand the meaning of goodness and to discern what is good.

The usual rendering of this logion, both in the ancient versions and the modern translations, is the rather flat cliché, "a good understanding," considering a substantive qualified by an epithetic adjective. Yet the Hebrew may very well be viewed as a noun in the construct state, followed by the noun for "what is good." The deeper meaning of "good" is often beyond easy discernment. Wisdom, at its beginning, may have to distinguish between two levels of goodness, so that a sage, after a total review of Israel's vision of the divine wonders, will be capable of perceiving the better behavior in private morality and in social ethics.

A final note on the chanting of praise permits the poet to cover the 22 letters of the Hebrew alphabet for the acrostic form of the psalm.

DATE AND THEOLOGY

The multiple glances at the marvels of God's work in nature and history pass over the national debacles. Because of the psalmist's apparent intention to praise the Lord in both a small "chapel" of devotees and in a large assembly hall, we may have here a product of Persian Judaism.

It has been suggested that Psalm 111 was composed for an autumn festival celebrating the covenant. If, however, the acrostic form points to a pilgrimage, it is probable that memory and the memorial (vv. 4-5, 9) allude to the exodus, when Moses said to the people, "Remember that day when you came out of Egypt, from the house of servitude, for it was with his powerful hand that Yahweh made you leave it" (Exod 13:3). Observe these amazing affinities with Ps 111:4, 5, 6, and 7.

If this psalm was composed for the Passover, the earliest Christians, who were Jewish and ate the Passover meal before the crucifixion and the rebirth of Jesus in their visions of the risen Christ, adopted the motif of "redemption" from Egypt by singing Ps 111:9. They spoke of the Passover as the feast that was later called "Easter," as the birth of life, the birth of the new man, delivered from sin and from the fear of death.

Significantly, the motif of God's righteousness, in the first strophe of the psalm, becomes in the last strophe "His praise will endure forever" (v. 10c). It is because those who practice wisdom will be able to understand the deeper meaning of "goodness."

The movement throughout the psalm may provide another element of theological evolution. The power of God's works in nature and in history, his holiness, and a full reverence for his name, "He who causes to be," become the source of a new power: weakness and even death will lead to a new form of strength (v. 8). Easter is the folly of wisdom (1 Cor 1:27).

PSALM 112

The Happiness of the Righteous Man

1. *Hallelujah!*

I

	Aleph	*Happy is the man who fears the Lord,*
	Beth	*Who delights greatly in his commandments,*
2.	Gimel	*His posterity shall be heroic on earth;*
	Daleth	*The generation of the godly shall be blessed!*
3.	Hê	*Wealth and riches shall be in his house,*
	Waw	*And his righteousness shall stand forever.*
4.	Zayin	*A light arises from darkness on [his] uprightness.*
	Heth	*[He shall be] gracious, compassionate, and just.*
5.	Teth	*The goodness of man makes him gracious, and he lends;*
	Yodh	*He conducts his affairs with discretion.*

II

6.	Kaph	*Surely he shall never be moved;*
	Lamedh	*The righteous shall be remembered forever.*
7.	Mem	*He shall not be afraid of evil tidings;*
	Nun	*His heart is fixed, trusting in the Lord;*
8.	Samekh	*With a firm heart, he fears nothing;*
	Ayin	*He can look down upon his enemies.*
9.	Peh	*He gives lavishly to the poor;*
	Sadheh	*His rectitude shall last forever;*
	Qoph	*His pride rises up in honor.*
10.	Resh	*The evil man sees it and is enraged;*
	Shin	*He gnashes his teeth and collapses;*
	Taw	*The desires of the evil man come to nought.*

BIBLIOGRAPHY

P. Auffret, "Essai sur la structure littéraire des Psaumes CXI et CXII," *VT*, XXX (1980), pp. 257-64; C. Barth, *Die Errettung vom Tode in den individuellen Klage- und Dankliedern des Alten Testaments* (Zollikon, 1947); G. Bornkamm, "Der Lohngedanke im Neuen Testament," *EvT* (1946), pp. 143-66; S. Mowinckel, "Marginalien zur hebräischen Metrik," *ZAW*, LXVIII (1956), pp. 97-123.

FORM

Like Psalm 111, Psalm 112 is an acrostic poem. Each half of the ten verses begins with a word whose initial letter follows from *Aleph* to *Taw*. Probably Psalm 112 was meant to be a sequel to Psalm 111. Both of them may have been parts of pilgrimage litanies. The first was to praise the wonders of Yahweh's work in nature and in history. The second celebrates the happiness of the righteous man, who is blessed by the Lord. A sharp warning to the scoundrel concludes the celebration of the upright man.

Both psalms contain thematic and even verbal similarities: "delight" (v. 1; cf. Ps 111:1); "the godly" (v. 2; cf. Ps 111:2); "righteousness stands forever" (v. 3; cf. Ps 111:3); "compassionate ... just" (v. 4; cf. Ps 111:4); "fixed" (v. 8; cf. Ps 111:8). The meter is quite regular (mostly 3+3), but the rhythm enlarges its beat (to 4+4), especially in the second strophe.

The two-strophe structure generally follows the pattern of this kind of hymnic song (three bicola), but the last substrophe forms two tricola, perhaps to respect the 22 letters of the alphabet. As is sometimes the case for acrostic poems (cf. Psalms 9–10; 25; 34; 37; 111; 119; 145; Prov 31:10-31; Lam. 1:1-4; Nah 1:2-8), the need to maintain the alphabetic order of letters compels the psalmist to use some well-known sentences, proverbial or otherwise.

COMMENTARY

Strophe I: Exultation for the Upright Man (vv. 1-5)

Strophe I is an exclamation of good wishes for the man who delights in the Lord's commandments. "Happy" rather than "Blessed" is the meaning of the Hebrew word, a plural construct, derived from the verb "to go forward," "to enjoy a movement of inner progress," perhaps "to lead in procession." However, the man whom the Lord has "blessed" receives from the psalmist the expressed hope of "bon voyage!" It is a word of encouragement: a dynamic formulation of good wishes for progress, safe journey toward the goal of well-being. The man's posterity is included in this interjection. In a tribal culture that survives the evolution of society, such an expectation of success includes the man's descendants. The second and third generation will behave with selfless bravura in order to help others in distress. Heroism is the by-product of social solidarity.

Wealth will accompany his happiness and permit him to act generously toward others (v. 3). He will lend to the poor in need. The implication would prevent the "lender" from charging exorbitant interest. As a wise businessman, he will act after reflective consideration (v. 5). To fear Yahweh out of love for him opens knowledge of one's responsibilities, especially if one is conducting a successful business. In moments of crisis, the truly pious man will not fall into a state of depression. His colleagues, his associates, and his clients will see a light rise over him from darkness (v. 4).

Strophe II: A Steady Heart Will Not Flinch (vv. 6-10)

Firmness of character will result from being God fearing. Decisions will be taken advisedly, and maintained. A "fixed" heart suggests not only control over passing emotions but also clarity of judgment before making a decision. An inner strength is the secret of success in business.

The man who calmly and intelligently enters into dialogue with Yahweh will not fail. The fear of God — that is to say, the awareness of God's honor — delineates the qualities of the social leader. He shares part of his wealth with the poor. His reputation for generosity will not die with him in his old age. His family will carry on. Unlike the scoundrel who sees and is enraged (v. 10), he is motivated by a "humble pride" that is anchored in the honor of God.

DATE AND THEOLOGY

The author of Psalm 112 used Psalm 111 as a model. The date is therefore also postexilic, when Jewish communities spread throughout the Persian Empire and wealth was both a cause and a result of social interdependence. Just as the poet of Psalm 111 had praised the deeds of the God who sealed an alliance with his people, so also the poet of Psalm 112 describes the qualities of the man who finds "delight" in the commandments of this alliance. The result of this sequential intention was a change from a concern for theology to an interest in the psychology of a man of substance. The ideal of manhood in Psalm 112 is worth the psalmist's assent, but he does not observe that riches, like political power, are apt to degenerate into moral satisfaction. Family responsibility can easily become family egocentricity.

Perhaps the final blast on the scoundrel is a veiled injunction to a successful, God-fearing man whose children and grandchildren, brought up in wealth, no longer delight in the philanthropy of their ancestors. An accumulation of riches to opulence may lead to happiness, although transience remains for

Us, the most fleeting of all.[1]

The person who fears the Lord and is animated by rectitude will give lavishly to the poor, but he will "conduct his affairs with discretion."

PSALM 113

The Name of the Lord Be Praised

1. Hallelujah.

I

Praise, O you servants of the Lord,
Praise the name of the Lord!
2.   *Blessed be the name of the Lord!*
From this time forth and forevermore.
3.   *From the rising of the sun to its setting*
May the name of the Lord be praised!

4.   *The Lord is high above all the nations;*
His glory is high above the heavens.
5.   *Who is like the Lord our God?*
The One who has raised his throne very high!

II

6.   *He stoops to look down*
On the heavens and earth.
7.   *He raises the destitute from dust;*
From mud he lifts up the poor.

---

1. Rainer Maria Rilke, "The Duino Elegies," tr. J. B. Leishman and S. Spender (New York, 1939), p. 73.

8.   *He makes them sit with princes,*
            With the princes of his own people;
9.   *He gives a home to the barren woman;*
            A mother of sons becomes filled with joy!

Hallelujah.

BIBLIOGRAPHY

P. C. Craigie, "Psalm 113," *Int*, XXXIX (1985), pp. 74-78; F. Crüsemann, *Studien zur Formgeschichte von Hymnus und Danklied in Israel,* WMANT XXXII (Neukirchen, 1969), pp. 134ff.; O. Grether, *Name und Wort Gottes im Alten Testament,* BZAW LXIV (Giessen, 1934); L. Knopf, "[*môshibi*] vocem cum [*shûbh*] 'werden' conjungit: Der die Unfruchtbare der Familie zur frohen Mutter von Kindern werden lässt," *VT*, IX (1959); Clinton McCann, Jr., *A Theological Introduction to the Book of Psalms* (Nashville, 1993), pp. 79-82; I. W. Slotki, "Omnipresence, Condescension and Omniscience in Psalm 113,5-6," *JTS*, XXXII (1931), pp. 367-70; J. T. Willis, "The Song of Hannah and Psalm 113," *CBQ*, XXXV (1973), pp. 129-54.

FORM

The Hallelujah psalms were used by pilgrims on the highways, marching in processions toward a site of common worship. Like several hymns of this category, they have only two strophes, each of which may be divided into two substrophes. A pilgrim song was generally short since it had to be learned, words and music, by the common people, not just by professional singers or priests and Levites. All pilgrims together were "servants of the Lord."

The rhetorical movement progresses swiftly: (1) the exhortation to praise the name of Yahweh, which is repeated six times; (2) the declaration of a supercosmic majesty of Yahweh: it is so immense that it exceeds the enormous limits of the universe; (3) yet Yahweh's compassion manifests itself to the destitute of Israel; (4) social equality sets the elect people apart from all the nations of the earth; (5) even the barren woman will become the mother of sons.

Not only does the last wonder present a close affinity between Ps 113:9 and the Song of Hannah, the mother of the prophet Samuel (1 Sam 2:10), but also a single theme — the victory and triumph song on Yahweh's exploits — unites the two poetic pieces (Ps 113:1-9, and 1 Sam 2:1-10).

COMMENTARY

Strophe I: Praise of the Name (vv. 1-5)

It is not obvious that Psalm 113 is a cultic hymn related to the ceremonial of a yearly feast. The "servants of Yahweh" do not seem to be priests and Levites, a hierarchic elite. While a pilgrimage leads worshipers toward a synagogue or the sanctuary of Zion, the majesty of Yahweh is stunningly spread beyond the already immense wideness, the height and the depth of the cosmos — heaven and earth. This supercosmos includes Yahweh's dwelling or throne, which is situated beyond the highest part of the universe. A fortiori, the Lord is royally seated above all the nations of the earth.

Strophe II: Yahweh's Compassion for Israel's Destitute (vv. 6-9)

In the ancient Near East, the elect people offered a unique aspect: social equality in a still hierarchic community. Simple people sit with princes. There are class distinctions within the people of Yahweh, but the destitute are raised from the dust, and the poor are not compelled to languish in the mud (lit., "dung"). Even the barren woman becomes the mother of sons and is joyful.[1] A home assigned to her will not be taken away, that is, a marriage is not to be severed on account of her sterility (Ezra 10:2, 14; Neh 13:23). However, nothing is told of male sterility, and the distinction is still between "sons" and the birth of daughters.

DATE AND THEOLOGY

Psalm 113 is not only a Hallelujah Psalm and a pilgrim song, but it also belongs to the Hallel Collection (Psalms 113–118). In modern Judaism, this hymn is chanted at the first blessing of the Passover cup of wine. In Christian usage, Psalm 113 belongs to the vespers of Easter Day, when praise of God's wonder of wonders is celebrated. In effect, the relationship between Psalm 113 and the Song of Hannah includes far more than the joy of being the mother of sons; it presents itself as the model to Psalm 113 almost in its totality.[2] The Lord is to be

1. The text of 1 Samuel 2–10 is uncertain. See G. Bressan, "Il cantico di Anna," *Bib*, XXXII (1951), pp. 503-21; XXXIII (1952), pp. 67-89; I. H. Eyberg, "Notes on the Text of Samuel Found in Qumran Cave 4," in *Studies in the Book of Samuel* (1960), pp. 1-97; P. A. H. de Boer, "A Syro-hexaplar Text of the Song of Hannah: I Sam. ii, 1-10," in *Festschrift G. R. Driver* (Oxford, 1963), pp. 8-15.
2. Cf. Craigie, "Psalm 113," pp. 146-47, and the many references therein; see also Willis, "The Song of Hannah," pp. 140-41.

praised for his triumph over Israel's enemies. There is none like Yahweh (1 Sam 2:2; Ps 113:5). While the Egyptian and Ugaritic literatures offer similar exclamations on the incomparability of their favorite deities, the emphasis of both Hannah's Song and Psalm 113 lies on the wonder that moves much farther than sunrise and sunset because it not only involves all the nations of the earth but it also presents an ideal of social equity for the elect people (vv. 7-9), unheard of among other nations.

While the Song of Hannah may have originated in the Shiloh sanctuary (cf. 1 Sam 3:3; 4:3-4), the psalm explodes the bournes of cultic worship. As in the case of the glory seen by the prophet Isaiah that spreads over the whole earth (Isa 3:6), this psalm presents a veritable revolution in political systems and social ethics.

Since the date of Hannah's Song is most probably ancient, close to the dawn of the monarchy, or at least part of the Deuteronomic literature — see, for example, Deut 32:36, 43 on the formula "servants of Yahweh" — Psalm 113 may have come from a date before or after the exile. Most probably, as a pilgrim song, Psalm 113 originated, if it was composed on the model of 1 Sam 2:1-10, as a song for the processional of worshipers to a synagogue, during Persian times.

Praise adds aesthetics to gratitude for seeing a wonder, perhaps unexpectedly spelled out by Joseph Addison,

> When all thy mercies, O my God,
>   My rising soul surveys,
> Transported with the view I'm lost
>   In wonder, love, and praise.

The hymnic exhortation of Psalm 113 does not rest on a first person subjectivism. The singer conceals himself as the unknown mouthpiece for the community of God.

PSALM 114

Rushing out of Egypt

I

1. *When Israel rushed out of Egypt,*
      Jacob's house, from a people of strange tongue,
2. *Judah became his sanctuary,*
      And Israel his dominion.

II

3. *The Sea saw it and fled;*
      The Jordan turned around backward.
4. *The mountains skipped like rams,*
      And the hills like lambs.

III

5. *What ails thee, O Sea, that thou fleest?*
      And Jordan, that thou turnest around backwards?
6. *O mountains, why do you skip like rams?*
      O hills, like lambs?

IV

7. *Tremble, O Earth,*
      At the presence of the Master,
      The presence of Jacob's God,
8. *Who turns the rock into a pool of water!*
      The flint into a fountain of water!

BIBLIOGRAPHY

J. Halbe, "Passa-Massot-Fest im deuteronomischen Festkalendar," *ZAW,* LXXXVII (1975), pp. 147-68; idem, "Erwägungen zu Ursprung und Wesen des Massotfestes," *ZAW,* LXXXVII (1985), pp. 324-45; O. Kaiser, *Die mythische Bedeutung des Meeres in Agypten, Ugarit und Israel,* BZAW LXXVIII (Giessen, 1959); H.-J. Kraus, "Gilgal — Ein Beitrag zur Kultusgeschichte Israels," *VT,* I (1951), pp. 181-99; idem, "Zur Geschichte des Passah-Massot-Festes im Alten Testament," *EvT,* XVIII (1958), pp. 47-67; idem, *Worship in Israel* (Oxford, 1966), pp. 161ff.; J. Langlamet, "Gilgal et les récits de la traversée du Jourdain," *Cahiers de la Revue Biblique,* XI (1969), pp. 7-58; A. Lauha,

"Die Geschichtsmotive in den alttestamentlichen Psalmen," *Annales academiae scientiarum Fennicae* (Helsinki, 1945); N. Lohfink, "Ps 114/115 (M und G) und die deuteronomische Sprachwelt," in *Festschrift H. Gross* (Stuttgart, 1986); H. Lubsczyk, "Einheit und heilsgeschichtliche Bedeutung von Ps 114/115 (113)," *BZ*, XI (1967), pp. 161-73; P. Luis, "Ps 114 (116), 1," *VD*, XVIII (1938), pp. 262-68; B. Renaud, "Les deux lectures du Ps 114," *RSR*, LII (1978), pp. 14-28; H. Spieckermann, *Eine Theologie des Psalters* (Göttingen, 1989), pp. 150-56; E. Vogt, "Die Erzählung vom Jordanübergang Jos 3–4," *Bib*, XLVI (1965), pp. 125-48; C. Westermann, *The Praise of God in the Psalms* (Richmond, Va., 1965).

FORM

This psalmodic sketch about the exodus and the crossing of the Jordan affects a theatrical swiftness and an almost humoristic apostrophe to the elements of nature. It should be considered as a sequence of four quatrains, each of two bicola, with an emphatic tricolon toward the end (v. 7bc) because it carries the key motif of the entire poem on God's presence, Jacob's God.

Some commentators see no strophic divisions, or they discern only two strophes (vv. 1-4, 5-8), but a segmentation between vv. 2 and 3 is too abrupt, and the thematic division clearly separates vv. 1-2 from vv. 3-4 into distinct strophes. Similarly, an obvious distinction sets apart vv. 7-8 from vv. 5-6.

An epic progress imposes itself:

Strophe I: the exodus from a land with a foreign speech, the mark of a strange nation; Strophe II: the Sea, the river Jordan, the mountains, and the hills: all of them act out a cosmic dance (vv. 3-4); Strophe III: these are addressed directly as scenic characters in a play (vv. 5-6); Strophe IV: the mountains no longer skip; they are admonished to tremble before the Lord's presence.

The form of the psalm is unusual and enigmatic: it is not a prayer of supplication, nor does it fit the traditional style of hymns, starting with imperatives to exhort worshipers on what to sing, or participial declarations of divine wonder and majesty. Sapiential elements are also absent, as well as reviews of sacred history with the people's thankfulness or ingratitude. Simply, the sketch is anchored on the fabulous "events" or "legends" of divine acts of marvels, bringing together the exodus itself with the turning around of the river Jordan and the piercing of the rock in the desert horrors of waterless wastes.

COMMENTARY

Strophe I: The Specific Missions of Israel and Judah (vv. 1-2)

A few critics suppose that Psalm 114 was truncated from a longer poem, including Psalm 113 (cf. LXX). Indeed, the psalm begins with a subordinate clause, "When Israel rushed out of Egypt . . ." Yet this conjecture is superfluous, for the style is intentionally succinct and provocative. The Hebrew text merely offers an indication of time, "When Israel . . ." The translation "rushed out" is permissible, for the traditions of "leaving" Egypt pile up to the institution of the Passover, the death of the Egyptians' newborn children, and the actual departure (Exod 12:37-39) in which hurry is clearly implied.

Jacob's "tribe" for "Jacob's house" is justified, for it refers to the conglomeration of all of Jacob's descendants. The Egyptians are described pejoratively as a people of a strange tongue. Foreign languages are generally considered an evil.

The name "Israel" is used first (v. 1a) for designating the whole family of Jacob, and then (v. 2b) it seems to be an "Israel" differentiated from "Judah." This may point to the ten "tribes" of northern Israel, split from the Davidic dynasty after the death of Solomon. Yet it may well be that the second mention of "Israel" stresses that the "sanctuary," the temple of Zion, stands for Judah, and "dominion" (v. 2b) for Israel in general, the "house" of Jacob. The reference to the specific missions of the two entities would be quite appropriate after the reform of Josiah, when the uniqueness assigned to the temple of Zion was imposed on the entire land. The exodus would then acquire a multiple meaning: deliverance from slavery, freedom from the adoration of the forces of nature personified as deities, and preparation for the covenant on Mount Sinai.

The ironical questions hurled at the Sea, the Jordan, the mountains, and the hills became a single command, ordered to the Earth itself, as if these various elements of nature were actors, vividly played on a stage!

COMMENTARY

Strophe I: Judah's and Israel's Missions (vv. 1-2)

The departure from Egypt and the crossing of the Jordan are evoked with the quick splash of a painter's brush. Every word counts. The name "Israel" changes meaning from one verse to the next. At first it seems to suggest the generic, all-involving designation of the Hebrews, as it fits the patriarchal origin of the people. The name "Israel" alludes eloquently to the ancestor's fight with God (Gen

32:24-32). It becomes "Jacob's house," which summons the whole posterity as well as the mystery of election.

Strophe II: The Dancing Insecurity of Nature (vv. 3-4)

The Sea, the mountains, and the hills are spoken to as personified villains. The Sea saw and fled. Ironically, the vestige of the mythical Monster who was vanquished at creation, according to ancient Near Eastern beliefs, is addressed ironically as a coward. The Jordan turns back as a defeated army in retreat. The mountains, the very symbol of solidity, behave like rams, and the hills like lambs. Nature bows before the people of God. The universe is both demythicized and remythicized in order that the singers may celebrate the power of Yahweh.

Strophe III: Satirical Humor on Nature's Fright and Confusion (vv. 5-6)

The rhetorical mockery is as brisk as repartee in commedia dell'arte. The Sea, symbol of pre-creative chaos, deserves a capital "S" as the cosmic enemy of God, but the question, with playful sympathy, asks, "What ails thee, O Sea?"

Strophe IV: Submission before the Sovereign (vv. 7-8)

Suddenly the text abandons the tone of mockery and adopts the style of military command or of prophetic condemnation, "Tremble! O Earth!" When the metaphors recall the rudeness of Habakkuk, some exegetes wish to correct the verb, a feminine imperative meaning "to turn," "to waltz," and not simply into "to shake," "to tremble" like a woman in labor (LXX) but into an entirely different word, in its construct state, signifying "the whole" (of the earth), in part because the noun for "Master" or "Sovereign" stands by itself, without an article. Neither the Hebrew MSS nor the ancient versions, as likewise the thematic sequence, would justify this emendation. The feminine possessives in v. 2ab, referring obviously to Yahweh, are inexplicable.

   The MT yields a remarkable progression, from "mountains," images of solidity and durability, to "the Earth," metaphor par excellence of terrestrial stability. The conjectural correction would also weaken the crispness of the epic. "The presence," literally "face," of the cosmic master is immediately identified as "Jacob's God," and the linking of "Jacob's house" (v. 1) with "Jacob's God" brings a climactic thrust to the entire psalm. The motif of "presence" is repeated, so that the bicolon becomes a tricolon (v. 7).

   The final statement on the splitting of the rock for drinking water (v. 8) inserts with only one example the tribulations endured by the tribes in the desert of Sinai (Exod 17:1; Num 20:1ff.; Deut 8:15; Ps 107:35; Isa 48:21). It also, and in a sublime way, completes the tribute to the Lord of wonders.

DATE AND THEOLOGY

The date is an unsolvable puzzle. Stylistic reminiscences of the "theophany" do not necessarily dictate that Psalm 114 adorned a ceremonial feast. The poet has composed a little gem of elocution, perhaps to be sung by two or three soloists and answered antiphonally by a choir. The element of playfulness is theologically the distant equivalent of the Song of Songs, and even of the tale of Esther. The psalm introduces a light touch, compelling meditations on the proper relationship between the Lord and nature. It also proposes in dialogical form the sense of wonder before the goodness of the Lord and the awe of his presence.

"The world is charged with the grandeur of God," muses Gerard Manley Hopkins. Why should the false claims of Israel and its consequent disasters, with its pride and its guilt, prevent playful realism from the true lovers of God? The fear of the void still experienced before the Sea, the awe produced by the sight of the Mount Hermon snows and the mortal harshness of thirst during the long summers, will not hinder the singing of hymns of praise. The universe bows before the Presence.

PSALM 115

Not unto Us, O Lord!

Preamble

1.   *Not unto us, O Lord, not unto us,*
          But unto thy name give glory!
          For the sake of thy mercy and thy fidelity!
2.   *Why should the nations say,*
          Where is their God, pray tell?
3.   *Our God is in the heavens;*
          He does whatever he pleases.

I

4.   *Their idols are silver and gold,*
           The work of men's hands.
5.   *They have mouths but do not speak;*
           Eyes, but do not see.
6.   *They have ears, but do not hear;*
           Noses, but do not smell.
7.   *They have hands, but do not feel;*
           Feet, but do not walk;
           Neither speak they through their throats.
8.   *Those who make them are like them;*
           So are all those who trust in them.

II

9.   *House of Israel, trust in the Lord!*
           He is their help and their shield.
10.   *House of Aaron, trust in the Lord!*
           He is their help and their shield.
11.   *You who fear the Lord, trust in the Lord!*
           He is their help and their shield.
12.   *The Lord has been mindful of us; may he bless us!*
           May he bless the house of Israel!
           May he bless the house of Aaron!
13.   *May he bless those that fear the Lord,*
           The small with the great.

III

14.   *May the Lord give you prosperity,*
           To you and also to your children.
15.   *May you be blessed by the Lord,*
           Who made heaven and earth.
16.   *The heavens are the Lord's heavens,*
           But he gave the earth to the sons of Adam.
17.   *The dead do not praise the Lord,*
           Nor any that go down into silence.
18.   *As for us, we will bless the Lord*
           From this time forth and forevermore.

Hallelujah.

BIBLIOGRAPHY

C. Barth, *Die Errettung von Tode in den individuellen Klage- und Dankliedern des Alten Testament* (Zollikon, 1947); O. Grether, *Name und Wort Gottes im Alten Testament,* BZAW LXIV (Giessen, 1934); A. Hurvitz, "The History of a Legal Formula, *kol 'ašer ba'ares 'asah* (Psalm CXXXV, 6)," *VT,* XXXV (1982), pp. 257ff.; H.-J. Kraus, *Theology of the Psalms* (Minneapolis, 1986), pp. 13ff.; H. Lubsczyk, "Einheit und heilsgeschicht-liche Bedeutung von Ps 114/115 (113)," *BZ,* XI (1967), pp. 161-73; K. Luke, "The Setting of Psalm 115," *Irish Theological Quarterly,* XXXIV (1967), pp. 347-57; H.-D. Preuss, *Die Verspottung fremder Götter im Alten Testament,* BWANT XII (Stuttgart, 1970), pp. 251ff.; H. Spieckermann, *Eine Theologie des Psalters* (Göttingen, 1989).

FORM

This psalm appears to be part of some ceremonial liturgy, when priests were blessed by the Levitical singers. The meter is quite regular (3+3; 3+2; 2+3). Different soloists and choristers as well as the congregation seem to have been assigned dialogical parts. A preamble (vv. 1-3) introduces three strophes, each of which has five bicola (except one tricolon, v. 7). Hymnic style is used here and there, especially in Strophe II, where an antiphonal refrain confers a special blessing on the "house of Aaron." The gist of Strophe I — a mockery of idolaters — is almost exactly quoted in another poem (Ps 135:15-18), which suggests some hymnic fragments, ready to be sung, floated before they were assigned to specific pieces. Here the blessing is invoked not only for the priests but also on the house of Aaron, and elsewhere on the "house of Israel" and the "house of Levi" (cf. Ps 135:19-20). The ceremonial for which Psalm 115 collected from various fragments is beyond identification.

COMMENTARY

Preamble: Glory to the Name (vv. 1-3)

A solemn invocation displays a keen knowledge of the ambiguity that tends to corrupt any religion. This knowledge feeds either theocentricity and social altruism, or egocentricity, with ecclesiastical and political pride as well as disastrous illusions. "Glory" is a concept that originated with the pompous honor accorded to princes, kings, and leaders in general. Cultically, it was born in the golden splendor of sacred objects, like the statues of cherubim, placed in the innermost room of a sanctuary.

"Name," on the contrary, conveyed the idea of the Sinai Deity's creative power. The name "Yahweh" probably meant, "He who causes to be," "He who brings into being" (Exod 3:15).

While "glory" found its source in cultic ceremonies, "name" involved the cosmic creativity of God, both the master of nature and the elector of the most precious people. Here the theology of glory and the theology of the name coalesce, for the originator of both realities is not man but God himself.[1] "Glory" *(kabhod)* easily becomes self-glory. Under the sway of the great prophets, the psalmist is aware of this ambiguity. His poem shows that divine glory, in the final analysis, belongs to the splendor, the wonder, the illuminative element of the creative flash. The senses of "sight" (glory) and of "hearing" (name) become one. Divine mercy and fidelity are the causes of the glory of the name.

The nations ask immodest questions. Even in the midst of military defeat, humiliation, death, and persecution, Israel may laugh at the illusive belief in human glory, its own and that of other nations. Even hidden under the events of disaster, God's name remains intact in the heavens and can give the Lord the freedom and the strength to do "whatever he pleases."

Strophe I: The Emptiness of Idolatry (vv. 4-8)

As the nations had asked Israel, "Where is now their God?" the singers reply, "Silver and gold are not alive."

Strophe II: Admonition to Israel and Her Priests (vv. 9-13)

The appeal to "the house of Israel" and to "the house of Aaron" implicitly admits the importance of the priesthood, set apart for the specificity of cultic functions, with stress on animal sacrifices. The antiphonal refrains sum up the ancient trust in a Lord who will succor and protect (vv. 9-11). The respect of Yahweh for his name (which implies far more than his reputation) stresses all of his activities among the nations as well as within his elect people. His name will manifest itself through his fidelity. He will deliver the new generation of those who have been severely punished. All those who fear the Lord seek to live in accordance with the standards of the Sinai Covenant.

The people of Israel may have been "seared . . . , scared, blessed," and often brought to death for their toil and betrayals, but a core of them has not erred. These will receive this peculiar mode of living that is involved in "blessing," among the small people in communion with the great (v. 13; Ps 113:8).

---

1. See S. Terrien, *The Elusive Presence* . . . (San Francisco and New York, 1978), pp. 138-52.

Strophe III: The Gift of Prosperity (vv. 14-18)

The freedom and power of God in the heavens (v. 3) are now seen in "the heavens' heavens." They are cited as the concomitant of his fidelity.

The startling consequences of trust in divine fidelity are now spelled out for a double conclusion to the entire psalm: (1) blessing for existence on earth is pledged by the Creator; the sons of Adam, to whom the earth was granted, are now invited to receive anew the opportunity to behave responsibly, within a united community where the small are received with *('im)* the great. An ethical sociology of brotherhood will require political as well as ecclesiastical expression. (2) Let the sons of Israel live a long time upon the earth, for "the dead do not praise the Lord." Death means eternal sojourn in the realm of silence (v. 17).

DATE AND THEOLOGY

In early Judaism, at the beginning of Persian ascendancy, when the Babylonian grip began to be more lenient and a limited freedom permitted the expectation of a decent future, this psalmist assembled bits of musical poetry. Like Second Isaiah, he predicted a restoration. Synagogal congregations may already have sung hymns of gratitude. God is free to save; he does what pleases him (v. 3). No sense of national transgression still haunts the psalmist.

The editors of the Psalter placed together Psalms 114 and 115 because they observed, no doubt, the similarity in ironic verve and even impetuosity against idolaters. The association of this poem with a yearly feast of covenant renewal remains hypothetical.

Just at the end of the exile, the ethical justice demanded by the great prophets was now related to the Levitical laws, many of which were orally transmitted, but which were now written down in the prevision of a finished Pentateuch. When Israel is assembled, standing before its God (Deut 29:10), the actuality of a serene future is then registered, and this anticipation is partly experienced as a present reality.

The regimen of religion by law may have sown the seeds of legalism, in spite of the preamble and its warning against national self-glory (v. 1). Justification by faith, as discerned and formulated by the apostle Paul, St. Augustine, Martin Luther, and John Calvin, among others, was often confused in the Christian churches with semi-Pelagianism, the seed of ecclesiastical self-glory. *Sola gratia* and *sola fides* do not mean the futility of works, but the centrality of God. "Not unto us give glory!"

PSALM 116

Escaping from Death

I

1. *I love the Lord, for he heard my voice*
   And my supplications.
2. *He inclined his ear toward me,*
   And I shall invoke him all my days.
3. *The bonds of death had surrounded me,*
   And the Angst of the grave had seized me;
   I had become the prey of deep distress and pain.

4. *But I called on the name of the Lord:*
   O Lord, save my life!
5. *The Lord is merciful and just;*
   The Lord is full of compassion.

II

6. *The Lord preserves the simpleminded;*
   I was brought low, but he saved me.
7. *Return, O my soul, to thy quietude,*
   For the Lord dealt bountifully with thee.

8. *In effect, he withdrew my life from death,*
   My eyes from tears, my feet from falling.
9. *I shall walk in the presence of the Lord*
   In the land of the living.
10. *I was confident, and thus I said,*
    Yes, I was brutally harmed.

III

11. *I even said, in my anguish,*
    Every man is a liar.
12. *What shall I render to the Lord*
    For all his bounties toward me?

13. *I will lift up the cup of salvation*
    And call on the name of the Lord;
14. *I will pay my vows to the Lord*

In full view of his entire people.

15.   *Is it not too hard for the eyes of the Lord*
        To see the death of all those who love him?

IV

16.   *Yes, my Lord, because I am thy servant,*
        I am thy servant, the son of thy handmaid,
        Thou hast loosed my bonds.
17.   *I offer thee a sacrifice of thanksgiving*
        And call on the name of the Lord.

18.   *I will pay my vows to the Lord*
        In the full view of his entire people,
19.   *In the courtyards of the Lord's house,*
        In the very midst of thee, Jerusalem!

Hallelujah.

BIBLIOGRAPHY

P. Auffret, "Essai sur la structure littéraire du Psaume 116," *Biblische Notizen*, XXIII (1984), pp. 32-47; M. L. Barré, "Psalm 116: Its Structure and Its Enigmas," *JBL*, CIX (1990), pp. 61-78; C. Barth, *Die Errettung vom Tode in den individuellen Klage- und Dankliedern des Alten Testaments* (Zollikon, 1947); F. Crüsemann, *Studien zur Formgeschichte von Hymnus und Danklied in Israel*, WMANT XXXII (Neukirchen, 1969), pp. 243-46; S. B. Frost, "Asseveration by Thanksgiving," *VT*, VIII (1958), pp. 380-90; H. L. Ginsberg, "Psalms and Inscriptions of Petition and Acknowledgment," in *L. Ginsberg Jubilee*, I (New York, 1945), pp. 159-71; H. Gressmann, "Der Festbecher," in *Festschrift für E. Sellin* (Leipzig, 1927), pp. 55-62; O. Grether, *Name und Wort Gottes im Alten Testament*, BZAW LXIV (Giessen, 1934); P. Joüon, "Ben 'amateka . . . Filius — ancillae tuus," *Bib*, XXIII (1942), pp. 190-91.

FORM

Some exegetes suggest that this hymn of thanksgiving, chanted by an individual, may have been the result of an editorial compilation that combined two independent fragments, vv. 1-9 and vv. 10-19. The LXX and Jerome divide this hymn into two independent psalms. Indeed, the style of v. 10 may indicate the beginning of a new poem. The present Psalm 116 contains repetitions, expressions of gratitude mixed with invocations of the divine name, a soul dialogue, and a declaration of confidence, with a double commitment to fulfill one's vows.

Compositional disorder may not be denied, but since the central theme is escape from death or from a grave sickness, one cannot expect a logical and rhetorical flow. Psalm 116 seems to be the cry of a man who was convulsed by the terror of final annihilation.[1] He prayed to his Lord for a reprieve and was overwhelmed with his sudden release.

Structural analysis is possible and even probable. Strophe I is a multiple supplication answered (vv. 1-3 + 4-5); Strophe II describes healing from a mortal malady (vv. 6-7 + 8-10); Strophe III conveys a commitment to thank God (vv. 11-12 + 13-15); Strophe IV proclaims a triumphant testimony in the temple of Zion (vv. 16-17 + 18-19). It will be noted that Strophes I, II, and III contain two substrophes, with an equilibrium of 3+2, 2+3, 2+3, but Strophe IV contains two substrophes with one tricolon (v. 16). Such a structure leads from the vivid memory of deep distress to the joyful expectation of singing before God's "entire people" in the sanctuary of Zion, and — as the poet stresses with obvious glee — "in the very midst of *thee,* Jerusalem!"

COMMENTARY

Strophe I: Prayers Answered (vv. 1-3 + 4-5)

The Hebrew text reads, "I love because Yahweh has heard . . ." (v. 1). It is not necessary to displace the divine name and read, "I love Yahweh because he. . . ." The poem of Job presents syntactic constructions of a similar aspect. The verb in the imperfect, "he hears," covers both the past and the continuous present tenses. No textual correction is needed. Thanksgiving hymns generally begin with such a declaration (cf. Pss 18:1; 30:1). The cry "I love" without a direct object reveals the absolute degree of the psalmist's passion for his God.

Strophe II: Saved from Death (vv. 6-7 + 8-10)

The memory of a deep distress is so recent and strong that the patient, while thankful for his healing, still shivers over the terror he has endured (cf. Pss 6:4; 18:4). The invocation of the holy name is typical of the Hallel psalms. Not only is Yahweh "merciful and just" (note the sequence of the epithets), but he is also and supremely "compassionate," a term that conveys the connotation of the womb of a mother.

The "simpleminded" are not only endowed with an open mind to wis-

---

1. Cf. H.-J. Kraus, "Vom Leben und Tod in den Psalmen," in *Biblisch-theologische Aufsätze,* IV (Neukirchen, 1972), pp. 258-77.

dom (Prov 9:11) in the good sense, but, pejoratively, they may also be persons of intellectual and spiritual mediocrity (Prov 1:22; 14:18). Having pledged to walk now "in the presence of the Lord," the former patient will appreciate the land of the living.

Strophe III: Commitment to Rites of Gratitude (vv. 11-12 + 13-15)

Again, the name of the Lord is invoked while a ritual cup is lifted and drunk as a symbol of thanks, the antithesis of the "cup of wrath" (cf. Isa 51:17, 22; Lam 4:21, 32-33). At the same time he will pay his vows.

Nevertheless, why did he retrospectively say, in his anguish, that "every man is a liar"? Was it that he indirectly insisted on his veracity in promising libation and the fulfillment of his vows? The last question of the strophe (v. 15) slyly raises the hope of life everlasting. Against the general denial of a life beyond the grave and the Hebraic insistence on final annihilation — perhaps as a polemical contradiction to the Egyptian culture of sophisticated undertakers — the psalmist uses an indirect aspect of his superlative love of God: he sympathizes with the anguish Yahweh must feel — so he supposes — at the death of God's human lovers. He does not go as far as the sapiential psalmist who affirms his hope in eternal communion with his God, saying, "I am always with thee . . . , then thou wilt receive me into glory" (Ps 73:23-24), but he boldly hints at God's sadness over the idea of eternal death for his devotees. Is it not that he wishes to promulgate a positive suggestion of life everlasting?

Strophe IV: In the Midst of Thee, Jerusalem (vv. 16-17 + 18-19)

The singer now claims the highest stage of devotion by twice calling himself "thy servant" or, more probably, "thy slave" (cf. Ps 143:12), "son of thy handmaid" (v. 16; cf. Exod 23:12; Ps 86:16). Not only will the singer repeat his intention to fulfill his vows (cf. Pss 61:8; 66:13), but he also seems to rejoice greatly over his solemn project to perform his rites "In the courtyards of the Lord's house," "In the very midst of thee, Jerusalem!" The holy city is now personified and addressed in a lyrical dialogue.

DATE AND THEOLOGY

The sudden interjection, not to the Lord, but to the city of the holy temple, "thee, Jerusalem," points to a date apparently close to the reconstruction of Zion at the end of the sixth century. To pay one's vows before a large assembly reflects the central motivation of worship in postexilic Judaism at the navel of the earth. The myth of the omphalos, inherited from worldwide beliefs (Shechem, Delphi, etc.), may have yielded a form of national hubris, with all its adjacent grounds for religious corruption as well as sociological and political coherence.[2]

The theology of Psalm 116 strengthens the faith of those caught by grievous disease and becomes the channel of their return to living. It also interplays between individual and collective hymnology. More strikingly still, it may have contributed to the development of the belief in the resurrection of the dead.

PSALM 117

Praise the Lord, All Ye Peoples!

1.   *Praise the Lord, all ye nations!*
         Adore him, all ye peoples!
2.   *For his goodness is mighty over us,*
         And the Lord's fidelity will last forevermore.
       Hallelujah.

BIBLIOGRAPHY

R. Martin-Achard, *Israël et les nations — La perspective missionnaire de l'Ancien Testament, Cahiers theologiques* XLII (Neuchâtel and Paris, 1959).

FORM AND COMMENTARY

This Hallelujah psalm is a hymn of praise of unusual brevity. Through the use of imperatives, the nations of the world are invited to praise the God of Israel (cf. Pss 22:27; 47:1; 72:11; 100:1; 113:2).

Whether these summons should follow the conversion of the "heathen" peoples is not clear (cf. Isa 49:6-7; 55:4-5).

2. S. Terrien, "The Omphalos Myth and Hebrew Religion," *VT,* XX (1970), pp. 315-38.

PSALM 118

Liturgy for Temple Pilgrims

I. The Lord Is Good

1. *Praise ye the Lord, for he is good;*
   For his loving grace endures forever!
2. *Let Israel be pleased to say,*
   For his loving grace endures forever.
3. *Let the house of Aaron say,*
   For his loving grace endures forever!
4. *Let those who fear the Lord be pleased to say,*
   For his loving grace endures forever!

II. The Lord Is for Me

5. *From the midst of distress I called to the Lord;*
   The Lord answered me and set me free.
6. The Lord is for me! *I do not feel any dread.*
   What can any human being do to me?
7. The Lord is for me! *He is my helper.*
   As for me, I look boldly upon those who hate me.

III. Better Seek Refuge

8. Better seek refuge in the Lord
   Than put one's trust in any man.
9. Better seek refuge in the Lord
   Than put one's faith in princes.

IV. In the Name of the Lord

10. *All nations surrounded me;*
    In the Lord's name I cut them to pieces.
11. *They surrounded me, encircled me;*
    In the name of the Lord I cut them to pieces.
12. *They encircled me like bees,*
    But they became extinct like a fire of brambles.
    In the name of the Lord, I cut them to pieces.

V. The Lord Is My Strength

13. *[They] pushed me to make me fall,*
    But the Lord came to my help.
14. The Lord is my strength, *I shall celebrate him.*
    It is he who has saved me.

IV'. The Lord's Right Hand

15. *A cry of triumph and of salvation*
    Is heard in the tent of the righteous!
    The Lord's right hand has acted with power.
16. *The Lord has raised his right hand;*
    The Lord's right hand has acted with power.
17. *I will not die, for I shall live,*
    And I shall tell the works of the Lord.
18. *The Lord chastised me harshly,*
    But he did not send me to death.

III'. Open for Me the Gates!

19. *Open for me the gates of righteousness!*
    I shall enter through them; I shall praise the Lord!
20. *Here is the portal that leads to the Lord!*
    Through this portal enter the righteous.
21. *I praise thee, for thou didst answer me,*
    And thou art for me salvation.

II'. The Cornerstone Is a Miracle

22. *The stone that the builders rejected*
    Is now the cornerstone;
23. *This came into being from the Lord,*
    And is now a miracle for our eyes.
24. *This is the day that the Lord has made;*
    May we rejoice in it and be glad.

I'. The Lord Is Good

25. *Save us, we beseech thee, O Lord!*
    Please, give us success!
26. *Blessed be he that comes in the name of the Lord!*
    We shall bless you from the house of the Lord.
27. *The Lord is God; he illuminates us*

> For the processional, holding palm fronds
> As far as the horns of the altar.

28.   Thou art my God! I celebrate thee!
          My God, I exalt thee!

29.   Celebrate ye the Lord, for he is good,
          And his fidelity endures forevermore.

BIBLIOGRAPHY

P. R. Ackroyd, "Some Notes on the Psalms," *JTS*, XVII (1966), pp. 392-99; E. Beaucamp, "Plaidoyer pour le Psaume 118," *Vie spirituelle*, CXVI (1967), pp. 64-67; O. Becker, "Psalm 118,12," *ZAW*, LXX (1958), p. 174; H. A. Brongers, "Die Wendung *b^ešem jhwh* im Alten Testament," *ZAW*, LXXVII (1965), pp. 1 ff.; M. Cahill, "Not a Cornerstone! Translating Ps 118, 22 in the Jewish and Christian Scripture," *RB*, CVI (1999), pp. 345-57; F. Crüsemann, *Studien zur Formgeschichte von Hymnus und Danklied in Israel*, WMANT XXXII (Neukirchen, 1969), pp. 217-23; M. et G. Dorival, *La Chaîne palestinienne sur le Psaume 118* (Paris, 1973); G. R. Driver, "Psalm 118, 27: [*'išrû-ḥag*]," *Textus*, VII (1969), pp. 130-31; B. D. Eerdmans, "Essays on Masoretic Psalms," *OtSt*, I (1942), pp. 205-96; idem, "Foreign Elements in Pre-exilic Israel, Ps. 118," *OtSt*, I (1942), 126-38; idem, "Thora Songs and Temple Singers in the Pre-exilic Period," *OtSt*, I (1942), pp. 162-75; S. B. Frost, "Asseveration by Thanksgiving," *VT*, VIII (1958), pp. 380-90; R.. M. Hals, "Psalm 118," *Int*, XXXVII (1983), pp. 277-83; P. Haupt, "Schmücket das Fest mit Maien!" *ZAW*, XXXV (1915), pp. 102-9; E. Kutsch, "Deus humiliat et exaltat: Zu Luthers Übersetzung von Psalm 118,21 und 18,36," *ZTK*, LXI (1964), pp. 193-220; S. E. Loewenstamm, "The Lord Is My Strength and My Glory," *VT*, XIX (1969), pp. 464-70; H. S. May, "Psalm 118 — The Song of the Citadel," in *[Memorial] E. R. Goodenough — Numen Supplement*, XIV (Leiden, 1968), pp. 97-106; J. L. Mays, "Psalm 118 in the Light of Canonical Analysis," in *Canon, Theology, and Old Testament Theology*, Festschrift B. S. Childs (Philadelphia, 1988), pp. 299-311; J. Meysing, "A Text Reconstruction of Psalm 117 (118), 27," *VT*, X (1960), pp. 130-37; J. J. Petuchowski, "*Hoshi'ah-na* in Psalm 118,25: A Prayer for Rain," *VT*, V (1955), pp. 266-71; W. Robinson, "Psalm 118: A Liturgy for the Admission of a Proselyte," *Church Quarterly Review*, CXLIV (1947), pp. 179-83; A. Schulz, *Kritisches zum Psalter* (Münster in Westfalen, 1932); T. F. Torrance, "The Last of the Hallel Psalms," *EvQ*, XXVIII (1956), pp. 101-8; P. Vanbergen, "Le Ps. 117 (118), une Eucharistie qui éclaire l'Eucharistie de Jésus," *Questions liturgiques et paroissiales*, XLV (1964), pp. 65-81; cf. idem, "Le Psaume de l'Octave de Pâques (Ps 118), voici le jour que fit le Seigneur," *Assemblées du seigneur*, XLIII (1964), pp. 30-49.

FORM

This psalm appears to be a conglomeration of independent fragments, some hymns, and others complaints or laments. There are, to be sure, a number of repetitions and irregularities, but Psalm 118 also appears to have been composed by a skillful organizer. He proposes to help with songs some pilgrims marching to the temple of Zion; thus, toward the end of his litany he addresses the gates of the sanctuary for a climactic entrance.

The strophic structure of hymns is here modified by the intermission of complaints, which generally calls attention to a central verse or strophe. "The Lord is my strength" (v. 14) stands out between the beginning and the ending of the psalm, with the joyful declaration, "The Lord is good" (vv. 1 and 29). The strophes are of various lengths, but the triple affirmation on the goodness and the strength of the Lord provides an architecture toward a mixed genre, "the hymnic lament," with alternation of community singing with individual and even personal reflection and meditation. Thus, the following structure is proposed:

    I. *The Lord Is Good* (vv. 1-4)
        II. From Distress to Invocation of the Name (vv. 5-7)
            III. A Better Refuge in the Lord (vv. 8-9)
                IV. Foreign Nations Defeated (vv. 10-12)
                    V. Core Strophe: *The Lord Is My Strength* (vv. 13-14)
                IV'. The Lord's Right Hand (vv. 15-18)
            III'. Open for Me the Gates (vv. 19-21)
        II'. The Cornerstone Is a Miracle (vv. 22-24)
    I'. *The Lord Is Good* (vv. 25-29)

The ascending strophes (vv. 1-12) alternate the invitation to praise (vv. 1-4) with an individual lament (vv. 5-7) and two complaints (vv. 8-9 and 10-12). Then comes the core strophe (vv. 13-14) on the triumphant affirmation, "The Lord is my strength." Finally the descending strophes, renew the invitation to collective praise and relate it to the Lord's right hand (vv. 15-18), the pilgrims' request for the gates of the temple to open (vv. 19-21), and the entry into the sanctuary with the remark on the cornerstone (vv. 22-24). The communal request concludes the entire poem with a final mixture of personal prayer and an invitation to praise. The psalm ends as it began, with a sung exaltation on the goodness of the Lord (vv. 25-29).

COMMENTARY

Strophes I-IV. The Lord Is Good (vv. 1-12)

The ascending strophes begin with a mystical exaltation of the Lord that is translated into an invitation addressed to (a) the house of Israel (see the LXX and Ps 115:9), meaning the popular community at large; (2) the house of Aaron, namely, the priests who participate in the ascent toward Zion; and (3) the elite, not of an institutional hierarchy, but of outstanding devotion to Yahweh. "Fear" means not terror or dread but, when constructed with the divine name, "passionate love that seeks complete devotion." These three groups, from the larger to the smaller, thrice sing the same refrain, "His loving grace endures forever."

The second strophe reveals that the psalmist has encountered a grave crisis. While adversaries abound and have surrounded him, the shout of victory is now repeated, "The Lord is for me!" It becomes a refrain, presumably for a single voice, symbol of all three groups mentioned previously. "He set me free," literally, "He opened for me a large space," where I could breathe and escape the entrapment. The prospect of defeat is now transformed into triumph, but the post-drama recollection leads to a comparison between human help and divine refuge.

The granting of freedom is expressed in nomadic terms, which persisted throughout the settled history of Israel (Pss 4:1; 31:8; 66:12; cf. Gen 26:22). The text does not suggest that this was a release from a dungeon or a citadel. Nor does it indicate that the hymnist remembers the divine jurisprudence by which a persecuted or pursuit victim would find "protection" within the sanctuary, waiting for the verdict of acquittal, as is suggested in some individual complaints.

Protection from "princes" cannot be relied on. Not only does the soloist repeat his faith in God as refuge through a refrain, which may have been sung antiphonally by a group of liturgical singers, but he also claims, in royal terms, that he escaped from a military entrapment by foreign nations. The style is that of royal psalms. A threefold refrain, "In the name of the Lord I cut them to pieces," clinches the validity of this interpretation. The king was probably involved in the processional pilgrimage, and the psalmist attributed a significant part to the military commander.

Core Strophe: The Lord Is My Strength (vv. 13-14)

The Hebrew text reads, "Thou didst push me" (v. 13), as if an accusation were directed against the Lord, but the LXX, Syr., and Vulg. imply the same verb in the passive mode, "I was pushed," in order to make me stumble and fall. "But

Yahweh came to my help" and "Yahweh is my strength." The psalmist wishes to tell, publicly, lyrically, musically, the benevolent deeds of Yahweh (v. 17). The sentence may be elliptical, but it succinctly develops the preceding one: Yahweh came to my help, he was my help, for his strength is shared by my weakness, and it transmutes my weakness into strength, the very power of God.

The recital of the recent past, a scenic passage from mortal danger to living victory, immediately brings the commitment of absolute dependence and joy in complete confidence, "I shall celebrate him." The psalmist remembers his professional vocation. He wishes both to sing praises and to accompany himself on a musical instrument. The plucking of a stringed cithara or lute accentuates the rhythm and the color of the canticle. The king is now safe, and the psalmist lends him the words that will initiate musically a joyful gratitude.

Strophes IV'-I': Pilgrims at Last Enter the Temple (vv. 15-29)

The right hand of the Lord was raised, and the enemy defeated. Songs of victory are sung in the tents of the fighters, now at ease. The king breathes with an amazing awareness of having escaped death (vv. 17-18). On the threshold of the sanctuary, and in the face of the closed portals at the entrance, the king shouts liturgically, "Open for me the gates of righteousness," and he invites his army to follow. At this point, the pilgrims are all assembled but no longer divided into three groups (vv. 2-4), for the *ecclesia* now faces the unification of diverse elements.

Strophe II' sounds at first like an intrusion. What is the miracle of the cornerstone (vv. 22-23)? It has been suggested that a proverb is cited here. There is little doubt that the pilgrims are startled by the architecture of the portals. The translation "cornerstone" is not necessarily an error, for the meaning is not "stone at the corner." As in several languages, for example, in the French "pierre angulaire," the Hebrew describes the shape of the stone, with its angular sides, not its position at the side of the edifice. A cornerstone may mean a capstone, a keystone, or a copestone, which exactly completes the arch of a large bay in its center to insure its solidity. In general, the term designates the fundamental stone. This is the way the LXX understood the Hebrew words (cf. Matt 21:41; Acts 4:11; but cf. Isa 28:16; 1 Pet 2:6-7; cf. also Eph 2:20).

The miracle — *mirabile dictu* — does not refer to the aesthetic equilibrium of the edifice, but indicates its mystical transmutation into a spiritual reality. Centuries before the story of Jesus was told by the early Christians, some psalmist had the courage to transcend the ideology of the temple as the center of the universe and to use its capstone as the symbol of an eternal, supraearthly, supra-geographical gift of the Lord to his people, hitherto seduced by the foreign myth of the omphalos.

The experience of divine presence outside of geographic space and the annual calendar of feasts is not generally affirmed by the psalmists,[1] who were, after all, professional functionaries of the temple. However, when such a universal availability is implied, the word "miracle" is not an oriental hyperbole. The sanctuary of Zion, in its historical foundation (2 Sam 6:1-11; 1 Kgs 6:1), does not require, or deserve, the description of "marvel" or "miracle" (cf. Ps 139:6), something beyond human demonstration or understanding. Nevertheless, its allegorical configuration, even its literal implication, indicates that the Lord, at any time and in any place, demands a mode of designation that includes duration and sometimes ecstasy. A most intimate communion with the divinity arises from the will of Yahweh: "This came into being from Yahweh" (v. 23).

At the threshold of this openness and supracultic hagiocentrism, the psalmist who led the pilgrimage stands on a boundary line. "This day that the Lord has made" (v. 24). Strophe I' crowns a tri-optic approach with two supplications of finality: "Save us, we beseech thee" — there are still some signs of uncertainty ahead in the international situation — and "give us success." What is salvation without an increase in the birthrate or without an increase of fertility in the soil?

It is possible that such a petition is not only aiming at lasting peace but also a devastating drought, and begs for rain.[2] The "Save us" prayer may also be the sign of a continuous sense of national guilt (Pss 12:1; 20:9; 28:9; 60:5; 108:6).

The words of admiration for the stones of the temple by the disciples of Jesus (Matt 21:9) introduce an apt citation of the psalm, with the proper interpretation. The validity of such an exegesis is strengthened by the preceding and following context: (1) "This is the day that the Lord has made" (v. 24) remains an obscure statement, special and even unique, probably eschatological, beyond the cultic calendar of the time — Sabbath or one of the yearly feasts, from Passover to Tabernacles. The Lord introduces a day above the spatial and temporal limits of temple ceremonial. (2) "Blessed be he" can hardly be a new monarch about to be enthroned since the military captain, in royal terms, has already been alluded to in the recall of distress (vv. 8-9, 10-12). The blessing of this mysterious figure is first demanded or predicted by the psalmist alone (v. 26) and then becomes a plurality of figures, to be blessed by the community at large, pilgrims ready to enter, or worshipers already in the temple, priests, princes, and the common but devoted crowd.

The psalm ends with a personal exclamation, "Thou art my God! I celebrate thee!" (v. 28). The hymn is ambivalent, presenting the psalmist sometimes speaking for a king, sometimes for himself, and sometimes for a community of worshipers.

---

1. Cf. "The Psalmody of Presence," in Terrien, *The Elusive Presence*, pp. 278-332.
2. See Petuchowski, "*Hoshi'ah-na* in Psalm 118,25," pp. 266-71.

DATE AND THEOLOGY

The antiphonal refrains, which suggest a pilgrimage as well as a procession with palms, do not prevent personal supplications. Psalm 118 stands in favor of a postexilic date, just after the building of the second temple. Yet the psalmist expresses his hope for the end of history. He also speaks for himself as the prophet of the messianic King. The wonder of his own life, saved from death, easily becomes the symbol of Israel, whose distress is not ignored. But Israel will survive through the grace and fidelity of God, who endures forever.

The faith of the psalmist is stronger than the memory of his suffering. To be sure, "What has once been lived through cannot possibly be effaced," said Nicholas Berdyaev, but faith engenders a hope even for the long future. Messianic hope, which Judaism devised after the disappearance of its Davidic kings, was inherited by early Christianity as the expectation of the reign of God in history.

PSALM 119

An Acrostic Litany

I. Aleph

1. *Happy are people whose way is undefiled,*
   Who walk the way of the Lord!
2. *Happy are those who observe his testimonies,*
   Who seek him with their whole heart!
3. *They also do no iniquity,*
   For they walk in his ways.

4. *It was indeed thou who didst command us*
   To keep diligently thy precepts.
5. *If only my ways were firm enough*
   To observe and keep thy statutes!
6. *Then I would not be ashamed*
   When I look at all thy commandments.

7. *I would praise thee with an upright heart,*
   When I learned thy righteous decisions;

8. *Thy precepts I shall observe and keep;*
       Oh! forsake me not utterly!

II. Beth

9. *Wherewith shall a young man cleanse his path?*
       By observing thy word;
10. *With my whole heart do I seek thee;*
       Let me not wander from thy commandments!
11. *Thy word have I conserved in my heart,*
       That I might not sin against thee!

12. *Blessed art thou, my Lord!*
       Teach me thy statutes!
13. *With my lips I enumerate*
       All the judgments of thy mouth.
14. *I have rejoiced in the way of thy testimonies*
       Even more than in any riches.

15. *I will meditate on thy precepts,*
       And have respect for thy paths.
16. *I will find delight in thy statutes;*
       I will not forget thy word.

III. Gimel

17. *Deal bountifully with thy servant,*
       That I may live and keep thy word.
18. *Open thou my eyes, that I may behold*
       The wonders of thy law!
19. *I am a stranger upon the earth;*
       Hide not thy commandments from me.

20. *My soul is worn away at all times,*
       Longing for thy judgments.
21. *Thou hast rebuked the proud; let them be cursed.*
       They have erred from thy commandments.
22. *Roll away from me reproach and contempt,*
       For I have kept thy testimonies.

23. *Princes take their seat and speak against me,*
       But thy servant meditates on thy statutes;
24. *Thy testimonies also are my delight;*
       My counselors are thy precepts.

IV. Daleth

25.   *My soul is covered with dust;*
        Quicken thou me according to thy word!
26.   *I have told thee my ways, thou didst answer me;*
        Teach me thy statutes!
27.   *Make me understand the way of thy precepts,*
        So I shall meditate on thy marvelous works.

28.   *My soul melts in tears, from deep grief;*
        Redress me according to thy word.
29.   *Remove far from me the way of lying,*
        And grant me the grace of thy law.
30.   *I have chosen the way of truth,*
        And assimilated thy judgments.

31.   *I have clung to thy testimonies;*
        O Lord, do not put me to shame!
32.   *I will run the way of thy commandments,*
        Because thou hast opened my heart.

V. Hê

33.   *Teach me, O Lord, the way of thy precepts,*
        And I shall keep it to the end.
34.   *Give me intelligence, that I may keep thy law,*
        That I might observe it with my whole heart.
35.   *Make me march on the path of thy commandments,*
        For in it I am delighted [to go]!

36.   *Incline my heart to thy testimonies,*
        And not toward covetousness.
37.   *Turn away my eyes from beholding vanity,*
        And make me live in thy way!
38.   *Strengthen thy word for thy servant,*
        As it addresses those who fear thee!

39.   *Turn away the reproach I fear,*
        For thy judgments are good.
40.   *Behold! I long after thy precepts;*
        Make me live within thy righteousness!

VI. Waw

41.   *Let thy gracious love come to me, O Lord!*
        Even thy salvation, according to thy word!

42.   *Thus I shall have an answer for anyone who attacks me,*
        For I trust in thy word.

43.   *Take not utterly out of my mouth the word of truth,*
        For I have hope in thy judgments.

44.   *Then I shall observe thy law constantly,*
        Forever and ever.

45.   *I shall walk in all freedom,*
        For I study thy precepts.

46.   *I shall speak of thy testimonies*
        Before kings without shame,

47.   *I find my delight in thy commandments,*
        Because I love them!

48.   *I lift up my hands to thy commandments;*
        I love them, and I wish to meditate on thy statutes.

VII. Zayin

49.   *Remember thy word to thy servant,*
        Thanks to which thou makest me hope:

50.   *This is the consolation in my misery,*
        For thy word enables me to live!

51.   *Arrogant men have sorely derided me,*
        But I have not deviated from thy law.

52.   *I remember thy judgments of old,*
        O Lord, and I am comforted.

53.   *Seeing the evildoers, horror has seized me;*
        They have forsaken thy law.

54.   *Thy precepts are for me as beautiful as psalmodies*
        In the house where I am a guest.

55.   *At night I remember thy name, O Lord!*
        And I observe thy law.

56.   *The wealth that truly belongs to me*
        Is to preserve and observe thy commandments.

VIII. Ḥeth

57.   *My lot, O Lord, may I say it?*
        Is to observe thy words.

58.   *I entreat thy favor with my whole heart;*
        Have mercy upon me, according to thy words!

59. I have scrutinized my ways,
    And wish to align my steps with thy testimonies.

60. I made haste and delayed not
    To keep thy commandments;
61. Though caught in the pits dug by the wicked,
    I have not forgotten thy law.
62. At midnight I arise to give thee thanks
    For thy right judgments.

63. I am the companion of all those who fear thee,
    And of those who keep thy precepts.
64. The earth, O Lord, is full of thy mercies;
    Teach me thy statutes!

IX. Ṭeth

65. Thou hast dealt well with thy servant,
    O Lord, according to thy word;
66. Teach me good discernment and knowledge,
    For in thy commandments I trust.
67. Before I was afflicted I erred,
    But now I observe thy word.

68. Thou art generous and actest generously;
    Teach me thy statutes.
69. Arrogant men have forged lies against me,
    But I keep thy precepts with my whole heart.
70. Their heart clogged with fat,
    But as for me, my delights are in thy law.

71. It was good for me to have been afflicted,
    That I might learn thy statutes.
72. The law thou utteredst is more precious to me
    Than thousands [of pieces] of gold and silver.

X. Yodh

73. Thy hands made and fashioned me;
    Give me intelligence for learning thy commandments.
74. Those that fear thee will be glad to see me,
    Because I have hope in thy word.
75. I know, O Lord, that thy judgments are right,
    And that thou afflictedst me on account of thy fidelity.

76. *Is it not thy fidelity that comforts me?*
    As thou didst promise thy servant?
77. *Let thy tender mercies come unto me,*
    That I may live, for thy law is my delight.
78. *May the arrogant be put to shame,*
    For they have twisted [truth] into lies!
    But I will meditate on thy precepts.

79. *Let those who fear thee come back to me,*
    And those who know thy testimonies.
80. *Let my heart so well fulfill thy precepts*
    That I may not be put to shame.

XI. Kaph

81. *My soul is longing for thy salvation,*
    And I hope in thy word.
82. *My eyes are worn out, waiting for thy word;*
    When will you have pity on me?
83. *Though I am like a smoked wineskin,*
    I have not forgotten thy precepts.

84. *How many more days will thy servant be alive?*
    When wilt thou condemn my persecutors?
85. *Arrogant men have dug pitfalls for me,*
    But this does not conform to thy law!
86. *All thy commandments are right;*
    Come to my help! I am wrongly harassed.

87. *They have almost eradicated me from the earth;*
    But as for me, I did not forsake thy precepts.
88. *By thy grace let me live!*
    That I may keep the testimonies of thy mouth!

XII. Lamedh

89. *Forever, my Lord!*
    Thy word is secure in the heavens!
90. *Thy faithfulness is for all generations;*
    Just as thou didst establish the earth, and it abides!
91. *Days stand by thy appointment,*
    For the universe is thy servant.

92. *If thy law had not been my delight,*
    Then I should have perished in my misery.

93.   I shall never forget thy precepts;
            By them thou makest me live!
94.   I am thine! Save me!
            For I have studied thy precepts.

95.   Scoundrels lie in wait to destroy me,
            But I attend to thy testimonies.
96.   I have seen a limit to all perfection,
            But thy commandment is infinitely ample.

XIII. Mem

97.   How I love thy law!
            All day long I meditate on it.
98.   Thy commandments have made me wiser than my foes,
            For they are mine forever.
99.   I have more understanding than all my teachers,
            For my meditation is thy testimonies.

100.   I understand things far more than the aged,
            Because I keep thy precepts.
101.   I avoid all paths leading to evil,
            In order to observe thy word;
102.   I do not depart from thy judgments,
            For thou indeed didst teach them to me.

103.   How sweet are thy words on my palate;
            Yea, better than honey to my mouth.
104.   Through thy precepts I gain understanding;
            Therefore I hate any path of duplicity.

XIV. Nun

105.   Thy word is a lamp unto my feet,
            A light unto my path;
106.   I have sworn and shall keep my oath
            To observe the judgments of thy righteousness;
107.   I am very much afflicted;
            Give me life, O Lord, according to thy word!

108.   Accept, I beseech thee, the offering of my prayers,
            O Lord! And teach me thy judgments.
109.   Constantly at the risk of death,
            Yet I do not forget thy law.

110. *Evil men have laid a snare for me,*
      But I have not erred from thy precepts.

111. *Thy testimonies I take as a precious inheritance forever,*
      For they are the rejoicing of my heart.

112. *I incline my heart to perform thy statutes,*
      As an eternal privilege, to the end.

XV. Samekh

113. *I hate double-minded people;*
      But thy law do I love.

114. *Thou art my shelter and my shield;*
      I hope in thy word.

115. *Depart from me, ye evildoers;*
      For I will keep the commandments of my God.

116. *Uphold me according to thy word, that I may live,*
      And let me not be put to shame by a deceiving hope!

117. *Sustain me and I shall be saved;*
      Then I shall always have regard for thy statutes.

118. *Thou rejectedst all those who err from thy statutes,*
      For their cleverness is vain.

119. *Thou countest as dross all the evil men of the earth;*
      Therefore I love thy testimonies.

120. *My flesh trembles from fear before thee,*
      And from awe before thy decisions.

XVI. Ayin

121. *I have acted with rectitude and justice;*
      Do not deliver me to my oppressors!

122. *Guarantee the well-being of thy servant;*
      Let not the arrogant men oppress me!

123. *My eyes are failing, I wearily wait for thy salvation,*
      And for the word of thy justice.

124. *Deal mercifully with thy servant,*
      And teach me thy statutes!

125. *I am thy servant; give me understanding,*
      That I may know thy testimonies!

126. *Lord, it is time to act;*
      They have violated thy law.

127.   *Yea, I love thy commandments*
        More than gold, even most refined gold,
128.   *Because I find thy precepts right in all cases,*
        And I hate all the ways of lying.

XVII. Peh

129.   *Thy testimonies are wonderful;*
        Thus my soul preserves and observes them.
130.   *As thy word unfolds, it illuminates;*
        It gives understanding to the simple.
131.   *My mouth is wide open; I am panting,*
        Because I long for thy commandments.

132.   *Turn toward me and give me thy grace!*
        It is thy wont for those who love thy name;
133.   *Straighten my steps by thy command,*
        And let no iniquity dominate me!
134.   *Redeem me from the oppression of men,*
        That I may keep thy precepts.

135.   *Make thy face shine upon thy servant!*
        And teach me thy statutes.
136.   *Streams of tears run from my eyes*
        Because people do not keep thy law.

XVIII. Ṣadhe

137.   *Righteous art thou, O Lord;*
        And upright are thy judgments.
138.   *Thy testimonies, which thou hast ordered,*
        Are rightness and faithfulness itself!
139.   *My zeal has consumed me,*
        Because my foes have forgotten thy words.

140.   *Thy word is surely well tested;*
        Therefore thy servant loves it.
141.   *I am of small stature, and despised,*
        But I do not forget thy precepts.
142.   *Thy righteousness is righteousness forever,*
        And thy law is the truth.

143.   *Trouble and anguish have taken hold of me,*
        Yet thy commandments are my delight.

144.   *The righteousness of thy testimonies is everlasting;*
        Give me understanding, and I shall live.

XIX. Qoph

145.   *I call thee with my whole heart;*
        Answer me, O Lord, I will keep thy statutes.
146.   *I cried unto thee; save me!*
        That I might keep thy testimonies.
147.   *I arose before dawn and cried;*
        I hoped in thy word.

148.   *I open my eyes before I hear the night watches,*
        That I might meditate on thy word.
149.   *According to thy lovingkindness, hear my voice!*
        O Lord, by thy best judgment let me live!
150.   *They draw nigh, those that follow after mischief;*
        They are far away from thy law.

151.   *Thou art near, O Lord;*
        And all thy commandments are the truth.
152.   *Long ago I have known of thy testimonies,*
        That thou hast founded them forever.

XX. Resh

153.   *Consider my affliction, and deliver me,*
        For I do not forget thy law.
154.   *Plead my cause, and be my redeemer!*
        Let me live, according to thy word.
155.   *Salvation is far from evil men,*
        For they seek not thy statutes.

156.   *Many are thy tender mercies, O Lord!*
        According to thy judgments, let me live!
157.   *My persecutors are many, and also my enemies;*
        But I do not swerve from thy testimonies.
158.   *I beheld the transgressors; and I was grieved*
        Because they kept not thy word.

159.   *Consider how much I love thy precepts!*
        Let me live, O Lord, according to thy lovingkindness!
160.   *The foundation of thy word is truth,*
        And every decision of thy righteousness is forever.

XXI. Shin

161.   *Princes have persecuted me without cause,*
    But my heart trembles only at thy words.

162.   *I rejoice at thy sayings,*
    As one that finds great spoil;

163.   *I hate and abhor lying,*
    But thy law do I love.

164.   *Seven times a day do I praise thee*
    Over thy right decisions,

165.   *There is great peace for the lovers of thy law;*
    They find there no stumbling block.

166.   *I have hope for thy salvation, O Lord!*
    And I practice thy commandments.

167.   *My soul has observed thy testimonies,*
    And I love them exceedingly.

168.   *I have kept thy precepts and thy testimonies;*
    And all my ways are open before thee.

XXII. Taw

169.   *Let my cry come near to thy face, O Lord!*
    Give me understanding according to thy word!

170.   *Let my supplication come near to thee!*
    Deliver me according to thy word!

171.   *My lips shall utter thy praise,*
    Because thou hast taught me thy statutes.

172.   *My tongue shall speak of thy word,*
    Because all thy commandments are right.

173.   *Let thy hand be my succor!*
    For I have chosen thy precepts.

174.   *I have longed for thy salvation, O Lord!*
    And thy law is my delight.

175.   *Let my soul live! And it shall praise thee.*
    May thy judgments be my help!

176.   *I have gone astray like a lost sheep;*
    Seek thy servant, for I do not forget thy commandments.

BIBLIOGRAPHY

P. Auffret, "Structures littéraires dans le Psaume 119," in *Voyez de vos yeux*, VTSup XLVIII (Leiden, 1993), pp. 319-414; see rev. in *JBL*, CXIV (1995), pp. 304-5; S. Bergler, "Der längste Psalm — Anthologie oder Liturgie?" *VT*, XXIX (1979), pp. 257-88; P. E. Bonnard, *Le Psautier selon Jérémie* (Paris, 1960), pp. 207-18; M. Dahood, "Note on *me'ereṣ*, instead of *ba'eres*: cf. 11QPsᵃ," *CBQ*, XXXII (1970), p. 254 (on Ps 119:87); A. Deissler, *Psalm 119 (118) und seine Theologie* (München, 1955); H. Duesberg, "Le miroir du fidèle: Le Ps 119 (118) et ses usages liturgiques," *BVC*, XV (1956), pp. 87-97; J. E. Eaton, "Proposals in Psalms CCIX and CXIX," *VT*, XVIII (1968), pp. 557-58; F. François et F. Pierre-Yves, "La grâce de ta loi: Lecture spirituelle du Psaume 118 [119]," *Vie monastique*, XXI (1988); D. N. Freedman, *Psalm 119: The Exaltation of Torah* (Winona Lake, Ind., 1999); J. Graham, *With My Whole Heart: A Devotional Commentary on Psalm 119* (London, 1962); O. Grether, *Name und Wort Gottes im Alten Testament*, BZAW LXIV (Giessen, 1934); B. Heyne, "Zu Ps 119,75, und 67," *ZAW*, LI (1933), p. 175; H.-J. Kraus, "Freude an Gottes Gesetz," *EvT*, XI (1951), pp. 337-51; idem, "Zum Gesetzesverständnis der nachprophetischen Zeit," *Biblisch-theologische Aufsätze* (Neukirchen, 1972), pp. 179-94; M.-F. Lacan, "Le mystère de la prière dans le Ps. 119," *Lumen vitae*, XXIII (1955), pp. 125-42; J. D. Levenson, "The Source of the Torah: Psalm 119 and the Modes of Revelation in Second Temple Judaism," in *Festschrift F. M. Cross* (Philadelphia, 1987), pp. 559-74; J. L. Mays, "The Place of the Torah-Psalms in the Psalter," *JBL*, CVI (1987), pp. 3-12; J. Clinton McCann, Jr., *A Theological Introduction to the Book of Psalms: The Psalms as Torah* (Nashville, 1993), pp. 30-32; F. M. Moos, "Pourquoi l'Église applique-t-elle certains psaumes à la Sainte Vierge (Ps. 119-133)?" *Vie spirituelle*, XCVIII (1958), pp. 186-208; H. L. Moran, "Note on Ps. 119:28 [*d.l.ph.*], 'collapse,'" *CBQ*, XV (1953), pp. 10-11; H. P. Müller, "Die hebräische Wurzel [*s.i.h.*]," *VT*, XIX (1959), pp. 361-71; G. Ostborn, *Tora in the Old Testament: A Semantic Study* (Lund, 1945); H. Parzen, "Psalm 119 — A Study in the Origins of Pharisaic Religion," *The Reconstructionist*, XIII (1947), pp. 19-20; T. Penar, "Lamedh vocativi exempla Biblia Hebraica," *VD*, XLV (1967), pp. 32-46 (Ps 119:26); G. Perdue, *Wisdom and Cult* (Missoula, Mont., 1977), pp. 303-12; A. Robert, "Le sens du mot loi dans le Ps. 119," *RB*, XLVI (1937), pp. 182-206; idem, "Le Psaume 119 et les Sapientiaux," *RB*, XLVIII (1939), pp. 5-20; J. Schreiner, "Leben nach der Weisung des Herrn . . . ," in *Festschrift H. Gross* (Stuttgart, 1986), pp. 395-424; K. Seybold, "Die Redaktion der Wallfahrtpsalmen," *ZAW*, XCI (1979), pp. 247-68 (Psalms 119, 135, and 136); W. Soll, *Psalm 119: Matrix, Form and Setting* (Washington, 1991); W. M. Soll, "The Question of Psalm 119," *JBL*, CVI (1987), pp. 687-88; J. P. M. van der Ploeg, "Le psaume 119 et la sagesse," in *La Sagesse de l'Ancien Testament* (Gembloux and Louvain, 1979), pp. 82-87; C. Vermès, "The Thora Is a Light," *VT*, VIII (1958), pp. 436-38; C. Westermann, *The Living Psalms* (Grand Rapids, 1984), pp. 294-96; R. R. Williams, *The Perfect Law of Liberty: An Interpretation of Psalm 119* (London and New York, 1952).

FORM

Acrostic compositions, of which Psalm 119 is an extraordinary example, were apparently held in esteem by the singers of the first or second temple (cf. Psalms 9; 10; 25; 34; 37; 111; 112; 145; Lamentations 3), but Psalm 119 is the longest (176 verses) in the Psalter. It was probably preserved because it was sung as a litany of 22 strophes, each made of 8 bicola. The initial word of each strophe begins with a letter of the Hebrew alphabet (aleph, beth, etc.). Such a linguistic tour de force may have aroused the admiration of the singers and copyists. It also helps to explain the diversity of critical views on the style of the psalm. Some call it a masterpiece; others admit its monotony of repetitiousness and even mediocrity of inspiration.

The acrostic form may have compelled the poet to produce a number of prosaic declarations on the main topic, which revolves about the love of the author for Yahweh's law and eight synonyms (commandments statutes, precepts, testimonies, etc.). The literary genre defies a single classification since the psalm is a collection of didactic affirmations, praise, lament, thanksgiving, confession of faith, and songs of trust. It is indeed more than "a mixed psalm." One characteristic, however, is constant: that of personal and even subjective supplication to Yahweh.

While the word "litany" may not be strictly adequate, the modern use of this word applies to a lengthy repetition of identical responses by the congregation to a liturgist's enunciation of divine virtues, attributes, or activities.

The prevailing meters (3+2; 3+3; 4+4) suggest thematic development, but attempts to discover an ascending or descending movement have been futile.

COMMENTARY

Strophe I: Aleph (vv. 1-8)

Happiness is familiar to sapiential masters and temple singers (Prov 8:32; Hos 1:2; 2:2; cf. Deut 28:11, 14). Blessing is a ritual gesture transmitting the virtue or even the sanctity of a patriarch or priest; happiness is a dynamic exclamation, a send-off with the wish for a bon voyage. *Ashrê* is probably derived from a verb of movement, "to step forward." Here people are complimented for unblemished ways or behavior. The psalm begins with felicitations and greetings directed toward the future.

Strophe II: Beth (vv. 9-16)

The psalmist introduces himself as a young man. The need to "cleanse his path" implies that for him, not yet a mature man, discipline is harder to attain and maintain. There is also an affinity with sapiential poetry (Ps 119:72, 127; Prov 1:4, 8, 10, 15; Eccl. 11:5). In addition, there is a preference of wisdom over wealth (v. 14; cf. Job 28:13, 19; Prov 3:14, 15).

Strophe III: Gimel (vv. 17-24)

This young man is precocious in his thinking, for he remarks that he does not belong to the earth, or that his terrestrial existence is transitory (cf. Deut 10:19; Ps 39:12). His faith isolates him from the majority of earthly beings. He is also the target of princes who "take their seats" as judges. He opposes his own counselors — spiritual realities — to those who determine the politics of the nation. But is he completely innocent of his psychological depression (v. 28)?

Strophe IV: Daleth (vv. 25-32)

The soul *(nephesh)* is not the Greek or modern *psychē,* but this word designates the deeper being in its totality. When it is in distress, the soul is short of breath and fears mortal danger. "Quicken me" is a petition, "Let me live" or "Keep me alive" (v. 25). Divine grace can "teach," another sign of sapiential influence. The Syr. reads "I desire" instead of "I have assimilated" (v. 30).

Strophe V: Hê (vv. 33-40)

The wisdom atmosphere continues, as Yahweh is compared to a master teacher. So also does the dynamism of the "happy" declaration.

Strophe VI: Waw (vv. 41-48)

The plea intensifies its interiority. "Gracious love" has to come directly (cf. LXX) without intellectual decision, or, rather, mobilizing the willingness to see Yahweh's love in granting the Law. The ritual gesture of the lifted hand makes the prayer as ardent as the words.

Strophe VII: Zayin (vv. 49-56)

The petition assumes that by using the word "thy servant," the suppliant will be able to obtain an answer more readily. But what is "the house" where the poet feels like "an invited guest"? It is generally assumed that the designation (v. 54) alludes to the earth itself. Some translate, "the house of my pilgrimage." The context, however, with its comparison of the Law's beauty to that of "psalmodies," clearly makes an allusion to the temple. This young man is apparently a sacred singer, not a professional cultist.

Strophe VIII: Ḥeth (vv. 57-64)

No claim is made for family wealth or status. To observe God's words is a sufficient and plenteous heritage. "Caught in the pits" is probably a better translation of an obscure MT ("The cords of the wicked ensnared me"). Again the Lord appears as a master teacher; the psalmist follows the sapiential tradition and unconsciously composes his prayer in the light of his intellectual training. The prayer is also articulated on the cosmic amplitude of the sapiential horizon with the splendid observation that the earth is full of God's mercies.

Strophe IX: Ṭeth (vv. 65-72)

Suffering, understood as a punishment but viewed as a teaching method for improvement, can be useful and even legitimate. The psalmist, again self-presented as "thy servant," quietly thanks his divine sovereign, "Thou hast dealt well" (v. 65), "Thou art generous" (v. 68), "It was good for me" (v. 71). The enemies fail to understand, for their hearts are dulled with self-indulgence ("clogged with fat").

Strophe X: Yodh (vv. 73-80)

The language of wisdom persists (cf. Job 10:8), but unlike the Jobian relapse in protest, the poet of this psalm finds joy in remembering his having been made and fashioned by the God who now corrects him (v. 73).

Strophe XI: Kaph (vv. 81-88)

Yet the trials, the testing, and the persecution from human foes, arrogant, envious, and calumniating, have not eased. A wineskin scorched with smoke is the very symbol of mortal danger. The ambiguity of correction and the pedagogical aspect of severe discipline arise from the image of the wine, which, exposed to heat as improvement, also risks destruction. The heat of the flames may burn out the skin and lose the wine. The servant of God, once more self-designated as the all-devoted assistant of God, begs for the end of his torture (v. 84), either physical or psychological.

Strophe XII: Lamedh (vv. 89-96)

Now the singer renews his praise: God's word is firm and therefore enduring, like heaven and earth (vv. 89-90). The concept of servitude as a privilege is applied not only to man but also to the universe. It receives a cosmic dimension. Yet the human foes have almost succeeded in murdering the patient (v. 87).

Strophe XIII: Mem (vv. 97-104)

From the love that God has shown in revealing his Law, the poet passes easily to the love of man for this Law. Moral obedience is transfigured into inner effusion of a highly emotional nature. To say that the Law "is mine" is to use the language of a lover rather than the language of an ethicist (v. 97). Soon the sapiential tone reappears: "my teachers" and "the aged," venerable masters of wisdom (v. 99), belong to a lower order of knowledge than the grip of the divine testimonies.

Strophe XIV: Nun (vv. 105-112)

Psalm 119:105 is perhaps the best-known verse of the entire psalm! "Thy word," as a lamp or a light, is still a metaphor of movement forward as suggested by the initial felicitation on happiness; it has been understood in a restricted sense, or perhaps with the cognitive awareness of canonical authority for the whole of "scriptural" theology. Rather, with the amplitude of diversity that it most likely possesses in this context (see below), the word should not be taken as a singular noun (cf. some Heb. MSS, LXX, and Syr.). It is at least a broadly psychological designation of the Law. In Psalm 119, prayer is a "free-will offering," a cultic term that here transcends the sacrificial ritual of temple worship, either before or after the exile. The psalmist uses this imagery only once with the apparent intention of "spiritualizing" the whole system of adoration, even in the temple of Zion.

Doing the loving act of performing God's statutes is "an eternal privilege, to the end" (v. 112). Whatever happens, in life or in death, the psalmist swears fidelity in following the Law, which he considers an inheritance as precious as ever. Such fidelity is not the result of submission: it is the manifestation of the most profound and lasting joy.

Strophe XV: Samekh (vv. 113-120)

Double-minded people, formerly rendered as "vain shouts," are translated as "skeptics" in the Greek etymological sense and modern usage. These men are really "doubters" (cf. Arab. "cleft branches"); they do not commit themselves to any law. Their intellectual suspense amounts to a vacuum. For the psalmist, on the contrary, total devotion leads to complete belief in divine protection. This time God is compared in military terms to "a shelter" and "a shield."

The poet is now seeking salvation. He repeats as a refrain a frantic desire for life, not relying on a false hope. He still trembles from fear, but this is not the terror of death. Rather, a lover of God "fears" to fall short of God's beloved expectations.

Strophe XVI: Ayin (vv. 121-128)

Asking more than ever for inclusive renewal in a "salvation" that seems to be desperately delayed (v. 123), the psalmist, twice in a single strophe (vv. 122, 124), proudly reaffirms his status as a "servant," for the renewed claim of total devotion leads to the belief that Yahweh will finally be moved to action. This time the plea is abruptly stated, "Lord, it is time to act!" (v. 126).

Prayer, in the Hebrew mentality, may at times contradict the rules of elegant politeness. Prayer may then sound like a military command. Such is the sublime freedom of love! Such also is pathos in its extremity.

Strophe XVII: Peh (vv. 129-136)

The lover of God has reached the ultimate degree of terror. Nevertheless, he still can have recourse to praise (v. 129). The literal meaning of the next demand expostulates on "the unfolding of thy word" (v. 130). The meaning is uncertain, but it probably refers to the beginning of exegetical hermeneutic! The physical condition of the patient, which may justify such an extremity of requesting, then receives an extremity of complaint: "Mouth wide open, I pant, unable to breathe as if I were strangulated." The "soul" is not mentioned, but its reality, as a free throat suddenly obstructed implies, makes the petition more forceful.

Denial of transgression, which might be judged today as self-adulation, must be viewed in the context of mortal peril. The psalmist fights for his life. He requests "redemption"! Then the sky clears and lightens, as once more "servanthood" is presented as an argument to convince, while streams of tears flow from his eyes.

The face of God will "shine" on his servant. The shining of God's face is like a rising sun, the symbol of renovation, the forerunner of a new term of life. It appears just as in Aaron's blessing (Num 6:24)!

Strophe XVIII: Ṣadhe (vv. 137-144)

Is the patient of small stature or just of low social status? The Hebrew word for "small" is ambiguous. The word "despised" keeps the ambiguity. Perhaps self-depreciation is another way of moving God to beneficent intervention. What is the "zeal" that consumes? Is it simply the desire to convert his contemporaries toward an ethical way of living?

Strophe XIX: Qoph (vv. 145-152)

The prayer has veered into several cries (vv. 145, 146, and 147). The more the foes despise the Law, the closer "they draw nigh" to the man of sorrows. Yet his trust in the nearness of the divine and his faith in the truth of the commandments do not vacillate.

Strophe XX: Resh (vv. 153-160)

A plea for the redeemer is repeated more as a new assertion of God's magnificent quality, his "tender mercies," probably a plural of majesty. It accompanies the unhesitating belief that the foundation of God's word is truth (v. 160). There is no room for any doubt, skepticism, or double-mindedness. One can thus repeat the cry, "Let me live!" (vv. 156, 159). The Lord is not at this time again compared to a teacher, but supremely imagined as a lawyer for the defense (v. 154), and indeed the "savior" (v. 155). His tender mercies are once again invoked, and the demand to live must banish the recurring horror of death. The truth of God's word appears "from the beginning." Truth anticipates all stories of revelation in Israel: no Sinai, no Moses, no Samuel, no prophet. Just God's word at creation.

Strophe XXI: Shin (vv. 161-168)

Princes are once again accused of tormenting the psalmist (cf. v. 23), who then prays "seven times a day." A schedule for ritual devotions is still in the formative stage (cf. Pss 5:8; 59:16; 88:13; Dan 6:10).

Strophe XXII: Taw (vv. 169-176)

The final stanza of the poem adds soberly, and yet with a restrained sense of drama, the summing up of the preceding requests. The agony has not abated; the expressions of hope in extremity still abound: "cry, supplication, succor, longing, help"! Yet the tone of the concluding plea, while it remains as ardent as ever, adds a note of intimate tenderness, "Let my cry come near to thy face!" The word for "visage," or "face," is in general a metaphor of presence. Here it seems advisable to preserve the Hebraic literalism, "near to thy face." It summons an imagery of mystical communion rarely formulated as well elsewhere.

Moreover, at the end of his litany, the psalmist links his deliverance to an outburst of praise that contains a solemn promise: "My lips shall utter thy praise," as well as "speak of thy word" (vv. 171-172). The poet is determined to share his "good news" with others. The psalm ends as a decision to preach a "gospel," not spoken but sung.

The psalmist is a singer as well as a sage. He sublimates his trial into music. Yet, for the last time, the Lord is compared to a teacher.

The ultimate confession is quite surprising, "I have gone astray like a lost sheep." The image of the sheep intimates silently the theological notion of "The Good Shepherd." With the begging, "Seek thy servant," he needs to be found again.

DATE AND THEOLOGY

It is difficult to assign a specific date for the composition of this psalm — a masterpiece of acrostic organization, although this feature may have been the cause of its stylistic monotony as well as of the anthological character of its citations.

Psalm 119 is filled with expressions and details that seem to have been borrowed from the whole of the oral and written traditions of Israel — a nascent "scripture" from its earliest days to Persian Judaism. Affinities between many formulas and the Jeremianic oracles or stories, however, may not be ignored or missed. The sapiential way of formulating the religious basis of morality has received constant attention throughout the commentary. But the affinities with Jeremiah and Jeremianic literature need to be stressed.

For example, "Thou [God] art generous and actest generously" (Ps. 119:68); cf. "I will turn away from doing good to them" (Jer 32:40). The enemies of the psalmist are similar to, if not identical with, those of the prophet (vv. 86-87; cf. Jer 11:9; 16:11). The teachers of wisdom, whom the psalmist admires but to whom he assigns second place (v. 99; cf. Jer 9:22-23), expresses suspicion and even hate against the faithless (v. 158; cf. Jer 3:7-20; 9:1). "There is great peace for the lovers of thy law" (v. 165; cf. Jer 6:15, 21). In both the psalm and the Jeremianic circle, even princes are persecutors.

Many other similarities may be observed, especially the need to search God "with the whole of [one's] heart," a stylistic feature prominent throughout the psalm, in Jeremiah, and in Deuteronomy.

There is not the slightest allusion to the exile in the psalm; and the foes are arrogant Judahites, but not invading strangers. The date may therefore be sometime between the reform of Josiah (622 B.C.E.) and the end of the kingdom of Judah (598 or 587 B.C.E.).

The theology of the psalm, it has often been maintained, rests on the love of the Law, which, for some commentators, designates the Pentateuch, and thus might point to a time close to Ezra and Nehemiah. But nowhere in the psalm is there a sign of the Pentateuchal traditions, prohibitions, legislation, or priestly concerns. Yet we find the word "torah" (used 25 times), "testimonies" (21 times), "commandments" (22 times), "judgments" or "decisions" (23 times), "word" or "oracle" (19 times), and "sayings" (24 times). In the same area of "legal" observance, the words "way," "road," and "path" appear 13, 5, and 2 times respectively.

The great diversity of these synonyms clearly prevents the identification of the word "torah" with the Pentateuch. Neither could "the word of God" designate canonical Scripture. Here may be the beginning of a trend toward a synthesis of various types of divine revelation, but it shows that God communicates with human beings, including a woman (2 Kgs 22:14), in many different ways, through sages, prophets, and other mediators of the divine will. The terms used vary; they cannot be taken literally. What counts is that they are uttered by human intermediaries of "the mouth of God."

In summary, the theology of Psalm 119 stresses, among other themes, the following points:

1. To seek God's presence, and even "to be near his face," is the primary condition of learning the will of God.

2. The word of God is to be received as a dynamic thrust, for it is food from his mouth — anthropomorphically speaking — to be received, eaten, and digested again and again.

3. The transgressions of doubters should be cause for pathetic concern but not brutal intervention by God's devotees. Hence the sharing of one's conviction leads, not to imposition, but to the "preaching of the gospel" (good news) with an intensity and respect that transform acceptance not only into joy but also into the awareness of an "apostolic vocation" for all.

4. The Law is not static but dynamic. It moves "on the way." It cannot be frozen forever in the century of its revelation. The biblical theologian's responsibility is to hold, at every moment of disquisition, the human description of Yahweh's will and activity as that of a continuous Creator, of an evolving "Savior."

Man's lot or inheritance is not a possession received from the past but a commitment of the past interpreted for the future.

5. The last theme is sober but also promising: the theologian of God's word or words must first and ultimately remember that consciousness of the lost sheep will color every intellectual search, and that one must become avail-

able to the initiative of a transcendence that is also an immanence of vulnerability. There cannot be any theological undertaking without humble and open spirituality.

Revelation is never far from inspiration.

PSALM 120

A Pilgrim Song for Peace

1. A Song of Ascents.

I

> In my deep distress, to the Lord I cried,
> And he answered me.
2.   Deliver my life from lying lips, O Lord,
> And from a deceitful tongue!

II

3.   What will be inflicted upon thee,
> Deceitful tongue, and even more?
4.   The arrows of a warrior, sharpened
> On the flaming embers of juniper?

III

5.   Woe is me, that I sojourn in Meshech,
> That I dwell in the tents of Kedar!
6.   Too long for my soul have I remained
> With those who hate peace!
7.   I am for peace, but when I speak,
> They are for war!

BIBLIOGRAPHY

P. Auffret, "La collection des Psaumes des Montées comme Ensemble Structure," in *La Sagesse a bâti sa maison* (Fribourg and Göttingen, 1982), pp. 439-62; H. W. Brekelmans, "Some Translation Problems . . . [Ps 120:7]," *OtSt*, XV (1969), pp. 170ff.; F. Crüsemann, *Studien zur Formgeschichte von Hymnus und Danklied in Israel*, WMANT XXXII (Neukirchen, 1969), pp. 155-56; K. Seybold, *Die Wallfahrtpsalmen: Studien zur Entstehungsgeschichte von Psalmen 120–134* (Neukirchen, 1978).

FORM

This individual lament of distress is made up of three short strophes: I: A Prayer Is Heard (vv. 1-2); II: A Malediction Is Thrown (vv. 3-4); III: A Self-malediction Is Expressed (vv. 5-7).

The meter is quite regular, chiefly 3+2 and 2+3.

Strophe I: A Prayer Is Heard (vv. 1-2)

Psalm 120 is the first of the Songs of Ascents (Psalms 120–134), which were used by pilgrims marching toward the temple. The selection of this piece for opening the subcollection of the Songs of Ascents is certainly unexpected. The psalmist has been the victim of vicious calumnies and seems still to be threatened by personal enemies. He may have been accused falsely of crimes, and his life has been put in danger. The structure of this concise poem is composed in a peculiar form, neither that of a complaint nor that of a hymn; the psalmist has received a divine answer, but he continues to beg the Lord (mentioned only twice) to intervene in his favor. This indicates an uncertain but somber situation.

Strophe II: A Malediction Is Thrown (vv. 3-4)

No longer a petition to Yahweh, the psalm hurls a malediction at an adversary directly addressed in the second person singular, condemning his deceitful tongue. The bitterness is of an unusual intensity. The irony is aggressive: What kind of arrows, so trenchant, so mordant, may really be those so poetically burning in flaming juniper? They are arrows of a "warrior," a hero of warfare, well known for his bravura.

Strophe III: A Self-malediction Is Expressed (vv. 5-7)

The poet is ashamed of himself because he has lived a long time in a pagan environment. Meshech is perhaps in the extreme north of the Holy Land (Gen 10:2), although the LXX translates μοσχοί, apparently a population living as far north as the Caucasus. Kedar is the desert of northern Arabia (Gen 25:13; Isa 42:11), where nomads lived alone in tent (Jer 49:29, 31) but appear to have had encounters with the Assyrians of Esarhaddon and Ashurbanipal. Did the psalmist actually emigrate to these foreign regions, for business or cultural purposes? The silence of the psalm may have been clear to the pilgrims, who had not experienced the same crisis. In any case, the singer claimed to be a peaceful man. Why did he menace his foe with mortal arrows? Apparently he was seduced by advantages in the midst of people who deceived him, for they hate peace. The "Woe is me!" clearly reveals personal guilt, of which the singer does not feel that he is forgiven. "Too long for my soul have I remained. . . ." The word traditionally translated "soul" may include the power and the eagerness to live, and does not mean the psyche of Hellenistic or modern times. Here the psalmist admits that his inner being has been corrupted by his long sojourn among those who "hate peace" and whose tongues are deceitful.

Against whom did the people wage war? Or is it that they spoke of war but meant domestic quarrels (cf. Pss 3:6; 35:3)? And what was the occasion for them to lie about the singer's behavior? The succinctness of the poem — a literary quality — leaves the situation obscure.

DATE AND THEOLOGY

As a pilgrim song, Psalm 120 belongs to postexilic times, when the early Jews prospered commercially and financially throughout the Persian Empire. The poet is a devotee of Yahweh, especially if he joined a pilgrimage to the Jerusalem temple, as implied by the very texture of his meditation. Perhaps the reference aims at the religious syncretism that contaminated his soul and led him to undermine the pacifism of his previous beliefs out of respect for others. Was his devotion to the Judaism of his time weakened and softened by his tolerance? Did the friends among whom he lived come to deceive him for reasons that at last proved to have been false? "Peace" is "health," the search for which may contradict indifference and *laissez-faire*. At all levels of human relations, it may mean active and efficient intervention. Perhaps the lines of Wordsworth may be appropriate.

> He raised his eye
> Soul-smitten; for, that instant did appear
> Large space ('mid dreadful clouds) of purest sky,
> An azure disc — shield of Tranquility,
> Invisible, unlooked for, minister
> Of providential goodness ever nigh?

A soul-smitten devotee of Yahweh returns to the catechism of his fathers, and he implicitly asks pardon, in order to live a new life.

PSALM 121

The Lord Is Thy Keeper

1. *Song of Ascents.*

I

I lift up mine eyes to the mountains:
From where shall my help come?
2.   My help will come from the Lord,
Who made heaven and earth.

II

3.   He will not allow thy foot to stumble;
Thy keeper will not fall asleep;
4.   Behold! He will neither slumber nor sleep,
The guardian of Israel.

III

5.   The Lord is thy keeper!
The Lord is thy shade on thy right hand.
6.   The sun shall not smite thee by day,
Nor the moon by night.

IV

7.   The Lord will keep thee from all evil;
He will protect thy life.
8.   The Lord will keep thy going out and thy coming in,
From this time forth and forevermore.

BIBLIOGRAPHY

P. Auffret, "La collection des Psaumes des Montées comme Ensemble Structure," in *La Sagesse a bâti sa Maison* (Fribourg and Göttingen, 1982), pp. 439-62; H. Blakeney, "Psalm 121,1-2," *Expository Times*, LVI (1944-45), p. 111; C. R. Ceresko, "Psalm 121: A Prayer of a Warrior?" *Bib*, LXX (1089) pp. 496-510; O. Eissfeldt, "Ps. 121: Stat crux, dum volvitur orbis," in *Festschrift H. Lilje* (Berlin, 1959), pp. 9-14; cf. idem, "Psalm CXXI," *Kleine Schriften*, III (Tübingen, 1966), pp. 494-500; H.-J. Kraus, "Der Lebendige Gott," *Biblisch-theologische Aufsätze* (Neukirchen, 1972), pp. 1-36; J. Morgenstern, "Psalm

121," *JBL*, LVIII (1939), pp. 311-23; P. H. Pollock, "Psalm 121," *JBL*, LIX (1940), pp. 411-12; E. Schick, "Ich hebe meine Augen auf," in *Beitrachungen zum 121. Psalm* (Basel, 1947); O. R. Sellers, "[Psalm 121]," *JNES* (1946), pp. 90-91; S. Terrien, *The Psalms and Their Meaning for Today* (Indianapolis and New York, 1952), pp. 220-27; P. Volz, "Zur Auslegung von Ps 23 u. 121," *Neue kirchliche Zeitschrift*, XXXVI (1925), pp. 576-85; J. T. Willis, "An Attempt to Decipher Psalm 121:2b," *CBQ*, LII (1990), pp. 241-51; cf. idem, "Psalm 121 as a Wisdom Poem," *Hebrew Annual*, II (1987), pp. 435-50.

FORM

The four regular strophes of this poem, with two bicola each, suggest the form of a hymn, but little in the course of this psalm hints at the genre of praise. Nevertheless, trust in the Creator of the universe may be a hymnic element. There are two difficult problems that affect the form and meaning of the song. (1) Is the second line of the first strophe a statement or a question? (2) Who is the person to whom the beneficent care of Yahweh is affirmed, seven times plus one, in favor of Israel? Could the genre of the psalm be a sapiential dialogue?

COMMENTARY

Strophe I: Are the Mountains a Menace? (vv. 1-2)

Why should the psalmist look up at some rocky or even snowy heights, like Mount Hermon, the Antilebanon, and the Lebanon? The traditional understanding was that the help of Yahweh is somehow confirmed by the sight of majestic mountains, marvelous witnesses to the God who created the earth besides the heavens. The sight of the heights conveys the power and the concern of the keeper.

It is indeed likely that the second line is syntactically distinct from the first, and that the adverb "from where?" indicates a fateful interrogation, implying that the mountains shelter or constitute a deadly peril. Was it that the poet, before undertaking his pilgrimage to Jerusalem, dwelt in a region of sharp cliffs, ravines, and caverns that concealed wild animals and even robbers, and that the pilgrimage itself passed through mountainous and dangerous defiles?

To be sure, no mountaineer in those days climbed the summits at the risk of unexpected and sudden weather changes, with avalanches or heavy frosts. But the hilltops were the seats of ancient sanctuaries, inherited from the Canaanites, which were strongly condemned (Lev 26:30; Ps 78:58). The high places were supposed to be destroyed when Israel entered the Holy Land (Deut

33:29); yet many of them were erected by the kings themselves, Solomon (1 Kgs 11:7), Rehoboam (1 Kgs 14:23), and several other monarchs (2 Kgs 17:9). Some of these hilltop shrines were torn down by Asa (1 Kgs 15:14), Jehoshaphat (1 Kgs 22:43), Jehoash (2 Kgs 12:3), Amaziah (2 Kgs 14:4), Azariah (2 Kgs 15:4), and Jotham (2 Kgs 15:35). Manasseh restored some of these high places (2 Kgs 21:3). Josiah defiled and cut to pieces a number of them (2 Kgs 23:5-15), but his reform at this point is not clearly stated.

The high mountains, like Mount Hermon, were not involved in this persistent syncretism, but shrines on the hills represented a cultic threat that continued over centuries. Psalm 121 may well have been a Song of Ascents in which the devotee of Yahweh began his pilgrimage to Zion and at once feared but still desired the worship on the "high places."

Strophe II: The Guardian of Israel (vv. 3-4)

On account of such ambiguity, the pilgrim, whom the psalmist now addresses, will resist and reject the attraction of these half-pagan, half-Yahwistic places of worship. His foot might hesitate here and there, but the Lord will not permit stumbling confusion. He is the keeper of the pilgrim, but above all he is the keeper of Israel. His vigilance knows no letup, intermission, or negligence.

Strophe III: The Pilgrims Will Be Safe (vv. 5-6)

The psalmist now anticipates all the possible perils on the trip to Jerusalem. Day and night the travelers will be exposed to the heat of the sun or the brightness of the moon, even more than sunstrokes in daylight, with more deleterious effects (2 Kgs 4:19; Jonah 4:8). As Bedouin women know well, dyed rugs or clothes will fade more quickly and thoroughly under moonlight than from the sun. The pilgrim will receive from Yahweh the shade of his right hand. This anthropomorphism compares the Lord to a shepherd (cf. Psalm 23). He shelters his sheep and lambs from the rudeness of nature. *Creatio continua* adds itself to *Heilsgeschichte.*

Strophe IV: The Intimacy of the Lord's Protection (vv. 7-8)

There seems to be an enlarging of the certainty that the God of Israel is master of history as well as the God of individual life. The "going out" and "coming in" broadens the purpose of the pilgrimage, which primarily refers to entering and leaving the sanctuary. It envisions all the breathing and heart beating and palpitating of earthly life. Probably it embraces not only going out to work but also coming in to rest in the evening.

DATE AND THEOLOGY

A Song of Ascents was especially used in postexilic times, when the Diaspora had spread the Jews into the Persian Empire, but its origin may have preceded the exile.

In the simplest terms, the psalmist uses the drama of departure on a hazardous journey as a metaphor for all of terrestrial existence. The last strophe might even add to creation and holy history the sleep of death, suggested by the final word, "evermore." Is this a hope for a perpetual cradling of safety (cf. Ps 73:24)?

Singing Psalm 121 in a cultic pilgrimage transforms its original use from geography to mortal existence. The pagan gods may sleep (1 Kgs 18:27), but the guardian of Israel does not even slumber. At the end of the day, Yahweh will transmute the going out into an eternal coming in.

It is generally agreed that Hebraic religious thinking seems to have reacted bluntly against the Near Eastern myths on death, especially those of the Egyptian culture of undertakers. Yet communion with the divine and the fullness of divine presence was sometimes so intense and so demanding, as with Enoch ("God took him," Gen. 5:24) or Elijah (2 Kgs 1:11-12), that a few singers of the psalms, like the poet of Psalm 121, hinted at eternal life.

Even Nietzsche could lend to Zarathustra a defiance of death, bold and tender at the same time:

When, thou well of eternity! thou joyous awful, noontide abyss! when wilt thou drink my soul back into thee?

Charles Péguy appears to answer,

Blessed is he who hopes
And who sleeps.

PSALM 122

Pray for the Peace of Jerusalem

1. *Song of Ascents. For David.*

I

> *I am full of joy when they say unto me,*
> > *Let us go to the house of the Lord!*
2. > *Our feet are stopped, standing*
> > *At thy gates, O Jerusalem!*

II

3. > *Jerusalem! City built as a castle*
> > *Joined together within itself,*
4. > *It is there that the tribes ascended,*
> > *The tribes of the Lord!*
> *The community for Israel*
> > *To praise the name of the Lord.*
5. > *For there they sat on thrones for justice,*
> > *The thrones of the house of David.*

III

6. > *Ask for the peace of Jerusalem!*
> > *Those who love thee, may they enjoy their rest!*
7. > *Let peace be within thy towers,*
> > *And tranquility in thy palaces!*

IV

8. > *For the sake of my brothers and friends,*
> > *May I really say, Peace to thee!*
9. > *For the sake of the house of the Lord, our God,*
> > *I shall seek happiness for thee.*

BIBLIOGRAPHY

A. Alt, "Das System der Stammesgrenzen im Buch Josua," in *Festschrift Sellin* (Leipzig, 1927), pp. 13-24; H. Donner, "Psalm 122," in *Festschrift F. C. Fensham*, JSOTSup 48 (Sheffield, 1988), pp. 81-91; H. Horst, "Recht und Religion im Bereich des Alten Testaments," *EvT,* XVI (1956), pp. 49-75; J. Jeremias, "Lade und Zion: Zur Entstehung der Ziontradition," in *Festschrift G. von Rad* (1971), pp. 183-98; H.-J. Kraus, *Theology of the Psalms* (Minneapolis, 1986), pp. 73-106; idem, *Worship in Israel* (Oxford, 1966), p. 181; M. Mannati, *Les Psaumes* (Paris, 1968), IV, pp. 129-35; S. Mowinckel, *The Psalms in Israel's Worship* (New York and Nashville, 1962), I, pp. 90, 185; M. Noth, "Das System der zwölf Stämme Israels," BWANT I (Neukirchen, 1930); W. H. Sellinger, Jr., *Psalms: Reading and Studying the Book of Praises* (Peabody, Mass., 1990), pp. 18, 138; C. Westermann, *The Living Psalms* (Grand Rapids, 1984), pp. 280-82.

FORM

The structure of this poem presents four strophes: three of two bicola each, and one strophe of three bicola (I: 1-2; II: 3-5; III: 6-7; IV: 8-9). Strophe II is noticeably longer than the first, for it stresses the topic of the psalm, which is not a song of Zion but a eulogy of Jerusalem. The meter is generally regular (3+2; 2+2), which points to the quiet style of the composition.

COMMENTARY

Strophe I: The Joy of Going to the House of the Lord (vv. 1-2)

The psalm is introduced properly as a Song of Ascents. "For David" is probably an editor's heading intended to preface the surprising shift of concern from "the house of the Lord" to Jerusalem, a Davidic city par excellence. "The house of the Lord" implies a post-Solomonic era, even a time following the construction of the second temple in the Persian period. The singer is ready, with great joy, to join a pilgrimage toward the sanctuary of Zion. To be standing at the gates of the city of Jerusalem recalls the success of the pilgrimage and the cause of the shift of concern from the sanctuary of Zion to the greatness of the civil institutions to be listed in the second strophe.

Strophe II: Architecture, Tribal Rallying, and Seat of Justice

Walls and towers, tightly built, make Jerusalem a model (vv. 3-5) of architecture. The tribes of Israel may have sent representatives to Jerusalem from the time of Solomon (1 Kgs 4:7-19), but the reference to the rallying of the tribes may be, in the Persian period, the dedication of the second temple (Ezra 6:17). The memory of such an event and the seat of royal tribunals (Deut 17:8; 1 Kgs 7:7) is rather vague, but it is summoned by the poet to indicate the sociological and political functions of Jerusalem during the Davidic monarchy as the capital not only of Judah but also of the whole of Israel. The Hebrew text uses the perfect tense "they sat" on account of the past character of the recollection.

The commandment for all the males of Israel to present themselves before the Lord implies the singleness of the national sanctuary, and does not specify the tribes (Exod 23:17; 34:23).

Strophe III: Prayer for the Peace of Jerusalem (vv. 6-7)

The request for national supplication for peace implies a contemporary or recent risk of war from a foreign enemy or a civil revolt that threatens the security of the inhabitants of the Davidic city. The psalm does not include any precise indication.

Strophe IV: The Singer's Own Commitment (vv. 8-9)

Psalm 122 is conceived by an individual artist, but his horizon embraces his brothers and friends. His motivation to seek the happiness of Jerusalem is, first of all, "for the sake of the house of the Lord." Yet no further detail suggests a cultic ritual. Zion is the center of Israel, thus presumably the center of the universe as well, and the concern of the psalmist does not require any justification.

DATE AND THEOLOGY

This short hymnic poem may have been prophetic or sapiential, for it is more interested in admiring the city than in worshiping Yahweh in Zion. If Psalm 122 was composed originally as a Song of Ascents, it was destined to stimulate the morale of pilgrims from the Diaspora in postexilic times. The prayer reflects traditional Yahwism. The Lord will not separate political considerations from religious devotion.

Other hymns of the Psalter appear to favor a worldwide spreading of divine presence. Jewish attachment to the city of Jerusalem depends largely, but not entirely, on the uniqueness of the sanctuary in Zion, but a Diaspora Jew, in his local synagogue, anticipated the geographical breadth of a William Blake, who envisioned a worldwide devotion to social compassion and to the advent of peace, confessing,

> I will not cease from mental fight,
> Nor shall my Sword sleep in my hand,

Till we have built Jerusalem
In England's green and pleasant land.

This is true not only for England but for any land without a spirit of exclusive possessiveness.

PSALM 123

Our Eyes Look at the Lord

1. Song of Ascents.

I

    I lift up mine eyes to thee,
      [For] thou art enthroned in the heavens.
2.   *Behold, as the eyes of servants*
      Are fixed on the hand of their masters,

II

    As the eyes of a handmaid
      Are looking at the hand of her mistress,
    So our eyes look at the Lord, our God,
      Till he gives grace to us.

III

3.   *Have mercy upon us, Lord, have mercy upon us!*
      For we received more than our share of scorn.
4.   *Our soul, for far too long, has been*
      Despised by the proud and arrogant.

BIBLIOGRAPHY

W. A. M. Beuken, "The Main Theme of Trito-Isaiah: The Servants of YHWH," *JSOT*, XLVII (1990), pp. 67-87; F. M. T. De Liagre Bohl, "Hymnisches . . . in den Amarna Briefen aus Kanaan," in *Opera Minora* (Groningen, 1953), pp. 375-79; H. Goeke, "Gott, Mensch und Gemeinde in Psalm 123," *BibLeb*, CXXXI (1966), pp. 234-88; A. Maillot and A. Lelièvre, *Les Psaumes*, III (Geneva, 1969), pp. 147-49; C. Westermann, *The Living Psalms* (Grand Rapids, 1984), pp. 42-46.

FORM

The shortness of this Song of Ascents and the strangeness of its form are unusual. The comparison of the Lord to a master of servants, in the plural, differs strophically from the comparison of the Lord to the mistress of a handmaid, in the singular. The psalmist appears to have divided his poem into three strophes of two bicola each. Such a structure suggests the genre of hymn, but the begging for grace denotes the *Gattung* of lament. Moreover, the singer at the beginning is an individual, whereas the begging for mercy (v. 3) is a communal enterprise. What is the keyword of the entire psalm: an appeal to God by a lonely singer? a communal complaint against the arrogant (v. 4)?

The meter is quite regular (3+2) but lengthens itself toward the end (3+2+2).

COMMENTARY

Strophe I: The Psalmist as One of the Servants (vv. 1-2ab)

The singer affirms his total devotion to the Lord, and he wants to obtain a vision of the divine presence (cf. Pss 2:4; 11:4; 115:3, 16). His eyes are fixed on God's hands. To lift up the eyes is a gesture of deep longing. While God is enthroned in the heavens — a sign of his kingship — his transcendence is not inaccessible. God's crowd of helpers, like royal attendants, wait for a single hint before going into action.

Strophe II: The Psalmist Is the Lord's Handmaid (vv. 2cd)

The comparison moves beyond the imagery of royal majesty. The link between God and man is feminine, intimate and tender. The Lord is close to his psalmic devotee, like a mistress to a handmaid who symbolizes beggars for mercy and waits for the slightest sign of intervention.

Strophe III: Begging for Divine Grace (vv. 3-4)

A repeated supplication, "Have mercy upon us" could be rendered "Grace us!" The Hebrew verb means not only "have mercy" but also, in archaic English,

"Grace us," that is to say "Transform us into thy treasure," make us receive this divine quality that incorporates us into thy closest family (cf. Ps 51:4).

The word "soul" might be translated "throat," which would fit the context of "to be sated," but the rendering "soul" covers the whole of physical and emotional beingness. Contempt by the "arrogant" includes the selfishness of the nonchalant, who remain spectators indifferent to the "arrogant." The pride of these men is the fruit of egocentricity and results in antisocial behavior.

DATE AND THEOLOGY

It is not possible to decide whether the authors of scorn and contempt are Jewish, in which case those who beg for mercy are the victims of nouveaux riches, or belong, on the contrary, to members of the Persian upper class, in which case those who pray for God's mercy symbolize the people of Israel, now scattered in the Diaspora. At any rate, the date appears to be postexilic, with pilgrims on their way to a rebuilt Jerusalem.

The theology emerges from an intense piety. The intimacy between God and the psalmist leads to a new approach. Divine grace may flourish in mercy (v. 4).

PSALM 124

The Lord Was on Our Side

1. Song of Ascents. For David.

I

    If the Lord had not been on our side
      [Let Israel thus repeat!]
2.   *If the Lord had not been on our side,*
      When men rose up against us,

II

3.   *Then they would have swallowed us alive,*
      For their ire was kindled against us;

4.   *Then a flood would have swept us away,*
            A torrent would have passed over our being;
5.   *Then they would have passed over us,*
            The waters with a raging foam!

III

6.   *Blessed be the Lord, who has not delivered us*
            As a prey for their teeth!
7.   *Our lives escaped like a bird from the fowlers' net!*
            The net broke, and we were free!
8.   *Our help is in the name of the Lord,*
            Who made the heavens and the earth.

BIBLIOGRAPHY

J.-N. Aletti and J. Trublet, *Approche poétique et théologique des Psaumes: Analyses et méthodes* (Paris, 1983), pp. 245ff.; F. Crüsemann, *Studien zur Formgeschichte von Hymnus und Danklied in Israel*, WMANT XXXII (Neukirchen, 1969), pp. 161-68; O. Grether, *Name und Wort Gottes im Alten Testament*, BZAW LXIV (Giessen, 1934); F. Horst, "Segen und Segenshandlungen in der Bibel," *EvT*, VII (1947), pp. 23-37; J. Schreiner, "'Wenn nicht der Herr für uns wäre'?" *BibLeb*, X (1969), pp. 16-25; I. W. Slotki, "The Text and the Ancient Form of Recital of Psalm 24 and Psalm 124," *JBL*, LI (1932), pp. 214-26.

FORM

This invitation to sing a Hymn of Thanksgiving may be divided into three strophes, each of which begins with a key word: Strophe I, "if not, if not" (vv. 1b-2); Strophe II, "then, then, then" (vv. 3-5); Strophe III, "blessed, our lives, our help" (vv. 6-8). In addition, the meter appears to punctuate such a division: Strophe I, 2+2+2, 2+2+2; Strophe II, 3+3, 3+3, 3+3; Strophe III, 2+2+2, 3+2, 3+3.

COMMENTARY

Strophe I: Let Israel Thus Repeat (vv. 1b-2)

The prelusive strophe invites the people of God to repeat what disaster might have occurred if Yahweh had been absent or unwilling to protect them (cf. Pss 27:13; 94:17; 119:92). Who are the "men" who rose up against the people of God? The psalmist is silent on their identity.

Strophe II: The Imagined Disaster as a Flood (vv. 3-5)

The psalmist pursues his comparison between a human enemy and a natural calamity. He then indulges in a bit of epic lyricism. The magnitude of the supposed catastrophe underlines the magnitude of the Lord's intervention. It is likened to a cosmic beast, possibly to the Near Eastern myths of creation.

Strophe III: The Invitation to Bless God (vv. 6-8)

The image of the world beast is continued (v. 6), but the deliverance summons the theme of a bird in a net (cf. Prov 7:23; Amos 3:5). A blessing of God is unusual when conferred by human beings other than priests.

The "name" of Yahweh, "He causes to be," is invoked as the manifestation of God's creation and historical activity. The Lord has selected the slaves in Egypt to be holy people, just as he made heaven and earth.

DATE AND THEOLOGY

As a Song of Ascents, Psalm 124 was used by pilgrims in the postexilic period. The theological implication of such a hymn unites in the mind of the singer the beneficent myth of creation and the Creator's continuing providence in history. While the identity of the enemy — domestic or foreign — is not revealed, one can easily believe that early Judaism saw gratefully that the Babylonian horrors had allowed a remnant to survive and to prosper. But an enormous problem was raised by the idea that Yahweh had taken sides against his own. Why the destruction of Jerusalem and of the temple of Zion? Why the killing of many Judahites and the exile of many survivors?

The question of theodicy is not asked. It is the psalmist's faith, however, that permits him to thank the Lord for the restoration of the Judahites as Jews in the religious sense of the word. *Heilsgeschichte* does not mean a history of healing and salvation without concern for moral sanctions, but confidence in Yahweh overcomes the most critical disorder.

Judaism persists through the centuries, and Christianity, one of its offspring, depends on the survival of its worldwide ethic and vision.

PSALM 125

Confidence in the Lord

1. *Song of Ascents.*

I

> Those who trust in the Lord are like Mount Zion:
> It is unshakable and stands forever.

2.   Jerusalem! Mountains surround her,
> Just as the Lord surrounds his people
> From henceforth and forevermore!

3.   The scepter of evil men will not lie heavy
> Over the domain of the righteous,
> And the righteous will not shake hands with iniquity.

II

4.   Extend thy goodness to those who are good
> And to the upright in their heart,

5.   But those who follow tortuous ways,
> Let the Lord chase them away
> With the workers of magic.
> Peace be on Israel!

BIBLIOGRAPHY

P. Auffret, *La Sagesse a bâti sa maison* (Fribourg and Göttingen, 1982), pp. 135-38; W. Beyerlin, *Weisheitliche Vergewisserung mit Bezug auf den Zionskult: Studien zum 125. Psalm* (Fribourg and Göttingen, 1985); W. Zimmerli, *Grundriss der alttestamentlichen Theologie* (Stuttgart, 1972), pp. 128ff.

FORM

This short psalm, perhaps accidentally truncated, contains two strophes: the first one is made of one bicolon and two tricola (vv. 1-3); the second comprehends one bicolon and only one tricolon. A fragment of a longer strophe may have survived. The wish for the peace of Israel (v. 5a) may have been part of an original third strophe. However, this strange construction may have reflected the difference of style between proverbial meditation (vv. 1-3) and prayer to the

Lord, immediately returning to an indirect form of speech. Even the proverbial style mixed wisdom and cult in both strophes (vv. 1 and 5).

COMMENTARY

Strophe I: Durability of Both Faith and Cult (vv. 1-3)

The sapiential style may well have informed the primary concern of the singer, when he compared trust in Yahweh to the solidity of Mount Zion. His confidence in the Lord is like the architecture of the sanctuary; it will never fail. Moreover, the topography of Jerusalem and environs shows that the surrounding hills, like the Mount of Olives and Mount Scopus, north and northeast of the temple, symbolize the endurance of the covenant, the people's selection, and the solidity of Mount Zion.

Yet the historical situation is most critical. A scepter of evil men lies heavy on Israel. Fortunately, the people includes "the righteous," who may be a designation of the entire chosen people (v. 2) or a small minority of singers, priests, and disciples of the great prophets. The intensity of their faith is sufficient to explain why Yahweh will preserve their domain. They will not enter into a social compromise with the workers of astrology and sorcery. Is this an allusion to the Judahites who, in the time of Jeremiah, collaborated with the Babylonian invaders, or, on the contrary, persisted in believing that the nation and its sanctuary were invincible?

Strophe II: The Workers of Iniquity (vv. 4-5)

The invasion and the long agony of Jerusalem announced such an event as the violation of the temple. The poet falls on his knees, so to speak, and invokes divine succor. At this point, "the upright" clearly designate the few who are good. The psalmist dissociates himself from "those who follow tortuous ways." The Lord is asked to exterminate them, together with the astrologers and magicians who, in violation of Josiah's reforms (2 Kgs 23:16-20), had recourse to practices that attempted to force the divine will with human techniques.

DATE AND THEOLOGY

If the scepter of evil men that lay heavy on Israel, like that of Babylon, the date will be approximately the end of the seventh and beginning of the sixth centuries B.C.E. The psalm was preserved as testimony to a divine sanction that threatened the elimination of the people of God from the face of the earth. It could be used after the exile as a catechetic reminder for the pilgrims of the Diaspora marching toward the second temple in the restored Jerusalem that the Lord was still granting goodness to the good.

The retribution of benevolence toward those who are "good" and "upright in heart" is traditionally held by some of the wise (cf. 15:29). The theology implied by this belief is open to a number of risks, one of which is religious pride. The anthropology of "goodness" persists both in Judaism and Christianity, in spite of a bold retort attributed to Jesus. When a certain ruler asked him, saying, "Good teacher, what shall I do to inherit eternal life?" Jesus is remembered as having said, "Why callest thou me good? None is good, save one, even God" (Mark 10:17-18; Luke 18:19). Another Gospel corrected the logion into the following, "Why askest thou me concerning what is good?" (Matt 19:17). Some manuscripts do not accept the humility attributed to Jesus. Perhaps they argued the theology of Psalm 125.

PSALM 126

The Lord Did Great Things for Us

1. *Song of Ascents.*

I

    When the Lord brought back the captives of Zion,
      We thought we were dreaming;
2.   *Then our mouths were filled with laughter,*
      And our tongues with gleeful cries;
    Then the nations would say,
      The Lord did great things for this people.
3.   *Indeed, the Lord did great things for us,*
      And we were overjoyed.

II

4.   *Bring back, O Lord, [all of] our captives,*
      Like torrents of water in the Negev!

5.   *Those who sow seeds while weeping*
          Will reap with shouts of delight.

6.   *One man goes sowing in tears,*
          Carrying his bag of seeds,
          But when he returns, with shouts of joy,
          His arms will be full of sheaves.

BIBLIOGRAPHY

E. Baumann, "Struktur-Untersuchungen im Psalter II," *ZAW,* LXII (1950), pp. 140-44; W. Beyerlin, *We Are Like Dreamers: Studies in Psalm 126* (Edinburgh, 1982); M. Dahood, [review of W. Bardtke], *CBQ,* XXX (1970), pp. 86-90; E. Dietrich, [*shûbh shebhûth*], in *Die endzeitlichen Wiedersuchungen im Psalter II,* BZAW XL (Giessen, 1925); F. Hvidberg, *Weeping and Laughter in the Old Testament* (Leiden, 1962); J. Morgenstern, "Psalm 126," in *Festschrift Millas-Vallicrosa,* II (Barcelona, 1956), pp. 111-17; R. Mosis, "'Mit Jauchzen werden sie ernten': Beobachtungen zu Psalm 126," in *Festschrift H. Reinelt* (Stuttgart, 1990), pp. 181-201; A. Gonzales Nañez, "Cual torrentes del Neguev," *Estudios bíblicos,* XXIV (1965), pp. 349-60; A. Rose, "Le Psaume 126 (125): Joie d'un peuple que son Dieu fait revivre," *Feu nouveau,* IX (1966), pp. 16-26; J. Strugnell, "A Note on Ps 126,1," *JTS,* VII (1956), pp. 239-43.

FORM

The Songs of Ascents were apparently collected together, not because they all belonged to the same genre of hymnology, but because they were used by pilgrims from the Diaspora during the Persian period. The pilgrims sang them as they marched toward the new sanctuary of Yahweh on Mount Zion. Indeed, several Songs of Ascents mention Zion (Pss 122:1, 6, 9; 132:13; 134:3). Psalm 126 presents a peculiar form because it was intended for those pilgrims who knew of the first return of exiles from Babylonia (after 538 B.C.E.). They may not have witnessed this return, but they learned about it, and sang their thanksgiving for the amazing intervention of Yahweh.

The poem comprehends two strophes of four bicola each (vv. 1-3, 4-5). Strophe I celebrates retrospectively the wonder and the joy of the great news. The second strophe, however, begs for the completion of the deliverance and the assembling of all. The supplication continues with the hope that irrigation of the sterile Negev, between the Sinai desert and the Holy Land, would produce ample and magnificent harvests, sufficient for a numerous and famished population.

The meter confirms the strangeness of the form, with its central articulation of themes (vv. 2-3). The hymnic exultation of the first strophe is couched in the unusual rhythm of 4+2; 4+2; 4+2; 4+2, whereas the survival of a partial captivity and the fear of famine compel a meter of *qinah* in symmetrical alternation, 3+2; 2+2; 3+2+2+2 (vv. 4-6). A hymn followed by a lament demands a core verse; it is found at the end of Strophe I and at the beginning of Strophe II.

COMMENTARY

Superscription (v. 1a)

The Hebrew title, "Song of Ascents," is followed in the Syriac with "Word of David on Haggai and Zechariah when they came back from deportation."

Strophe I: Joy at the First Return (vv. 1b-3)

The Hebrew MSS, as well as the ancient versions, vary at several points. The first line literally may mean, "In Yahweh's return from the captivity of Zion," which implies that at the time of the destruction of the Zion sanctuary, in 587 B.C.E., with the death and the exile of the majority of the population, Yahweh left the defiled site of the holy mountain and somehow moved to Mesopotamia with his deported people. However, the verb "to return" may be viewed as a causative, and the translation "brought back" is possible (cf. 2 Sam 19:33; Isa 30:15; 52:8; 63:17; Ezek 43:2). The ancient versions also seem to have read a causative mode (see LXX, Syr., Vulg.). Moreover, the text may signify "the captivity from Zion."[1] Some translators in modern times prefer to read, "Restore the fortunes of Zion."[2]

It appears that Strophe I, of joy and thanksgiving, means a partial return, so that the prayer for a second return would have asked for a liberation of all the captives (v. 4a).

---

1. The words *shûbh shebhûth* are found many times, with different meanings (Deut 30:3; Jer 29:14; 30:3, 18; 31:23; 48:47; Hos 6:11; Amos 9:14; also Pss 14:7; 53:6; 85:1).

2. E. Baumann, "[*shûbh shebhûth*]: Eine exegetische Untersuchung," *ZAW*, XLVII (1929), pp. 35-36; J. Gray, "Kingship of God in Prophets and Psalms," *VT*, XI (1961), pp. 1-29; N. M. Sarna, "Epic Substratum in the Prose of Job," *JBL*, LXXVI (1957), p. 17; S. Terrien, *Job: Commentaire* (Neuchâtel, 1963), p. 272; Beyerlin, *We Are like Dreamers*, pp. 3-4; M. Dahood, *Psalms III*, AB XVIIA (Garden City, N.Y., 1970), *in loc.*

Strophe II: Supplication for a Total Return and New Prosperity (vv. 4-6)

It is probable that for several years after the deliverance (538 B.C.E.) the situation was less than pleasant (Isa 59:9-11), and that an increase of the population in the Holy Land, presumably stricken by lack of rain and other disasters, would render the crisis even more severe. Hence the rather unexpected vision of gushing waters flowing from the rocks in the Negev. The psalmist's evocation of successful agriculture is also unusual (cf. Hag 2:18-20). Most of Strophe II rejoices with a farmer who spreads with tears seeds of grain carried in the farmer's bag (cf. Amos 9:13). His sowing will be done in chagrin, but the harvest will be magnificent.

DATE AND THEOLOGY

The traditional translations of vv. 1 and 4 are probably correct. The psalmist rejoices profusely over the complete return from Mesopotamia. Yet the early years were filled with uncertainties. Judaism was born as a religion freed from a political government. The Judahites became the Jews. The congregations of Yahweh worshipers contained individuals who had to "convert from their sins" (Isa 59:20; Hag 2:14). As a disciple of the prophets and the wise, the psalmist was possessed by a faith that triumphed over doubt and confusion. He prayed for a new world order. He may also have thought, beyond the proximate future, of the end of time, when history would come to its fulfillment.

Eschatology found its roots in divine kingship. It took hold of Judaism through the crises of the Persian, Hellenistic, Maccabean, and Roman centuries. Some Jews became the first Christians because, among other symbols, they learned the image of the sower throwing his seeds on all sorts of ground waiting for the final harvest they called "the kingdom of God" (Mark 4:3-20). Like Judaism, Christianity fell from the original vision. "The harvest truly is plenteous, but the laborers are few" (Matt 9:37).

PSALM 127

Unless the Lord Builds the House

1. Song of Ascents. For Solomon.

I

If the Lord does not build the house,
Its builders work on it in vain.
If the Lord does not watch over a city,
Its guards stay awake in vain.

2.   *In vain do you rise at dawn,*
      Or delay your evening rest,
Those who eat the bread of idols. . . .
[A true God] will give prosperity to his beloved.

II

3.   *Indeed, sons are the Lord's inheritance,*
      The fruits of the womb in reward;
4.   *Like arrows in a warrior's hand,*
      Thus are the sons of one's youth.

5.   *Happy is the warrior*
      who has filled his quiver with them.
      They will not be put to shame, for they will overpower
      The enemies at the gate.

BIBLIOGRAPHY

F. Bussby, "Note on *šēnā'* in Psalm 127,2," *JTS*, XXXV (1934), pp. 306-7; M. Dahood, "The *aleph* in Psalm CXXVII,2," *Orientalia*, XLIV (1975), pp. 103-5; E. Edwards, "A New Interpretation of [*ken yitten lidhihu šēnā'*]," *Expository Times*, LIV (1942-43), pp. 225-26; J. A. Emerton, "The Meaning of *šēnā'* in Psalm CXXIV,2," *VT*, XXIV (1974), pp. 15-31; P. J. Estes, "Like Arrows in the Hand of a Warrior (Psalm CXXVII)," *VT*, XLI (1991), pp. 304-11; H. Gese, *Lehre und Wirklichkeit in der alten Weisheit: Studien zu den Sprüchen Salomos und zu dem Buch Hiob* (Tübingen, 1958); V. Hamp, "'Der Herr gibt es Seinen im Schlaf," in *Festschrift J. Ziegler* (Würzburg, 1972), pp. 71-79; M. C. Huyck, "Psalm-City: A Study of Psalm 127," *Worship*, XL (1966), pp. 510-18; C. C. Keet, *A Study of the Psalms of Ascents* (London, 1979), pp. 54-63; L. Köhler, *Hebrew Man* (Nashville, 1956), pp. 101-2; P. D. Miller, Jr., "Psalm 127 — The House That Yahweh Builds," *JSOT*, XXII (Feb. 1982), pp. 119-32; idem, *Interpreting the Psalms* (Philadelphia, 1986), pp. 131-

37; H. Schmidt, "Grüsse und Glückwünsche im Psalter," *TSK*, CIII (1931), pp. 141-50; K. Seybold, "Die Redaction der Wallfahrtspsalmen," *ZAW*, XCI (1978), pp. 247-68 (esp. p. 254); E. Slovonic, "Toward an Understanding of the Formation of Historical Titles in the Book of Psalms," *ZAW*, XCI (1979), pp. 370-71.

FORM

In its superscription, Psalm 127 is either offered or attributed to Solomon. Was it because he was remembered as the builder of the temple in Zion and the master of sapiential poetry? The poem is made up of two strophes of eight bicola each, and each strophe may be divided into two substrophes (vv. 1 and 2, 3-4+5). The composition is quite symmetrical and regular, but its themes appear, at first sight, entirely disparate: from house builder and city guard (Strophe I) to the blessing of sons and well-equipped warriors (Strophe II).

In addition, the rhythm varies between the two strophes: it is at first quite coherent (3+3; 3+3; 3+3; 3+3), but rather mixed in Strophe II (4+3; 3+2; 2+2; 2+4; 2+2). Was it that the psalmist first composed a unified poem (Strophe I)? Then did he, or someone else, add a few lines of heterogeneous origin?

While several commentators think of two different psalms eventually brought together, exegetical pursuit may help to discover a principle of coherence that unites the entire poem.

COMMENTARY

Strophe I: Godlessness and Human Failure (vv. 1-2)

This psalm begins with emphatic repetitions, such as "if . . . , if . . . ," followed by a didactic address to Yahweh (twice) and a play on the Hebrew assonance of the verb "whoever builds" and a noun of similar sound, "a house."

The second line deals with a slightly different topic (the uselessness for a guard to watch for the safety of a city at night), but both statements reinforce each other, with "vain," "useless," and even include a third "vain" at the start of the next bicolon (v. 2).

The expression "to build a house" is commonly employed in the Psalms and elsewhere with startlingly different meanings: (1) literally, "to erect any stone edifice for the inhabitation of anyone, even a king" (2 Sam 7:27; cf. Deut 8:12); (2) a metaphor for "to build a dynasty" (Gen 16:2); (3) a sacred act in making "the house of the Lord" (Ps 78:68). Did the poem suggest the inclusion of all these meanings?

A parallel line (v. 1c) introduces another example of futility, when a night watchman guards a city without God (cf. Pss 102:16; 147:2). In all these cases, the clear implication is that the only keeper, guardian, and protector is Yahweh.

In the second substrophe (v. 2), the poet directly addresses conscientious and experienced workers who spend long hours at their labor, from early morning to late evening, but without faith in the Lord. They "eat the bread of idols." The Hebrew words yield an uncertain sense, perhaps "the bread of toils" or "sorrows" (Gen 3:16 [childbirth labor]; Prov 5:10; 10:22; 14:23; cf. Pss 106:36, 38; 139:24). The adverb *kēn*, "like," might be a noun (Pss 110:7; 128:4) or an adjective, "true," "honest." The last word of v. 2 is also obscure. Some take it to mean "sleep" (cf. Ps 132:4; Prov 6:4), and others see it as the term for "prosperity, success, happiness."[1]

The syntactic liaison remains meaningless, with the plural immediately followed by a singular: "Those who eat the bread of idols [a true God?] will give prosperity to his beloved" (Deut 33:12; Pss 60:7; 108:7; Isa 5:1; Jer 11:15).

Strophe II: Progeny of Sons, Divine Inheritance (vv. 3-5)

The builders of the house are blessed with a progeny of sons. The fruits of the womb may be meant to include daughters. The father of many sons is like a warrior whose quiver is full of arrows. Quite clearly, the psalm develops succinctly two sapiential sayings. The builders and the sons of the Lord's inheritance form a consonantal paronomasia; so also are "the strong man" and the "war hero" endowed with bravura (vv. 4 and 5). Thus the unity of the psalm, not a composition of two independent psalms, is subtly and convincingly implied. Human work is successful only with Yahweh as keeper and protector.

Such protection, believed to be divine, is granted against foreign enemies and also against domestic adversaries who will testify falsely against innocent victims, since the city gate has always been used as the local tribunal (Deut 21:19; 25:7; Amos 5:12).

DATE AND THEOLOGY

Like other Songs of Ascents, this psalm may have been conceived in the sapiential circles of Judahite kings, perhaps at the court of Hezekiah. It bears no trace of a dark cloud of national disquietude. It perhaps admires the dynasty of David, without defending it as a glorious concern on the part of Yahweh. The allusion to Zion as the sanctuary is discreet but undeniable, and the city of Jerusalem is the

---

1. Cf. M. Dahood, *Psalms III*, AB XVIIA (Garden City, N.Y., 1970), pp. 223-24. The translation of *ken* without a definite article as "The Reliable" is doubtful.

unique symbol of the Lord's benediction. From total reliance upon divine help, the poem moves swiftly from the happiness of the fathers to that of their sons. There is no mention of gratitude for a wife or a mother, although "the fruits of the womb" are exalted, perhaps out of respect for femininity.

The theological meditation of the Fourth Gospel, like this psalm, affirms that without the aid of the divine mystery for human openness, even a member of the apostolic circle "can do nothing" (John 16:5).

PSALM 128

The Lord Bless Thee from Zion

1. Song of Ascents.

I

> *Happy is anyone who fears the Lord;*
> *He who will walk in his ways.*
2. *Upon the labor of thy hands*
> *Thou shalt nourish thyself;*
> *Happiness and prosperity will be thine.*

II

3. *Thy wife will be like a fruitful vine*
> *In the alcove of thy house;*
> *Thy sons, like the green shoots of olive trees*
> *All around thy table.*

III

4. *Behold! The brave man will be blessed*
> *Who fears the Lord.*
5. *May the Lord bless thee from Zion!*
> *And thou wilt see with joy the happiness of Jerusalem*
> *All the days of thy life.*
6. *Also, mayst thou see the sons of thy sons!*
> *Peace be on Israel!*

BIBLIOGRAPHY

F. Horst, "Segen und Segenshandlungen in der Bibel," *EvT,* LXXII (1947), pp. 23-37; C. C. Keet, *A Study of the Songs of Ascents* (London, 1969), pp. 63-68; P. D. Miller, Jr., *Interpreting the Psalms* (Philadelphia, 1986), pp. 136-37; S. Mowinckel, *Psalmenstudien,* V: *Segen und Fluch in Israelskult und Psalmdichtung* (Oslo, 1924); J. Pedersen, *Israel: Its Life and Culture,* I-II (Oxford, 1926), pp. 182-212; H. Schmidt, "Grüsse und Glückwönsche im Psalter," *TSK,* CIII (1931), pp. 141-50; G. Wehmeier, *Der Segen im Alten Testament* (Basel, 1970).

FORM

This short psalm, which was used during a pilgrimage to Zion from some distant Diaspora, mixes sapiential salutations with priestly blessings. The congratulations are expressed in the third person singular, while the blessings are addressed to an individual, perhaps a fellow traveler, in the second person singular (cf. vv. 1 and 4 with vv. 2, 3, and 5). It is constructed in three strophes that in diverse ways insist on the joy of progeny. The psalm ends with a sedate wish for the peace of Israel. The rhythm (chiefly 3+2) is lengthened once into 4+3, perhaps to emphasize the importance of individual freedom (v. 2ab).

COMMENTARY

Strophe I: Happiness of the God-fearing Farmer (vv. 1bc-2)

The exaltation that wishes happiness originates in the sapiential circles. It means a salutation that differs from a benediction that originally is a cultic sentence and gesture that involve a transmission of power, as in the patriarchal blessing. The word "happy," on the contrary, derives from a verb that means "to go forward," "to run relentlessly toward a goal." Happiness has a dynamic significance, a reality of movement, that the Latin *beatus,* with the substantive *beatitude,* fails to convey. Clearly happiness depends on "marching" and even "running in the Lord's ways."

The fear of Yahweh does not signify terror at his ire or judgment; rather, it suggests "awe" at the immediate presence of the divine. But it does not involve a sense of guilt. The fear of God belongs to the sphere of passionate commitment that is "afraid" to displease or disappoint a lover.

Strophe II: Happiness of the Bridegroom, Future Father (v. 3)

The fruits of the womb lead to subtle praise of a bride and potential mother. Sexual love is implied by "the alcove of thy house" (v. 3b). The Hebraic devotion to the religious aspect of genealogy leads to thankfulness for the fertility of a loving wife. The image of a woman compared to a grapevine bearing grapes leads to the other image of happy descendants likened to olive shoots. More than wheat or honey, the oil from olives is a symbol of successful agriculture. The sons are praised with their mother as the sources of therapeutic enjoyment, like excellent wine (cf. Ps 104:15).

Strophe III: The Happiness of the City of Jerusalem (vv. 4-6)

From dynamic exaltation and exultation, the psalmist finds a climax in the blessing from Zion. Moving from a wisdom reflection to a cultic benediction, his concern is to praise not mortal man but the champion. Thus endowed with the spiritual eating and drinking of a celebration at the temple, he is endowed with true bravura. He will see "with joy" the prosperity of Jerusalem.

The verb "to see" is here constructed not with a direct object but with an indirect link by a preposition. This semantic nuance is generally ignored by modern translators (cf. other examples in 2 Kgs 10:16; Isa 52:8; Jer 29:32; Mic 7:9). To see the city in a political, economic, sociological, and religious "boom" will raise the blessed pilgrim to new heights of enjoyment. Mystical spirituality does not oppose or condemn physical play, for wine rejoices the heart of man. Dynamic "beatitude" enhances the aesthetic pleasure of religion and earthly living.

DATE AND THEOLOGY

As the Songs of Ascents accompany the travelers who direct their steps toward the Holy City, they anticipate the jubilation of a service of worship in the house of the Lord.

During Persian times, in spite of some moments of difficulty with the functionaries of the empire, Judaism developed a nonpolitical form of sociological coherence. Priestly legalism without excess offered a ritual of moral behavior, both national and individual, that respected sapiential openness to debate and diversity. The joy of Zion could be received, admired, and expected, no longer with the syncretistic dangers inherent in the glorification of the omphalos myth inherited from the Canaanites and common to many religions and cultures, including the vagaries of Shechem, Delphi, and many other sites in oriental and occidental history.[1] Christianity, unlike Christendom, might discover in a symbolic Zion or Jerusalem, together with Judaism and Islam, a source of stability and of deep unity.

PSALM 129

Often Oppressed, Never Done For

1. *Song of Ascents.*

I

    "Many times since my youth they oppressed me,"
      Let Israel say!
2.   *Many times they oppressed me since my youth,*
      But they never prevailed against me.

II

3.   *On my back plowmen plowed;*
      They cut long furrows.
4.   *The Lord is just: he severed*
      The cords of evil men.

III

5.   *May they be ashamed and forced to turn back,*
      All those who hate Zion!
6.   *Let them be like grass over the roofs*
      That dries up before it grows!

IV

7.   *With it the reaper will not fill his hand,*
      Nor his arms the binder of sheaves,
8.   *And those that will pass by will not say,*
      "Let the blessing of the Lord be upon you!"
      We, however, shall bless you in the name of the Lord.

---

1. Cf. S. Terrien, "The Omphalos Myth and Hebrew Religion," *VT*, XX (1970), pp. 315-38.

BIBLIOGRAPHY

J.-N. Aletti and N. Trublet, *Approche poétique et théologique des Psaumes: Analyses et méthodes* (Paris, 1982), pp. 228ff.; F. Crüsemann, *Studien zur Formgeschichte von Hymnus und Danklied in Israel*, WMANT XXXII (Neukirchen, 1979), pp. 168ff.; C. C. Keet, *A Study of the Psalms of Ascents* (London, 1969), pp. 68-74; A. Maillot et A. Lelièvre, *Les Psaumes*, III (Genève, 1968), pp. 168-70; M. Mannati, *Les Psaumes*, IV (Paris, 1968), pp. 164-68; C. Westermann, *The Living Psalms* (Grand Rapids, 1984), p. 54.

FORM

This psalm differs in tone from the other Songs of Ascents. Its form is that of a hymn with four strophes, with two bicola for the first three strophes and composed with such regularity in the first three strophes that its rhythm remains symmetrically uniform (3+2). The fourth strophe lengthens itself with a final tricolon. Verse 8 ends with an echo of v. 1, bringing together the dual destiny of Israel in history, from mortal trials to an uncanny power of survival.

As a liturgical piece for several singers in antiphony (vv. 1bc, 2, 8c), this Song of Ascents, like most of the others, mentions Zion, even when it is an object of hate for the enemies of the nation (v. 5). But for the pilgrims, Zion is the symbol for complete devotion.

COMMENTARY

Strophe I: The Survival of Israel (vv. 1b-2)

One of the most astonishing features of ancient Near Eastern history is the endurance of Israel under duress. The people that called itself chosen by Yahweh suffered again and again from the attacks of neighbors. Here Israel is bidden to repeat, "Many times have they oppressed me since my youth" — meaning military defeats and foreign occupation — Egyptian slavery, opposition of Canaan and its neighbors, conquest and occupation from Assyria and especially Babylon — but never extermination.

What began as the rehearsal of a national lament blossoms forth into the celebration of Israel's constant renewal. One can easily see how the first editor of these songs would bring together Psalm 129 after Psalm 128, for the peace that Israel had missed for so many years would require the repeated singing of its tragic misfortunes as well as its amazing power of endurance.

Even since its youth, from the desert of Sinai to the ferocious battles for the conquest of the Promised Land, Israel was threatened, invaded, decimated, and exploited, but never annihilated.

Strophe II: The Lord, After All, Is Just (vv. 3-4)

The pilgrims, on their way to Jerusalem, would recall the horrors of the past with images of agricultural hardship. The oppression of Israel is compared to the wounding of the soil. Perhaps the memory of the servitude in Egypt revives dramatically the exhaustion of the fathers who were forced to plow and to dig furrows in the Nile Delta and mines of lapis lazuli in the Sinai Peninsula. Here national pride moderated by gratitude instills the claim, "They never prevailed against me."

The cultic ceremony for which the poet appears to have composed the psalm is unknown (cf. Pss 118:2ff.; 124:1-2), but the singing of it fits the ultimate destination of the pilgrims.

Strophe III: Maledictions against the Enemies (vv. 5-6)

Like other national laments, this psalm presumes the election of Israel as a special people, together with the promise of the Holy Land. The enemies are the "haters of Zion." It is difficult, if not humanly impossible, even for devout religionists to acknowledge or discern their own responsibility in the bellicose conflicts that accompanied the conquest of the Holy Land. They were indeed the invaders. The Canaanites, Philistines, Syrians, even in some ways the Assyrians and Babylonians, considered Israel as the invaders. But the Hebrews were sincere devotees of their God, different from the divinities of their neighbors. Religious wars are the most cruel and inhuman of all international conflicts, for they involve a confusion between political ambition and metaphysical imagination.

The psalmist uses another metaphor from agricultural architecture: the grass seed sown on the house roofs soon dries up, just as the adversaries of Yahweh are exterminated.

Strophe IV: No Blessing but Benediction (vv. 7-8)

The reapers and gatherers of sheaves have empty hands and arms, for the enemies gained nothing to preserve. Their work is useless, for they are missing the blessing from Yahweh (vv. 7-8a). This Song of Ascents must have been intoned by priests, who blessed cultically in the name of Yahweh (v. 8c).

DATE AND THEOLOGY

The poetic survey of Israel's trials over many centuries suggests a postexilic date. In the Persian period, Judaism looked forward to a relatively secure destiny. If there are still "haters of Zion," they would be desiccated like grass on rooftops (cf. Ps 103:15-16; Isa 37:27; 40:6ff.).

This review of destructive brutality, always followed by a renovation, may be viewed as a timeless prediction of events more recent than the Psalms' composition and original use: the Hellenistic war, leading to the Hanukkah (168-165 B.C.E.), the Roman extermination and destruction of the second temple (C.E. 68-70), the many massacres and expulsions of Jewish communities, culminating in the monstrous Holocaust of the twentieth century, always penultimate, never final. Such a history points to the timelessness of Psalm 129, with its theology at once simple and difficult to accept or to be comprehended by "the goyim," who thought of themselves as Christians! The Lord does not prevent the cruelty of the recurrent persecutions. He prevents only the elect people from being wiped out. Theodicy is beyond rational explanation. Is Israel's sense of uniqueness dependent on the uniqueness of its faith? Yahweh stands beyond human imagination. The name of Yahweh — "He causes to be whatever he causes to be" — underlines the final benediction offered in the psalm. The Lord is not one who answers the prayers of national supremacy. He teaches a justice that transcends human morality but eventually dominates persecution.

"War is as much a punishment to the punisher as to the sufferer," wrote Thomas Jefferson. The nations of the world will know peace when religion discovers its universality.

PSALM 130

De Profundis

1. *Song of Ascents.*

I

    Out of the depths
      I cried to thee, O Lord!

2.   *My Sovereign, hear my voice!*
    May thine ears be attentive to the sound of my supplications!
3.   *If thou, O Lord, shouldst mark iniquities,*
    My Sovereign, who could stand?

II

4.   *But there is forgiveness with thee,*
    That thou mayest be feared;
5.   *I waited for the Lord; my soul waited,*
    And I hope for his promise;
6.   *My soul [waits] for my Sovereign*
    More than watchmen for the morning,
    Yea, than watchmen for the morning.

III

7.   *May Israel wait for the Lord!*
    For with the Lord there is steadfast love,
    And with him plenteous redemption;
8.   *And he, himself, will redeem Israel*
    From all its iniquities.

BIBLIOGRAPHY

N. Airoldi, "Note critiche ai Salmi," *Augustinianum*, X (1970), pp. 174-80; J.-N. Aletti et N. Trublet, *Approche poétique et théologique des Psaumes: Analyses et méthodes* (Paris, 1982), pp. 202ff.; R. Arconada, "Psalmus 129/130 (De Profundis) retentus, emendatus, glossatus," *VD* (1932), pp. 213-19; P. Auffret, *La Sagesse a bâti sa maison: Ps. 130* (Fribourg and Göttingen, 1982), pp. 514-21; W. Brueggemann, *The Message of the Psalms* (Minneapolis, 1984), pp. 104-6; C. H. Cornill, "Psalm 130," in *Festschrift K. Budde* (Giessen, 1920), pp. 38-42; E. Dell'Oca, [Psalm 130], *Rivista bíblica*, XXVI (1964), pp. 10-15; R. C. Dentan, "An Exposition of an Old Testament Passage," *Journal* of *Bible and Religion*, XV (1947), pp. 158ff.; F. James, *Thirty Psalmists* (New York, 1938), pp. 135-40; C. C. Keet, *A Study of the Psalms of Ascents* (London, 1969), pp. 74-82; R. A. Marrs, "A Cry from the Depths (Ps 130)," *ZAW*, C (1968), pp. 81-90; J. Clinton McCann, Jr., *A Theological Introduction to the Book of Psalms* (Nashville, 1993), pp. 86-90; P. D. Miller, Jr., "Psalm 130," *Int*, XXXIII (1979), pp. 176-81; idem, *Interpreting the Psalms* (Philadelphia, 1986), pp. 138-43; Š. Porúbčan, "Psalm 130,5-6," *VT*, IX (1959), pp. 322-23; W. H. Schmidt, "Gott und Mensch in Psalm 130 (Formgeschichtliche Erwägungen)," *TZ*, XXII (1966), pp. 214-53; N. H. Snaith, *The Seven Psalms* (London, 1964), pp. 86-96; J. J. Stamm, *Erlösen und Vergeben im Alten Testament* (Bern, 1940); H. Thielicke, *Out of the Depths*, tr. G. W. Bromiley (Grand Rapids, 1962); J. Tromp, "The Text of Psalm CXXX, 5-6," *VT*, XXXIX (1989), pp. 100-103; P. van Imschoot, "Ps 130 (Vulg, 129)," *Collationes Gandavenses*, XXVI (1939), pp. 217-21; P. Volz, "Psalm 130," in *Festschrift K. Marti* (Giessen, 1925), pp. 287-96; C. Westermann, *The Living Psalms* (Grand Rapids, 1989), pp. 116-22.

FORM

This psalm appears to be composed of three strophes, the second and third of which include a tricolon (vv. 6 and 7). The first two strophes seem to be an individual supplication (vv. 1b-3 and vv. 4-5). The third strophe is an exhortation to Israel in the third person singular. The meter is quite irregular other than in Strophe I (3+3; 3+2; 3+3), namely, 3+2; 4+2; 4+2 and then, for v. 6, 3+2; 4+3; 4+2; 4+2; finally, in vv. 7-8, 3+3+3; 3+2. Several commentators, in view of the thematic and metrical changes, suggest that Psalm 130 was made of two disparate fragments. Others think that the prayer of supplication is sung by a collective "I" in the name of Israel and that the psalm is therefore a unity, although the third strophe has only two stichoi.

COMMENTARY

Strophe I: A Cry from the Depths (vv. 1b-3)

An individual singer finds himself in profound distress. No specification of his plight is indicated. The "depths" have for centuries been understood as "the abode of the dead." Even today, in many countries, the Latin title *De profundis* is used for invitations to a funeral.

The name *Yahweh*, revealed to Moses at the vision of the burning bush, is here coupled with another, *Adonai*, "My Sovereign" (cf. vv. 3 and 6). It may be an attempt to render the prayer even more intense than if it was addressed to the liberator from slavery. It is the plural of majesty of the name *Adôn*, which may have an aesthetic as well as political connotation (cf. the Greek *Adonis*?). Immediately the semantic allusion to the dead is linked to "transgressions" as if the phenomenon of death were the result of a condemnation of sin!

The depths are often associated with the "deep waters," and death is separation from God, as is guilt that remains after committing a crime (cf. Ps 69:2, 4; Isa 51:10; Ezek 27:34). The psalmist appears to reject the notion of death as the consequence of culpability. The context of the condemnation of Adam and Eve is quite different, for it deals with the human desire for immortality (Gen 3:3). Yet the poet had to introduce the wonder of divine forgiveness (v. 4) in his soft but clear negativism: How could the Lord, my Sovereign, "mark iniquities," implying "forever"?

Strophe II: The Fear of Divine Forgiveness (vv. 4-6)

The psalmist does not fear divine forgiveness, but he understands the peculiarly Hebraic sense of "fearful love." Even a pre-Islamic saying grasped, at the human level, the notion of fear, not terror, without the expectation of punishment for sinfulness. Here "fear in love" comes from passionate intimacy. The lover becomes fearful when he risks disappointing his lover, or failing to reach the sublime expectation of pleasing perfectly.

In Hebraic poetry the secret of the fear of God is the justified humility of "missing the mark" (etymological origin of the Hebraic meaning of sin!).

Faith is love in fear. To wait for "my Sovereign" is to recognize that the presence of God may be delayed, even elusive, until a full manifestation of it explodes into a psychological upheaval of spiritual vision or audition.

Strophe III: The Redemption of Israel (vv. 7-8)

These verses are a stylistic volte-face with a change of theme and a subtle explanation of theology. Israel is pressed to "wait for the Lord" (v. 7). The choice of another verb for "wait" and "hope" is most significant. Strophe II's "I waited for the Lord" (v. 5) has now become "May Israel wait for the Lord!" (v. 7). Without a doubt the individual lamenter from the depths, in Strophes I and II, is not aware of transgressions that deserve death, but the exhortation to Israel finds a hope of redemption in the Lord's marvelous forgiveness of national iniquities. Israel's hope is intense, radical, profound, and in some way devastating because the guilt is deep. It is true that the human petition to God for "not marking iniquities" is a passionate plea, and that the psalmist hopes "more than watchmen for the morning" (twice), but the exhortation to Israel is different. It implies a national appeal to repent and to create equality between rich and poor. The great prophets discerned without equivocation that the elect people would survive only with the steadfast love that enacts a solemn drama of "redemption." From Amos and Hosea to Jeremiah and Ezekiel, prophetic schools became aware of Israel's fall into spiritual slavery. Only the "buying back" or the redeeming of their freedom, involving a "plenteous" payment, would insure the perenniality of Israel in the history of humankind.

DATE AND THEOLOGY

The Songs of Ascents are quite diverse, in form, in genre, and in theology. It would seem that the editors of proto-collections, like those of the Songs of Ascents, have brought together a number of pieces of disparate origins like hymns, individual supplications, sapiential sayings, and prophetic judgments of national failure. This last theme characterizes the final crowning of Psalm 130. Yet the prophetic stringency leads to a Deutero-Isaianic exultation of divine love.

Many theologians, especially St. Augustine and Martin Luther, have found in Psalm 130 the gist of the gospel, announcing salvation "nevertheless." Redemption is not earned by humankind but — as its etymology shows — is "purchased" or bought by God at great pain and a high price. The nominal expression "plenteous redemption" is immediately followed by the verbal insistence "He, himself, will redeem Israel" (vv. 7 and 8).

To redeem a prisoner of high standing is to buy his freedom. A ransom has to be paid. The steadfast love of the Lord will gather and offer his own son, as in the story of the sacrifice of Isaac by his father Abraham. Redemption calls symbolically for the burden and wrenching of self. The use of the word "redemption" necessitates a new theology.

While other Songs of Ascents may have led indirectly to a semi-Pelagian bargaining with a deity at the marketplace, Psalm 130 begins with a cry of distress from the depths of death itself, but it becomes a metaphor strangely demanding the paradoxical language of "the death of God." In communion or affinity with a people in perdition, God offers himself. The longing of Israel for this certitude ends in a monumental sense of security.

The awareness and acceptance are not conducive to human negligence or lassitude. "There is forgiveness with thee, that thou mayest be feared." This kind of fear includes an "awe" that renders man able and willing to work, not in order to obtain an indulgence and to deserve life instead of death, but as a participation with an apotheosis that unveils truth, displays a sanctification of doubt, and strengthens the intent to find God and ride in his chariot. In the words of Emily Dickinson, the Lord says, "Arms of Mine—sufficient phaeton."

PSALM 131

Proud Play with Humility

1. *Song of Ascent. From David.*

I

> *Lord, my heart is without pretense,*
> > *And my looks are not haughty.*
> *I have taken no part in grandiose actions*
> > *Or in marvels beyond my scope.*

II

2.   *Far from this! My desires are moderate and quiet*
> > *Like those of an infant at his mother's breast;*
> *Yes, my desires are like those of an infant.*

III

3.   *Let Israel wait for the Lord*
> *From henceforth forevermore.*

BIBLIOGRAPHY

W. Beyerlin, *Wider der Hybris des Geistes: Studien zum 131. Psalm* (Stuttgart, 1982); P. A. H. de Boer, "Psalm 131,2," *VT*, XVI (1966), pp. 287-92; A. Maillot, "Israël, compte sur le Seigneur (Ps. 131)," *BVC*, LXXVII (1967), pp. 26-37; G. Quell, "Struktur und Sinn des Psalms 131," in *Festschrift L. Rost* (Berlin, 1967) pp. 173-85.

FORM

This short psalm consists of three strophes. The first one has two bicola (v. 1b-e); the second has one tricolon (v. 2); and the third has one swift bicolon (v. 3). The strophic shortening articulates a crescendo of themes, from self-praise to an exhortation for Israel to wait humbly for the Lord. As a Song of Ascents sung in a pilgrimage toward Jerusalem, Psalm 131 is placed intentionally right after Psalm 130, for both pieces terminate in a similar way. The meter's irregularity (3+2; 2+2; 2+3; 3+3; 4+2) may fit the progress of the song from egocentricity to national concern.

COMMENTARY

Superscription (v. 1a)

The attribution of this psalm to David reflects the psychological contradictions that affected the temperament of the man who founded the royal dynasty in Jerusalem. David appeared to be at once proud and humble, strong and weak, restrained and extravagant, a devotee of the covenant and a murderer. Moreover, he was a gifted charmer and a thaumaturgical figure.

Strophe I: Claiming Moderation (v. 1b-e)

In Hebraic anthropology, the heart was viewed as the seat of intelligent and reasonable decisions. The Hebrew verb (v. 1d) means "to be swollen, to be high, to exalt oneself, and to claim superiority." The psalmist at once denies that he has ever been pretentious beyond his capacities, or that he has looked down upon his fellowmen. Literally the MT means, "My eyes do not look haughtily at others." To substantiate this egocentric display of humility, the poet affirms playfully that he has never taken part in ambitious, extravagant designs and that he has never been seduced into attempting to perform marvels, or miracles exceeding his normal strength.

Strophe II: Sated and Satisfied like a Babe (v. 2)

The psalmist continues his defense even more emphatically by stating that his soul, here the seat of desire, has been easily tamed. Literally he wants to say, "I have smoothed, composed, silenced, or appeased — even leveled my desires." Then he compares himself to a well-fed infant, sated and entirely satisfied, at his mother's breast or in his mother's arms.

   As in another Song of Ascents, the poet repeats his claim to sufficiency. Poetic parallelisms may have been the evidence of sapiential style.

Strophe III: Let Israel "Wait" in Hope for the Lord (v. 3)

The sudden shift from self-praise to a hidden warning for Israel in its apparent impatience does not represent a non sequitur. On the contrary, the proud play on the humility of this individual becomes a lesson for the elect people. Just as the singer responds to accusations of indulging in foolish grandeur, so he also concludes that Israel transcends charges of national extravagance. The plea is motivated by the psalmist's hope that Israel's "waiting" for the Lord will last forever.

DATE AND THEOLOGY

Such a poem is addressed to Yahweh, but it does not constitute a prayer of supplication. Its third strophe seems to be an objective exhortation to the holy people, who, like the poet himself, has been "boasting" about its achievement and imperial ambitions, out of proportion to its size, ability, and vocation.

Many years later, in the first century of Christendom, seized by a somewhat similar ambiguity of a proud play with humility, the apostle Paul declared that he was "chief of sinners." The psalm was still seeking preeminence for the dynasty of David in spite of military disasters and political oppression. He could easily be one of the pilgrims of the early postexilic Diaspora, on their way to Zion, for he was curiously influenced by the great prophets of the eighth and seventh centuries, especially Jeremiah. He knew the perils of religious hubris.

Like Christian churchmen and the liberated members of Judaism in the early days of the Persian era, the psalmist had to learn that "nationalism is an infantile disease." It is "the measles of mankind" (Albert Einstein, "To Sylvester Viereck," 1921).

The belief in being chosen may well corrupt "waiting for the Lord." Today, "It is everywhere self-evident that *we* are on the side of Light, *they* on the side of Darkness," wrote Aldous Huxley ironically *(The Devils of Loudun).* The church is nothing but a sect if it pretends (cf. Ps 131:1) to be superior to other churches or so-called "pagan" religions. The urge to wait for the Lord is an invitation, dramatically urgent, "to walk humbly with [one's] God" (Mic 6:8).

PSALM 132

Lord, Remember David

1. Song of Ascents.

I

> *Lord, remember David,*
> > *And all the hardships he endured!*
> 2.   *He swore an oath to the Lord;*
> > *He vowed this to the Mighty One of Jacob:*

3.　　　*I will not enter the tent [or] my house,*
　　　　　Nor ascend a bed for my rest.

4.　　　*I will not allow my eyes to sleep,*
　　　　　Nor even close my eyelids,

5.　　　*Till I find a place for the Lord,*
　　　　　A residence for the Mighty One of Jacob.

II

6.　　　*Behold, we heard the news in Ephrathah;*
　　　　　We found it in the fields of Jaar.

7.　　　*Let us go to his residence,*
　　　　　And prostrate ourselves before his footstool.

8.　　　*Arise, O Lord, to the place of thy rest,*
　　　　　Thou, and the ark of thy majesty!

9.　　　*Thy priests are robed in righteousness,*
　　　　　Thy devotees shout with joy,

10.　　*On account of David, thy servant!*
　　　　　Do not reject thy Anointed!

III

11.　　*The Lord has sworn his oath to David;*
　　　　　He will not come back from his truth:
　　　　　"I will set on thy throne a fruit from thy loins.

12.　　*If thy sons observe my covenant,*
　　　　　And the precepts I have taught them,
　　　　Even their sons, forever,
　　　　　Will sit upon thy throne."

13.　　*Yes, the Lord has chosen Zion;*
　　　　　He ardently desired it for his house:

14.　　*"It is the place of my rest forever;*
　　　　　I shall reside here, for it was my very wish.

Envoi

15.　　*I shall abundantly bless its resources,*
　　　　　Give its poor their fill of bread,

16.　　*I shall clothe its priests with salvation,*
　　　　　And its devotees will sing with joy.

17.　　*There I shall make a horn sprout for David,*
　　　　　And light a lamp for my Anointed;

18. *I shall clothe his enemies with shame,*
    But as for him, his crown will flourish."

BIBLIOGRAPHY

F. Asensio, "El Psalmo 132 y la 'Lámpara' de David," *Gregorianum*, XXXVIII (1957), pp. 310-16; A. Bentzen, "The Cultic Use of the Story of the Ark in Samuel," *JBL*, LXVII (1948), pp. 37-53; R. A. Carlson, "David and the Ark in 2 Samuel 6," in *Festschrift E. Nielsen* (Leiden, 1993), pp. 17-23; G. A. Davies, "The Ark in the Psalms," in *Festschrift S. H. Hooke* (Edinburgh, 1963), pp. 51-61; O. Eissfeldt, "Psalm 132," *Welt des Orients*, II, 5/6 (1959), pp. 480-83; T. E. Fretheim, "Psalm 132: A Form-critical Study," *JBL*, LXXXVI (1967), pp. 289-300; H. Gese, "Der Davidsbund und die Zionserwählung," *ZTK*, LXI (1964), pp. 10-26; D. Hermann, "Die Königsnovelle in Ägypten und in Israel," in *Wissenschaft Zeitschrift . . . Leipzig*, III (1953-54), pp. 33ff.; D. R. Hillers, "Ritual Procession of the Ark and Ps 132," *CBQ*, XXX (1968), pp. 49-55; C. B. Houk, "Psalm 132: Literary Integrity and Syllable-Word Structures," *JSOT*, VI (1978), pp. 41-48 (with responses by R. E. Bee and C. B. Houk, pp. 54-57); A. R. Johnson, "Hebrew Conceptions of Kingship," in *Myth, Ritual and Kingship*, ed. S. H. Hooke (Oxford, 1958), pp. 204-35; idem, "The Role of the King in the Jerusalem Cultus," in *The Labyrinth*, ed. S. H. Hooke (London, 1945, pp. 71-111; idem, *Sacral Kingship in Ancient Israel* (Cardiff, 1955); C. C. Keet, *A Study of the Psalms of Ascents* (London, 1969), pp. 86-101; H.-J. Kraus, *Königsherrschaft Gottes im Alten Testament*, BHT XIII (1951); idem, *Worship in Israel* (Oxford, 1966), pp. 182ff.; N. Kruse, "Psalm cxxxii and the Royal Zion Festival," *VT*, XXXIII (1983), pp. 279-97; A. Laato, "Psalm 132: A Case Study in Methodology," *CBQ*, LXI (1999), pp. 24-37; P. Nel, "Psalm 132 and Covenantal Theology," in *Festschrift F. C. Fensham*, JSOTSup XLVIII (Sheffield, 1988), pp. 188-91; E. Nielsen, "Some Reflexions on the History of the Ark," VTSup VII (1959), pp. 166ff.; M. Noth, "David und Israel in 2 Sam. 7," in *Festschrift A. Robert* (Paris, 1958), pp. 122-30; idem, "Gott — König — Volk im Alten Testament," *ZTK*, XLVII (1950), pp. 157-91; idem, "Jerusalem und die israelitische Tradition," *OtSt*, VIII (1950), pp. 28-46; J. R. Porter, "The Interpretation of 2 Samuel 6 and Psalm 132," *JTS*, V (1954), pp. 161-73; G. A. Rendsburg, *Linguistic Evidence for the Northern Origin of Selected Psalms* (Atlanta, 1990), pp. 87-90; A. Robinson, "Do Ephrathah and Jaar Really Appear in Psalm 132⁶?" *ZAW*, LXXXVI (1974), pp. 220-22; L. Rost, "Sinaibund und Davidsbund," *TLZ*, LXXII (1947), pp. 129ff.; idem, *Die Überlieferung von der Thronnachfolge Davids*, BWANT III, 6 (Neukirchen, 1926); J. Schreiner, *Sion — Jerusalem Yahwes Königssitz* (München, 1963), pp. 47-56; M. Simon, "La prophétie de Nathan et le temple," *RHPR*, XXXII (1952), pp. 41-58; H. von den Bussche, "Le texte de la prophétie de Nathan sur la dynastie Davidique," *ETL*, XXIV (1948), pp. 37-53; G. von Rad, "Erwägungen zu den Königspsalmen," *ZAW*, LVIII (1940/41), pp. 216-22; idem, "Das judäische Königsritual," *TLZ*, LXXII (1947), p. 211.

FORM

This psalm is neither a prayer of supplication nor a hymn, although it includes some requests to the Lord (vv. 1b, 8-10) and quotes verbatim oracles from the same Lord (vv. 11c-12, 14-18). Like some hymns, it is composed of three strophes: Strophe I (vv. 1b-5), Strophe II (vv. 6-10), and Strophe III (vv. 11-13). The poem ends with four bicola (vv. 14-18) that stress the significance of the Lord's revelation of his intent. Each strophe is divided in two substrophes. One tricolon appears (v. 11) to stress the oracular declaration of the Lord's oath to David.

The meter is generally regular (3+3), with one emphatic tricolon (the oath to David, v. 11) and the promise to cause a horn, symbol of success, to flourish upon David and his dynasty (v. 17: 4+3).

The placing of this psalm among the Songs of Ascents may well indicate that pilgrims marching to Jerusalem were eager to connect the two themes: Zion and David's dynasty.

COMMENTARY

Strophe I: David's Oath to the Lord (vv. 1b-5)

The initial part of Strophe I is a liturgical appeal for the Lord to "remember" David and his painful afflictions. "Remember," when applied to God, is a sort of euphemism for "Pay attention" (Neh 5:19; Pss 25:6ff.; 74:2, 18, 22; 89:47, 50). Psalm 132, sung by different voices, may have been composed for some cultic ceremonial not mentioned elsewhere in the literature of Israel or Judah. Such a ceremony,[1] perhaps implied by the Deuteronomic stories of 2 Samuel 6 and 7, may have been a covenant festival, a Zion festival, or an enthronement festival, any one of which perhaps was celebrated annually on the first day of Sukkôth (Tabernacles). Any one of these hypotheses is possible, but no demonstration has so far been convincing.

The "hardships" endured by David may have been the long struggle with King Saul's forces, or the difficulties David encountered in bringing the ark to Jerusalem (2 Sam 6:6-15; 1 Chr 15:5-14). According to legendary traditions, which contain elements of historical truth, the king made a vow to the Lord that he would select a place of "rest" for "the Mighty One of Jacob." This designation of Yahweh, literally "the Bull," seems to reflect, with other words, a northern origin of the psalm (cf. v. 5; also Pss 24:6; 44:4; 46:7, 11; 49:13; Isa 49:26; 50:16).

David's vow to select a place of rest for the Lord was most probably re-

---

1. Cf. A. Caquot and P. de Robert, *Les livres de Samuel* (Genève, 1994), pp. 412-36.

lated to the belief that Zion was the navel of the world. Claims to that effect had been made previously for the sanctuaries of Dan and Shechem, but Zion's Rock was probably endowed with this significance by the Jebusites long before David finally conquered the fortress (2 Sam 4:5-9). Zion was David's choice because he may have agreed with the Canaanite myth. Although this is not explicitly mentioned anywhere, the history of the temple in the book of Kings and the Prophets, for better or for worse, amply supports the hypothesis of the omphalos myth in Zion.[2]

Strophe II: Zion and the Davidic Dynasty (vv. 6-10)

The tenacity with which the kings of Judah and later the Jews, from the postexilic restoration to our day, have held the sacrality of Zion is affirmed by the poet of Psalm 132 with unusual eloquence (vv. 7-10, 14-15). Choristers now sing corporately, as if they were the fathers who had discovered the uniqueness of the site. "Ephrathah" is most probably "Ephraim" (cf. Judg 12:5) rather than a designation of Bethlehem, where the ark was never kept, and "Jaar" seems to have been another name for Kiriath-jearim, where the ark was preserved for many years (1 Chr 13:5). As worshipers prostrate themselves before the ark — Yahweh's footstool — priests are assembled (v. 9).

In this psalm the ceremonial reflects a critical situation: the "Anointed," namely, a king of the Davidic line and the semantic model in later years for the "Messiah" to come, is threatened with foreign or domestic opposition (v. 10). The psalmist now moves forward from the time of David to a period within the centuries of the monarchy. He thus expresses his devotion to the king as the servant of the Lord.

At the same time Yahweh's presence in the temple belongs to the deepest convictions of the singers. The Lord's residence is real, in a mode that is never clearly formulated. God, the Lord of heaven and earth, "rests" or allows his "name" to be invoked in the sanctuary, but he remains untouchable and invisible.[3] The ark brings sacramentally his power and his majesty (v. 9).

Strophe III: Will David's Sons Observe the Covenant? (vv. 11-13)

During the centuries of the Davidic monarchy (960-587 B.C.E.), cultic prophets interpreted the demands of the Lord. Some of them asked for royal integrity

2. S. Terrien, "The Myth of the Omphalos and Hebrew Religion," *VT*, XX (1970), pp. 315-38; bibliographies on pp. 318-19.

3. S. Terrien, "The Metaphor of the Rock in Biblical Theology," in *God in the Fray: Festschrift W. Brueggemann* (Minneapolis, 1998), pp. 157-71.

and ethical rectitude for the government in tenure. This psalm holds that the Davidic Covenant is as conditional as the Sinai Covenant. It is not mythicized as eternal. It rests on a national standard of ethics to be applied in history.

Yet the utmost desire of the Lord is to dwell through some mode in Zion. The mode of this dwelling is not defined, but the motif of Presence is intermingled with the site of Zion and the behavior of both king and nation (vv. 11-12). The affinities of Psalm 132 to Nathan's prophecy (2 Sam 7:4-16) and Solomon's prayer of dedication of the temple (1 Kgs 8:23-33) have been noted.

Envoi: A Lamp and a Horn for the Anointed (vv. 14-17)

The oracle announces the prosperity that will prevail in covenant, kingship, and Zion and cooperate amicably in a dynamic way (v. 15).

The covenant precepts remain unformulated. For an age when the Torah became more a cultic law than an ethical guide, it would appear that the psalmist, the disciple of the great prophets, favors a self-offering in totality rather than the minutiae of food prohibitions and other practices, which were chiefly legal reactions against Canaanite rites.

The metaphor (v. 17) of a lamp as light, just as a symbol of successful maturity (1 Kgs 11:36 and 2 Kgs 8:19), coalesces with the virtues of royal government and mingles them as the secret of the covenant way, so that Israel may truly be a priestly kingdom for all the nations of the earth (Exod 19:5).

DATE AND THEOLOGY

Psalm 132 was apparently composed in preexilic times, during the reigns of the Davidic dynasty, but its use, by pilgrims marching toward Zion, confers upon it a theological firmness often absent in other royal psalms. God elects Israel to serve him; the king as well as the priests must be respectful of the link that unites the site of Zion to the Davidic dynasty.

The psalm is silent on the corrupting influence played by the myth of the omphalos. It required drastic action during the reform of Josiah (2 Kgs 23:4-15) and vitiated the alliance between the theological strictness of the great prophets and the monarchy during the long years of Judah's agony before its final submission to the Babylonian army (587 B.C.E.).

Nevertheless, hope in ultimate salvation, not based on ritual legalism, became the *raison de vivre* advocated by this psalmist. The fervent attachment to the geographical sacrality of Zion prevented Judaism from following its vocation toward a worldwide spirituality. It also explains in large measure the exclusivism and arrogant presumption of many so-called "Christian" churches. It prevents them, to this day, from recognizing their sectarian pride and the limitation of their idealism. From the beginning of the Christian era, churches have often denied their openness to global humanity. It seems impossible for Christendom to open up and to incarnate the psalmist's expectation of a universal blossoming of the "horn." The "crown" (Ps 132:11) belongs symbolically to "one of David's descendants," if not physiologically at least existentially (Acts 2:30-35).

Gregory of Nyssa entertained a vision of worldwide harmony when he wrote, "The Maker of all prepared beforehand, as it were, a royal lodging for the future king."

PSALM 133

Friendship and Benediction

1. Song of Accents. For David.

I

    Behold! How pleasant, how sweet
      For brothers to dwell together!
2.   *It is like precious oil spread on the head,*
      That descends on the beard,
    The beard of Aaron that descends
      To the hem of his robes.

II

3.   *It is like the dew of Hermon*
      That descends on the hills of Zion.
    There the Lord bestows his blessing:
      Life! Forevermore!

BIBLIOGRAPHY

P. Auffret, "Essai sur la structure littéraire du psaume 133," *Biblische Notizen*, XXVI (1985), pp. 22-34; A. Berlin, "On the Interpretation of Psalm 133," in *Directions in Biblical Hebrew Poetry*, ed. E. R. Follis, JSOTSup XL (Sheffield, 1987), pp. 141-47; H. Gunkel, "Psalm 133," in *Festschrift K. Budde*, BZAW XXXIV (Giessen, 1920), pp. 69-74;

K. Horst, "Segen und Segenshandlungen in der Bibel," *EvT*, VII (1947), pp. 23-37; O. Keel, "Kultische Brüderlichkeit in Ps 133," *Freiburger Zeitschrift für Theologie und Philosophie*, XXIII (1976), pp. 68-80; C. C. Keet, *A Study of the Psalms of Ascents* (London, 1969), pp. 102-7; O. Loretz, "Die Ugaritistik in der Psalminterpretation," *UF*, IV (1972), pp. 167-69; G. H. Rendsburg, *Linguistic Evidence for the Northern Origin of Selected Psalms* (Atlanta, 1990), pp. 91-93; J. M. Rosenstiehl, "Un commentaire du Psaume 133 à l'époque intertestamentaire," *RHPR*, LIX (1979), pp. 559-65; A. Schultz, *Kritisches zum Psalter* (Münster in Westfalen, 1932), pp. 62ff.; W. G. E. Watson, "The Hidden Simile in Psalm 133," *Bib*, LX (1960), pp. 108-9.

FORM

Like Psalm 132, which precedes it immediately in the Psalter, this poem is neither a lament nor a prayer of supplication. It exhales the joyfulness of a hymn, but it contains only two substrophes of three and two bicola. One may decide that it is made of only one strophe in the sapiential style. The theme is the beauty and sweetness of brotherhood, which are compared to those of the ritual oil poured on the head of Aaron (Strophe I) or to the dew of Mount Hermon (Strophe II). Both comparisons evoke the blessing of Yahweh. What kind of brotherhood is here praised?

COMMENTARY

Strophe I: The Delights of Fraternal Friendship (vv. 1b-2)

A number of exegetes take the word "brothers" in its literal sense, siblings of the same family, including half-brothers and nephews (cf. Gen 13:6-7; 27:42-42; etc.). The levirate law (Deut 25:5) indicates the importance of the fraternal bond in ancient Israel. Family coherence, it is argued, may also result from economic considerations, so that property would not be divided among many inheritors. However, examples of family dissent are as common as those of family harmony. As late as the first century c.e., the parable of Jesus on the two brothers (Luke 15:11-32) alludes to a less-than-ideal fraternal relationship. The figurative use of the word "brother" for artists who live together in the precincts of the temple appears to be common in sapiential circles (Job 30:29; Prov 18:9). Those who admit that Psalm 133 is a wisdom poem ignore the sapiential use of the word "brothers" in a figurative sense. Is not the beauty and sweetness of brothers dwelling together a marvel of friendship worth noticing?

The comparison of fraternal unity among professional musicians may well be that of precious oil flowing down on the hem of Aaron's robes.[1]

Strophe II: The Dew from Mount Hermon (v. 3)

The flowing of the dew from Mount Hermon to Mount Zion seems to be a geographical impossibility. The nine thousand-foot mountain is visible from Jerusalem but at a distance of two hundred miles. It has been suggested that Aaron received on his head not the sacramental oil but "cinnamon unguent" that was brought to the hill of Zion. Two Coptic documents of a late date propose this possibility.[2] The allusion to Aaron, the high priest (Exod 29:7; Lev 6:3), would be quite normal in postexilic times, when second temple Judaism had access to the sacerdotal traditions written down as part of the Torah (Exod 31:10; cf. Ezra 7:1-5). The robes of Aaron (plural) suggest liturgical vestments proper for a ceremonial blessing (Num 6:24-26). The psalmist insists on "the blessing of Yahweh" that is implied by a ritual gesture in a solemn ceremony, raised to the level of divine acceptance, approbation, and intervention.

DATE AND THEOLOGY

Since the so-called "priestly code" may have been transmitted orally during the monarchy, the date of Psalm 133 may have been earlier than postexilic times. At any rate, the benediction of Yahweh seems to be the ultimate meaning of the comparison with the beauty and sweetness of brotherhood. The sapiential style is now transformed by a cultic usage, but the sacerdotal atmosphere does not imply the minutiae of a legalistic diet and other prohibitions and prescriptions of the finished Pentateuch. This singer, a functionary of the temple of Zion, had been exposed to the disciplines of the wise and the great prophets. This short psalm favors a theology of existential salvation. True fraternity rests on the open outgoingness of God's effective benediction.

> Man liveth not by Self alone,
>> But in his brother's face. (William Blake)

---

1. The masculine plural "robes," rather than the MT feminine (v. 2d), was the probable original; cf. J. van der Ploeg, "Fragments d'un manuscrit de psaumes de Qumrân (11Ps^b)," *RB*, LXXIV (1967), pp. 408-12.

2. O. von Lemm, *Koptische Miscellen . . .*, cited by Rosenstiehl, "Un commentaire du Psaume 133," p. 560, n. 4; also K. H. Kuhn, "A Coptic Jeremiah Apocryphon," *Le Muséon*, LXXXIII (1970), p. 304; cited in Rosenstiehl, "Un commentaire du Psaume 133," p. 561.

PSALM 134

All Night Long, Bless Ye the Lord

1. *Song of Ascents.*

I

> Behold! Bless ye the Lord,
>   All of you, servants of the Lord!
> You who stand in the house of the Lord
>   All night long!

II

2. Lift up your hands toward the sanctuary,
      And bless ye the Lord!
3. May the Lord bless thee from Zion,
      The maker of heaven and earth!

BIBLIOGRAPHY

W. F. Albright, "Notes on Psalms 68 and 134," in *Festschrift S. Mowinckel* (Oslo, 1955), pp. 1-12; P. Auffret, "Note on the Literary Structure of Psalm 134," *JSOT*, XLV (1989), pp. 87-89; F. Crüsemann, *Studien zur Formgeschichte von Hymnus und Danklied in Israel*, WMANT XXXII (Neukirchen, 1969), pp. 78-79; F. Horst, "Segen und Segenshandlungen in der Bibel," *EvT*, VII (1947), pp. 23-27; C. C. Keet, *A Study of the Psalms of Ascents* (London, 1969), pp. 107-11.

FORM

This brief poem, the last of the Songs of Ascents, is made of two strophes of two bicola each. Strophe I is an appeal to the servants of Yahweh (v. 1b-e). Strophe II is addressed to outsiders who remain unidentified, perhaps fellow pilgrims on their way to Zion (v. 2). A third exhortation is sung to Yahweh himself; from Zion, God is asked to bless a single personage who is unnamed, perhaps the choirmaster, perhaps the king himself.

The name "Yahweh" appears three times in Strophe I and twice in Strophe II (vv. 2-3). The meter, at first uniform (3+2; 3+2; 3+2; 3+2; 3+2) is enlarged for the last stichos (3+3). While Yahweh is not praised directly, the style appears to be suitable for the hymnic genre.

COMMENTARY

Strophe I: Appeal to the Servants of the Lord (vv. 1b-2)

The summons startlingly begins with a sapiential injunction, "Behold!" Blessing the Lord is the prerogative of those who stand all night in the sanctuary (Isa 30:29). Are they priests or Levitical musicians?

Strophe II: Divine-Human Reciprocity (vv. 2-3)

The psalmist now addresses outsiders, pilgrims within sight of the temple. To lift up the hands in a ritual gesture has become the opportunity of those who will bless the Deity, an act of praise and thanksgiving. Benediction is "saying good things." It is not the same as the blessing of human beings, nor could it be a transfer of power from man to God. Finally, the hope of a blessing from God, Creator of heaven and earth, is the supreme gift. It is promulgated from Zion, a sacerdotal symbol uniting finitude to infinity, a logical impossibility but a sublime ultimate of the gift of Presence.

DATE AND THEOLOGY

With its diversity of gestures, sayings, and persons, Psalm 134 may have concluded a ceremonial feast, the exact meaning of which is now lost. If the unknown figure addressed in Strophe II is a king, the date would be preexilic, and the poem would have been preserved as the crowning "Song of Ascents" during postexilic times. As a royal psalm, this poem might have been sung in the eschatological hope that the "Anointed One" would come as "the Messiah" at the end of time. Communion between God and man would proffer the final apotheosis of human history.

The reference to Zion, the key to the Songs of Ascents, indicates that nocturnal worship energizes the chorus (1 Chr 9:33) and, as in Psalm 150, affirms that man is not alone in the immensity of the universe. The Creator still creates.

PSALM 135

The Lord of Nature and History

I

1. *Hallelujah! Praise the name of the Lord;*
    Give praise, servants of the Lord
2. *Who stand in the house of the Lord,*
    In the courts of the house of our God!

3. *Praise the Lord, for the Lord is good!*
    Play music, for his name [is] sweet as a lyre.
4. *For it is Jacob whom the Lord chose for himself,*
    Israel, for his precious treasure.
5. *As for me, I know that the Lord is great,*
    And that our Sovereign is above all the gods.

II

6. *All that the Lord pleased, he did!*
    [He, the maker of] heaven and earth,
    Of the seas and all the abysses!
7. *He raises clouds from the ends of the earth,*
    And lightnings he changes into rain,
    Forcing out the wind from its storehouses.

8. *In Egypt he smote the firstborn,*
    Those of man as of beasts;
9. *He sent signs and marvels*
    In the very midst of thee, O Egypt!
    Against Pharaoh
    And all his servants!

III

10. *He smote many nations,*
    And he slew mighty kings —
11. *Sihon, king of the Amorites,*
    And Og, king of Bashan,
    And all the kingdoms of Canaan —
12. *And he gave their lands in heritage,*
    In heritage to Israel, his people.

13. *Thy name, O Lord, endures forever!*
    Thy memory, O Lord, from generation to generation!
14. *For the Lord vindicates his people,*
    And has compassion on his servants.
15. *The idols of the nations are silver and gold,*
    The work of the hands of men.

IV

16. *They have mouths but do not speak;*
    Eyes, but do not see;
17. *Ears, but do not hear;*
    Nor is there any breath in their mouths.
18. *Those who make them are like them,*
    All those who trust in them.

19. *House of Israel, bless the Lord!*
    House of Aaron, bless the Lord!
20. *House of Levi, bless the Lord!*
    You who fear the Lord, bless the Lord!
21. *Blessed be the Lord from Zion!*
    Inhabitant of Jerusalem,
    Hallelujah!

BIBLIOGRAPHY

P. Auffret, *La Sagesse a bâti sa maison* (Fribourg and Göttingen, 1982), pp. 536-48; E. Baumann, "Struktur-Untersuchungen im Psalter II," *ZAW*, LXII (1950), pp. 144-48; E. Bonnard, *Le Psautier selon Jérémie* (Paris, 1960), pp. 219-22; W. Brueggemann, *The Message of the Psalms* (Minneapolis, 1984), pp. 59-60; F. Crüsemann, *Studien zur Formgeschichte von Hymnus und Danklied in Israel*, WMANT XXXII (Neukirchen, 1969), pp. 127-29; A. Lauha, "Die Geschichtsmotive in den alttestamentlichen Psalmen," *Annales academiae scientiarum Fennicae* (Helsinki, 1945); M. Noth, *A History of Pentateuchal Traditions* (Englewood Cliffs, N.J., 1981); R. Pytel, "Zur Exegese von Psalm 135,17," *Folia orientalia*, XI (1969), pp. 239-44; K. Seybold, "Die Redaktion der Wallfahrtpsalmen," *ZAW*, XCI (1979), pp. 247-48; G. von Rad, *Wisdom in Israel* (Harrisburg, Penn., 1972), pp. 177-79; W. Zimmerli, *Erkenntnis Gottes nach dem Buche Ezechiel*, Abhandlungen zur Theologie des Alten und Neuen Testaments XXVII (Zürich, 1954).

FORM

This hymn is composed of four strophes, remarkably regular, each of which contains three substrophes, begins and ends with Hallelujah, invites praise in Strophe I (vv. 1-5), declares that Yahweh's rule over nature is marvelous, and continues with the evocation of the exodus (vv. 8-9) and the "inheritance" of the land in Strophe III (vv. 10-12). It insists on the uniqueness of Israel's election in Strophe III (vv. 13-15) and the inanity of idolatry in Strophe IV (vv. 16-18), and it concludes with a summons to bless Yahweh rather than praise him in Strophe IV (vv. 19-21).

The meter is almost as regular as the strophic structure, a characteristic that seems to imply that the poet was professionally trained in the art of prosody.

COMMENTARY

Strophe I: Play Music for the Lord's Name (vv. 1-5)

A Hallelujah psalm (cf. Psalms 111–113) addresses the "servants of Yahweh" as all the members of the community at worship (cf. Ps 134:1). Gathered inside the sanctuary and its courtyards, they may be the priests as well as the Levitical singers. The praise of the name, however, rather than the glory of the Lord, suggests the language of prophets instead of that of priests. This "name" designates more than reputation and fame; it means the whole intervention of Yahweh in the life of the community. It is as sweet as a lyre (v. 3). Orchestral music is to support the words sung by the chorus.

"Yahweh is great," "above all the gods"; their existence here is not denied, for it appears to be taken for granted (v. 5). Nevertheless, Strophe III will insist on the total emptiness of their images (cf. v. 15).

Strophe II: The Continuous Creator (vv. 6-9)

The greatness of Yahweh emerges from the wonder of his creation, not only heaven and earth but also the tempests of the high seas and the dread of the great abyss (v. 6). Weather changes, sudden storms, and diluvial rains, all of gigantic amplitude, are the result of his work (vv. 6c-7). Hence the plagues of Egypt, which prepare for the momentous event of the exodus, are so extraordinary that Egypt, the most powerful empire at the time, is ironically addressed in the second person singular. It became Yahweh's defeated adversary.

Strophe III: The Inheritance of the Land (vv. 10-15)

The country that had been promised falls into the hands of Israel as a gift. The battles that led to the possession of Canaan are not spelled out, for they are the victory of the Lord. The elect people receives the land as its heritage (v. 12).

The sojourn in Sinai and the Mosaic covenant are ignored. Moses is unknown. The traditions that have been preserved elsewhere (Exod 12:29; Num 21:21-24, 33-35; Josh 2:2-13; etc.) do not seem to capture the poet's interest; the same is true of the annual celebration of the Passover.

Strophe IV: Not Only the Praise but the Blessing (vv. 16-21)

After stressing that the images of the gods, made of silver and gold by human hands, are lifeless, the final strophe returns to the exhortations of Strophe I. However, the summons is more intense, for it is addressed to the official classes of cultic functionaries who became preeminent in postexilic Judaism: the priests — house of Aaron — and the singers of psalms — house of Levi. It will be observed that the expression "house of Levi" is not mentioned elsewhere in the entire Psalter (cf. Pss 115:9-10, 12; 118:2-3). Moreover, the poem that began as an invitation to praise Yahweh's name ends with an order to cultic officials as specialists of blessing and benediction. Blessing generally indicates the conferring of divine power upon human beings and was originally practiced by the patriarchs and later by the sacerdotal and Levitical classes. Blessing is here invited as a ritual of adoration to God by cultic officials.

The origin of Zion is unclear. Did the Jebusites already think of it as the center of the world, the navel of the earth?[1]

DATE AND THEOLOGY

Psalm 135 has been called "a mosaic of quotations" selected and gathered to display the Lord as master of nature and history. Its poetic affinities are many (cf. vv. 1-2 with Ps 134:1; v. 3 with Ps 127:1; v. 4 with Deut 7:6; v. 5 with Exod 18:11; v. 6 with Ps 115:3; v. 8 with Ps 136:10; vv. 10-12 with Ps 136:17-22; v. 13 with Exod 3:15; v. 14 with Deut 32:36; vv. 15-20 with Pss 113:4-6; 118:2-4).

The date of this amalgam must be postexilic. Besides these quotations and reminiscences, an almost verbatim citation in vv. 6-7 is borrowed from the Jeremianic literature (Jer 10:13-14; cf. Isa 41:6-7). The psalm may have been composed as a viaticum of consolation for the exiles whose faith was shattered. The

---

1. S. Terrien, "The Omphalos Myth and Hebrew Religion," *VT*, XX (1970), p. 338.

psalmist expresses here, in spite of the adverse circumstances of Babylonian oppression, perhaps the very dawn of hope with the successes of Cyrus. The singer is thrilled at the greatness of the Lord (Jer 10:6) and his mockery of foreign idols (Jer 10:9, 14).

Nevertheless, the poem received its final form when Zion was again viewed as the center of the earth. In its present form, the psalm was composed as a liturgy that was suitable for a cultic celebration at some festival. Similarly, the other Hallelujah psalms hailed the goodness and delights of Yahweh (cf. Ps 54:6).[2]

A solo voice (v. 5) embroidered the sublime confession of faith in the immensity of Yahweh's power and the status of this Sovereign *(Adonai)* above all the gods of the foreign empires. To follow the ancient beliefs that personified the forces of nature is precisely to confuse the Lord God with lifeless idols. Yahweh orders, stirs up, and restrains the physical forces that foreigners have deified: clouds, lightnings, and rain.

In a burst of religious patriotism, the psalmist rejoices over the election of Israel by a God who is unique among the gods worshiped by foreign nations, and whose uniqueness translates itself into the uniqueness of Israel. When patriotism is founded on the motif of divine election and is not submitted to a religious and ethical judgment like those of the oracles of the great prophets, from Amos to Ezekiel, it quite easily descends into vulgar chauvinism. The universal mission becomes blurred and even nonexistent. Where in this psalm surges the memory of the covenant hope for Israel to be "a priestly nation"?

The prophet Jonah learns that God has compassion for Nineveh, the barbarous enemy of the people that has been elected, the very symbol of mortal calamities (Jonah 4:11).

Edith Cavell, the English nurse who was executed by the Germans during the World War I (1915), said the night before her death, "Standing as I do in view of God and eternity, I realize that patriotism is not enough. I must have no hatred or bitterness toward anyone."

A hymn like Psalm 135, rejoicing in a continuous Creator, demands respect and admiration for a people that passed through centuries of discrimination, persecution, and assassination. At the same time, the theology of Psalm 135 requires a new perspective, placing the elect people in the midst of an earthwide humanity.

The Christian church became an arrogant sect when it took itself to be the New Israel, uniquely chosen and exclusive of other nations or religions. This hymn to the Creator of all humankind is marred, like other psalms of Zion, when it yields to the temptation of theological imperialism.

2. Cf. H.-J. Kraus, *Theology of the Psalms* (Minneapolis, 1984), pp. 59-67.

PSALM 136

A Litany of Praise

Prelude

1.	Praise the Lord, for he is good,	For his mercy is forever!
2.	Praise the God of gods,	For his mercy is forever!
3.	Praise the Sovereign of sovereigns,	For his mercy is forever!

I

4.	The sole doer of great miracles,	For his mercy is forever!
5.	The intelligent maker of the heavens,	For his mercy is forever!
6.	Who stretched out the earth over the waters,	For his mercy is forever!

II

7.	He made the great luminaries,	For his mercy is forever!
8.	The sun, which rules by day,	For his mercy is forever!
9.	The moon and stars to rule by night,	For his mercy is forever!

III

10.	He struck Egypt in its firstborn,	For his mercy is forever!
11.	He led Israel's exit from its midst,	For his mercy is forever!
12.	With mighty hand and outstretched arm,	For his mercy is forever!

IV

13.	He split in two the Sea of Reeds,	For his mercy is forever!
14.	And made Israel pass through its middle,	For his mercy is forever!
15.	He shook off Pharaoh and his army into the Sea,	For his mercy is forever!

V

16.	Leading his people through the desert,	For his mercy is forever!
17.	He smote mighty kings,	For his mercy is forever!
18.	He slaughtered famous kings,	For his mercy is forever!

VI

19.	Sihon, king of the Amorites,	For his mercy is forever!
20.	And Og, king of Bashan,	For his mercy is forever!

21. *And he gave their country in heritage,*	For his mercy is forever!
22. *In heritage to Israel his servant.*	For his mercy is forever!

VII

23. *He remembered us in our humiliation,*	For his mercy is forever!
24. *And rescued us from our enemies,*	For his mercy is forever!
25. *He provides food for all creatures,*	For his mercy is forever!
26. *Give praise to the God of the heavens!*	For his mercy is forever!

BIBLIOGRAPHY

L. Alonso-Schökel, "Psalm 136 (135)," *VD*, XLV (1967), pp. 129-38; W. H. Bellinger, Jr., *Psalms . . .* (Peabody, Mass., 1973), pp. 78, 145; W. Brueggemann, *The Psalms and the Life of Faith* (Minneapolis, 1995), pp. 176, 178; F. Crüsemann, *Studien zur Formgeschichte von Hymnus und Danklied in Israel*, WMANT XXXII (Neukirchen, 1969), pp. 74-76; P. D. Miller, Jr., *Interpreting the Psalms* (Philadelphia, 1986), pp. 40-41, 74-75; M. Noth, *A History of Pentateuchal Traditions* (Englewood Cliffs, N.J., 1981); J. Obermann, "An Antiphonal Psalm from Ras Shamra," *JBL*, LV (1936), pp. 21-44; C. Westermann, *The Living Psalms* (Grand Rapids, 1984), p. 274.

FORM

This psalm is a litany of praise, preceded by a prelude of three bicola. The body of the hymn contains seven strophes, the first five of which are made of three bicola, and the last two of four bicola. The divisions between the seven strophes after the prelude are thematically justified: the first three bicola summon a community of singers to praise the Lord, while the seven strophes that follow unfold and partially develop the catechism of Psalm 135: the Lord of nature and history is thus remembered as the unique and intelligent Creator (Strophes I and II). Then the protector of Israel at the exodus and the conquest of the land becomes the savior from humiliation (Strophes III to VII). Psalm 136 adds what the poet of Psalm 135 had omitted: Israel's military defeat and divine salvation. Only a single line, at the end, echoes the prelude by asking for the praise of Yahweh.

The litany offers 26 identical responses of the community at large. The meter is chiefly regular (3+3) with a lengthening (4+2) for important statements (vv. 4, 12, and 15).

Like its companion poem and probable model (Psalm 135), Psalm 136 is an assemblage of citations and reminiscences from other traditional evocations of Yahweh, the Master of nature and history.

COMMENTARY

Prelude (vv. 1-3)

The invitation to praise, reiterated three times, invokes Yahweh as "the God of gods"; Psalm 135 had placed him as greater than "all the gods" (v. 5).

Strophes I-II: Praise for the Prodigious Creator (vv. 4-9)

The making of the universe is the most stupendous of all miracles. Yahweh made the heavens with knowledge, wisdom, and understanding (v. 5). The Creator is an intelligent architect (cf. Deut 32:18; Prov 5:1). The making of the universe begins with "the great luminaries" — the sun and moon — whose seasonal alternations produce the distinctive repetitions of the calendar (vv. 7-9).

Strophe III-IV: From Egypt to the Sea of Reeds (vv. 10-15)

The slavery and the plagues of Egypt led to divine salvation. The Lord is compared to a manual worker — well muscled and intervening "with a mighty hand and outstretched arm" (v. 12). The splitting of the Sea in two may reflect a Canaanite expression: "I divide the sea from the sea."[1] Actually, the soil around the Suez Isthmus is so flat that an equinoctial low tide of the Red Sea would provide easy passage, while the next high tide would engulf Pharaoh and his army (vv. 14-15).

Strophes V-VI: From Sinai to Canaan (vv. 16-22)

Yahweh is credited with leading his people through the desert of Sinai, but traditions preserved elsewhere are ambivalent on this "leading." They show popular impatience, complaint, protest, and even rebellion, followed by divine retribution. As in Psalm 135, however, the kings of the Amorites and of Bashan are slaughtered by Yahweh, and the land of Canaan is a gift of inheritance, twice noted (vv. 21-22; cf. Ps 135:12).

Strophe VII: Defeat and Deliverance (vv. 23-26)

A remarkable addition to the recension of Psalm 135 appears in the ascription of grace now transforming defeat into deliverance. To be sure, the poet of Psalm

---

1. R. Dussaud, *Les découvertes de Ras Shamra (Ugarit) et l'ancien Testament* (Paris, 1937), p. 61.

136 does not justify, by moral judgment, his admission of humiliating calamity, but he marvelously ascribes the release to the perennial love of Yahweh.

He merely states, "[God] remembered . . . our humiliation" (v. 23). The sobriety and brevity of this allusion to a national disaster, which might have led to a final annihilation of the elect people, deserves notice and admiration.

Because God remembered, he rescued (v. 24). Here appears the key to the 26 antiphonal responses on the perenniality of divine grace. The Hebrew word for "grace" received extensive analyses. No single word will render the diversity of the Hebrew meanings: Mercy? Fidelity? Faithfulness? Compassionate love?[2] At the end of the litany, the singers are immersed within the Hebraic truth par excellence: Yahweh will never forget his people.

DATE AND THEOLOGY

The similarity and sometimes word-for-word coincidences with Psalm 135 render a postexilic date most probable. The recital of *Heilsgeschichte* at times short-circuits the theology of grace in times of distress as in times of peace. The fidelity of the Lord cannot fail. The faith of Psalm 136 demands comments from Psalm 135.

Yet the killing of the Egyptian firstborn, answered at once by the antiphonal refrain, "For his mercy is forever!" jars the best comprehension, not only of the modern reader but also of the other psalmists, of sapiential schools, and of prophetic worldviews. Covenant morality will not endorse such an inhuman religion.

Moreover, the universality of God's intent should breed a commitment to universal salvation, or at least to the elect people's sense of sacerdotal mediation between Israel and "the enemy."

Perhaps the awareness of Israel's mission toward the nations of the world is uncovered by implication in the penultimate bicolon (v. 25). "He provides food for all creatures." Literally, "He gives bread to all flesh." The expression "all flesh" includes all creatures of the earth, although some original singers may have looked at it in the restrictive sense of "all members of the elect people." Divine providence, even at the time of a risk of mortal danger, cannot ignore the immense variety of human beings, or at least the "enemy" nations of the ancient Near East. The psalmist has thought primarily of the need for plenteous harvests among those who survived the exile. Nevertheless, the poet may have been happily betrayed by his own words.

---

2. Among the many studies of the word *ḥesed*, see N. Glueck, *Ḥesed in the Bible* (New York, 1975).

•

A warning to victorious nations in any war may be issued here for the formulation of peace treaties (cf. comments on the theology of Psalm 135).

Peace, even in a recital of monstrous national woes that are now overcome, demands a corporate understanding of mutual forgiveness.

Peace *(shalom)* is the manifestation of health *(shalem)*.

PSALM 137

If I Forget Thee, Jerusalem

I

1.
    By the waters of Babylon —
        There we sat down and wept
        As we remembered Zion.

2.
    We hung our citharas on the poplar trees,
    That were in the midst thereof.

3.
    For there our captors asked us
        The words and melodies of a song,
    And our tormentors demanded mirth,
        "Sing to us a song of Zion!"

II

4.
    How can we sing a song of the Lord
        On foreign soil?

5.
    If I forget thee, Jerusalem,
        Let my right hand forget its cunning!

6.
    If I do not remember thee,
        Let my tongue cleave to the roof of my mouth,
    If I do not keep Jerusalem
        Above my highest joy!

III

7.
    Remember, O Lord, the children of Edom,
        The day of Jerusalem!

> *How they said, Raze it, raze it!*
> *Down to the foundations thereof!*

8. *O you, daughter of Babylon, doomed to die!*
> *Happy shall he be who requites of thee*
> *What thou hast done to us!*

9. *Happy shall he be that takes thy little ones*
> *And dashes them against the rock!*

BIBLIOGRAPHY

P. Auffret, "Essai sur la structure littéraire du psaume 137," *ZAW*, XCII (1980), pp. 346-77; I. Eitan, "The Identification of *Tiškaḥ yemini*; Ps 137,5," *JBL*, XLVII (1965), pp. 193-95; D. N. Freedman, "The Structure of Psalm 137," in *Festschrift W. F. Albright*, ed. H. Goedicke (Baltimore, 1971), pp. 187-206; K. Galling, "Erwägungen zur antiken Synagoge," *Zeitschrift des deutschen Palästina-Vereins*, LXXII (1956), pp. 163-78; A. Guillaume, "The Meaning of [*twll*] in Ps. 137,5," *JBL*, LXXV (1956), pp. 143-53; M. Halle and J. J. McCarthy, "The Metrical Structure of Psalm 137," *JBL*, C (1981), pp. 161-67; B. Hartberger, *"An den Wassern von Babylon"* . . . *Psalm 137* . . . *Jeremiah 51,* . . . *Edom-Tradition* (Frankfort and Bonn, 1986); H. Lenowitz, "The Mock — *Simḥâ* of Ps. 137," in *Directions in Biblical Hebrew Poetry*, ed. E. R. Follis, JSOTSup XL (Sheffield, 1987), pp. 149-59; F. Luke, "The Songs of Zion as a Literary Category of the Psalter," *Indian Journal of Theology*, XIV (1965), pp. 72-90; G. J. Ogden, "Prophetic Oracles against Foreign Nations and Psalms of Communal Lament: The Relationship of Psalm 137 to Jeremiah 49:7-22 and Obadiah," *JSOT*, XXIV (October 1982), pp. 89-97; H. Spieckermann, *Heilsgegenwart: Eine Theologie der Psalmen* (Göttingen, 1989), pp. 115-21.

FORM

This is one of the most beautiful poems of the Psalter, yet it ends with a monstrous imprecation. It consists of three strophes, symmetrically made of two substrophes. As in many other laments or complaints, its central core, which in this psalm comprises the entire second strophe (vv. 4-6), provides the key to the meaning of the whole psalm, the memory of Zion.

Within the strophic structure, there also seems to be a detailed symmetry of words. Most substrophes contain two bicola, although the first and the penultimate have tricola (vv. 1 and 8). Chiastic oppositions or parallel equilibriums display the professional competence of the poet; yet the lack of objective criteria in the identification of syllables renders an algorithmic analysis hypothetical; the ancient singers and modern exegetes need the thematic divisions of the strophic structure for the interpretation of the psalm.

COMMENTARY

Strophe I: The Melancholy of the Deportees (vv. 1-3)

In the first substrophe the psalmist recalls that during the captivity in Babylon, his fellow singers, seated on the banks of the waterways, were unable to sing or to play their musical instruments. The Hebrew text has "streams" or "rivers," but in the traditional versions, "the waters" is probably correct, for the soil of Mesopotamia ("Between Rivers") was full of canals and marshes.

The second substrophe suddenly interrupts the lyricism of the deportees' ritual "weeping," as the psalmist recalls that the Babylonian captors asked them for musical diversion. Perhaps they were not "tormentors" since they allowed the deportees to be idle, free from forced labor, and they may have wanted to compare the music of their captives with their own.[1] They wanted gaiety, even mirth, but the psalmist's fellow artists knew only laments, "the songs of Zion."

Strophe II: The Memory of Jerusalem (vv. 4-6)

Zion, the sanctuary that sheltered "the Rock" and its surrounding city of Jerusalem, had been burned and its foundations razed to the ground. How could they sing "songs of Zion" in the country of barbarous destroyers? Yet were they not in danger of forgetting their holy temple, the navel of the earth[2] and the Davidic site of anointed royalty?

The psalmist, now expressing his own thoughts, twice takes an oath not to forget Jerusalem, devastated as it was. His own poem had become a "psalm of Zion" (cf. Lam 2:10-11, 18; 3:48-49). A remarkable contradiction animates the core strophe. On the one hand, the psalmist refuses to sing a song of Zion on foreign soil; on the other hand, he is terrified by the possibility that he might forget the lines and the notes of these songs unless he rehearses them, even for the pleasure of hated victors. He swears twice, risking his own fluency, that his highest joy will remain with the memory of Jerusalem.

---

1. As late as the first half of the twentieth century, Arab Bedouin of (then) Transjordania could sing for hours a number of poems, accompanied by their musical instruments. Author's personal observation in 1934.

2. See S. Terrien, "The Omphalos Myth and Hebrew Religion," *VT,* XX (1970), pp. 315-38.

Strophe III: Imprecations on Edom and Babel (vv. 7-9)

Having taken a solemn oath preventing his oblivion of a distant land that may never again be the site of divine Presence and of the cosmic unity between heaven, earth, and the underworld, he now turns to the actual destroyers, those who had perpetrated the crimes of stealing the treasures of Zion and razing the holy edifice of Solomon to its very foundations. Nebuchadnezzar, the emperor of Babylon, employed Edomite mercenaries who encouraged the total annihilation of Israel's holy place (Ezek 25:12-14; Obad 8-15; cf. 2 Kgs 24:10-17; Lam 1:20-22; 3:64-66; 4:21; Ezek 35:5-9). The antagonism of Edom toward Israel, and vice versa, had begun in patriarchal times with the story of Jacob and Esau. It continued through the centuries till the Roman era with the rise of Antipater, an Idumean (Edomite) and father of Herod the Great.

The curse against the "daughter of Babylon" is even more gruesome in that it does not praise the divine Avenger, but salutes and declares "happy" anyone who will dash Babylonian babies against the rock, any cliff, or the "Holy Rock" that continued to stand above the ruins of the sanctuary.

DATE AND THEOLOGY

The psalm appears to have been composed in the early part of the sixth century. The poet may have witnessed the events he recalls, or he may have belonged to the rising second generation of the exile (587-??? B.C.E.). The theological presuppositions are similar to those of the other songs of Zion. For the modern exegete, these presuppositions are in need of an eschatological interpretation, when Babylon becomes a symbol of multiple and unending warfare (Rev 17:5). The imprecation, to slaughter babies, aims at the annihilation of the Babylonian people; it does not consider the grief of their mothers. Human vengeance misses the theocentric and somewhat noble attitude of "Vengeance is mine, . . . saith the Lord."

PSALM 138

Hymn of Personal Thanksgiving

1. *Of David.*

I

> I thank thee with my whole heart!
>> I celebrate thee in the presence of the gods!
2.
> Facing thy holy temple, I worship thee,
>> And I praise thy name for thy love and veracity,
> For thou hast magnified thy name
>> Even above thy promises.

II

3.
> The same day I call, thou answerest me!
>> This fortifies my soul!
4.
> All the kings of the earth praise thee, O Lord!
>> For they hear thy promises from thy mouth!
5.
> They sing about the ways of the Lord,
>> Since great is the glory of the Lord.

III

6.
> The Lord is sublime and yet cares for the humble,
>> But he knows the proud from afar.
7.
> If I step in the midst of trouble,
>> Thou bringest me back to life against mine enemies;
> Thou stretchest out thy hand,
>> And thy right hand saves me.

Envoi

8.
> The Lord is perfect on my behalf;
>> Thy mercy, O Lord, endures forever!
> Do not forsake the works of thy hands!

BIBLIOGRAPHY

C. Barth, *Die Errettung vom Tode in den individuellen Klage- und Dankliedern des Alten Testaments* (Zollikon, 1947); W. Brueggemann, *The Message of the Psalms* (Minneapolis, 1984), pp. 131-32; F. Crüsemann, *Studien zur Formgeschichte von Hymnus und Danklied in Israel*, WMANT XXXII (Neukirchen, 1969), p. 249; O. Grether, *Name und Wort Gottes im Alten Testament*, ZAW Beiheft LXIV (Giessen, 1934); H.-J. Kraus, *Theology of the Psalms* (Minneapolis, 1979), pp. 44, 74, 134; C. Westermann, *The Living Psalms* (Grand Rapids, 1989), pp. 197-200.

FORM

Psalm 138 was ascribed to David by the editors of the Psalter, perhaps because it affects the form of a hymn, but it is to be sung by an individual. It consists of three strophes of three bicola each, followed by an Envoi made of one tricolon.

The meter is irregular, but the composition is a lyrical affirmation of divine greatness that ends, at the very last stichos, as a swift petition. Meditation in the presence of Yahweh turns into a request for the whole of humankind.

COMMENTARY

Strophe I: Yahweh Will Be Praised in the Presencce of the Gods (vv. 1b-2)

The poet does not deny that the gods of other nations may exist, but he affirms the exclusivity of his own adoration. "With my whole heart" indicates at once that his intellect and his will are not divided. He implicitly rejects tensions between faith and doubt, and rejects any hint of duplicity.

Facing the gates of the Zion sanctuary, he prostrates himself rather than mildly bowing and inclining his head as a courteous salutation. His awareness of the divine Presence becomes supremely intense when he stands in the precincts of the temple and prepares to enter the holy place. Then, while waiting, he composes a hymn in which he praises the name of Yahweh. The "name" covers far more than the symbol of reputation or fame; it designates the Lord's activity in time and in space. Specifically, the name belongs to a theology of the word before it reflects a theology of sight. It flows from God's steadfast love and from God's manifestation of truthfulness that produces in human beings the responses of "confidence and "truth" as well as "truthfulness," both probably deriving from a common root, the "Amen" of the Jewish and Christian liturgies.

Strophe II: The Invocation of the Name (vv. 3-5)

Through the immediacy of the divine answer to his prayers, the psalmist receives the sensation of self-assurance, which largely contributes to his poetic inspiration; his *nephesh*, "soul" in the sense of inner self, weak as his ego may have been in the past, is now affirmed, or strengthened; he has become the master of difficult decisions. His horizon broadens his view of the world. Beyond his concern for Zion, the sanctuary that brings the Lord to the omphalos of the universe, he emphasizes with a newly discovered joy the time when foreign monarchs will praise Yahweh.

The universal quality of this future is so certain that it becomes a psychological present. The promise of a united humanity will be fulfilled. The "name" becomes the "glory" that will illuminate the entire earth, as it illuminates the heavens. It will flash a light for universal peace.

Strophe III: Sublimity and Concern for Humility (vv. 6-7)

The Lord is "exalted": he is "the highest." His position is unique. His supremacy may hardly be conceived. "Sublime" is Yahweh, but his infinite transcendence does not prevent him from inserting justice into his "humaneness" for the lowest of humankind. He distinguishes between the arrogant and the lowly, so much so that when enemies threaten the poet with death, Yahweh intervenes at once and effectively. Deliverance prefigures salvation in the totality of its sweep from terrestrial existence to eternal life.

Envoi: Perfection and Supplication (v. 8)

Now comes the crown of the poem, with a final affirmation of praise and an unexpected supplication. God's attitude toward the psalmist has been perfect. God is perfect on the poet's behalf. God has done everything for him. He has not only promised to fulfill his purpose for the future, but he already approves, *hic et nunc*, his devotee, in all aspects of existence. He will protect him from mortal attacks.

Yet the world situation is still precarious. The kingdoms of the earth still compete for their neighbors' land. Human beings persist in unjust and criminal covetousness. Israel, the elect people, still favors the rich at the expense of the poor. In the very midst of a hope for utopia, the psalmist is aware of human failures, ambitions, and oppression. Hence, as a final word, the prayer, "Do not forsake the works of thy hands!"

Without the vision and strength that lead to goodness, the human condition remains uncertain. It vacillates between good and evil. Creation is recalled at the very moment that one begs for ultimate salvation. How can the Creator forget the works (plural) of his hands, in their diversity? The poet, who has until now indulged in personal elation for a personal destiny, suddenly places himself at the center of a worldwide humanity. He demands universal communion for a universal salvation.

DATE AND THEOLOGY

The hymn of gratitude of this artist, praising the Lord for subjective happiness, now calls on the Creator to remember the works of his hands in their totality. The date of such a composition will remain uncertain. The psalmist faces the façade of Solomon's temple, or the second sanctuary, built in Persian times. The psalm is contemporary with a preexilic or postexilic century.

Psalm 138 is uncommon, for it blossoms into a worldwide perspective: "Thy merciful love endures forever." Never does the psalmist doubt, like the poet of Job, that the Lord is just, nor does he pray only for the devotees who prostrate themselves before entering the gates of Zion (v. 2). He praises Yahweh's benevolence toward him, but he expects the assent of "the kings of the earth." Yet he summons the Creator of humankind. The chef d'oeuvre of creation remains ambiguous, since Yahweh might forsake the works of his hands. The psalm, which appears at first to be self-congratulatory, at last melts into intercession for all.

PSALM 139

Shall I Flee from God's Presence?

1. *To the choirmaster. Of David. Psalm.*

I

O Lord, thou hast searched me and known me.

2.   *Thou knowest my downsitting and my uprising;*
        Thou understandest my thoughts afar off.
3.   *Thou winnowest my path and my lying down,*
        And art acquainted with all my ways.

4.   *For there is not a word on my tongue,*
        But lo! O Lord, thou knowest it altogether.

5.   *Thou hast beset me behind and before,*
        And laid thy hand upon me:
6.   *Such knowledge is too wonderful for me;*
        It is high; I cannot attain unto it.

II

7.   Whither shall I go from thy Spirit?
        Or whither shall I flee from thy presence?

8.   *If I ascend up into heaven, thou art there;*
        If I make my bed in Hades, thou art there!
9.   *If I take the wings of the morning,*
        And dwell in the uttermost parts of the sea,
10.   *Even there shall thy hand lead me,*
        And thy right hand shall hold me.

11.   *If I say, Surely darkness shall cover me,*
        And night shall encompass me about,
12.   *Even darkness darkens not from thee,*
        But night shines as day:
        Darkness and light are alike to thee!

III

13.   Yea, thou, thyself, didst form my inward parts;
        Thou didst weave me in my mother's womb!

14.   *I will praise thee, for I am awesomely and wonderfully made.*
        Marvelous are thy works!
        And this my soul knows well.
15.   *My frame was not hid from thee*
        When I was made in secret,
        Curiously wrought in the uttermost depths of the earth.
16.   *Thine eyes did see mine embryo, still imperfect;*
        And in thy book were written all my days,
        When there were yet none of them.

17.   *How precious are thy thoughts to me, O God!*
        How great is the sum of them!
18.   *If I should count them,*

They are more numerous than the sand;
When I awake, I am still with thee.

IV

19. Surely thou wilt slay the wicked, O God!
    Depart from me, therefore, you men of blood!

20. *For they speak against thee wickedly,*
    And thine enemies take thy name in vain.

21. *Do I not hate them, O Lord, that hate thee?*
    And am I not grieved by those who rise against thee?

22. *I hate them with perfect hatred;*
    I count them as mine own enemies.

23. *Search me, O God, and know my heart!*
    Try me and know my doubts;

24. *And see if there be any wicked way in me,*
    And lead me in the way everlasting!

BIBLIOGRAPHY

P. Auffret, *La Sagesse a bâti sa maison* (Fribourg and Göttingen, 1982), pp. 321-82; G. M. Behler, "Der nahe und der schwer zu fassende Gott: Eine biblische Besinnung über Psalm 139," *BibLeb*, VI (1965); idem, "Seigneur, tu me sondes et tu me connais," *Vie spirituelle*, L (1959), pp. 29-56: K. H. Bernhardt, "Zum Gottesvorstellung von Psalm 139," in *Festschrift G. Holz* (Berlin, 1965), pp. 20-31; P. E. Bonnard, *Le Psautier selon Jérémie* (Paris, 1960), pp. 223-32; idem, "Un Psaume pour vivre, Le Psaume 139 (138)," *Esprit et vie*, LXXXIV (1979), pp. 529-38; M. Dahood, "Congruity of Metaphor," VTSup XVI (1967), p. 196; G. A. Danell, "Psalm 139," *Uppsala Universitets Årsskrift* (1951), pp. 1-37; S. B. Frost, "Psalm 139: An Exposition," *CJT*, VI (1960), pp. 113ff.; T. H. Gaster, "A Canaanite Ritual Drama" (The Wings of Shahar), *JAOS*, LXVI (1949), pp. 69, 71-72; J. C. M. Holman, "The Structure of Psalm CXXXIX," *VT*, XXI (1971), pp. 298-310; idem, "Analysis of the Text of Psalm 139," *BZ*, XIV (1970), pp. 37-71, 198-227; H. Hommel, "Das Religionsgeschichtliche Problem des 139. Psalms," *ZAW*, XLVII (1929), pp. 110ff.; F. James, *Thirty Psalmists* (New York, 1938), pp. 49-56; R. Kilian, "In Gott geborgen: Eine Auslegung des Psalms 139," *Bibel und Kirche*, XXVI (1971), pp. 97-102; J. L. Koole, "Quelques remarques sur Psaume 139," in *Studia biblica et semitica*, Festschrift T. C. Vriezen (Wageningen, 1966), pp. 176-80; J. Krašovec, "Die polare Ausdrucksweise in Psalm 139," *BZ*, XVIII (1974), pp. 224-28; R. Lapointe, "La nuit est une lumière," *CBQ*, XXXIII (1971), pp. 397-402; H. B. Lovitt, *A Critical and Exegetical Study of Ps. 139* (New York, 1964); M. Mannati, "Psalm 139,14-16," *ZAW*, LXXXIII (1971), pp. 257-61; P. D. Miller, *Interpreting the Psalms* (Philadelphia, 1986), pp. 144-53; S. Mowinckel, "The Verb *śi^aḥ* and the Noun *śi^aḥ, siḥa*," *Studia theologica*, XV (1961), pp. 1-10; H. P. Müller, "Die Gattung des 139. Psalms," *Deutscher Orientalistentag*, I (1968), pp. 345-55; M. Picard, *La fuite devant Dieu* (tr. from German) (Paris, 1956); R. Pytel, "Psalm 139,15," *Folia orientalia*, XIII (1971), pp. 257-66; G. Rice, "The Integrity of Psalm 139,20b," *CBQ*, XLVI (1984), pp. 28-30; M. Saebø, "Salme 139 og visdomsdiktningen," *Tidsskrift for teologi og kirke*, XXXIV (1966), pp. 157-84; H. Schmidt, *Das Gebet des Angeklagten im Alten Testament*, BZAW XLIX (Giessen, 1928); N. Schmidt, ed., *Festschrift W. Eichrodt* (Zürich, 1970), pp. 263-76; A. Schulz, *Kritisches zum Psalter* (Münster in Westfalen, 1932), pp. 65ff.; H. Schüngel-Straumann, "Zur Gattung und Theologie des 139. Psalms," *BZ*, XVII (1973), pp. 39-51; K. Seybold, "Die Redaktion der Wallfahrtspsalmen," *ZAW*, XCI (1979), p. 24; P. W. Skehan, [On 11QPs[a], 1955], in *Studies in Israelite Poetry and Wisdom* (Washington, 1971), p. 48; D. Sölle, "Psalm 139," in *Die Hinreise* (Stuttgart, 1975), pp. 155-64; J. M. Steedman, "'Eyelids of the Morn': A Biblical Convention,'" *HTR*, LVI (1963), pp. 55ff.; S. Wagner, "Zur Theologie des Psalms CXXXIX," VTSup XXIX (1978), pp. 357-76; E. Würthwein, "Erwägungen zu Psalm 139," *TLZ*, LXXXI (1956), pp. 341-42; idem, *VT*, VII (1957), pp. 165-82; E. J. Young, *Psalm 139: A Study of the Omniscience of God* (London, 1965).

FORM

The form and the literary genre of this psalm are so exceptional that they have elicited a great variety of interpretations. The structure proposed herewith is notably regular. No textual alteration is accepted.

Psalm 139 consists of four strophes, each of which contains two substrophes of three plus two, double or triple verses. Every one of these four strophes is preceded by a separate title, unusually formulated with a single colon (v. 1) of three bicola (vv. 1, 7, 13, and 19). The meaning of these titles is clear:

Strophe I: God's Search and Knowledge of Me (v. 1)
Strophe II: Where to Flee from God's Presence? (v. 7)
Strophe III: The Marvelous Creation of Little Me (v. 13)
Strophe IV: God's Continuous Search of Me (v. 19)

The symmetry of the four strophes strongly indicates literary coherence and unity of composition (see diagram on p. 875).

The use of tricola at the end of Strophe II (v. 12), in preparation for a similar use of tricola in Strophe III, stresses the sense of wonder at embryology and the psalmist's self-analysis (vv. 14, 15, 16, and 18).

The meter varies substantially from beginning to end: 3+3 (vv. 3-13, 16, 18, 20, 23, 24); 3+3+3 (vv. 1, 2, 14, 15); 4+3 (vv. 17, 21, 23); 4+4 (v. 19). Such metrical complexity may correspond to emotional fluctuations on the poet's part. It does not necessarily indicate a plurality of authors.

	I		II		III		IV
1.	– – – – – – –	7.	– – – – – – –	13.	– – – – – – –	19.	– – – – – –
2.	– – – – – – –	8.	– – – – – – –	14.	– – – – – – –	20.	– – – – – – –
	– – – – – –		– – – – – –		– – – – – –		– – – – –
					– – – – – –		
3.	– – – – – – –	9.	– – – – – – –	15.	– – – – – – –	21.	– – – – – – –
	– – – – – –		– – – – – –		– – – – – –		– – – – –
4.	– – – – – –	10.	– – – – – – –	16.	– – – – – – –	22.	– – – – – – –
	– – – – – –		– – – – – –		– – – – – –		– – – – –
					– – – – – –		
5.	– – – – – – –	11.	– – – – – – –	17.	– – – – – – –	23.	– – – – – – –
	– – – – – –		– – – – – –		– – – – – –		– – – – –
6.	– – – – – – –	12.	– – – – – – –	18.	– – – – – – –	24.	– – – – – – –
	– – – – –		– – – – – –		– – – – – –		– – – – –
			– – – – – –		– – – – – –		

COMMENTARY

Superscription (v. 1a)

The postexilic editors of the Psalter attributed this poem to David, but called it simply "psalm to be sung with strings." The literary genre is uncertain. It presents semantic affinities with Job and Proverbs: Is it a psalm of wisdom? It praises Yahweh for wonderful works. Is it a personal hymn? It accepts divine scrutiny and asks for more. Is it a legal plea for God's judgment in a temple vigil? It begs Yahweh to slay the scoundrels. Is it a supplication for deliverance from the pursuit of enemies? The poet asks where he could flee from Yahweh's presence. Does he rebel against divine attention? There is a remarkable diversity of suggestions among exegetes. None is demonstrable.

Strophe I: God's Search and Knowledge of Me (vv. 1b-5)

The entitling of Strophe I (v. 1b) is terse and crisp. It affirms without qualification that God has scrutinized minutely the character and personality of the psalmist. It is an I-Thou exchange of the most intimate kind. The verb commonly translated "to search" signifies "to dig," with several nuances of meaning depending on the context. It is often found in sapiential poetry. God sees wisdom and "penetrates it thoroughly" (Job 18:27). "To scrutinize" is to examine critically (Job 29:16; Prov 18:17; 23:30). The related idea of "testing" occurs widely (Job 32:11; Ps 44:22; Prov 28:11; 23:30; cf. Deut 13:15; Judg 18:2; 2 Sam 10:3).

The second verb of this declaration is literally, "and thou hast known me," but ancient versions and modern translations prefer the present tense, "and thou knowest me." Divine knowledge begun in the past continues in the present. God knows every aspect of the psalmist's personality. The following lines illustrate both the profundity of the knowledge and the thoroughness of the search.

The main body of Strophe I (vv. 2-6), still couched in the I-Thou style of address, enunciates in some details the declaration of the title (v. 1b). The sitting and uprising as well the path and the lying down do not refer to a single experience, limited in time, as is sometimes claimed. On the contrary, they point to continuous attention on the part of God (vv. 3-4; cf. v. 5), an uninterrupted concern.

The plural "my thoughts" is preferable to the singular, for the Hebrew word does not refer to intellectual and philosophical reflections but means "my desire" and "my intention." God has encompassed the psalmist day and night, at home and abroad. God's hand has rested constantly upon his shoulders. This semimystical conviction is such a wonder that it cannot be fathomed in its causes and purposes. Does it imply that the poet is aware of the exceptional aspect of his inner life in comparison with the confessions of his fellow beings?

There is no need to consider such a psychology of the self as evidence of a prayer for a night of vigil prior to a ritual judgment (cf. Pss 7:8; 17:3; 26:1; 44:20; Jer 12:3).

Strophe II: Where to Flee from God's Presence? (vv. 7-12)

In Strophe II the psalmist asks an enigmatic question. Is it an indirect way of describing happily, but awesomely, the incredible presence of the Lord, in all places and at all instants? Or could it be a poetic way of confessing his lassitude and even a slight resentment before the overwhelming attention of the Lord? Could it not be a protest against the divine pursuit, unrelenting and implicitly demanding, that limits the poet's freedom to decide for himself and choose between severity and playfulness for his behavior?

The verb "to flee" assumes several senses, such as the act of moving swiftly away from a person or a situation that is dangerous, hostile, or intolerable (Gen 16:8; 31:27; Exod 2:15; 1 Kgs 2:7; 12:2; Job 27:22)? One flees from a battlefield or a natural catastrophe. Why should this exemplary and ardent devotee of Yahweh flee from the "Spirit" and the "face" of the Lord? The "Spirit" is the very core of divine reality, and the "face" designates symbolically the openness and the urge of God to reveal himself (cf. Jer 23:24; Amos 9:2). Going up to heaven, and down to the underworld where Yahweh is absent, with rare exceptions (Job 26:6; Prov 15:11; Amos 2:9; cf. Job 7:21?), as well as "taking the wings of the morning" (vv. 8-9), are poetic ways of expressing an extreme, irreversible, and inaccessible shelter, like "the uttermost parts of the sea" (v. 9b). The stress does not lie on the omnipotence, omniscience, and omnipresence of Yahweh, but it clearly refers to the innermost, although occasional, desire of the bewildered psalmist.

Again the problem must be faced in earnest. Why flee from God's Spirit and presence? Is the psalmist "tired" of constant inspection? Somehow, does such scrutiny spoil his independence, or is it that he hides himself from the almighty and omniscient God in order to conceal a secret sin? To flee from the Spirit of God and to succeed in such an enterprise mean that the poet would then believe that he possesses a distinct privilege either of having access to God's inner beingness (Pss 51:13; 104:30; 145:10; Isa 53:19-11; Jer 23:24; Hag 2:15) or of having the power to run away from his face. Even Moses was forbidden to see the face of God (Exod 33:11, 20).

If darkness and light are alike for Yahweh, then nobody is able to protect the self from God's judgment. Ascending to heaven may be reminiscent of Enoch, who "walked with God; then he was not, for God took him" (Gen 5:24). Or, again, of Elijah, whom Yahweh took up to heaven in a whirlwind (2 Kgs 2:1). The psalmist may have entertained the somewhat presumptuous hope that after death he would be received in glory (cf. Ps 73:24). Even descending into the underworld, like other mortals, would not be the sign of annihilation.

Strophe III: The Marvelous Creation of Little Me (vv. 13-18)

Nevertheless, the poet does not stumble under the threat of metaphysical hubris. His knowledge of embryology, probably gained from sapiential circles, does not induce in him the prideful illusion of standing apart from other specimens of humanity. The extreme complexity of his coming into being becomes only the source of his praise and astonished wonder at Yahweh's works. That a fetus would be made in secret is obvious, but why the belief that it is woven in "the uttermost depths of the earth" as well as in his mother's womb? There is here no contradiction: the language of poetry is simply to be taken symbolically. The view of mother earth, strange to the modern mind, was common in the ancient Near East as well as in classical Greece (cf. Plato, *Republic* 3.414c-e). Likewise the notion of a rigid and a-temporal "fixing," or pre-birth immobility, ahead of time, "of all my days," should not be confused with predestination as defined by the apostle Paul, Luther, Calvin, and even the Council of Trent.

Just as "the uttermost depths of the earth" point to divine omnipotence, so also the written "book" of future days represents an attempt to substantiate a desire to praise the Creator and his works. The present existence, which the psalmist enjoys, has been written in the book of the living (cf. Exod 32:32; Ps

68:29). For God, human concepts of past, present, and future, according to this ancient hymn and many others, do not affect the supratemporality of divine "eternity."

Strophe IV: God's Continuous Search of Me (vv. 19-24)

The entitling bicolon of the final strophe is so unexpected that many commentators believe it belongs to another psalm or, in any case, represents an alien addition. The beginning of Psalm 140 (vv. 2-6) breathes a similar passion against evil and evildoers. However, the remarkable structure of Psalm 139 and its final plea (vv. 23-24) invalidate such conjectures.

It may well be that the psalmist, by declaring vehemently his horror of scoundrels who commit evil deeds, is thereby affirming indirectly that he is not one of them. Perhaps he concludes implicitly with many other authors of individual psalms of complaint[1] that he had gravely suffered from the evildoers. This would be an obvious cause for his outburst of hatred: "Surely thou wilt slay the wicked, O God!" (v. 19). Let it also be observed that he does not refer to personal vengeance against his enemies. He trusts the intervention of a just and powerful God without even asking for it in prayer! The explosive assertion of hate is so passionate that its tone, not his thought, should be understood by the modern reader. One might be amazed at the relative restraint of a persecuted man whose faith dominates his instinct. God alone will avenge.[2]

This transposition of enmity into divine hostility comes from the psalmist's honest belief that his own adversaries are God's enemies (v. 20). This presumption is in one sense quite admirable, for it is based on an absolute certainty that the Creator of the world is not too busy to protect his own devotees.

The exclamation of horror before scoundrels may well explain, positively and favorably, the rather extravagant desire to flee the Lord's overwhelming "presence" and even "Spirit," as this was strangely sketched in Strophe II. It may, moreover, provide a clue to the meaning of the final substrophe (vv. 23-24). The poet rebels against a doting father who dictates every move and word of his adored child. Now, surprise! This harassed child asks for more "divine examination, scrutiny, and search." And even for testing and trial (v. 23).

This last petition is unexpected, but the context may clarify its origin: "Try me and know my doubts." The Hebrew word is different from the thinking, desire, or intent of the first strophe. Although it is generally translated sim-

---

1. See S. Terrien, "Amos and Wisdom," in *Festschrift J. Muilenburg* (New York, 1962), pp. 108-15.

2. E. Würthwein, "Erwägungen zu Psalm CXXXIX," *VT*, VII (1957), pp. 165-82; G. W. Anderson, "Enemies and Evildoers in the Book of Psalms," *BJRL* XLVIII (1965), pp. 18-29.

ply by "disquieting thoughts" (cf. Ps 94:19), its affinities with cognates derived, with a spelling slightly different, from the verb "to cleave," "to divide," suggest that the disquieting thoughts may in fact have been "divided opinions" (1 Kgs 18:21), close to the halfheartedness castigated by another sapiential psalmist (Ps 119:113). Let it not be forgotten that "doubt" or "divided opinion," like the Greek *skepsis,* does not mean a pejorative negativity but the ambiguity of reflection.

This poet has come to understand that the hatred of evil and evildoers might mirror a certain deviation in his own behavior, and that his strange desire to flee from God's presence and Spirit might reveal an ambivalence on his part that threatens the devotion of his fidelity. There might be in him "a wicked way" counterbalancing "the way everlasting" that he craves to follow.

DATE AND THEOLOGY

Many readers maintain that Psalm 139 is a ritual prayer of meditation on the omniscience of the Lord and on the marvels of his creative power, both cosmic and humanly minute. A different exegesis may be proposed: the traditional attributes of the Deity should be considered as the tools, not the purposes, of an extraordinary poem of supplication whose subjective imagination reveals an exceptionally intense intimacy with Yahweh and a bold familiarity sometimes displayed by the greatest mystics of Jewish, Christian, and Muslim milieus.

Similarity with the poem-discussion of Job and the Jeremiah oracles or confessions have been observed and listed. Like the man of Uz and the prophet from Anathoth, the psalmist exclaims with skill, finesse, and force, as if he were a religious acrobat who dances on the high wire without a safety net, "All my ways are known to thee, Lord!" Likewise, the prophet Jeremiah exults when he recalls, "Thou knowest! What comes out of my lips is already clear before thee" (Jer 17:16). Similarly, the Jobian poet, whose sapiential horizon includes the whole of humanity, declares, "[Thine] eyes are open to all the ways of humankind" (Job 23:10; cf. 31:4).[3]

Even before his birth, when he was being formed in his mother's womb, Jeremiah felt that he had been known by the Lord (Jer 1:5). Both the prophet and the psalmist use the image of "weaving." In similar terms, Job would say to Yahweh, "Thy hands have formed me and fashioned me" (Job 10:8; cf. Ps 139:15). Like Jeremiah (12:2-4), the sacred singer asked for the death of the evildoers, but he finally begs the Lord to search him, still, and to know his heart (Jer 12:3; cf. Ps

---

3. S. Terrien, *Job: Commentaire* (Neuchâtel, 1963), pp. 23-27; idem, "The Patmos Picture of Job Tightening His Belt for a Duel with Yahweh," in *The Iconography of Job through the Centuries: Artists as Biblical Interpreters* (University Park, Penn., 1996), pp. 38-39.

139:24). Both the prophet and the psalmist want to know the way that is ever-lasting (Ps 139:24; Jer 6:16).

While the poem of Job was most probably composed by a disciple who was well acquainted with the Jeremianic literature, in its oral form, the relation-ship between the prophet and the psalmist is obscure. Who influenced whom? In any event, the date of Psalm 139 will have to be found during the last years of the kingdom of Judah (609-587 B.C.E.).

The date of composition, even approximate, is important for the under-standing of this poem, whose literary genre is unique in the Psalter. It reflects a situation of national agony. After the battle of Carchemish (605 B.C.E.), the Egyptian domination of the kingdom of Judah was replaced by Babylonian oc-cupation. Following several years of humiliation and repression, King Zedekiah rebelled against the forces of the Babylonian king, and he was finally seized; his sons were slain in his presence, his eyes were gouged out, and he was taken to Babylon in fetters.

If Psalm 139 was composed by a sacred singer of the temple at a date pre-ceding its burning in 587 B.C.E., the evildoers were doubtless either Babylonian tyrants, Judahite traitors, or even Judahite patriots who violently opposed the courageous preaching of Jeremiah. They insisted that the sacredness of Zion would not protect the sanctuary forever. Thus, in a time of national and reli-gious agony, a sacred singer retreated within himself, confused by the hopeless-ness of the crisis. His psalm survived the catastrophe, for it proclaimed an un-shakable faith in Yahweh, the Jeremianic God of awesome judgment. No wonder the poet tried to flee such a God, anywhere on earth, or even in the darkness of death. Such a flight, however, was impossible for him since the God of prophetic condemnation was also the benevolent Creator. Praise him, the cosmic maker of the psalmist's mini-selfhood!

After an expostulation of hope that all evildoers, surely God's enemies, would be annihilated, his final plea concerns his own doubts and somehow his eagerness to learn a way of life, loving forever.

As he tries to find coherence from chaos, and a reason to survive presently in a world of existential menace, the psalmist assembles a number of different psalmodic motifs. The theological implications of his strange prayer of praise, more than anywhere else in the Psalter, emerge from his spirituality. His ability to exist in the midst of national and cultic extremity derives first from God's omniscience, which is an ambivalent reality, an obsessive quest, but also the ba-sis of human certitude. Divine attention to him in the past is the guarantee of divine protection in the future, even if the structure of society and of worship is dislocated.

Impersonal determinism is quite foreign to the affirmation that his words have already been written in the book of the living. Theological notions of preordination and predestination, so well hinted at by the apostle Paul and developed by St. Augustine, Thomas Aquinas, Luther, and Calvin, are irrelevant to this psalm.

The Geneva reformer and humanist as well as biblical expositor sometimes softened the bluntness of his language. He could leap from the psalm to modern culture and rebuttal when he commented,

> We are ashamed to let men know and witness our delinquencies, but we are so indifferent to what God may think of us, as if our sins were covered and veiled from his inspection.

Thus, the fanciful attempt to escape God's presence, and therefore God's judgment, even by courting an entrance into the world of the dead, is bound to fail and eventually to vanish.

Because the Latin translation of the line, "When I awake, I am still with thee" (v. 18), is given as *"Resurrexi, et adhuc sum tecum,"* it became attributed to the Christ at Easter. Omnipresence thus inspired the *modus vivendi* of divine vulnerability with new-beingness in immortality.

Like Job, bewildered by his trial and revolted by the sterility and the total misapprehension of orthodox monotheists, the poet is finally challenged by the Yahweh of total creation, who faces problems with Behemoth and Leviathan. The psalmist, until then unaware of God's being enmeshed in the enigma of cosmic evil, is overwhelmed with cognitive luminescence. Like Job, he declines the divine challenge of a duel with the God of hidden compassion, unnamed and unmentioned, but present in the movement of both minutiae and immensities (Job 40:2-3). The singer, with joyful and obstinate praise, dares to demand, "Know my doubts."

This hymn of praise adorns itself with a supplication and an interrogation. A forerunner of Christology, the poet is a theologian without knowing it. He brings wisdom thinking into prophetic realism, and composes for a doomed temple a song of adoration.

PSALM 140

Thou Art My God!

1. *To the choirmaster. Psalm. Of David.*

I

2.   *Lord, deliver me from malevolent men!*
        Preserve me from men of violence
3.   *Who premeditate evil deeds in their heart!*
        Every day they prepare to make war;
4.   *They sharpen their tongues like serpents*
        And secrete viper's venom between their lips.   Selah

II

5.   *Keep me, Lord, from the hands of wicked men!*
        Preserve me from men of violence
    Who prepare to make my steps stumble!
6.   *Arrogant men have concealed a snare to catch me,*
    And have woven cords into a net
        At the edge of my path to entrap me.   Selah

III

7.   *I said to the Lord, "Thou art my God!"*
        Pay attention to the voice of my supplication!
8.   *Lord! My Sovereign! Thou, the force of my salvation,*
        Who hast helmeted my head for the day of the fight.
9.   *Lord, do not grant the scoundrels their desire*
        Or the success of their evil plots!   Selah

IV

10.   *If those who surround me lift their heads,*
        Let the malice of their lips overwhelm them!
11.   *Let red-hot embers rain upon them!*
        And [God] will hurl them down into the Abyss! They will not rise.
12.   *Slanderers will not be left upon the earth;*
        Violent men will be chased without cease.

Envoi

13. *I know that the Lord does justice to the needy,*
     And he renders their rights to the poor.
14. *The just will then celebrate thy name;*
     Men of rectitude will dwell in thy presence.

BIBLIOGRAPHY

W. Beyerlin, *Die Rettung der Bedrängten in den Feindpsalmen der Einzelnen auf institutionelle Zusammenhänge untersucht,* FRLANT XCIX (Göttingen, 1970); H. Birkeland, *Die Feinde des Individuums in der israelitischen Psalmenliteratur* (Oslo, 1933); idem, *The Evildoers in the Book of Psalms* (Oslo, 1955); L. Kopf, "[*rwn*] so dass sie frohlocken," *VT,* IX (1959), p. 249; H.-J. Kraus, *Theology of the Psalms* (Minneapolis, 1986), pp. 131, 143; G. A. Rendsburg, *Linguistic Evidence for the Northern Origin of Select Psalms* (Atlanta, 1990), pp. 95-97; H. Schmidt, *Das Gebet der Angeklagten im Alten Testament,* BZAW XLIX (Giessen, 1928).

FORM

Although the meter of Psalm 140 is irregular, its four strophes and *Envoi* are symmetrically constructed. Each strophe contains three bicola, and the *Envoi* only two. The poem is articulated as a hymn, although it pleads for deliverance from enemies as if it belonged to the genre of individual complaint or lament. The *Envoi,* however, affects the form of a hymn on the celebration of Yahweh's name.

COMMENTARY

Strophes I and II: Supplication for Divine Help (vv. 2-4, 5-6)

The Hebrew text uses two different words, in the singular, and both terms signify "man." They probably are used in the collective, for the verbs that follow are in the plural. It may be that the psalmist has to face two types of adversaries. The expression, "they prepare to make war," is used only in sapiential style (cf. Prov 15:18; 28:25; 29:22). The "war" that they prepare seems to be a domestic entanglement rather than a foreign conflict.

Strophes III and IV: Urgent Quest in Imminent Danger (vv. 7-9, 10-12)

The prayer becomes more intense, and begins again with a striking affirmation of faith, "Thou art my God!" and "Thou, the force of my salvation." The imagery of a military casque ("Thou hast helmeted my head") and the comparison of vicious slander with wild animals indicate extreme terror at the crisis (Pss 9:15; 10:7; 58:4; 67:5; 141:9; 142:3). In the midst of the conflict, the enemies now "surround" the psalmist. His situation becomes so desperate that he yields to a dramatic style of defense. In v. 9b, the *Selah* is misplaced, as the word for "they lift up" belongs clearly to v. 10a. Several words have an uncertain meaning, but the general sense is clear.

Envoi: Praise of the Name (vv. 13-14)

The end of the poem is not an editorial addition, but subtly links the prayer that precedes it with an act of gratitude for the Lord's intervention, "Yahweh does justice to the needy." The psalmist places himself among "the just," "the men of rectitude." His celebration of the Lord's name shows that he "dwells" in the Lord's presence. Although Zion is not mentioned, many exegetes discern a cultic allusion here.

DATE AND THEOLOGY

It may be that Psalm 140, composed after a conflict with scoundrels, was concluded as a hymn. If the extermination of the slanderers is expected "from the earth," the psalmist's horizon was worldwide and perhaps understood eschatologically. On the other hand, "earth" without the article may designate the country, the territory of the Holy Land (cf. Exod 20:12). The expression "dwell in the Lord's presence" may rather indicate living permanently in spriritual communion with God. The psalm may well have pointed to a member of the Diaspora, far from Zion, who is surrounded night and day by the most intimate company of his Lord.

PSALM 141

Give Ear to My Voice!

1. *Psalm. Of David.*

Prelude

Lord, I called thee; make haste toward me!
Listen to my voice when I call thee!
2. *May my prayer be like incense in thy presence!*
My hands are lifted up, like an evening offering.

I

3. *Lord, mount a guard over my mouth,*
A watch over my lips.
4. *May my heart not incline to any evil,*
To share the wicked deeds of scoundrels,
With men who practice magic;
I will not eat their dainty food.

II

5. *May the upright correct me kindly;*
Let them rebuke me, like oil on my head!
But the scoundrels, let them not anoint my head,
For my prayer will be against their evil deeds.
6. *Let their judges hurl them against a rock,*
But let them hear my pleasant words!

III

7. *As when one plows and cuts furrows in the soil,*
Our bones are scattered toward the abode of the dead.
8. *Thus I turn my eyes to thee, O Lord, my Sovereign, for near thee,*
I seek refuge!
Do not abandon my life!
9. *Keep me away from the trap they set against me,*
The snare wrought by the magicians.

Postlude

10. *Let the scoundrels fall into their own nets,*
While I escape, going on my way!

BIBLIOGRAPHY

J. B. Burns, "An Interpretation of Psalm CXLI 7b," *VT,* XXII (1972), pp. 245-46; A. Caquot, "L'énigme du Psaume 141," *Positions luthériennes,* XX (1972), pp. 14-26; D. Gualandi, "Salmo 141 (140)," *Rivista biblica* (1958), pp. 219-33; H. Junker, "Einige Rätsel im Urtext der Psalmen," *Bib,* XXIV (1943), pp. 197-212; R. Pautrel, "Absorpti sunt juncti Ps 141:6," *RSR,* XLIV (1950), pp. 219-28; G. A. Rendsburg, *Linguistic Evidence . . . Northern Origin of Select Psalms* (Atlanta, 1990), pp. 99-102; R. Tournay, "Le Psaume 141," *VT,* IX (1959), pp. 58-64; R. J. Tournay, "Psaume CXLI: Nouvelle interprétation," *RB,* XC (1983), pp. 321-33.

FORM

The text of this psalm, especially of vv. 5-7, has been poorly preserved. The syntax is obscure, and diverse readings among the Hebrew manuscripts, including the Dead Sea Scrolls fragment, have rendered the textual problems almost beyond solution. Some scholarly proposals, especially those of Caquot ("L'énigme du Psaume 141") and Tournay ("Psaume CXLI") are attractive but remain conjectural. The translation offered above is likewise hypothetical.

Psalm 141 is a personal prayer of mixed genres. It is composed of three strophes of three bicola each (vv. 3-4, 5-6, 7-9), as if it were a hymn, but the prelude (vv. 1b-2) and postlude (v. 10) embrace an individual complaint.

COMMENTARY

Prelude: Invocation (vv. 1b-2)

The opening supplication is almost a rebuke to a silent God. The petitioner is acquainted with cultic rites, for he compares his urgent cry to the smoke of incense and the evening offering. But he seems far away from the shrine of Zion, or at least he ignores the sanctuary, using cultic practices as symbols of his devotion wherever he stands and whenever he prays.

Strophe I: Request for Self-Restraint (vv. 3-4)

The wise often advise caution in conversation and debate (Prov 13:3; Sir 22:27-29), but the poet's supplication goes farther than a simple request for restraint in speech. Unexpectedly, he asks for protection against himself. He is tempted to join "workers of nothingness," who seem to have been magicians, sorcerers, and necromancers, like the sinners (Deut 18:10-11) who were eliminated from the temple of the Lord during the reform of Josiah (2 Kgs 23:5-9).

Often interpreted as "workers of iniquity," such men believed that they could take power into their own hands. They were "practitioners of magic." By promising that he will not join them in their meals, the psalmist implicitly admits that he is attracted for a deeper reason than just "their dainty food." A devotee of Yahweh is tempted to claim divine power while he is only a "worker of nothingness."

Strophe II: Correction by the Righteous (vv. 5-6)

The friends of the poet seek to warn him of his religious lapse. He might accept their chastisement, for they correct him with love that is indeed similar to divine fidelity. Syntactic connection, however, is lacking, and the Hebrew text is uncertain. Similar uncertainty concerns the next line, "let them not anoint my head" (v. 5b). Is there a rebuke of the righteous, or a refusal to be enticed by the magicians? Again, who are the judges who would throw the evil men on the rocks of the deadly cliffs? And who are those who should hear the poet's "pleasant words"?

Strophe III: Do Not Abandon My Life! (vv. 7-9)

The imagery of agriculture enables the poet to ask passionately for Yahweh's nearness and communion. Divine presence will produce a refuge in his chaotic mind. The temptation from the magicians is not yet conquered. They lost his cooperation, and they seek to entrap him. As the plowman carves the ground in tracing his furrows, sorcerers unearth bones, perhaps in a ritual of necromancy. The edge of the underworld is near. *Death* is the ultimate result of the entrapment.

Once more the Hebrew text is uncertain. Some scholars correct "our bones" to "their bones" (cf. some Hebrew MSS, LXX) and thus find in Strophe III some continuity with Strophe II. However, the supplication persists, for the peril has not yet abated. "Do not abandon my life!" (v. 8). In its intensity, this last plea implies the hope that life on this earth still has meaning and deserves to be protected.

DATE AND THEOLOGY

This psalm was probably composed in postexilic times, perhaps before the construction of the second temple. The psalmist cries out on account of his persistent terror against the magicians whom he rejected. They became dangerous enemies. Thus he has not yet escaped, and the silent God must act now.

If the interpretation of the practitioners of magic is correct, the psalmist may still be divided between a strict faith in Yahweh and his enemies, popular seducers who use techniques that deny the freedom of God. The literatures of Assyro-Babylonia, Egypt, and Ugarit include major myths that were permeated by magical rites,[1] and the history of Judah contains several allusions to magicians, sorcerers, and necromancers (Deut 18:10-11; 2 Kgs 23:4-15; Isa 3:2-3; Jer 27:7; Ezek 13:18-20).

Waiting for ultimate salvation, this suppliant finally reveals his steadfast triumph over the attraction of all forms of superstition.

PSALM 142

Supplication of a Lonely Man

1. *Psalm. Of David. When he was in the cave. Prayer.*

I

2. *With my voice I cry to the Lord;*
    To the Lord I supplicate with my voice.
3. *I pour my complaint before him;*
    Before him I will tell my trouble.
4. *When my spirit within me is fainting,*
    Thou, thyself, wilt be watching my path.

II

On the road where I walk
    They have concealed a snare for me.
5. *Look on my right and see!*
    No one takes notice of me;

---

1. L. W. King, *Babylonian Magic and Sorcery* (New York, 1896); R. C. Thomson, *The Reports of the Magicians and Astronomers of Nineveh and Babylon* ... (1900); G. Conteneau, *La magie chez les Assyriens et les Babyloniens* (Paris, 1947); F. Lixa, *La magie dans l'Égypte antique*, I, II, III (1925); A. Lods, "La magie canaanéenne," *RHPR* (1927), pp. 1-16; idem, "Du rôle des idées magiques dans la mentalité israélite," in *Old Testament Essays* (1927), pp. 75-76; C. H. Ratschow, *Magic and Religion* (Gütersloh, 1946); G. B. Vetter, *Magic and Religion* (New York, 1958).

> *All refuges are denied me;*
> *Nobody cares for my life.*

III

6. *Lord, it is to thee that I cry!*
   I say, Thou art my refuge!
   My portion is in the land of the living!
7. *Attend to my cry, for I feel very low;*
   Deliver me from those who are pursuing me;
   They are stronger than I am!
8. *Bring my very being out of prison,*
   That I may praise thy name!

Envoi

> *The righteous will surround me,*
> *As soon as thou art generous to me.*

BIBLIOGRAPHY

W. Beyerlin, *Die Rettung der Bedrängten in den Feindpsalmen* . . . , FRLANT XCIX (Göttingen, 1970); W. Brueggemann, *The Psalms and the Life of Faith* (Minneapolis, 1995), pp. 71, 74; H. Schmidt, *Das Gebet der Angeklagten im Alten Testament,* BZAW XLIX (Giessen, 1928).

FORM

This prayer song, to be intoned by a man in distress, is made up of three strophes. The first two have three bicola each, and the third strophe has two tricola and one bicolon. Probably the poet amplified the rhythm as the supplication became more passionate, but the last bicolon was a promise to praise the name. Thus the two genres are represented, complaint and hymn. The *Envoi* gathers together God's love and social approval (v. 8cd).

COMMENTARY

Strophe I: My Spirit Is Faint (vv. 2-4)

Ascribed to David in the cave (see 1 Sam 22:1; 24:4; Ps 57:1), this supplication arises from the terror of helplessness in the face of ferocious enemies. Through his loss of any divine or human protection, the poet shouts with a loud voice. He wants to be sure that a God who seems absent or mute will soon listen to an ultimate need. This overwhelming fear does not prevent sophisticated exchanges of words in elegant repetition (vv. 1cd-2). The vehemence of his appeal indicates both the extremity of his terror and the tenacity of his confidence in God, even a God who remains silent. The complaint is "poured" like a torrential cascade. The "spirit" of the sufferer is faint, and his breath is lost. Still, the prayer expects that Yahweh, ignorant of the drama, will look and see. Then he will certainly intervene.

Strophe II: Solitude and Hopelessness (vv. 4cd-5)

The "imprisonment" is not to be taken literally, as in other contexts (Lev 24:12; Num 15:34; Ps 107:10-16). Instead of a legal incarceration, the poet complains metaphorically of his own selfhood. In anticipation of his explicit lament over his psychological imprisonment, he states that, without friends, he is thrown into a mortal destiny. Not only do his enemies seek to entrap him, but Yahweh is no longer one of his refuges. The two horrors combine to announce a death, from persecutors and from his own selfhood. Nobody cares for his life (in the sense of *élan vital*).

Strophe III: Salvation and Praise (v. 8ab)

The poet at last demands far more than a temporary refuge. He cries out for liberation from his enemies and from his psychological separation from all. "Bring my very being out of my [emotional] prison." Then the lament will change into a hymn of praise to the name.

Envoi: Divine and Social Acceptance (v. 8cd)

In a society where solidarity of tribal and national relations is paramount, the final expectation is the gift of social approval. It inevitably will follow the intervention of Yahweh, which is not described but becomes evident. The land of the living will remain the devotee's home.

DATE AND THEOLOGY

This prayer song, overstepping and eventually conquering a desperate crisis, is of an uncertain date, but its form and poetic qualities may well point to the time of the monarchy. The experience of solitariness when life is threatened and death has to be faced with a sophisticated psychology of the self and a theology of elusive presence could be placed at the time of Judah's agony at the end of the seventh century (cf. Pss 38:12; 88:9, 19). Here is a persecuted loner whom society and God himself appear to have abandoned. Risks of entrapment do not undermine this man's faith. Practical providence does not, by its absence, keep the mind of the Hebrew devotee from postponing skeptical conclusions, for it knows the meaning of waiting. A psalm is composed to be sung as a sign of unfailing expectation. The lamenter is intimately aware of the compassionate quality of Yahweh. That is the chief reason for his hope in praising the divine name.

The theology of the name is held over against the theology of glory, for it places the hearing of the word over the seeing. It counts on time. The name of "Yahweh," "He causes to be," revealed in the scene at the burning bush, brings creation back from the past and promises re-creation for the future. To praise the name is to know God and to abide through a glimmer of his mystery (Pss 23:3; 25:11; 31:3; 106:8; 109:21; 148:5, 13).

PSALM 143

Teach Me to Do Thy Will

1. *Psalm. Of David.*

I

> *Lord! Hear my prayer!*
> > *Listen to my supplication!*
> *On account of thy faithfulness*
> > *Answer me, and also for thy justice.*

2. > *Let there be no judgment against thy servant,*
> > *Although no human being can be found righteous before thee.*

II

3. > *An enemy has pursued my very being;*
> > *He has crushed my life to the ground;*
> *He has forced me to live in the dark,*

Like those who have long been dead.
4.   *My spirit faints within me,*
       And my heart is numb.

III

5.   *I remember the days of old;*
       I meditate on all that thou hast done;
       I ponder the work of thy hands;
6.   *I stretch my hands toward thee.*
       My soul is athirst for thee
       Like a desiccated land.

Core Verse

7. *Answer me at once, O Lord!*
    My spirit is faint.
Do not hide thy face from me
    Lest I be like those who go down to the Pit!

III′

8.   *In the morning show me thy love,*
       For in thee I trust.
    Reveal to me the way I should go,
       For I lift up my soul toward thee!

II′

9.   *Deliver me from mine enemies, Lord!*
       I flee toward thee as my refuge!
10.   *Teach me to do thy will,*
       For thou art my God!
    Let thy good spirit
       Lead me on level ground!

I′

11. *For the sake of thy name, O Lord, make me live!*
    In thy justice, bring my soul out of trouble!
12. *For the sake of thy fidelity, thou shalt exterminate mine enemies*
    And cut off all the foes of my life,
       For I am thy servant.

BIBLIOGRAPHY

R. Arconada, "Psalmus 142/143 retentus, emendatus, glossatus," *VD*, XIII (1933), pp. 240-46; W. Beyerlin, *Die Rettung der Bedrängten in den Feindpsalmen* . . . , FRLANT XCIX (Göttingen, 1970); O. Grether, *Name und Wort Gottes im Alten Testament*, BZAW LXIX (1934); H.-J. Kraus, *Theology of the Psalms* (Minneapolis, 1986), pp. 24-40; H. Schmidt, *Das Gebet der Angeklagten im Alten Testament*, BZAW XLIX (Giessen, 1928); W. Schottroff, *Gedenken im Alten Orient und im Alten Testament*, WMANT XV (Neukirchen, 1964).

FORM

This is perhaps a Vigil psalm, made up of quotations from several other prayers, that a falsely accused individual would be allowed to say during the night of his asylum in the sanctuary, waiting for the next morning's oracle of acquittal. The gathering of diverse fragments of invocation might explain the irregularity of the meter. The psalm, however, has a symmetrical structure. Three ascending strophes plead for a divine audience (I, vv. 1b-2); confess persecution at the hands of enemies (II, vv. 3-4); and express hope for salvation by identifying Yahweh as the continual Creator (III, vv. 5-6). The first three strophes climax in a core petition (v. 7), where the peril of death renders the pleading more urgent still. The concluding three strophes are built on the motifs of refuge, perhaps a temple-asylum vigil, and the theology of the name (vv. 8, 9-10, 11-12).

COMMENTARY

Strophe I: Appeal to a Silent God (vv. 1b-2)

In great distress the poet asks the Lord for an answer. He appeals to God's sense of justice, but adds that none is sinless in the divine presence. He therefore hopes that the hitherto mute God will answer the prayer without judging the petitioner, who confidently claims to be Yahweh's servant. The kind of righteousness that is lacking in human beings seemingly displays a legalistic character of reward and punishment (v. 2) that jars with the initial invocation, "on account of thy faithfulness." The suppliant's perspicacity leads him to expect a higher theological level of divine-human relation: "Let there be no judgment against thy servant."

Strophe II: The Endurance of Suffering (vv. 3-4)

The adversary pursues the sufferer's "soul," which here assumes the significance of "inward beingness." An enemy has crushed to the ground the poet's life — a symbolic use of a fight-to-the-finish — then excommunicated him and isolated him from society, as if he had been incarcerated in an empty cistern without light (v. 3). This is another image of mortal expectation. Thus the enemy, who must have been a magistrate or judge of high standing, has attacked the hero's most sensitive element. The center of the persecuted man's personality is his spirit, the manifestation of his will to live, and his heart, the seat of his intellect.

Strophe III: *Creatio Continua* (vv. 5-6)

Appeal is now uttered indirectly to the God who gives and maintains life on earth. The poet's "soul" *(nephesh)* desires God without qualification. The image of thirst, once experienced, remains the most awful sign of existential need. To say, "My soul is athirst for thee" (v. 6), sounds like a cry of passion.

Core Strophe: Renewal of the Appeal (v. 7)

All three elements of prayer are now repeated in brief rehearsal: (1) cry for deliverance; (2) human faintness in divine absence; (3) descent into the Pit — the lowest abode of death.

Strophe III': The Night of Waiting (v. 8)

In the temporary shelter of the shrine, perhaps expecting the oracle of acquittal "in the morning," the suppliant distills the catechism of his adolescence: (1) the Lord is to be revealed again; (2) the poet's "obstinate" confidence in that love has not disappeared; (3) the knowledge of God's will illuminates and sustains human behavior. In tune with these motifs (divine love, human confidence, and knowledge of God's will for the way), the psalmist sums up his request: "I lift up my soul toward thee!" The ascending motion still belongs to man.

Strophe II': Refuge, Teaching, and Spirit (vv. 9-10)

The survival of the enemies still presents a threat. God's refuge must be permanent. Clearly, if the language of temple asylum before morning continues, the image of demanding lasting reality is far more profound, durable anywhere, and therefore inclusive in time and space. But the renewed man needs to be taught again not only God's will but also the power and the manner with which to do this will. Man's ability to behave properly is to be explained by Yahweh, the Teacher. The ascendent movement indicated by the sentence, "I flee toward thee as my refuge," transmutes the imagery of temple asylum for a night, waiting for a priestly oracle in the morning, to a lifetime shelter, anywhere on the earth and any time on the calendar.

In this eloquent instance, the night of vigil may have been the source of the poetic language now innovated by the psalmist, but such a static origin has been absorbed by a vision of dynamic, ongoing movement, initiated by the "spirit" of the Lord.

Not only does the poet expect to be led by Yahweh's "spirit of goodness," or "good spirit," but he also envisions smooth travel "on level ground" (v. 10). The tortuous ride of the recent trial will now be the enjoyment of riding on a royal highway. He will walk in the wisdom of his teacher.

Strophe I': For the Sake of Thy Name, Free at Last (vv. 11-12)

The correspondence between the creative power of the name "Yahweh," "He who causes to be," has in the end invigorated the man whose prayer will be answered. If the singer is to live, the foes must be bound and immobilized: "Let my enemies perish!" (v. 12). In an age of harsh competition and murders, the prayerful man has no choice: the forgiveness of criminal accusers is out of question.

DATE AND THEOLOGY

Psalm 143 is the last of the so-called "Penitential Psalms" (Psalms 6; 32; 38; 51; 102; 130; 143). Although it does not confess any sin or transgression, it admits that no human being is pure before God (v. 2). Thus it affects a penitential tone (cf. Psalm 38). Does this indicate that the poet looks at his enemies as agents of divine correction for his own, undescribed, acts of rebellion? The citations of many laments with which Psalm 143 is composed probably refer to postexilic times, when anthologies of earlier poems were admissible in the temple cult. Nevertheless, the cruelty of the foes may also suggest the last years of the kingdom of Judah (605-587 B.C.E.), when a prophet like Jeremiah could be physically abused by the authorities.

The repeated appeals to God's answer and the unveiling of his face, like the unrestrained intimacy with Yahweh that the poet freely expresses, show a long acquaintance with the *Heilsgeschichte* of Israel (v. 5).

The theological presumptions are those of traditional Yahwism. Cultic ceremonial is not important for this member of the chorus, in preexilic or postexilic times. He rises directly to the divine transpersonality, without an intermediary like a priest or other officer of sacrificial worship. The request for God as the teacher of his will aims at a reality that goes beyond the commandments of covenant law. It may well indicate a sapiential influence.

While the Hebrew text reads, "I have hidden [my failings]" to thee (v. 9), the LXX reads, "I have fled," or "I flee toward thee." The flight toward Yahweh inserts a powerful energy, with a speedy movement of ascent, which itself shows the vigor of a man eager to receive lucid and forceful guidance from the "spirit" of the Lord. This word is relatively rare in the Psalter (cf. Ps 51:12-14). The "breathing" background of the word "spirit" reveals the marvel of living rather than of dying (Ps 31:5). It mitigates the terror of death, now dissipated.

The LXX and Vulg. not only, like the MT, ascribe Psalm 143 to David, but they add, "When his son [Absalom] pursued him." Thus they have seized the psychological complexity of the poem. Justice and fidelity go hand in hand when they describe the benevolence of Yahweh's spirit. Man does not possess personal righteousness, but he may count on God's righteousness. The psalm anticipates Pauline reflections on justification by faith. The "servant" grasps the joy of "Thou art my God!"

PSALM 144

The Song of a Happy Warrior

1. *From David.*

I

> *Blessed be the Lord, my rock!*
> *Trainer of my hand for battle,*
> *And of my fingers for war!*

2.
> *My love and my fortress,*
> *My citadel and my liberator,*
> *My shield who gives me shelter*
> *And subdues peoples under me!*

II

3.   *Lord, what is man that he deserves notice of thee,*
          And the son of man that thou shouldst think of him?

4.   *Mortal man is like a breath;*
          His days like a passing shadow.

5.   *Lord, bend open thy heavens and come down!*
          Touch the mountains and make them smoke!

III

6.   *Cast forth lightning and disperse my foes!*
          Shoot out thine arrows! Rout mine enemies!

7.   *Stretch thy hands from on high!*
          Save and deliver me from deep waters,
     From the hands of sons of barbarians,

8.   *Whose mouths speak lies,*
          And whose right arm is falsehood!

9.   *I will sing a new song to thee, O God;*
          On the ten-stringed harp I will play for thee!

III′

10.   *Thou who givest victory to kings,*
          And savest thy servant David.
     Rescue me from the malevolent sword,

11.   *And deliver me from sons of barbarians,*
     Whose mouths speak lies
          And whose right arm is the right hand of falsehood!

II′

12.   *May our sons be like green plants*
          Growing tall from their earliest days!
     And let our daughters be like shapely columns,
          Sculpted like those of a palace!

13.   *Let our barns be overfilled,*
          Offering all manners of goods!

I′

     May our ewes bring forth thousands,
          Myriads in our country farms!

14.   *Let our heifers be heavy with calves,*

> *Suffering no mischance or miscarriage!*
> *No cry of distress on our roads!*
15. *Happy the people for whom this is true!*
> *Happy the people whose God is the Lord!*

BIBLIOGRAPHY

E. Baumann, "Struktur-Untersuchungen im Psalter II," *ZAW,* LXII (1950), pp. 148-52; Z. W. Falk, "[*yaḥiṣ*]: Gestures Expressing Affirmation," *JSS,* IV (1959), pp. 268-69; J. J. Jeremias, *Theophanie: Die Geschichte einer alttestamentlichen Gattung,* WMANT X (Neukirchen, 1965); H.-J. Kraus, *Theology of the Psalms* (Minneapolis, 1986), pp. 107-11; R. T. O'Callagan, "Echoes of Canaanite Literature in the Psalms," *VT,* IV (1954), pp. 164-76; G. von Rad, *Der Heilige Krieg im alten Testament,* Abhandlungen zur Theologie des Alten und Neuen Testaments XX (Zurich, 1951); J. Ziegler, "Psalm 144,14," *Wort und Geschichte,* Festschrift K. Elliger (Neukirchen, 1973), pp. 191-97.

FORM

Several critics, debating the composition of this psalm, have suggested that it was made from two or three fragments, and that v. 9, with its intention to sing and play music, did not fit with the preceding or following context. Moreover, it has been maintained that the terminal blessings belonged not to a war song but to a harvest festival. Other scholars have also believed that the questions regarding man's frailty and mortality reflect sapiential poetry. Strophic analysis, however, supports the thesis of unity of composition, for a remarkable symmetry characterizes the entire poem: three strophes with bicola and occasionally a tricolon parallel each other, separated by a core verse (v. 9) that links the two sets of three strophes (vv. 1d-8, 10-15). The meter confirms this analysis by enlarging the core verse from the general rhythm of 3+2 in the first three and the last three strophes, to a spectacular 5+5, with the intention of singing and playing music.

COMMENTARY

Strophe I: Rock, Trainer, and Shield (vv. 1-2)

Title: The LXX adds: "against Goliath."

The psalm begins as a hymn, similar to the invocation of Ps 18:2-3. The singer is a happy warrior because he has received many signs of Yahweh's protection in the past, and he specifically thanks his Lord for having already "subdued peoples under me" (v. 2d). From the start, we are led to infer that Psalm 144 was composed for, or even by, a Davidic king, praising Yahweh in a royal feast, perhaps the ceremony of a new king's enthronement.

The accumulation of terms of endearment, military as these may be, is thrown at Yahweh in an act of jubilation that will reappear in the last three strophes. Among these manifold qualifications of God there appears in the Hebrew text a different and unexpected designation of Yahweh, "My love," which is reminiscent of the passionate cry, "I love thee" (Ps 18:2).

Strophe II: Sapiential Realism and Humility (vv. 3-5)

The questions on the fragility of human life seem at first to constitute a non sequitur. Yet, immediately after the reminiscent claim of victory over several peoples, the singer reminds himself of mortality and of the fragility of human existence in the presence of Yahweh. Even kings must die (cf. Job 7:17; Ps 8:4).

The two designations of "man" are significant: Adam, who yielded to Eve's desire to become immortal but was confirmed in his mortality (cf. Job 14:1-2; Pss 39:5, 11; 62:9).

Belief in divine transcendence may keep a God remote or even indifferent to human misery. The divine Presence may be elusive, but it will be still renewed after the so-called "death of God." Yahweh will bend, fold, cleave, and cut open the heavens in order to come mythically to earth. The psalmist does not express the active proximity of God to human fears and human trials as an "incarnation," but he willfully uses the forceful language of heavenly disruption (v. 5) that will become primordial in Christianity. We are reminded of the burning bush at the foot of Mount Sinai and of Elijah on Mount Carmel.

The last sign of divine intervention is a rarely acknowledged volcanic eruption (v. 5).

Strophe III: The Existential Instant of Life or Death (vv. 6-8)

"The Song of a Happy Warrior" cannot ignore moments of dire combat with their terror, either memories of a recent past or the acute striking of the present actuality. The language of the theophany uses lightning strikes that will disperse the enemy and thus save the hero from drowning in the deep waters. Here the poet's imagination remembers the symbol of immersion within the great Flood, or even the primal Ocean upon which the myths of creation would stage the foundations of the earth.

In the unfolding of a holy war the adversaries of the people of God are more than sons of aliens. One may translate "sons of barbarians," in the pejorative sense of the ancient term. Israel evoked the conquest of the Holy Land, not as the legitimate invasion of territories long occupied by the Canaanites and related ethnic groups but as the fulfillment of a divine promise of a gift or inheritance (Deut 33:2-3; Judg 5:4-5; Hab 3:4-6).

Core Verse: The Happy Decision to Praise (v. 9)

The promise to play music and to sing appears in a lament form. The mixed genres are theologically sound since the heat of the battle, with its uncertainties, does not prevent a certainty of triumph — a God-instigated victory. The professional musician emerges from the fracas of blood and death to the orchestral harmony. The jubilation thanks the Lord. Music becomes, par excellence, the channel of communion between humanity and divinity.

Strophe III': New Prayer for Salvation (vv. 10-11)

The repeated supplication for safety embroiders on the victories remembered in Strophe I (v. 2b). David is now honored explicitly by the epithet "thy servant" (v. 10b). The length of the Davidic dynasty — a phenomenal happening of over four centuries with uninterrupted lineage — includes the fabulous achievements of the Bethlehem shepherd, anointed by the prophet Samuel, buffeted by King Saul, dethroned by Absalom, and condemned by the prophet Nathan for adultery and murder. Nevertheless, David is now praised as a servant of the Lord. A poet places in the mouth of a Davidic king the risk of a malevolent sword. Here David overcomes his fright, for he serves the Lord. Here his enemies do not deserve to be taken seriously, for their claims are lies and falsehood. Yet the supremely courageous warrior will become the happy warrior.

Strophe II': Victory Leads to Posterity (vv. 12-13b)

Fertility in the fields and in the stables (v. 12) only reflects the vigor and beauty of sons and daughters in the realm of posterity.

Strophe I': Children and Wealth (vv. 13c-15)

The psalmist knows that warfare, when victorious, will be followed by territorial and agricultural success. Nevertheless, he prays that such wonderful results will be granted, largely and even abundantly, if he prays for safety from diseases and accidental mishaps. Then the cattle will multiply only with prayer (v. 14a). Victorious conflicts with foreign nations should produce a wealthy people, with numerous and healthy children. The beauty and vigor of sons and daughters is expressed according to the aesthetic trends of the time.

The Hebrew relative pronoun (v. 12a) yields no satisfactory syntax. The word was probably mispronounced and later misspelled from the sapiential formulation of a dynamic beatitude, "Happy will be the sons. . . !" This dynamic salutation is repeated in the final lines of the psalm (v. 15).

DATE AND THEOLOGY

If Psalm 144 was a royal canticle composed for a king of the Davidic dynasty, its date may have been in preexilic times. Yet it may have been composed during the Persian period, when the story of David from Bethlehem became a popular legend as a factor in the growth of the eschatological theology of later Judaism. The expression "tens of thousands of lambs" suggests the glorious expectation of the kingdom of God on earth.

The hero of this psalm became a happy warrior, for he looked beyond military triumph toward an era of universal peace. The uncertainties and horrors of warfare are not omitted, but the moral ambiguity of any military triumph is here ignored. Friedrich Nietzsche was bluntly correct when he wrote, "War makes the victor stupid and the vanquished vengeful."

Nothing in the psalm is told about the mothers, brides, and orphans of slain combatants. There is no hint of a critique of international conflicts. No judgment is offered on the psychological deterioration of surviving, but maimed, veterans. Psalm 144, more than any other poem of the Psalter, should be judged, not through an anachronistic comparison with modern cultures — although these are likewise inhuman — but according to a theology of Yahwism compromised by the institution of the monarchy.

The prophets of the eighth century may have been more astute than the psalmists, who were artistic functionaries of a shrine controlled by an anointed monarchy. Those prophets announced peace.

> They shall beat their swords into plowshares,
>   And their spears into pruning hooks;
> Nation shall not lift up a sword against nation,
>   Neither shall they learn war anymore.   (Mic 4:3 = Isa 2:4)

The Davidic Bethlehem became the Birth-of-Jesus Bethlehem in Christian tradition, often violated by Christendom itself; for it declared, on that night,

> No war, or battle's sound,
>   Was heard the world around;
> The idle spear and shield were high up hung.   (John Milton)

PSALM 145

Hymn to God, the King

1. *Praise. From David.*

I

	Aleph	*I shall exalt thee, my God, the King!*
		And bless thy name forever in perpetuity.
2.	Beth	*Every day I shall bless thee,*
		And celebrate thy name forever in perpetuity.
3.	Gimel	*The Lord is great and greatly to be praised;*
		His greatness is unsearchable.

II

4.	Daleth	*One generation shall celebrate thy works to another,*
		And proclaim thy heroic acts!
5.	Hê	*I shall recount the splendor of thy majesty,*
		And meditate on thy wonders.
6.	Waw	*People will speak of thy awesome power,*
		And I shall declare thy greatness.

III

7.	Zayin	*They shall recall the memory of thy immense bounty,*
		And celebrate thy righteousness.
8.	Ḥeth	*The Lord is gracious and full of love,*
		Slow to anger and faithful in his love;
9.	Ṭeth	*The Lord is good toward all creatures,*
		And his compassion embraces all of them.

IV

10.	Yôdh	*All thy creatures will praise thee, O Lord!*
		And thy devotees shall bless thee.
11.	Kaph	*They shall speak of the glory of thy kingship,*
		And proclaim the bravura of thy heroism,
12.	Lamedh	*Making known thy heroism to the sons of Adam,*
		And the glorious splendor of thy kingship.

V

13.	Mem	*Thy kingship is a kingship for all time,* *And thy reign shall last for all generations.*
14.	[Nun]	*The Lord is trustworthy in all his promises,* *And faithful in all his deeds.*
15.	Samekh	*The Lord upholds all those who stumble,* *And raises all those who are bowed down.*

VI

16.	ʿAyin	*The eyes of all hope in thee,* *And it is thou who givest them food in season.*
17.	Peh	*Thou openest thy hand and dost satisfy* *The desire of every living creature.*
18.	Ṣadhê	*The Lord is just in all his ways,* *And faithful in all his deeds.*

VII

19.	Qôph	*The Lord is close to all who invoke him,* *To all who call on him in sincerity.*
20.	Resh	*He fulfills the desires of those who fear him;* *He hears their cries and saves them.*
21.	Shin	*The Lord guards all who love him,* *But exterminates all scoundrels.*

Envoi

22.	Taw	*Let my mouth ever praise the Lord,* *And all flesh bless his holy name,* *Forever in perpetuity!*

BIBLIOGRAPHY

W. H. Bellinger, *Psalms: Reading and Studying the Book of Praise* (Peabody, Mass., 1990), p. 82; W. Brueggemann, *The Message of the Psalms* (Minneapolis, 1984), p. 28; idem, *The Psalms and the Life of Faith* (Minneapolis, 1995), pp. 47-49, 123-28; J. Carmody, "The Theology of Ps 145," *Bible Today*, XLIII (1969), pp. 272-79; F. Crüsemann, *Studien zur Formgeschichte von Hymnus und Danklied in Israel*, WMANT XXXVIII (Neukirchen, 1969), pp. 186, 229; D. N. Freedman and J. C. Geoghegan, "Psalms 119 and 145: Alphabetic Acrostic Psalms," in *Psalm 119: The Exaltation of Torah* (Winona Lake, Ind., 1999), pp. 19-23; D. N. Freedman and J. C. R. Kimelman, "Psalm 145: Theme, Structure and Impact," *JBL*, CXIII (1994), pp. 37-58;

O. Grether, *Name und Wort im Alten Testament*, BZAW LXIV (Giessen, 1934); F. Horst, "Segen und Segenshandlungen in der Bibel," *EvT*, VII (1947), pp. 23-37; A. R. Hulst, "*Kol basar* in der priesterlichen Fluterzählung," *OtSt*, XII (1958), pp. 28-68; L. Liebreich, "Psalms 34 and 145 in the Light of Their Key Words," *HUCA*, XXVII (1956), pp. 181-92; P. D. Miller, Jr., *Interpreting the Psalms* (Philadelphia, (1986), pp. 76-78; O. H. Steck, "Das Problem theologischer Strömungen in nachexilischer Zeit," *EvT*, XXVIII (1968), pp. 445-58; W. G. E. Watson, "Reverse Rootplay in Ps 145," *Bib*, LXII (1981), pp. 101-2; C. Westermann, *The Living Psalms* (Grand Rapids, 1989), pp. 221-29; idem, *The Praise of God in the Psalms* (Richmond, Va., 1965).

FORM

This psalm is, par excellence, a hymn of praise (cf. Psalms 33; 34; 103; 104; 111; along with those placed at the end of the collection, Psalms 146–150). It is the only piece in the Psalter with the simple superscription, "Praise." It presents a vocabulary typical of the hymnic style, with the words "bless," "proclaim," "promise," "fulfill," "greatness," "splendor," "glory," and so on. The meter is irregular, as if this poem had been collected from diverse sources, but its composition is unusually symmetrical, with seven strophes (the number 7 being a favorite of ancient times), of three bicola each. An *Envoi* concludes the whole (v. 22). It parallels the personal accent of the first line, "*my* God!" and the final exultation, "Let *my* mouth . . ." (v. 22).

Psalm 145 is an alphabetic acrostic poem, since each bicolon begins with a word whose initial is a letter of the Hebrew alphabet, taken in order (cf. Psalms 9–10; 25; 34; 37; 111; 112; 119). The initial letter *Nun* is accidently missing in the MT, but it was preserved in the ancient versions (LXX, Vulg., Syr.) and in the Dead Sea Scroll fragment. Some modern translations have different numbers for vv. 14-22.

COMMENTARY

Strophe I: My God, the King! (vv. 1b-3)

The only instance of the definite article before the appellation of the divine monarch provides a special power to the invocation. "The King!" may be the integration within the poem of the spoken announcement in public ceremonies. The apostrophe insinuates a stupendous sensation of confidence. The invocation already contains a vivid presence. The poet extols the Kingship of God, a unique divinity, different from any other belief in the ancient Near East. Hereditary monarchy was not, at first, the governmental system of the tribes delivered from Egyptian slavery. Charismatic leaders, from Moses and Joshua to their successors, the so-called "judges," could maintain a modicum of social fairness, but the invasion of the Philistines proved to be too disruptive, at least for a theocracy. The hereditary succession of monarchs may have been a device adopted from neighboring countries and put to the test by the prophet Samuel, who attempted to organize a relatively stable pattern of government, with Saul and then David.

Yet the psalmists, singers and players, who were functionaries of the Zion sanctuary, wished to preserve the transcending quality of an allegiance that was free from all human ambiguities.

Even as the devotees of Yahweh composed hymns for the ceremonies of human enthronement, Davidic kingship needed to be checked by disciplined reverence for the divine King. Whether or not there was a feast of enthronement for human monarchs is not proved, but this psalmist seems to proclaim the feast of a divine enthronement. "My God, the King!" is a cry of the heart, possibly a hidden protest against the Davidic dynasty.

Strophe II: Divine Work of Heroism (vv. 4-6)

Yahweh's kingdom is everlasting. It does not need an annual rite of renewal. This psalmist accumulates the acts of bravura ascribed to the Creator, according to the ancient myth of the cosmic fight between order and chaos. The heroism of the Creator becomes a primordial element of hymnic praise.

Strophe III: Divine Goodness (vv. 7-9)

After the heroic deeds of creation, the poet lists the holy qualities of the Lord: his immense bounty, his rectitude, his grace, his love, his compassion toward all living beings, human and animal. The memory of God's love is transmitted from generation to generation; this is the real power of Yahweh. The poet has moved from the subjectivity of his devotion to the corporate feelings of the cultic community.

Strophe IV: Universal Kingship (vv. 10-12)

Far more than the worshipers who are gathered in Zion, the whole of humanity, although they are "the sons of Adam," will acknowledge and celebrate the divine bravura (v. 12). Yahweh's "name" includes his glory (v. 11). All the living creatures of the world will someday worship the King! The psalmist opens up an eschatological perspective.

Strophe V: A Providence for Individual Persons (vv. 13-15)

Unlike human kingships, the reign of Yahweh will last forever. The language at this point may be influenced by Canaanite poetry (cf. Ugarit, III AB, A10), where eternity is claimed for historical monarchs. Not only will God be faithful to his promises, but he also, and specifically, "upholds those who stumble" (v. 15). The meaning of this verse is obscure. Is "falling" (literal translation of the MT) an image for "going astray," or should the text mean that those who "stumble" are the victims of entrapment? The second meaning is preferable, for the word "stumble" belongs to the same semantic category as that of the next line, "those who are bowed down." The sentence may refer to the needy or humble wrongly accused.

Strophe VI: The Feeding of the Hungry (vv. 16-18)

The intention of the poet once more requires some clarification. There are seasons of dry weather followed by famine. Does God answer the desires of those who are famished? Or does the psalmist repeatedly look forward to the *eschaton,* when the reign of God will benefit the whole of humanity? Once again it may be conjectured that hymns of praise anticipate the future liturgically and induce with joy a state of worship that transforms time into an eternal present.

Strophe VII: Sincere Prayer Is Always Answered (vv. 19-21)

The final strophe insists on the universality of God's concerns and the abundant sufficiency of his gifts. There is no trace of protest against the apparent injustices of nature and history. Nor is there an accusation against a God who may be silent and distant. The Lord's protection for those who love him may not be denied, but what is the meaning of the previous declarations of universal benevolence? Sapiential debate on divine rectitude is absent. Strict favor is distributed on those who "fear," namely, "passionately love" the Lord over against the evildoers, who will not escape final extermination.

Envoi (v. 22)

In a return to the self-efflorescence of his lyricism, the artist sums up all the stages of his incitement to praise with the voice of song. He hopes to enlist "all flesh" and to celebrate God's "holy name." Just as the love of Yahweh embraces all creatures, so also the singer exhorts the entire chorus, symbol of all humanity, to join him in the seven strophes of the hymn. Far beyond the cultic community, the vision of all nations, beginning with the last day of history, brings universal salvation to a single vocalic harmony.

DATE AND THEOLOGY

The theology of the name dominates the entire psalm. The "name" suggests a reality that lies around the spelling or appellation Yahweh, and goes far ahead of its syllabic sound. It includes a reputation justified by the fulfillment of promises; it also both reveals and conceals the unspeakable letters Y H W H spelled out for Moses at the scene of the burning bush (Exod 3:13). The name is an enigma and a dogma: God is the One who brings into being; he causes existence to happen; the psalmist is a personality who can test his origin and his destination. "I exist," for the Creator of the universe has extracted me from the void of nonbeing to introduce me for a moment into terrestrial life.

If the name is the first pole of this model of hymnology, the second is to confess, in the simplicity of childhood, that the Maker of beingness loves all the creatures of the earth.

In stunning objection to covenant particularism when it sets apart the priestly people from all other nations, the praise of the Creator who feeds and saves "all flesh" musically and mystically becomes the rallying cry till the end of the world. Because the theology of the name appeals to the "hearing" of the word rather than yielding to the popular attraction of "seeing" cultic mirrors of glory, it prepares for the survival of Judaism without a temple as well as a society. It also produces the simple but demanding discipline of authentic Christendom.

The "gospel" is "God's spell." To *hear* the Evangel is to enter the inclusiveness, not the exclusivity, of the *ekklēsia*, the assembly of those who hear the call *(klēsis)*. When the psalmist goes beyond his individualistic religion in order to sing the praise of a God of gods who loves all creatures, he hears the *aniconic* specificity of YAHWEH, whose name probably means, "The One who causes to be."

The community of those who "fear" to displease him was named the *qāhāl*, a Hebrew word that the Hellenistic Jews translated by the Greek word *ekklēsia*, later adopted by the early Christians.

The hymnist knows that "The Lord our God is God of gods, and Lord of lords, a great God, a mighty and an awesome one" (Deut 10:17). At the same time, "the Being of God is so comfortable, so convenient, so necessary to the felicity of mankind, that [. . . .] if God were not a necessary Being of Himself, He might almost seem to be made for the use and benefit of men" (John Tillotson, Archbishop of Canterbury, 1694).

PSALM 146

Mortality and Doxology

Prelude

1.   *Hallelujah!*

        O my soul, praise the Lord!
2.   *I will praise thee, O Lord, all my life;*
          I will celebrate my God till my death!

I

3.   *Do not put your trust in princes,*
        A son of Adam cannot bring salvation;
4.   *When his breath departs, he returns to dust;*
        On that very day his best plans perish.

II

5.   *Happy is the man whose help is the God of Jacob,*
        And whose hope is in the Lord, his God!
6.   *Maker of heaven, earth, the seas,*
        And all that is in them,
        Keeper of truth forever,
7.   *Restorer of rights for the oppressed,*
        Giver of bread to the famished!

III

8.   *The Lord unties the bonds of the prisoners;*
    The Lord opens the eyes of the blind;
    The Lord straightens those who are bowed down;
    The Lord loves the man of rectitude;
9.   *The Lord protects the sojourners;*
    [The Lord is feared by the whole earth,
        And all the inhabitants of the world
        Know the works he has created.]
    He is the comforter of orphan and widow,
        And he leads astray the scoundrels.

Postlude

10.　　*The Lord will be King forever!*
　　　O Zion! Thy God will last for all generations!

　　Hallelujah!

BIBLIOGRAPHY

W. Brueggemann, *The Message of the Psalms* (Augsburg, 1984), pp. 162-63; idem, *The Psalms and the Life of Faith* (Minneapolis, 1995), pp. 40-41, 126-28; F. James, *Thirty Psalmists* (New York, 1938), pp. 57-60; J. S. Kselman, "Psalm 146 in Its Context," *CBQ*, L (1988), pp. 587-99; H. Schmidt, "Grüsse und Glück im Psalter," *Theologische Studien und Kritiken*, CIII (1931), pp. 141-50.

FORM

This psalm affects a peculiar form: like some other hymns, it is framed between a prelude and a postlude declaring the poet's intention to praise the Lord, but its body is composed of three irregular strophes (?) or parts (?): Strophe I (vv. 3-4) seems to have been influenced by sapiential speculation, as it warns against the mortality of princes; Strophe II begins as a beatitude (v. 5) but soon shifts into the celebration of the Creator (vv. 6-7); Strophe III lists the acts of the Lord that benefit the oppressed (vv. 8-9).

Perhaps the diversity of its themes corresponds to the diversity of its form. Strophe III is unusual, for it begins with five monocola; each monocolon begins with the name of Yahweh, but the strophe ends with a traditional bicolon on the popular belief in retribution. The text itself is uncertain, for a Dead Sea Scroll fragment, 11QPs^a, adds a bicolon absent in the MT (see brackets), and the third part or strophe may not be determined accurately.

COMMENTARY

Prelude (vv. 1-2)

Psalm 146 is the first of the last hymns of the Psalter to begin with Hallelujah (cf. Psalms 147–150). The exhortation to praise the Lord is addressed by the psalmist to his own soul, as if a double personality divided the consciousness of his poetic impulses. This psychological dialogue soon becomes a single address, in prayer to the Lord; the psalmist commits himself to praise for his entire life. The phrase "till my death" (lit., "for the rest of my existence") may reflect a sapiential observation.

Strophe I: Warning to Fellow Singers (vv. 3-4)

Interruption of the hymnic form with a sapiential observation containing a warning to other singers should not be regarded as a political attack against the nobles, for it is inspired by the remembrance of the universality of death: we all die because we are the sons of Adam (cf. Gen 3:3). Here is no animosity against aristocracy, but simply profound sadness on the fate of all human beings. The psalmist expresses his regret that even the best intentions of noblemen are wiped out with their last breath.

Strophe II: Benevolence of the Creator (vv. 5-7)

As in most hymns, the themes for praise blossom pleasantly on the attention displayed by the God of Jacob, thus linking the present benevolence to the patriarchal election (v. 5). The goodness of the Creator appears especially in the cosmic harmony that seems to join heaven, earth, and the seas, with all that they contain and support (v. 6a). The thought of the strength of this gigantic organization of the world passes quickly to the reliability of God's promise (v. 6c) and to his sense of justice for the oppressed as well as to his generosity for the famished (v. 7).

Strophe III: A Litany on the Name "Yahweh" (vv. 8-9)

A special strophe forming an embryonic litany on the name of Yahweh describes in five or six single cola the providential graciousness of the Lord. The name YHWH begins each sentence and frames its appearance with participles, thus respecting the typical syntax of the hymnic style. It constitutes the summit of the entire psalm (vv. 7 and 9).

Postlude (v. 10)

The theme of Yahweh's eternal kingship, already prominent in Psalm 145, is declared anew (v. 10a). It is an echo of the prelude's address to "my soul," this time making Zion the object of the psalmist's final exhortation.

DATE AND THEOLOGY

Loving concern for Zion, without any specification of cultic reality or legality, has replaced the psychological awareness of the self (v. 10 versus v. 1). The brevity of the summons "O Zion! Thy God!" remains ambiguous. Does the myth of the earth navel survive in the restriction of the cult to this sanctuary? Is the "Rock" of Zion still the link from the realm of death to the glory of heaven?

The date reflects the postexilic Diaspora, when the second temple replaces the first, destroyed by the Babylonians (587 B.C.E.), as the principle of social coherence in the Persian Empire.

The theology of wisdom transforms the sternness of universal mortality to overwhelming joy in the elation of doxology.

While death remains the curse of the sons of Adam, life is the benediction of believers in Yahweh. "Happiness" is the dynamic march toward the goal of fulfilling dynamism. The probable etymology of the word makes happiness the faculty of growth. The litany spells out and yet preserves the mystery of God, who created a harmonious cosmos and induces justice in society. No room is left for the anxiety of theodicy. The Lord unties, the Lord opens, the Lord straightens, the Lord loves, the Lord protects. A tense affinity between justice and love concludes. Yahweh comforts and leads astray.

Once again, the theology of the name, which favors the sense of hearing over that of seeing, dominates the spirituality of spaceless and timeless adoration of the divine. "My God," "his God," and "thy God" (vv. 2, 5, 10) evolve from the subjective to communality of worship, with its objectivity of gratitude. One will note with attention the movement of praise from "my God" to "his God," and finally "thy God, O Zion!" The theological outlook embraces the passion of the individual, extends itself to the holy people, and crowns this ascension with the hope of universal worship in the presence of the eternal King.

PSALM 147

Restoration and Doxology

1.   *Hallelujah!*

Prelude

How good it is to celebrate our God!
How pleasant it is to praise him!

I

2.   The Lord is rebuilding Jerusalem;
          He gathers together the exiles of Israel!
3.   He heals the brokenhearted,
          And binds up their wounds.

II

4.   He counts the number of the stars,
          And he names each one of them.
5.   Our Lord is great and full of strength;
          As for his intelligence, there is no limit.

III

6.   The Lord sustains the needy,
          And throws scoundrels down to the ground.
7.   Celebrate the Lord with a thanksgiving hymn;
          Celebrate our God on the cithara.

IV

8.   He veils the sky with clouds,
          And prepares the rain for the soil.
          He grows green grass on the mountains;
9.   Thus he gives to cattle their pasture,
          And feeds young ravens when they cry.

V

10.   He takes no delight in the vigor of horses,
          Nor does he admire the agility of men's legs;
11.   But he takes pleasure in those who fear him,
          And in those who hope in his fidelity.

VI

12.   Jerusalem! Praise thou the Lord!
          And thou, Zion! Celebrate thy God!
13.   For he has reinforced the bars of thy gates,
          Just as he blessed thy sons in thy midst.

VII

14.   He brings peace to thy borders;
          He satisfies thee with the best wheat.

15.   *He sends his commands to the earth,*
        And his word runs around at once.

VIII

16.   *He spreads the snow like tufts of wool;*
        He scatters hoarfrost like ashes.
17.   *He throws his ice like morsels;*
        Who can resist his cold weather?

IX

18.   *He says a word, and he melts them;*
        He makes his wind blow, and the waters gush.
19.   *He proclaims his promise to Jacob,*
        His statutes and decrees to Israel!

Postlude

20.   *He has not done this for any other nation;*
        No other knows his judgments.

    Hallelujah!

BIBLIOGRAPHY

P. Auffret, *Hymnes d'Égypte et d'Israël: Étude de structures littéraires* (Fribourg and Göttingen, 1981), pp. 122-31; J. Blau, "Nāwā Thilla (Ps CXLVII,1): Lobpreisen," *VT*, IV (1954), pp. 410-11; W. Brueggemann, *The Message of the Psalms* (Minneapolis, 1984), pp. 163-65; J. Cazeaux, "Le Psaume 147," in *Critique du Langage chez les Prophètes d'Israël* (Paris, 1976), pp. 149-63; F. Crüsemann, *Studien zur Formgeschichte von Hymnus und Danklied in Israel*, WMANT XXXII (Neukirchen, 1969), pp. 131-34; H. L. Ginsberg, "A Strand in the Cord of Hebraic Hymnody," *Eretz Israel*, IX (1969), pp. 45-50; O. Grether, *Name und Wort Gottes im Alten Testament*, BZAW LXIV (Giessen, 1934); H. Haag, "Er tut Kund sein Wort (Ps 147,19)," in *Wort und Hoffnung* (Luzern, 1970); H.-J. Kraus, *Theology of the Psalms* (Minneapolis, 1986), pp. 46, 150, 157; P. D. Miller, Jr., *Interpreting the Psalms* (Philadelphia, 1986), pp. 74-78; see Psalm 47; J. J. Stamm, *Erlösen und Vergeben im Alten Testament* (Bern, 1940); W. G. E. Watson, "The Pivot Pattern in Hebrew, Ugaritic and Akkadian Poetry," *ZAW*, LXXXVIII (1976), pp. 239-53.

FORM

This psalm, carefully composed as a hymn, contains nine strophes of two bicola (one tricolon, v. 8) that are embraced by a prelude (v. 1) and a postlude

(v. 20) that respectively invite the chorus to praise and to delineate the Lord's compassion.

It is possible that the nine strophes should be grouped in three strophes of three parts each (vv. 2-7, 8-13, 14-19), but the diversity of themes remains after such a division. The poet has managed to juxtapose two different motifs within each bicolon, probably because his structural goal was to ally divine greatness in the universe with divine concern for animal and human vitality.

The meter is exceptionally uniform throughout the psalm (3+3 and 3+3+3).

COMMENTARY

Prelude (v. 1)

As in other hymns, especially the last four of the Psalter, the Hebrew exclamation and exultation, "Hallelujah!" "Praise the Lord!" sets the tone for the poem. Emphasis is laid on the artistic and spiritual pleasure of playing and singing in order to praise the Lord.

Strophe I: Rebuilding Jerusalem and Loving the Needy (vv. 2-3)

At once the power and the compassion of Yahweh are joined in a single quatrain. The restoration of the Holy City, like the return of the deportees from Babylon, is the work of God's hand (Pss 78:68; 87:1; 102:16). The healing of the brokenhearted is on the same level as sacred urbanism.

Strophe II: The Starry Night and Intelligence (vv. 4-5)

Immediately the greatness of God appears in the night sky. God made an immense number of stars (power), and he is able to count them and name them (intelligence). From the contemplation of the cosmic vastness, a majestic sign of the Creator's immense strength, the singer moves now to the wisdom of the world's harmony, seasonal rhythm, and equilibrium. The universe is not an accident of physics. Unlike the gods and goddesses imagined by the foreign nations of the ancient Near East, the one, almighty, intelligent Lord understands the purpose of his work.

Strophe III: Praise for the Ethical Divinity (vv. 6-7)

The old companionship of righteousness and compassion is recalled as another source of praise: Yahweh effectuates fair judgments and carries them out. Thanks are offered to the Lord of retribution. Divine morality insures the coherence of society.

Strophe IV: Rain and Fertility for Food (vv. 8-9)

From cosmic immensity, the poet moves on to the splendor of meteorology. The soil of the Holy Land requires an annual season of rain to assure its fertility. Green grass on arid hills becomes food for bullocks and heifers. Even young ravens, selected by the psalmist among other birds, receive an answer to their cry. The choice of the bird mentioned is significant: ravens, viewed as an ill omen by pagan antiquity, are noted in Israel for their astuteness (1 Kgs 17:4; Job 38:41; Prov 30:17; Isa 34:11).

The LXX adds at the end of v. 8 "green grass for the fields of the sons of Adam" (cf. Ps 104:14), thus changing the tricolon into two bicola.

Strophe V: War Techniques and Religious Devotion (vv. 10-11)

Then it seems that the psalmist ascribes to Yahweh a dislike for the art of equitation and the sport of horse racing. It will be noted, however, that horses were also harnessed to war chariots and that human agility in running was prized by the infantry. The psalmist opposes military equipment and athletics to the sustained love of Yahweh and faith in the validity of his promises. The fear of the Lord does not mean terror or dread, but the passionate desire not to disappoint him and the hope of spiritual triumph.

Strophe VI: The Summons to Jerusalem and Zion (vv. 12-13)

The Holy City and its temple, presumably rebuilt, are now addressed directly as actors in the new drama. The reinforcement of the city gates is ascribed to the Lord when actually it was performed by Nehemiah (3:3; 3:6; 12:27). Men, even governors, could not succeed without divine decision and supervision.

Once again, human work is made possible by the determination and the diligence of God, who is interested in the safety of Jerusalem. Safety and prosperity are to be the manifestation of divine providence for generations to come. The Lord has blessed the sons of Israel.

Strophe VII: Promise of Peace and Good Harvests (vv. 14-15)

The coupling of a promise of peace with good harvests depends on the speed and completeness in which the benevolent commands of the Lord reach the earth and instantaneously produce their fulfillment. The word promotes life.

Strophe VIII: The Beauty and Harshness of Winter (vv. 16-17)

The greatness of God in the universe, at creation and in its maintenance, continues to manifest itself in the double meaning of the cold season: the beauty of nature in the snow and ice, with its spectacular scenes, and also the hardship it inflicts on the poor, or the nomads. The compassion of God is not expressed here, but it may be implied in anticipation of the subsequent strophe.

Strophe IX: The Word of God at Springtime (vv. 18-19)

The psalmist hides himself behind the pulchritude of nature and its seasonal cruelty, but he yields to his aesthetic appreciation. At the same time he seems to insist, lyrically, on divine compassion, for he clearly admires the sliding of winter into the "miracle" of spring. At the word of God, the snow melts and the ice feeds the torrents of water. The Near East knows water as a precious gift, and the psalmist ignores both disastrous droughts and murderous floods in the narrow canyons that divide hills and mountains.

Praise does not have room for sapiential doubts on theodicy. But the marvels of nature culminate in the marvels of history — that is, the history of salvation. The name of the ancestor of Israel, Jacob, did not become a substitute for his insidious cheating of his brother's birthright, but it stressed the ambiguity of his "fight with God" (Gen 27:30; 32:24-32). The fighter with God becomes the true patriarch of Israel.

Although not explicitly mentioned, the Mosaic covenant is implied by the last stichos on the gift of Passover. It becomes the command to obey statutes and decrees (v. 19b). Although not mentioned by name, and not yet unified, the Torah is clearly implied, but not in the sense of the completed and written Pentateuch.

Postlude (v. 20)

Although they are not yet a unified Torah, statutes and decrees have been revealed to Israel alone, never to any other people. Does the psalmist, by this declaration, claim joyfully but implicitly the wonder of the election of the people of God? Judaism, for better sociological coherence and in spite of bitter divisions, was tempted to go further in feeling not only favored but also uniquely placed, in a position of superiority over the surrounding nations.

DATE AND THEOLOGY

Psalm 147 alludes to the return of the exiles from Babylon as well as to the construction of the second temple, probably the repairs carried out by Nehemiah (12:27); thus it points to a postexilic date, perhaps between ca. 500 B.C.E. and some years later.

Praise rests chiefly on the recital of creation and salvation. The psalmist interpenetrates mastery of nature and *Heilsgeschichte*. All the elements of life are given to humankind.

The postlude, the sublime crown of the hymn, offers a certain ambiguity in the sense of uniqueness implied by the favor manifested by Yahweh to Israel. The feeling of superiority over the surrounding nations is not stressed, and the risk of an arrogant pride issuing from separatism fails to be condemned, or endorsed. It is softened by the whole context of praise and its basis of humble gratitude.

The ambiguity of the postlude, however, was inherited by Christendom. To this day, a number of traditional churches tend to place other churches and other religions on a level of exclusion, or at least of dogmatic competition.

The poet of Psalm 147, as in several other hymns at the end of the Psalter, is specifically silent on the mysterious gift of election, and it is thereby open to a sober universality.

PSALM 148

Praise from the Universe

I

1.　　　*Hallelujah!*

　　　Praise the Lord from the heavens;
　　　　Praise him in the heights!
2.　　　*Praise him, all you his angels;*
　　　　Praise him, all you his hosts!

II

3.   *Praise him, sun and moon,*
          Praise him, all you shining stars!
4.   *Praise him, you heavens of heavens,*
          And you waters above the heavens!

III

5.   *Let them praise the name of the Lord,*
          For he gave an order and they were created,
6.   *And he established them forever and ever!*
          He set a rule that shall not be bypassed.

IV

7.   *Praise the Lord from the earth,*
          Sea monsters and all abysses,
8.   *Fire and hail, snow and mist,*
          Hurricane winds, carrying his orders!

V

9.   *Mountains and all of you hills,*
          Fruit trees and all of you cedars!
10.   *Wild animals and all of you cattle,*
          Reptiles and winged birds!

VI

11.   *Kings of the earth and all of you peoples,*
          Princes and all you judges of the earth!
12.   *Young men and you maidens,*
          Old folks together with children!

VII

13.   *Let them praise the name of the Lord,*
          For his name alone is sublime!
          His splendor covers earth and heaven!
14.   *For he has raised the honor of his nation,*
          Praise from all his devotees,
          From Israel's sons, people close to him!
          Hallelujah!

BIBLIOGRAPHY

P. Auffret, *La Sagesse a bâti sa maison: Étude de structures littéraires . . . dans les Psaumes* (Fribourg and Göttingen, 1982), pp. 383-404; E. Beaucamp and J. P. de Reles, "Le choral de la création en marche, Psaume 148," *BVC*, LXII (1966), pp. 31-34; W. Brueggemann, *The Message of the Psalms* (Minneapolis, 1984), p. 165; F. Crüsemann, *Studien zur Formgeschichte von Hymnus und Danklied in Israel,* WMANT XXXII (Neukirchen, 1969); J. L. Cunchillos, "Le Psaume 148: Hymne au Dieu inaccessible, Document religieux d'une mentalité conservatrice," in *Proceedings . . . Jewish Studies* (Jerusalem, 1981); A. H. Gardiner, *Ancient Egyptian Onomastica*, I-II (London, 1947); P. Grether, *Name und Wort Gottes im Alten Testament,* BZAW LXIV (Giessen, 1934); D. R. Hillers, "A Study of Psalm 148," *CBQ*, XL (1978), pp. 323-34; P. Joüon, "Les reptiles [*shereṣ*] et [*remes*]," *Bib,* XI (1940), pp. 152-58; A. Klawek, ". . . Ps 148," *Ruch Biblijny,* IV (1951), pp. 333-41; R. A. F. Mackenzie, "Ps 148, 14bc: Conclusion or Title?" *Bib,* LI (1970), pp. 221-24; P. D. Miller, Jr., *Interpreting the Psalms* (Philadelphia, 1986), pp. 71-72; L. Ruppert, "Aufforderung an die Schöpfung zum Lob Gottes . . . Ps 148," in *Festschrift H. Gross* (Stuttgart, 1986), pp. 275-96; H. Spieckermann, *Heilsgegenwart: Eine Theologie der Psalmen* (Göttingen, 1989), pp. 50-59; G. von Rad, "Hiob 38 und die altägyptische Weisheit," VTSup III (1955), pp. 293-301.

FORM

Some scholars have attempted to divide this psalm into three sections: first, vv. 1-6; second, vv. 7-13; and third, v. 14. This proposed structure suggests that sections one and two contrast with one another, and that the stichos, "Let them praise the name of the Lord" (vv. 5 and 13) repeats itself on account of a difference of themes between the two so-called sections. There is a narrowing of perspective, but no contrast. Moreover, a structure of seven quatrains, with two bicola each, is typical of a joyful mood. The seventh strophe concludes the poet's finale with two tricola (vv. 13-14).

COMMENTARY

Strophe I: The Summons of Celestial Beings (vv. 1-2)

Celestial elements are personified and become beings, like angels and the heavenly host of the sons of God in the opening folktale of Job (2:1). The poet does not have the power to summon the mythical inhabitants of the divine sphere, but he lyrically associates the whole universe with the hymnic symphony and chorus that he will direct in the course of a service of thanksgiving. His own words of exaltation include the heavenly spheres, before his horizon comes closer, as the hymn progresses. In the meantime, orchestral and vocal aesthetics are the controlled channels of a transcendental emotion.

Strophe II: The Heavens of Heavens (vv. 3-4)

The poet outdoes himself as he exhorts the moon, the sun, and the stars to join the concert and to render praise truly universal. He wishes to invite the totality of creation by summoning the heavens par excellence — cf. the Hebrew idiomatic "construction" of two identical nouns, "heavens of heavens," to join the Grand Magnificat. The infinitely distant heights of sublimity, the heavens' heavens, even the celestial ocean, do not confine the universe within a humanly conceived limitation in space. This is the language of a mystic. When the artist seeks to formulate in poetic metaphors the memory of his ecstasy, he must turn to the art of music. Ancient music knew the mathematical basis of its tunes, and it also acknowledged the overpowering force of its tonality and rhythms, which led to the realm of the ineffable.

Strophe III: The Invitation to Praise the Name (vv. 5-6)

For the cosmic ensemble in the playing and singing by nature and supernature, the poet now unveils the secret purpose of the hymn: "Let them praise the name of the Lord" (v. 5).

The theology of glory usually centered on the sacred objects of the innermost room of the temple mobilized the visual sense. It is absent from the concerns of this hymnologist. What counts for him is the theology of the name, which appeals to the sense of hearing. He ignores the ritual of Zion. The sacrificial system is absent. The high-priestly and priestly orders do not enter the preoccupations of this hymn. Creation is the subtone of "the name." YHWH means "He who causes to be" and not the "I am" of the LXX. The name refers not to the legislation of Leviticus but to the hearing of the word at the scene of the burning bush, near the foot of Mount Sinai (Exod 3:13; cf. 1 Kgs 19:11-13). The Mosaic covenant stands in the background, and it deals with ethics, not ritual gestures (Exod 19:3-6; 20:2-17). The parallel Decalogue (Exod 34:17-28) comes from another tradition. The "rule" (v. 6) associates human behavior and divine governance, which, in turn, are initiated by creation (cf. Gen 8:22; Job 28:26; 38:8; Prov 30:8).

Strophe IV: Praise from the Earth (vv. 7-8)

From the heavenly sphere, the concentricity of the horizon continues to be restricted as it enters the realm of the earth with its dry land and its oceans, with all the creatures that live in them. The listing of the sea monsters and all abysses includes a hidden allusion to the Near Eastern myth of a cosmic fight, which in its Hebraic adaptation leads to the creation of light, of order, and of stability. Thus a suitable environment for animal and human existence appears.

Closer still to the conditions of human safety are the meteorological disturbances — fire (lightning), hail, snow and mist, even hurricane winds that, in the end, are under control since they are acceptable as instant means of communication for divine commands.

Strophe V: Appeal to Cattle and Reptiles (vv. 9-10)

To be universal, the concert of praise requires inaccessible mountains and dry hills, as well as fruit trees and cedars, wild beasts and cattle, birds, and even reptiles, presumably dangerous, as these are listed side by side with the musical participants.

Strophe VI: Summons to All Classes of Society (vv. 11-12)

The exhortation to praise, finally, lists the great men of the earth, kings, princes, and judges, down to the youth, even to young girls, and old people. What counts is not social status. Even maidens are invited to sing praises in a predominantly male culture where females, on the whole, were ignored.

Strophe VII: Israel's Sons, A People Close to God (vv. 13-14)

Earth and heaven are syntactically married. The extreme transcendence proclaimed in the early part of the hymn is now attenuated. God is not absent, or indifferent, to his creation. The name of Yahweh, "He who causes to be," demands that the realm of God and the realm of humankind be sealed together (Gen 2:4). The universality of all the invitations to praise the name does not negate, for the sake of equanimity, the unique position of Israel's sons. The final summons is based on thankfulness to Yahweh for having raised "the horn" (translated in v. 14 as "honor") of those close to him. The horn (a symbol derived from the strength of the bullock) is the sign of might and therefore honor and new vitality (Pss 75:5, 10; 83:17, 24; 89:17). This is a cultic psalm, after all, originally destined to be sung in the sanctuary of Zion. Perhaps the sentence implies that the authentic sons of Israel are those who are close to the Lord.

The Hallel that terminates the psalm in the Hebrew text is absent from the Dead Sea Scroll fragment (11QPs^a).

DATE AND THEOLOGY

The hymns of praise are gathered at the end of the Psalter, as the crowning achievement of the collection. Not laments or supplications, but canticles of praise *(tehillim)* become the dominant element of the canonical book. The date is postexilic, and perhaps follows the restoration as well as the return of all the exiles, for Yahweh has raised the horn of his community of devotees.

Psalm 148 goes beyond other hymns in that it unites distance and intimacy. Even the heavens of heavens, the space that identifies divine sublimity with inaccessibility, stands within the musical reach of those singing and playing, even if the words must be considered poetic metaphors of exceptional boldness. Angels are the messengers who belong to the service of divine revelation. They are also in the service of human praise. The verbal laudation is transfigured into tones and tunes when it addresses "the name!" Here is a fabulous hint at the unexpected theology of the Incarnation. Such a hymn possesses ultimately an eschatological meaning. The anointed God-man is not mentioned, but some reality of this sort is implied (cf. Ps 132:17; Luke 1:69).

Foreign kings, nobles, and judges add their collaboration to the ceremonial. The era of divine royalty completes divine creativity. Let it not be forgotten that such words are not read but sung. Music at the level of the sacred is a language that pierces, or hits, the secret part of being. When music dazzles the mind, it presides over the early phases of ecstasy.

In his *Visions de l'Amen,* Olivier Messiaen may have thought of this psalm when he spoke of "airing from self, outside space and time." To enlist the universe in the singing of praise reflects mythical imagination. Modern doxology cannot be intoned as the literal expression of an outmoded cosmology. Yet it remains a collective response to the theologoumenon of Presence.

PSALM 149

A Song of Renewal

I

1.   *Hallelujah!*

Sing for the Lord a song of renewal!
His praise in the assembly of the faithful!
2. *Let Israel rejoice in his Maker!*
May the sons of Zion delight in their King!

II

3. *Let them praise his name with dancing!*
Play for him, tambourine and cithara!
4. *For the Lord shows favor to his people;*
He will crown the humble with salvation.

III

5. *Let the faithful exult in [God's] glory;*
Lying on their mats, may they cry for joy!
6. *Full-throated, let them exalt him,*
Holding in hand a two-edged sword!

IV

7. *To wreak vengeance upon the nations,*
And punishment upon all peoples;
8. *To bind their kings in chains,*
And their princes in iron fetters;
9. *To execute on them their written sentence.*
This will be an honor for all his faithful.
Hallelujah!

BIBLIOGRAPHY

W. Brueggemann, *The Message of the Psalms* (Minneapolis, 1984), pp. 165-67; idem, *The Psalms and the Life of Faith* (Minneapolis, 1995), pp. 124-28; A. R. Ceresko, "Psalm 149: Poetry Themes (Exodus and Conquest) and Social Function," *Bib*, LXVII (1986), pp. 177-94; F. Crüsemann, *Studien zur Formgeschichte von Hymnus und Danklied in Is-*

rael, WMANT XXXII (Neukirchen, 1969), p. 79; N. Füglister, "Ein garstiges Lied — Ps. 149," in *Festschrift H. Gross* (Stuttgart, 1986), pp. 81-106; H. Gunkel, "Psalm 149," in *Festschrift P. Haupt* (1926); H.-J. Kraus, *Theology of the Psalms* (Minneapolis, 1986), pp. 68-69; J. Moltmann, *Le Seigneur de la Danse* (Paris, 1972); W. O. E. Oesterley, *Sacred Dance* (Cambridge, 1923), pp. 159-60; J. Pedersen, *Israel: Its Life and Culture,* III-IV (Oxford, 1940), p. 452; C. Peters, "Psalm 149, in Zitaten islamischer Autoren," *Bib,* XXI (1940), pp. 138-51; A. Sendrey, *Music in Ancient Israel* (London, 1969), p. 441; R. J. Tournay, "Le Psaume 149 et la 'Vengeance' des Psaumes de Yahweh," *RB,* XCII (1985), pp. 349-58; M.-G. Wosien, *Sacred Dance: Encounter with the Gods* (New York, 1974).

FORM

This hymn of praise comprehends four strophes. The first three are quatrains, and the fourth is longer, made of three bicola, in order to strengthen the final exhortation (vv. 7-9). The meter is regular (3+3), with a slower rhythm (4+4) for the concluding exclamation (v. 9b). Throughout the poem, verbs are sometimes in participle form, sometimes in the jussive, and the last strophe contains, exceptionally, three infinitives with the prepositional prefix to indicate an intention, revealed only in the last line (v. 9b).

Strophes I and II summon to praise with music and dances, and Strophes III-IV appear to become a war song of victory.

COMMENTARY

Strophe I: Praise for the Maker of Israel (vv. 1-2)

The Hebrew text literally has "a new song," but the figure of speech does not mean that it is an original, hitherto unknown, work of art. It designates a canticle that deals with the future, transcending the present era. The psalm belongs to an eschatological hope (cf. Pss 33:3; 40:3; 96:1; 98:1; 144:9). It points to the renewal of all things, the newness of the world, and the arrival of everlasting life.

The invitation to praise is addressed to "the assembly of the faithful." In Hellenistic times, the Septuagintal Greek translators understood that the word for "assembly" meant not only a simple community but also "those who are called" *(ekklēsia).* To this day, Christians use this term for "the church." The Hebrew word for "faithful ones" did not originally designate a sect within the most orthodox form of Judaism, but simply those who respond fully and existentially to the Lord's love without attention to or obligation of ritual gestures, even sacrificial offerings. The hymnic motif of creation is here united to the cosmic origin of election. The rejoicing is about "one who made Israel," a participle that is used substantively, "Maker [of Israel]," who is also their King (v. 2). This sovereign is not comparable to the foreign monarchs, who appear in chains when the psalm reaches its termination.

Strophe II: Praise of the Name (vv. 3-4)

Music and dance were common in the ancient Near Eastern cults, especially those of Egypt. David is represented as dancing before the ark. The theology of the name, appealing to hearing rather than seeing, reaches its peak of intensity here. Musical instruments that produce sound with beat and plucking (tambourine and cithara) are religiously distinct from flutes and trumpets, which require blowing tunes that were later estimated to be too sensual.

Strophe III: God's Glory (vv. 5-6)

Until one reaches the last stichos (v. 6b), the psalm continues to sound like a hymn of praise. The text has literally, "Let the faithful exult in glory" (v. 5). Because the Hebrew word means "glory" and also "majesty" or "splendor," several commentators understand "in their own majesty" or "in the light of their coming triumph." The word "glory," even in the context of the theology of the name, appears to designate the transcendentality of God.

Toward the end of the strophe, however, the imagery of warriors at rest on their mats, keeping their double-edged swords at their sides and shrieking full-throated their cries of triumph, raises a bewildering question: How could a hymn of praise for the name of the Lord turn into a victory song after an apparently cruel war?

Strophe IV: Vengeance on Defeated Nations (vv. 7-9)

It seems that the praise of God, which was first articulated as "a song of renewal," literally, "a new song" (v. 1), has now become a victory song for those who stayed alive after the paroxysm of a fierce battle with foreign nations. The terror of facing death, and of being surrounded by death, might justify a cry for vengeance and a lust for the punishment of kings and nobles now captured (vv. 7-8). The faithful have escaped utmost peril, and it may be the memory of the heat of battle that, after triumph, demands forceful revenge and now expects that "honor" will be bestowed on heroic veterans (v. 9).

DATE AND THEOLOGY

For a long time such a psalm has been ascribed to the second century B.C.E., on account of the victories of Judas Maccabeus over the well-trained battalions of Antiochus IV Epiphanes (168-165 B.C.E.). The closing of the canon for the Psalter, before the period of Hellenistic Judaism, now generally accepted, prevents the possibility of such a dating, even if the *Asidaioi* are the *hasidim* of the psalm (v. 9; cf. 1 Macc 2:42; 7:13).

Since the formula "a new song" appears elsewhere in the sense of eschatological hope, could Psalm 149 announce, in metaphoric terms, the end of history with a cosmic Armageddon involving all the nations of the world? The poet is clearly recalling poetic and prophetic traditions of earlier days. The hymn of triumph attributed to Moses after the exodus sings of "a valiant warrior: Yahweh is his name" (Exod 15:34; cf. Ps 149:6, 7). There the enemy is quoted as saying, "I shall draw my sword and destroy them" (Exod 15:9). Allusions are offered not only to the exodus but also to the conquest (Exodus 15–20).

Miriam the prophetess danced at the sound of the tambourine (Exod 15:20; Jer 31:3-4; cf. Ps 149:3). The theme of the New Exodus will be actualized by Israel's "Maker" (Ps 149:2; cf. Job 35:10; Isa 54:2, 5).

The psalmist has also remembered the oracles of the prophet Hosea (7:14; 8:14). The psalmist's lack of concern for sacrificial rites (Ps 149:3, 5) echoes the prophet's astonishing declaration spoken by Yahweh, "It is steadfast love that delights me, not sacrifices" (Hos 6:6).

Vengeance is the intent of Yahweh in his fight against the goyim; here the word is probably understood as "the pagans" (Ps 149:7; cf. 2 Chr 20:17-29; Isa 61:2; 63:3). The double-edged sword, far from defending a veteran on his mat (Ps. 149:6), is probably a metaphor designating the powerful word of God through the semantic change involved in the risk of the spoken word (Prov 5:4; Sir 21:4). The double-edged sword may be a comparison, since the prefix "w" may be not "and" but "like" (cf. Job 5:7; Prov 26:25).

This hymn could hardly have been placed as the penultimate piece of the Psalter, between Psalms 148 and 150, if it had been a military song intoned as a sequence to a military fiat. As an eschatological aria of divine judgment, executing a written sentence (v. 9; cf. Isa 65:6) with the Lord's own sword (Isa 34:5-6), the hymn exalts, at the end of days, the final and bloody theophany. It is a song of newness, stretching human lust for vengeance into a divine avenging (Ps 94:1).

The distinction between human revenge and divine avenging must be respected. But the latter is still close to religious patriotism akin to national idolatry, for it attributes to God a sense of superiority similar to that of chauvinism.

The psalmist is still far away from the apostle Paul's exhortation, quoting Scripture (Deut 32:35): "Vengeance is mine, I will repay, saith the Lord." Then he added, "If thine enemy hungers, feed him; if he thirsts, give him drink, for in so doing thou shalt heap coals of fire upon his head" (Rom 12:20). The thought is still ambiguous.

William Cowper seems to have discerned the ambiguity of the psalmodic poet, and even that of the apostle Paul, when he wrote,

> *Him,* the vindictive rod of angry justice
> Sent quick and howling to the center headlong;
> *I,* fed with judgment, in a fleshly tomb, am
>   Buried above ground.

Even if the enemy belongs to the goyim — nations in the sense of pagans — the thought requires masterly moderation. By rejecting dissidents, Christians have established not "churches," but "sects." The *ekklēsia* is open to all. It becomes a sect when it excludes.

PSALM 150

The Final Praise, with Dance

I

1. *Hallelujah!*
    Praise God in his holy place!
        Praise him in the firmament of his strength!
2. *Praise him for his acts of heroism!*
        Praise him for his immensity!

II

3. *Praise him with the sound of the trumpet!*
        Praise him with lute and cithara!
4. *Praise him with timbrel and with dance!*
        Praise him with strings and with flute!

III

5. *Praise him with the sound of cymbals!*
     Praise him with the clapping of cymbals!
6. *Let anyone that has breath*
     Praise the Lord!
    Hallelujah!

BIBLIOGRAPHY

W. Brueggemann, *The Psalms and the Life of Faith* (Minneapolis, 1995), pp. 125-28, 192-97, 202-3, 211-13; F. Crüsemann, *Studien zur Formgeschichte von Hymnus und Danklied in Israel,* WMANT XXXII (Neukirchen, 1969), p. 79; H. Gressmann, *Musik und Musikinstrumente im Alten Testament* (Giessen, 1903); U. S. Leupold, "Worship Music in Ancient Israel: Its Meaning and Purpose," *CJT,* XV (1969), pp. 176-86; H. Seidel, "Ps. 150 und die Gottesdienstmusik im Altisrael," *Nederlands Theologisch Tijdschrift,* XXXV (1981), pp. 84-100; A. Sendrey, *Music in Ancient Israel* (London, 1969); M. Wagner, *Die Musikinstrumente des alten Orients* (Münster in Westfalen, 1950), pp. 43-44; E. Werner, "Musical Instruments," *IDB,* III (Nashville, 1962), pp. 469-76; C. Westermann, *The Living Psalms* (Grand Rapids, 1984), p. 211.

FORM

This final hymn of praise is composed of three quatrains, of two bicola each. The last of these appears to be shorter (v. 6b) since it summarizes the whole psalm with its summons to anyone who has breath (v. 6a). The naming of the Deity moves from "God" to "the Lord" (Yahweh; vv. 1 and 6), which indicates a movement from the theme of creation to that of salvation. The meter is regular (3+3), with the first stichos shorter (2+3). The imperative verb, "Praise God," or "Praise him," is used ten times, while the last exhortation to all creatures that breathe selects the optative (v. 6b). The orchestra is enlisted with seven groups of musical instruments, no doubt by respecting specific numbers.

COMMENTARY

Strophe I: Holy Place and Firmament (vv. 1-2)

The Holy Place designates the temple of Zion, the unique sanctuary, where full worship could be performed in postexilic times. According to the myth of the omphalos, or navel of the earth, the Holy Place brought together heaven and earth. It was like the umbilical cord of a newborn baby not yet severed from the mother's womb. The praise of God unites the firmament, with its enormous vault of strength (v. 1), and the greatness and immensity of the created world. The "acts of heroism" performed by the Creator secure the dry land of the earth surrounded by oceans.

The theme of the transcendence of God over nature thus presides over the orchestral ensemble of Strophes II and III. The Maker of the universe is a hero, for his habitat is spread from the measureless firmament to the earth's greatness.

Strophe II: The Timbrel and the Dance (vv. 3-4)

Wind instruments were not used in sacred music, with the exception of the shofar fashioned from the horn of a wild ibex, later a ram's horn (Josh 6:4; 1 Chr 15:28; 2 Chr 15:14; Hos 5:8). It was ascribed to the animal substituted for Isaac, just before Abraham's woeful sacrifice of his son (Gen 22:13). The shofar was blown, with its hoarse waves and siren warnings, before and after the most solemn occasions. During the Middle Ages, it was especially blown for the *Dies irae,* as in the *Tuba mirum* (Hab 3:1-19), and later on in masses of Requiem, as in the blast of sixteen silver trumpets for the "Grand 'Messe des Morts" by Berlioz.

Dancing, however, demanded the softer melodies of the plucked lute and cithara, other stringed instruments, and even a mysterious one (from a verb meaning "to love passionately"; v. 4), which is never mentioned in the lists of temple orchestras and was probably rejected in the rabbinical era as inducing erotic excitement (*Genesis Rabbah,* 30).

The all-calling hymn that concludes the Psalter does not object to praising God with dancing to the sound of the timbrel.

Strophe III: Anyone Who Has Breath (vv. 5-6)

The clapping of cymbals accompanies dancing, at the paroxysm of popular joy. The psalmist knew two kinds of cymbals, and invites for the praise of Yahweh anyone endowed with good breathing. No restriction is announced. The thrill of Yahweh's presence is open to all, possibly sinners and aliens from the wide world, perhaps also birds and animals like those creatures "of sea and land" that George Herbert summoned to praise the Almighty.

DATE AND THEOLOGY

The "Gloria" in the liturgy moves from penitence to gratefulness when grace is received and accepted. Music bestows on praise the virtue of a true reconciliation that foments peace. The postexilic date seems to be posterior to the trials of Ezra and Nehemiah. Theology, when chanted, receives the power of hope. It prays, "Thy kingdom come! May thy reign truly arrive!"

The psalm is not a supplication. Most notably, it ends the Psalter, side by side with Psalm 149, which rages with God's wrath against the nations; Psalm 150 brings the Psalter to its culmination through self-giving in pure religion. The call for divine avenging is now the implicit call for everything that breathes to praise the Lord.

Psalm 150, immediately succeeding Psalm 149, echoes the position of Psalms 1 and 2 in reverse order, which present the gift of selfhood (Psalm 1) and the image of a Lord who laughs at unbelievers (Psalm 2).

Those who sing the final hymn are anticipating the promise of a new song. Milton had it right when he wrote in *Paradise Lost:*

> The solemn pipe
> And dulcimer, all organs of sweet stop,
> [. . .] All sounds on fret by string or golden wire,
> Tempered soft tuning, intermixed with voice,
> Choral or unison; but then
> Explodes the demand of Praise.

For, at first, Milton had written:

> Open, ye everlasting gates; they sung,
> Open, ye Heavens, your living doors! let in
> The great Creator, from his work returned
> Magnificent, his six days' work, a World!

Psalm 150 is sunk in ancient mythology, but its truth may survive its obsoleteness as the roots of its faith grow even more solidly anchored in the age of global humanity.

ADDENDUM: PSALM 151 [?]

The Dead Sea Scrolls, in addition to having several fragments of poems including quotations of canonical psalms, also contain a composition that has been called "Psalm 151" (11QPs^a). It is not strictly speaking a "psalm," but a fictitious autobiography of young David (col. xxviii). It is absent from the canonical Psalter, although parts of it are found in some manuscripts of the LXX and in Syriac.

The text of this Qumran poem begins with the hymnal exhortation, "Hallelujah!" and bears the superscription, "From David, son of Jesse." The verses are formulated in the first person singular.

The following paraphrase is abbreviated:

> Young David tells how, younger than his brothers, he was herder for his father's sheep and goats. His hands made a flute and his fingers a cithara, so that he might render glory to the Lord. Although mountains and hills ignored him, trees exalted his words, and the flocks his deeds. God sent the prophet Samuel to anoint him with holy oil, as the Lord God had not chosen any of his brothers, but established him prince of his people, and sovereign of the sons of the covenant.

This poem neither supplicates nor praises. In it David celebrates his God and himself. The Qumran sectarians thus contributed to the development of the Davidic legend in the second or first centuries B.C.E.

For an extensive bibliography, see J. A. Sanders, *The Psalms Scroll of Qumran Cave 11* (11QPs^a), Discoveries in the Judaean Desert IV (Oxford, 1965); P. W. Flint, *The Dead Sea Scrolls and the Book of Psalms* (Leiden, 1997).

Index of Subjects

Gath, 126, 127

Gebal, 594

Genesis myth, 718-19

genres, 12

gestures, 854

Gihon, 753

Gilgal, 600, 602

giver of life, 717-18

gladness, 406

glory, 91, 97, 109, 127, 178, 278, 279, 283, 437, 479, 532, 608, 676, 723, 772-73, 877, 925

God: abandonment, 310, 360, 513; absence, 45-48, 160, 230, 351, 354, 539; anger, 112-13, 115; as bridegroom, 617-18; compassion, 404, 491, 617; distance and proximity, 711; enthronement, 87; eternity, 643, 698-99; faithfulness, 344, 513, 774; as father, 268, 269; fidelity, 200, 205, 260, 863; fingers of, 129; forgetfulness, 555; freedom, 774, 888; glory, 33, 211, 925; goodness, 161, 222, 268, 304, 412, 413, 472, 527, 616, 690, 730, 739, 783, 824, 905, 910; greatness, 557; as guide, 240; as healer, 241; hearing, 614; hiddenness, 140, 143, 235, 282, 284, 502-3, 557, 645; holiness, 127, 149, 407, 557, 681, 684, 687; hospitality, 173; as host, 241; immanence, 109, 132, 315, 711; impotence, 534; inattention, 664, 665; incomprehensibility, 256; judgment, 877; justice, 121, 150, 287, 311, 331, 347, 531; keeping oath, 637; as king, 377-79, 659-60, 679, 686-87, 827, 904-5; knowledge, 876; laughter, 83, 930; as liberator and Redeemer, 214; loneliness, 629-30; love, 113, 314, 316, 355, 362, 384, 460, 462; as majestic, 550; mighty deeds, 140, 141-42; as mother, 268, 269, 616; nearness, 513, 532, 533, 534-35; omnipotence, 276, 278, 279, 491, 554, 555, 557, 877; omnipresence, 877, 881; omniscience, 140, 293, 877, 879; passion, 109; as pastor, 239; as possession, 533, 535; power, 128, 223, 757, 774; presence, 45-48, 354, 455, 806, 881; as protector, 665; repentance, 116; righteousness, 200, 758, 896; as Rock,

656-57; as shepherd, 812; silence, 145, 271, 555, 557, 886, 893; sovereignty, 82, 445, 471; suffering, 475; transcendence, 109, 132, 198, 205, 279, 315, 491, 533, 609, 675, 711, 899, 929; universal rule, 481; vengeance, 574, 618, 663-64; vulnerability, 362, 414, 452, 469, 491, 516, 557; will, 144; wrath, 155, 198, 326, 450, 566, 567, 572, 573, 578-79, 638

godless, 164, 424

gold, 213, 520, 522

golden calf, 731, 752

Goliath, 31, 898

good, 758

good shepherd, 569, 580-81, 670

goodness, 241, 692, 758

gospel, 473, 480, 704, 747, 841, 907

Goudimel, Claude, 4

goyim, 572-74, 581, 837, 926-27

grace, 106-7, 113, 115, 161, 200, 216, 261, 365, 404, 408, 410, 435-36, 485, 614, 733, 818-19, 862-63

grape presses, 127

gratitude, 472

graven images, 568, 569, 680

graves, 492

greed, 570

Greek tragedy, 588, 590

green pastures, 672, 676

Gregorian chant, 112

Gregory the Great, 3

Gregory of Nyssa, 850

guilt, 255-56, 289, 293, 404-5, 406, 408, 409-10, 472, 474, 531, 733, 840

Gunkel, Hermann, 12, 13, 15, 41-42, 566, 660

Habakkuk, 769

Hagrites, 594

hail, 921

Hallel psalms, 764, 777

Hallelujah, 43, 60, 909, 914

Hallelujah psalms, 17, 19, 763, 779, 857, 859

Hammurabi, 693

handmaid, 818

Hanukkah, 837

happiness, 71, 98-99, 213, 248, 262, 284,

•

Index of Scripture and Other Ancient Sources

CPSIA information can be obtained at www.ICGtesting.com
Printed in the USA
LVOW08s1408190713

343745LV00002B/3/A